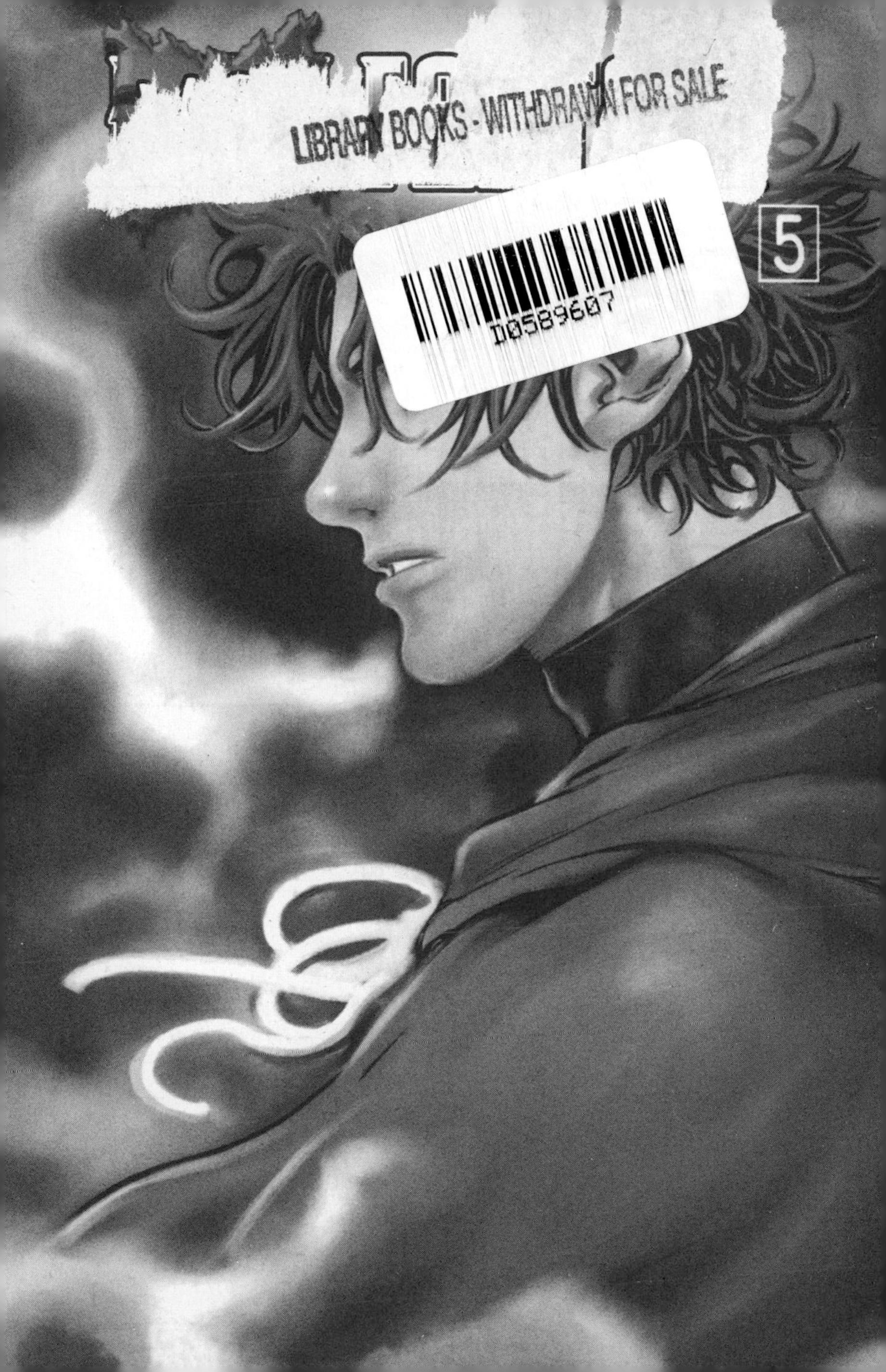
5

Last Fantasy Vol. 5
Story By Creative Hon
Art By Yong-Wan Kwon

Translation - Sora Han
English Adaptaion - Mike Wellman
Retouch and Lettering - StarPrint Brokers
Production Artist - Jennifer Carbajal
Graphic Designer - Fawn Lau

Editor - Luis Reyes
Digital Imaging Manager - Chris Buford
Pre-Production Supervisor - Erika Terriquez
Art Director - Anne Marie Horne
Production Manager - Elisabeth Brizzi
Managing Editor - Vy Nguyen
VP of Production - Ron Klamert
Editor-in-Chief - Rob Tokar
Publisher - Mike Kiley
President and C.O.O. - John Parker
C.E.O. and Chief Creative Officer - Stuart Levy

A  Manga

TOKYOPOP and  are trademarks or registered trademarks of TOKYOPOP Inc.

TOKYOPOP Inc.
5900 Wilshire Blvd. Suite 2000
Los Angeles, CA 90036

E-mail: info@TOKYOPOP.com
Come visit us online at www.TOKYOPOP.com

ISBN: 978-1-59532-530-1

First TOKYOPOP printing: July 2007
10 9 8 7 6 5 4 3 2 1
Printed in the USA

VOLUME 5

STORY BY CREATIVE HON
ART BY KWON YONG-WAN

HAMBURG // LONDON // LOS ANGELES // TOKYO

STORY THUS FAR

Tian—a low level, under-experienced magic user whose only effective spell is Fireball—and Drei—an exceptionally strong, exceptionally dumb warrior for whom the obvious is a complex understanding—are best friends and partners in a quest to gain as much gold as possible. However, every moment of financial prosperity is usually quickly followed by a succession of financial disasters, which usually leaves the duo clambering for food, shelter and the tools necessary to take on the big, wide, rich world yet again. However, when they arrived in the town of Yekacherin not too long ago, they found what they had never thought possible... gainful employment. Working as virtual slaves for Anna, the commander of the town's militia who prefers to be called its Queen, they are earning their keep, which is fortunate in a town that is being slowly taken over by a corporate retail conglomerate known as Rain Emblem. Rain Emblem is a convenient, one-stop shopping bazaar that is driving all of the small business in Yekacherin away. And as if that wasn't annoying enough, Mariel, the holy lady, is the liaison of a religious organization charged with helping the poor and destitute throughout the lands of Sobeetrook. Capitalism on your left, socialism on your right, a near fascist sheriff with a royalty complex in the middle...What are our heroes to do? Well, Tian falls in love only to find his young prostitute paramour brutally murdered. It wasn't the thief Nagi, as he thought...it was actually a disease that is turning the whole town into zombies. That is where we are now...

CONTENTS

CHAPTER 6

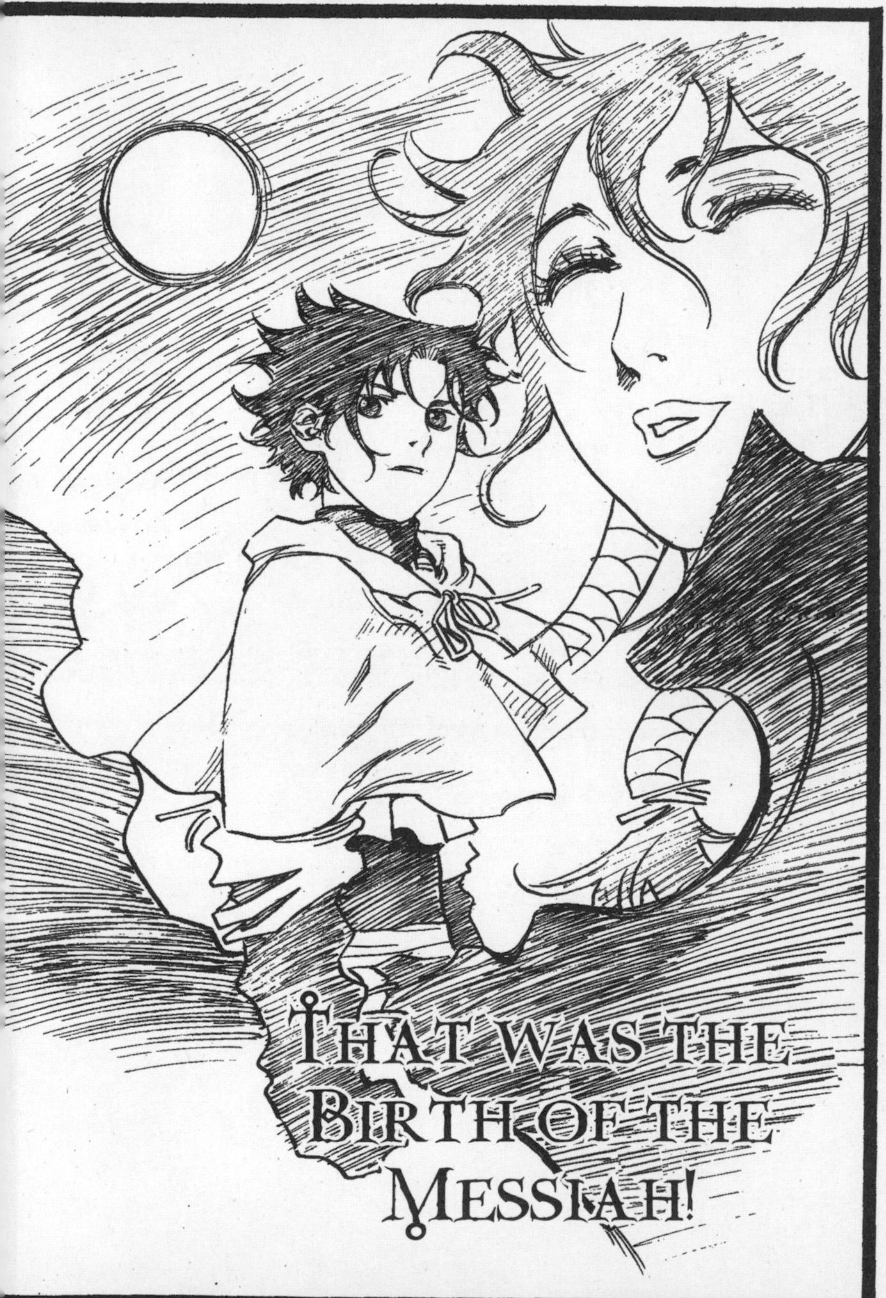
THAT WAS THE BIRTH OF THE MESSIAH!

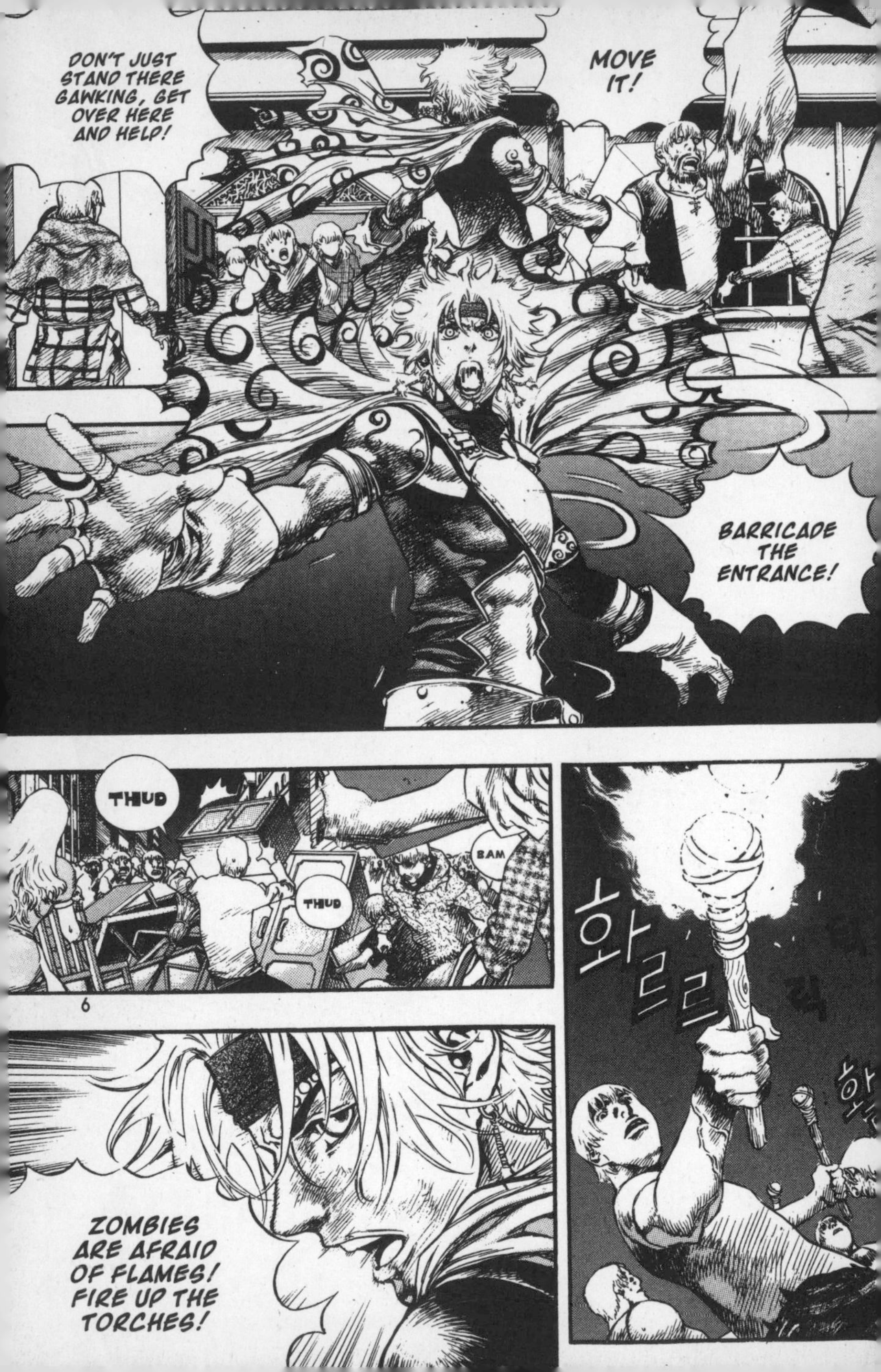
DON'T JUST STAND THERE GAWKING, GET OVER HERE AND HELP!
MOVE IT!
BARRICADE THE ENTRANCE!
THUD
BAM
THUD
ZOMBIES ARE AFRAID OF FLAMES! FIRE UP THE TORCHES!
화르르

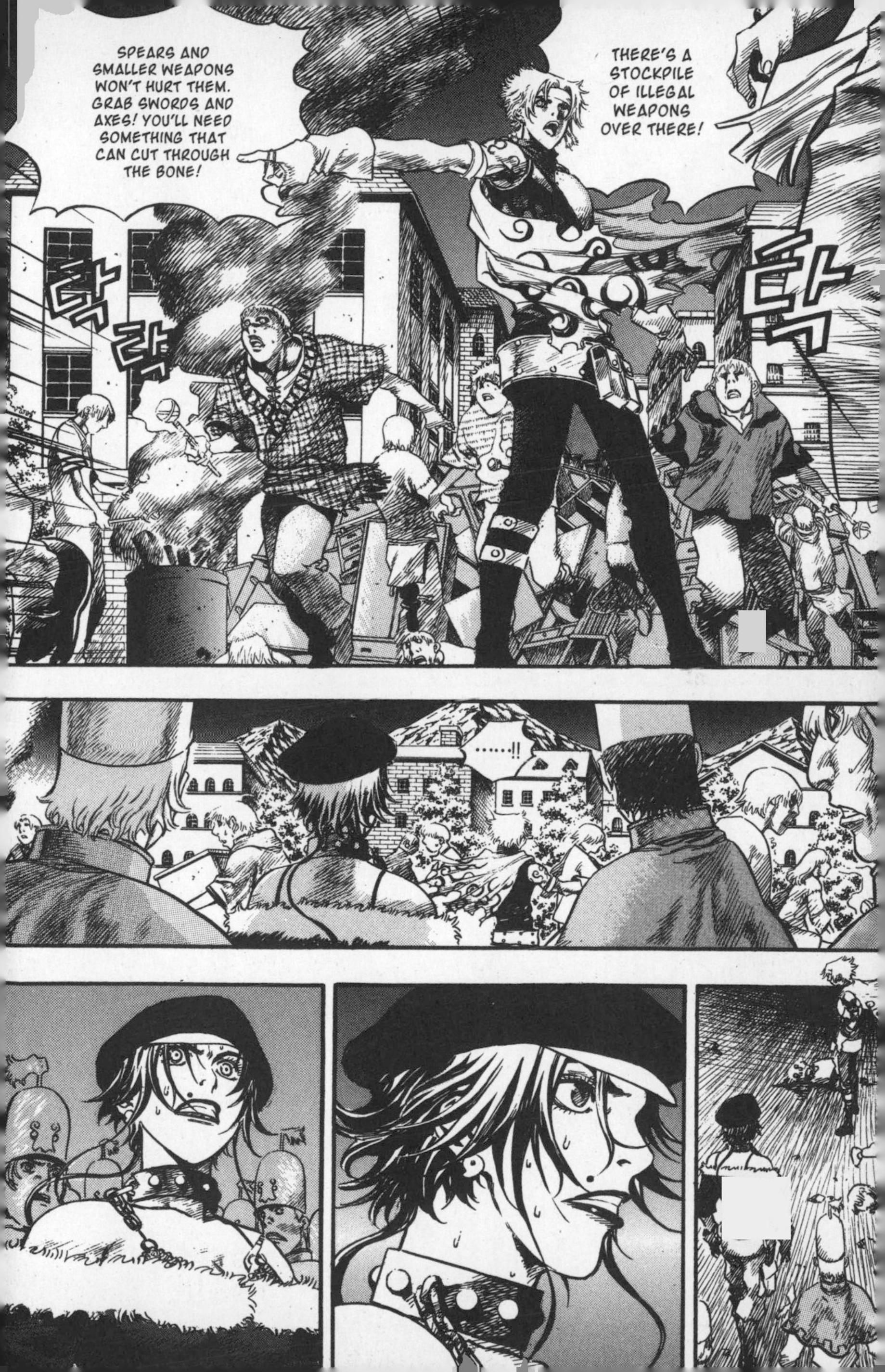
SPEARS AND SMALLER WEAPONS WON'T HURT THEM. GRAB SWORDS AND AXES! YOU'LL NEED SOMETHING THAT CAN CUT THROUGH THE BONE!
THERE'S A STOCKPILE OF ILLEGAL WEAPONS OVER THERE!
......!!

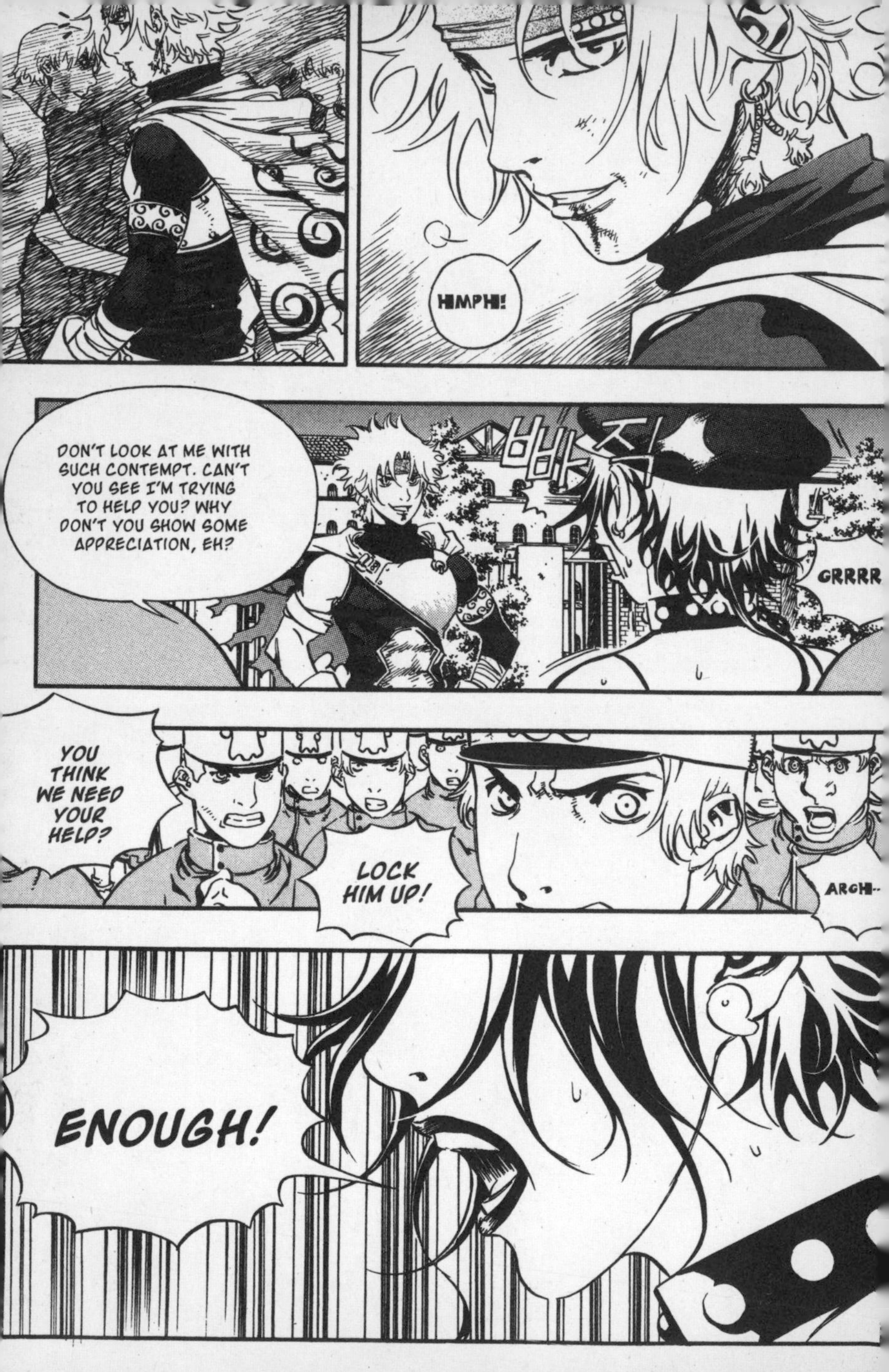
HMPH!
DON'T LOOK AT ME WITH SUCH CONTEMPT. CAN'T YOU SEE I'M TRYING TO HELP YOU? WHY DON'T YOU SHOW SOME APPRECIATION, EH?
빠직
GRRRR
YOU THINK WE NEED YOUR HELP?
LOCK HIM UP!
ARGH..
ENOUGH!

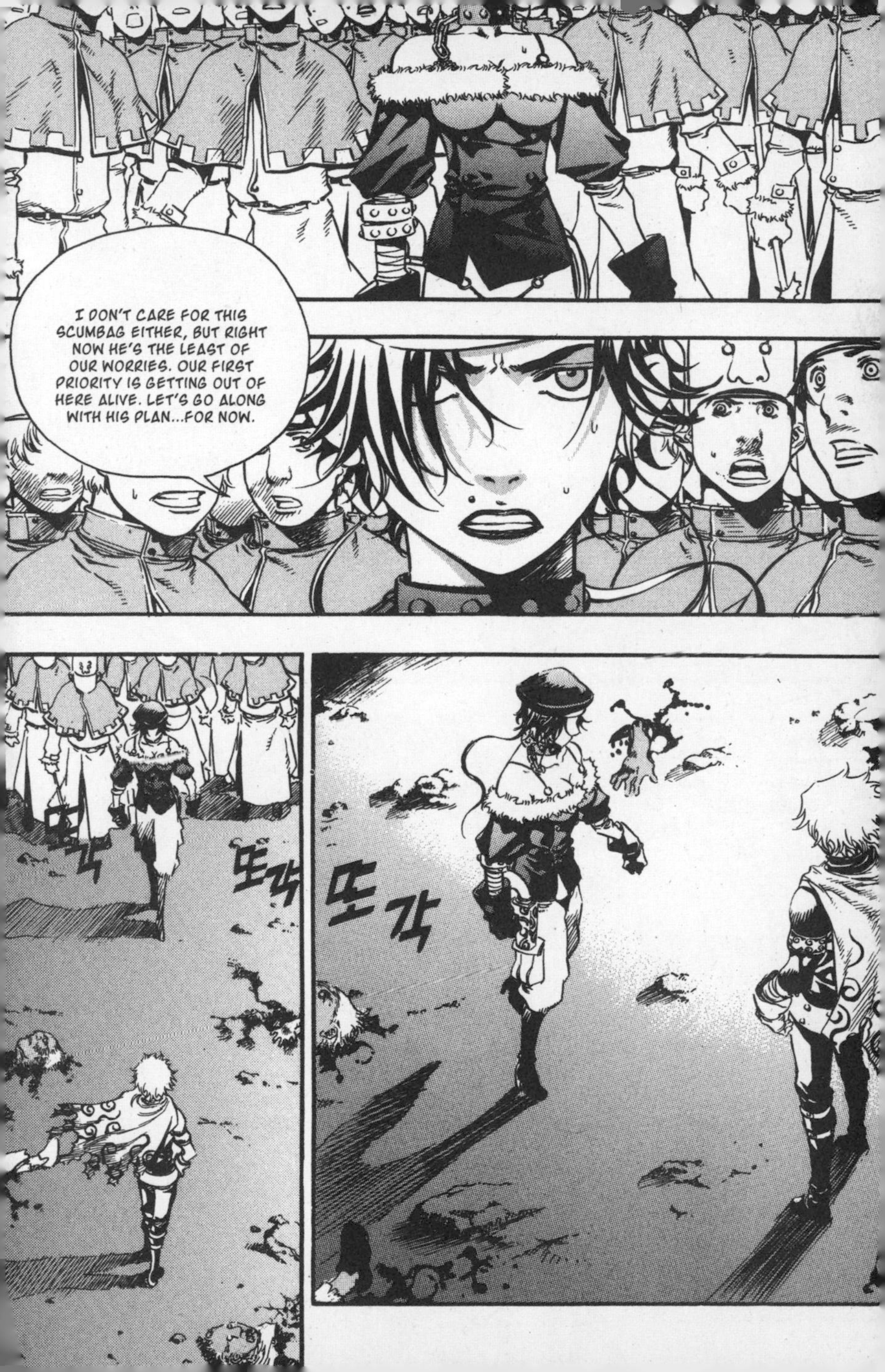
I DON'T CARE FOR THIS SCUMBAG EITHER, BUT RIGHT NOW HE'S THE LEAST OF OUR WORRIES. OUR FIRST PRIORITY IS GETTING OUT OF HERE ALIVE. LET'S GO ALONG WITH HIS PLAN...FOR NOW.
또각
또각

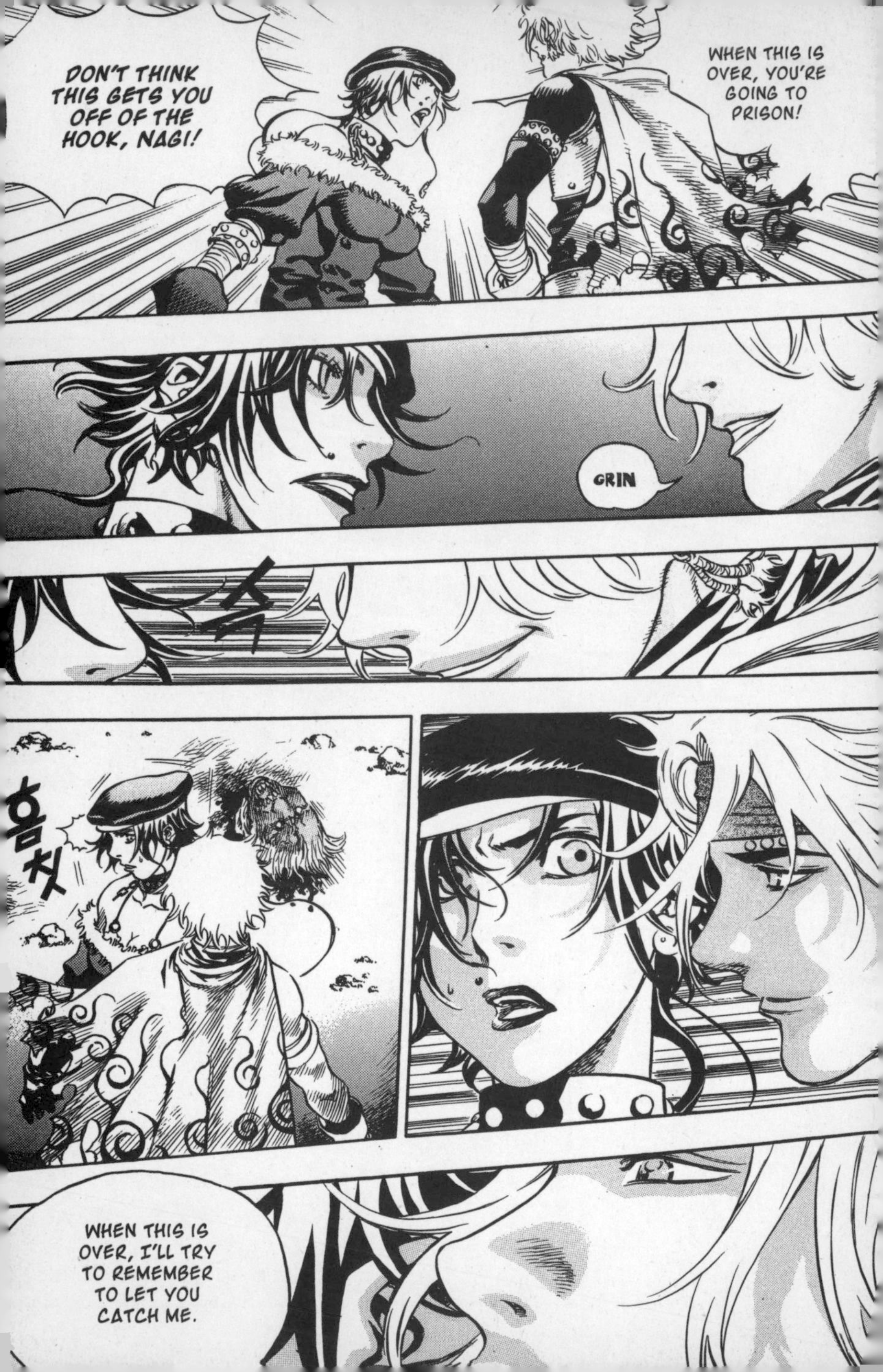
DON'T THINK THIS GETS YOU OFF OF THE HOOK, NAGI!
WHEN THIS IS OVER, YOU'RE GOING TO PRISON!
GRIN
슥
흠칫
WHEN THIS IS OVER, I'LL TRY TO REMEMBER TO LET YOU CATCH ME.

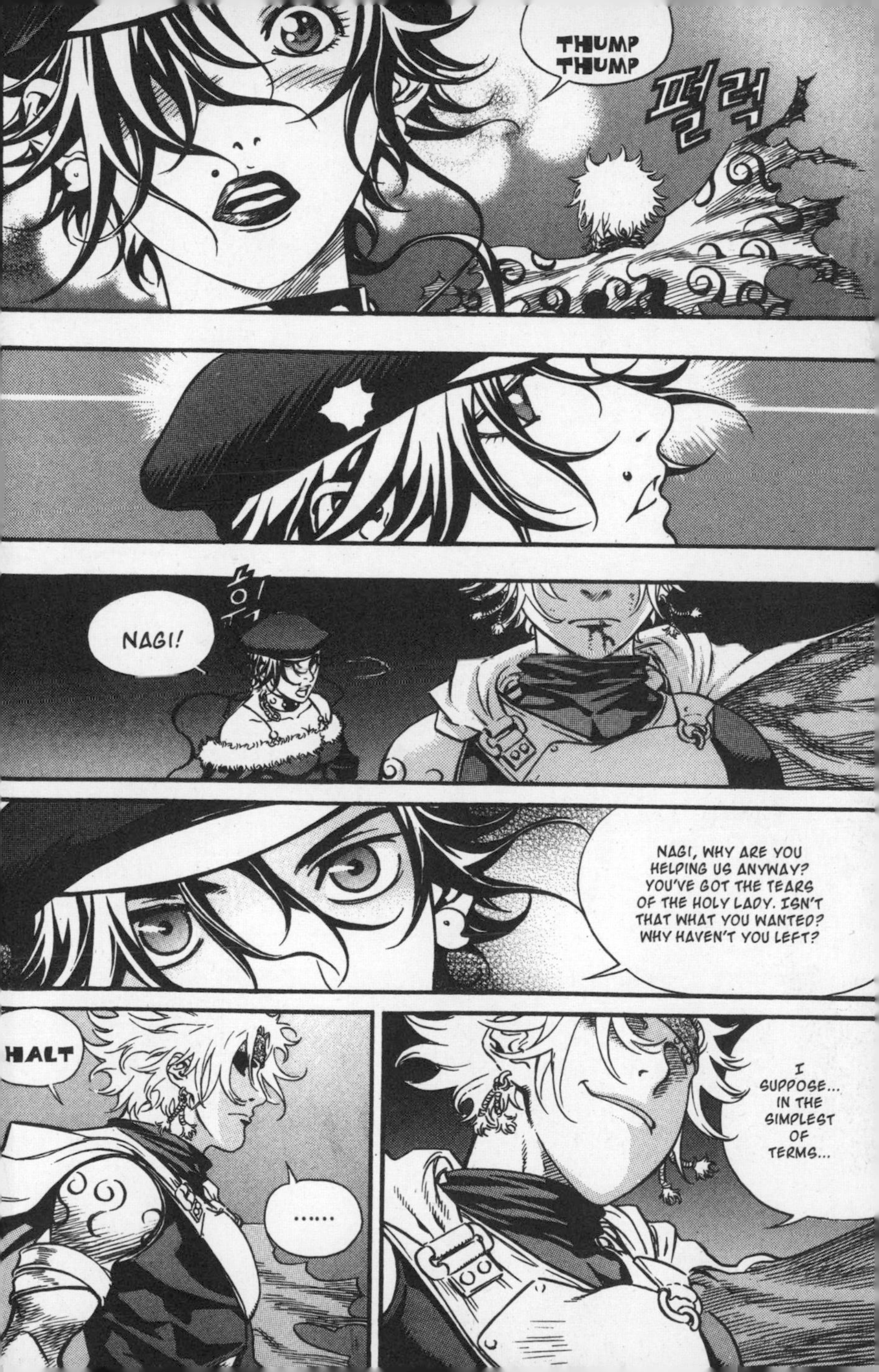
THUMP
THUMP
펄럭
NAGI!
NAGI, WHY ARE YOU HELPING US ANYWAY? YOU'VE GOT THE TEARS OF THE HOLY LADY. ISN'T THAT WHAT YOU WANTED? WHY HAVEN'T YOU LEFT?
HALT
......
I SUPPOSE... IN THE SIMPLEST OF TERMS...

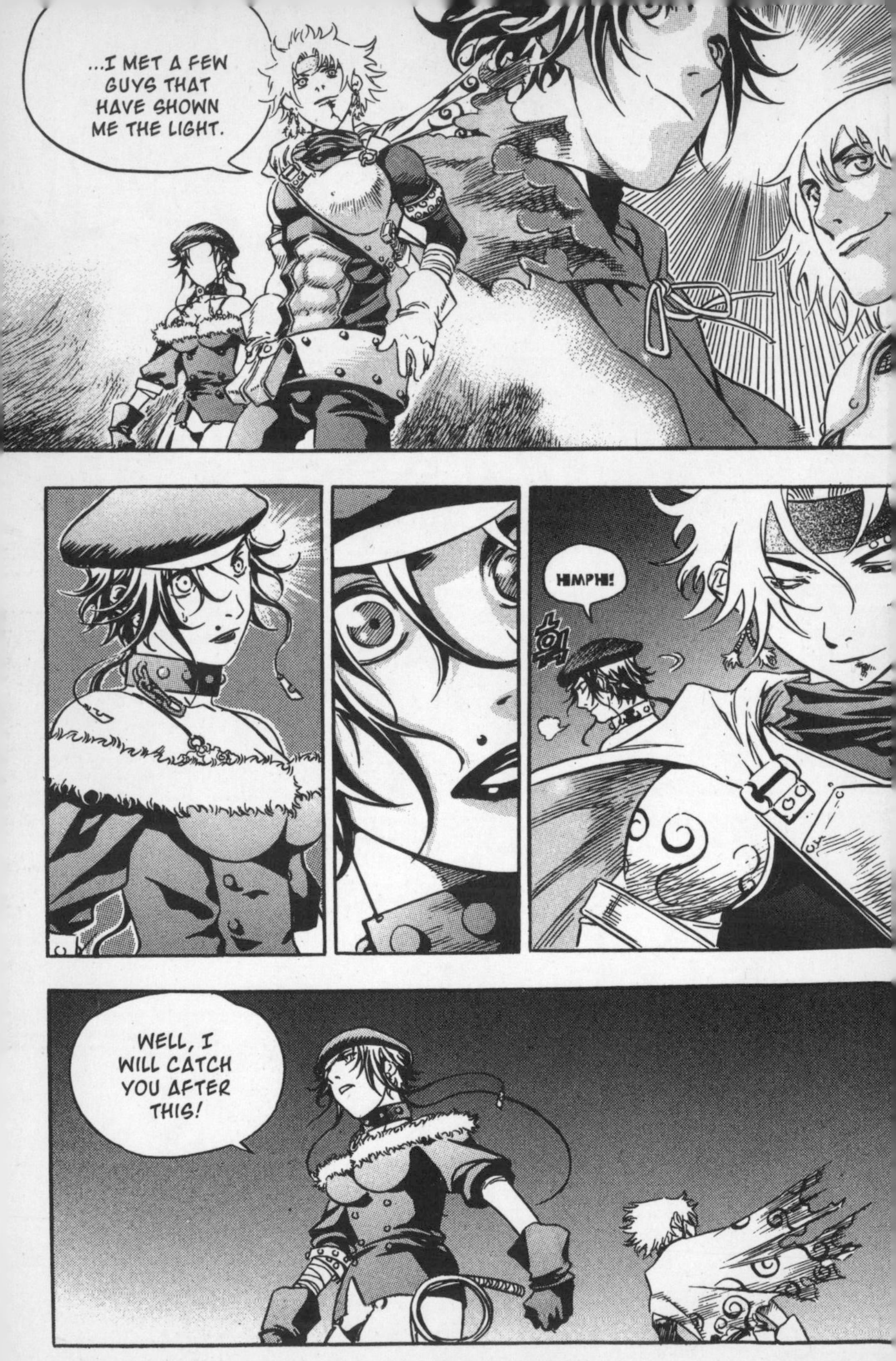
...I MET A FEW GUYS THAT HAVE SHOWN ME THE LIGHT.
HMPH!
WELL, I WILL CATCH YOU AFTER THIS!

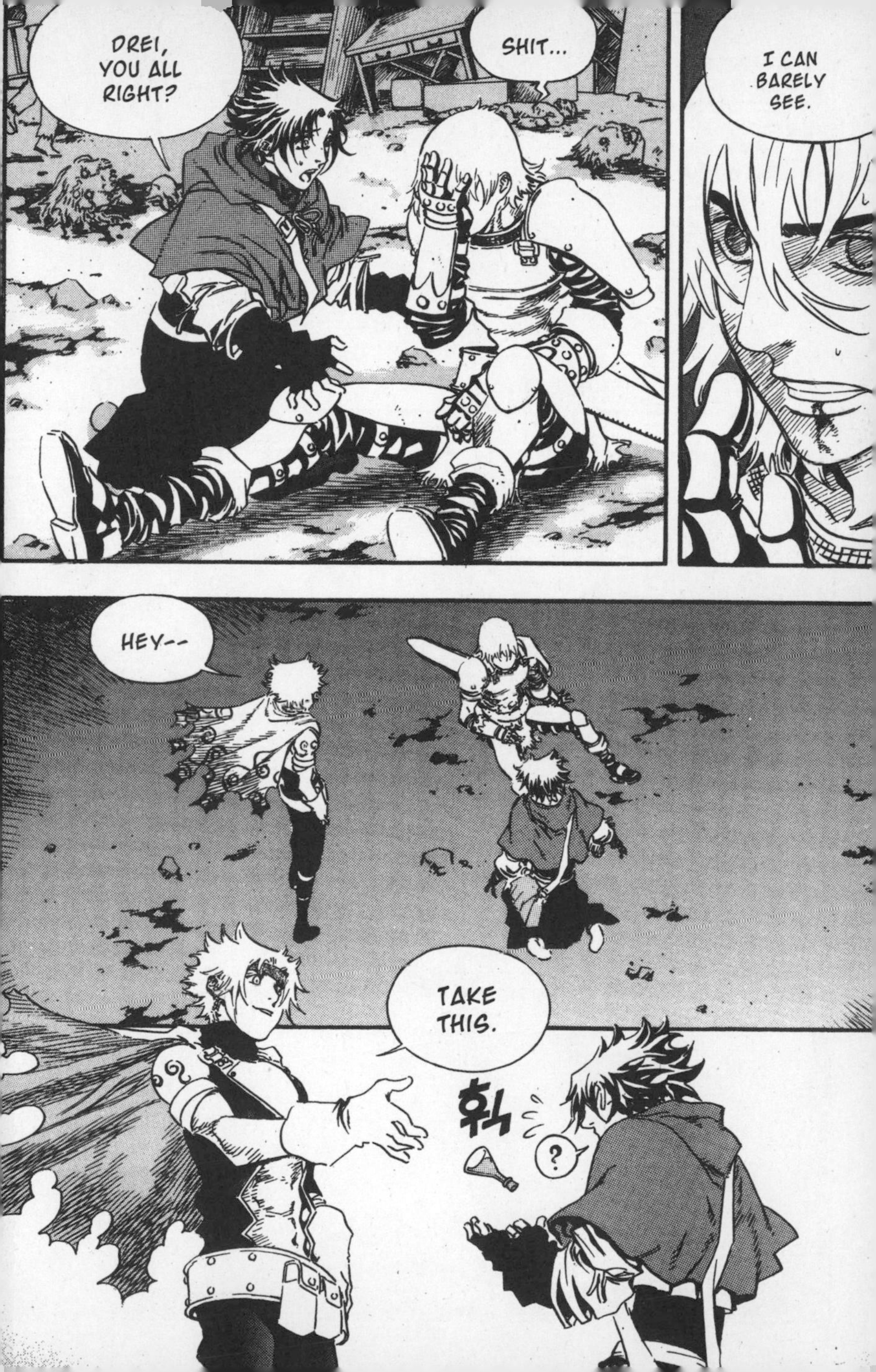
DREI, YOU ALL RIGHT?
SHIT...
I CAN BARELY SEE.
HEY--
TAKE THIS.
휘
?

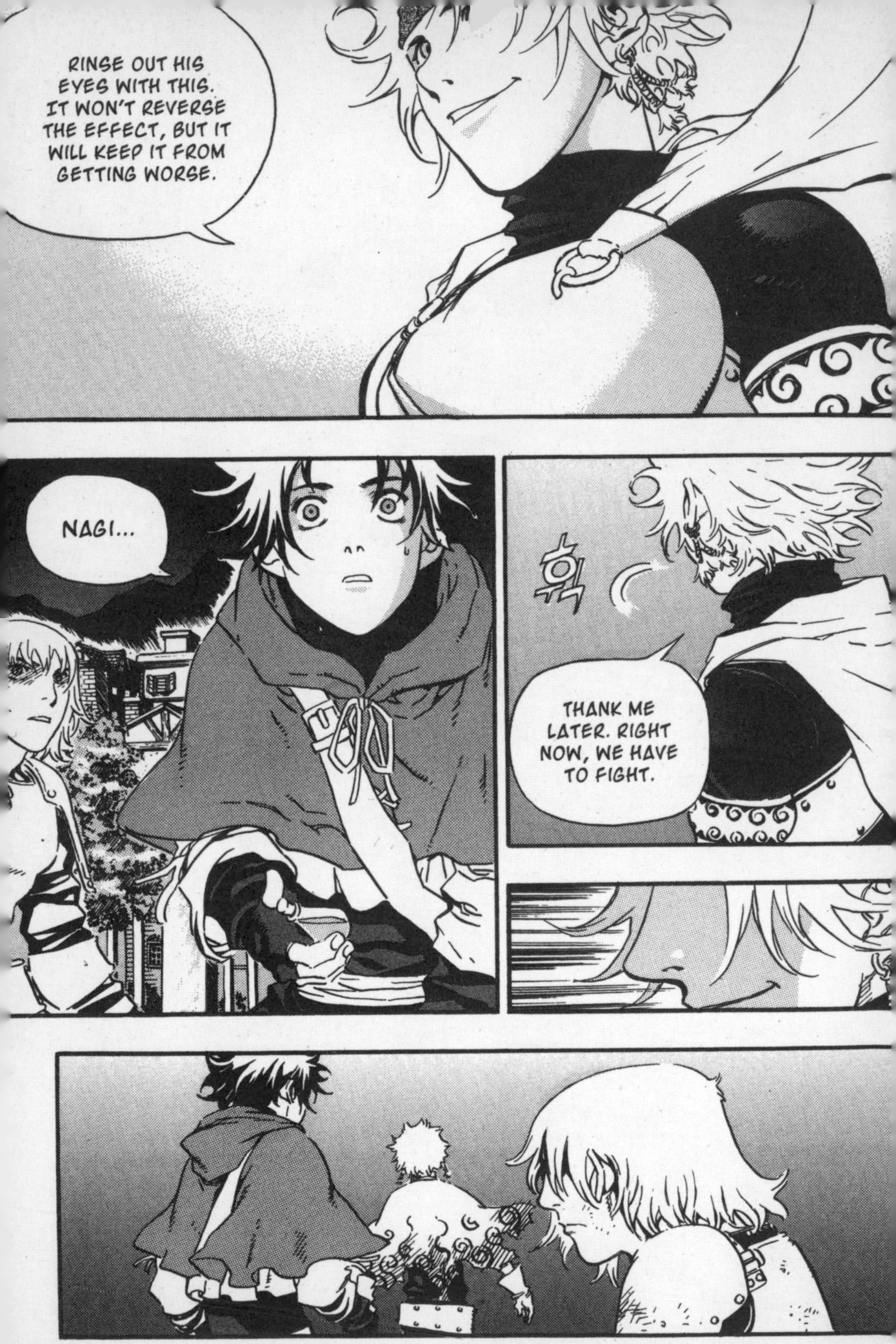
RINSE OUT HIS EYES WITH THIS. IT WON'T REVERSE THE EFFECT, BUT IT WILL KEEP IT FROM GETTING WORSE.
NAGI...
휙
THANK ME LATER. RIGHT NOW, WE HAVE TO FIGHT.

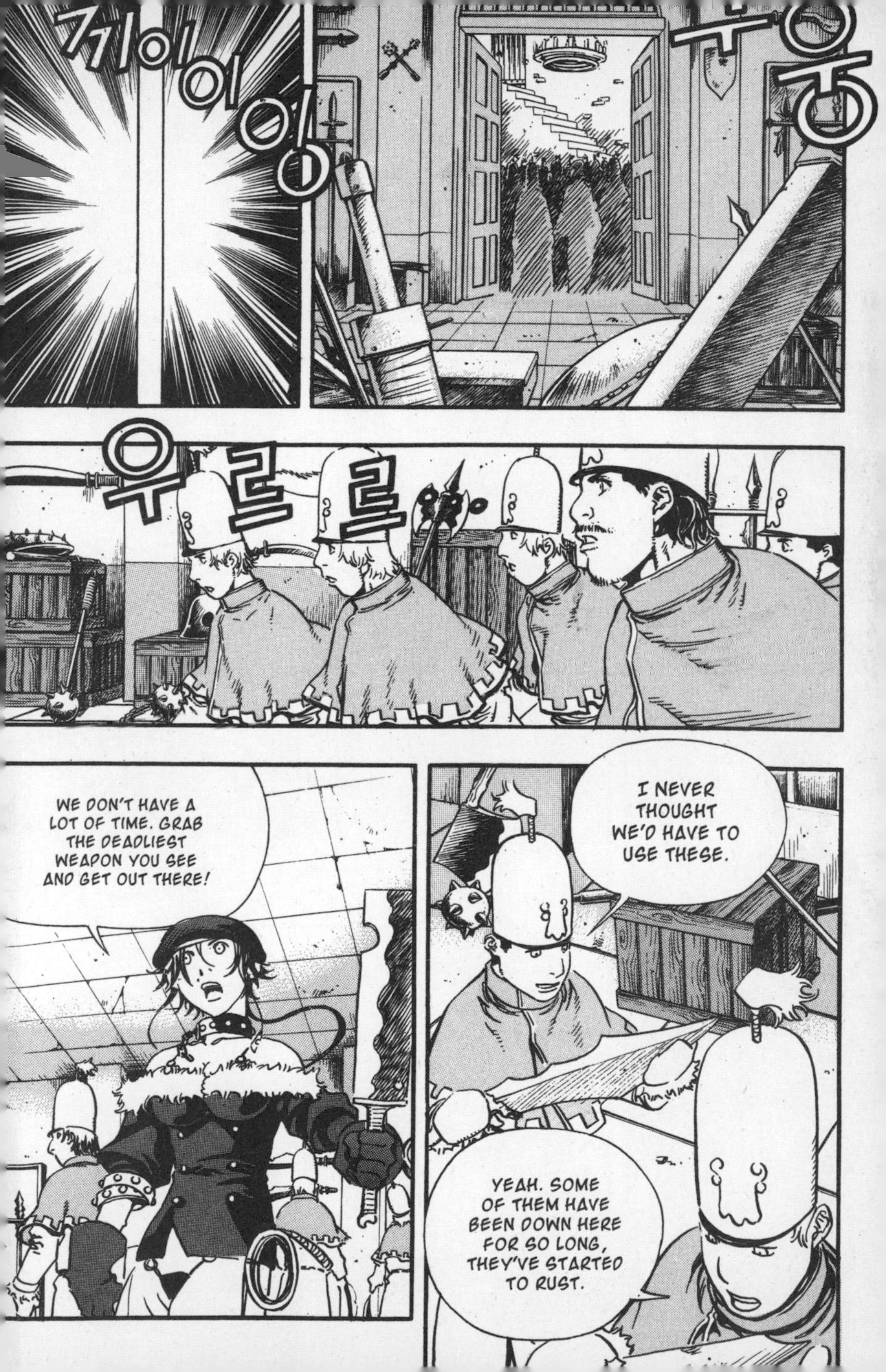
끼이이이잉
쿠웅
우르르
WE DON'T HAVE A LOT OF TIME. GRAB THE DEADLIEST WEAPON YOU SEE AND GET OUT THERE!
I NEVER THOUGHT WE'D HAVE TO USE THESE.
YEAH. SOME OF THEM HAVE BEEN DOWN HERE FOR SO LONG, THEY'VE STARTED TO RUST.

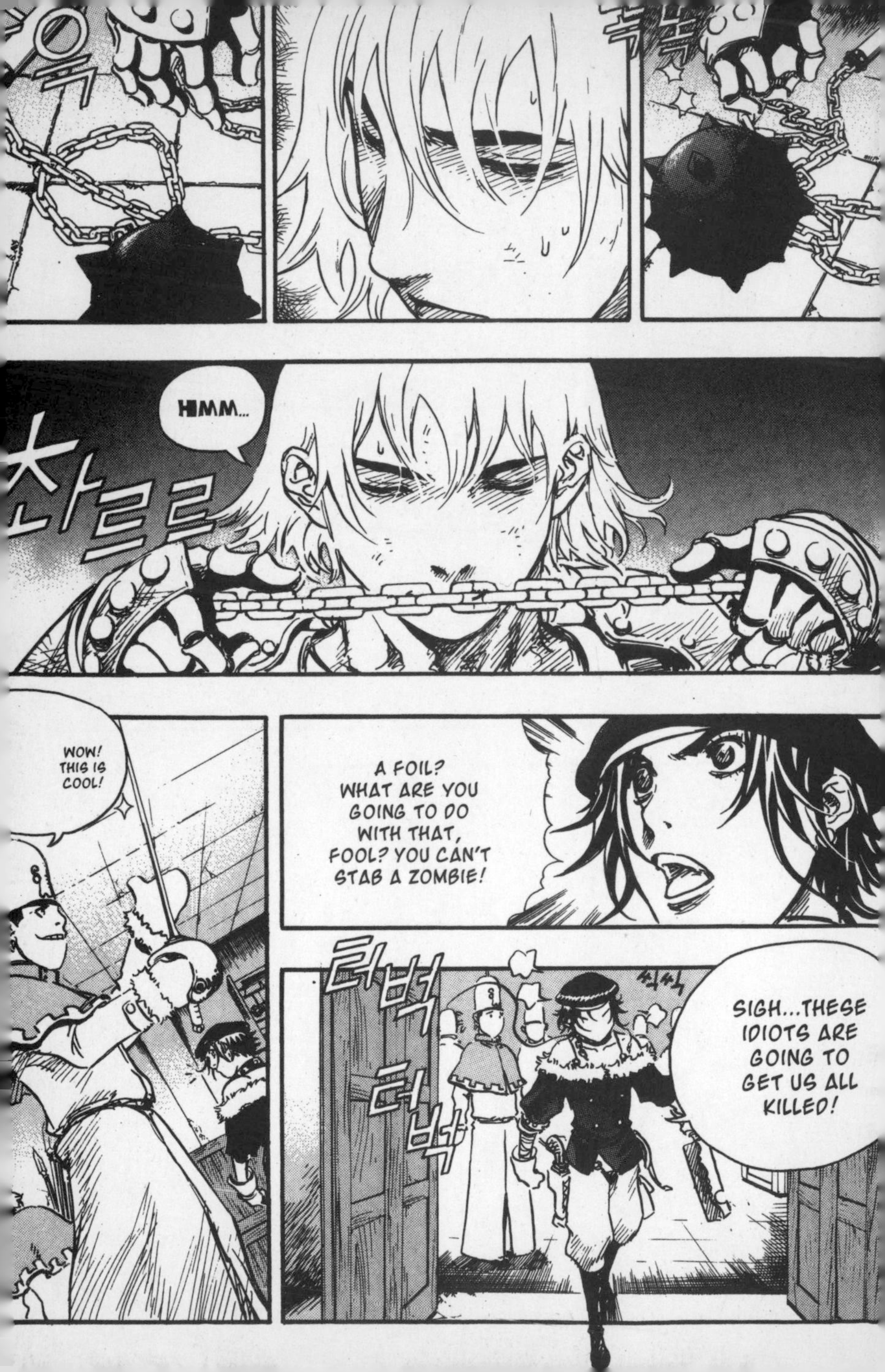

HMM...
WOW! THIS IS COOL!
A FOIL? WHAT ARE YOU GOING TO DO WITH THAT, FOOL? YOU CAN'T STAB A ZOMBIE!
SIGH...THESE IDIOTS ARE GOING TO GET US ALL KILLED!

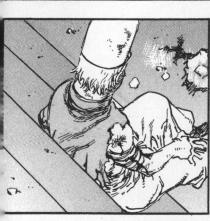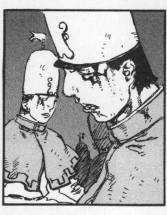

USELESS...

...FOOLS...

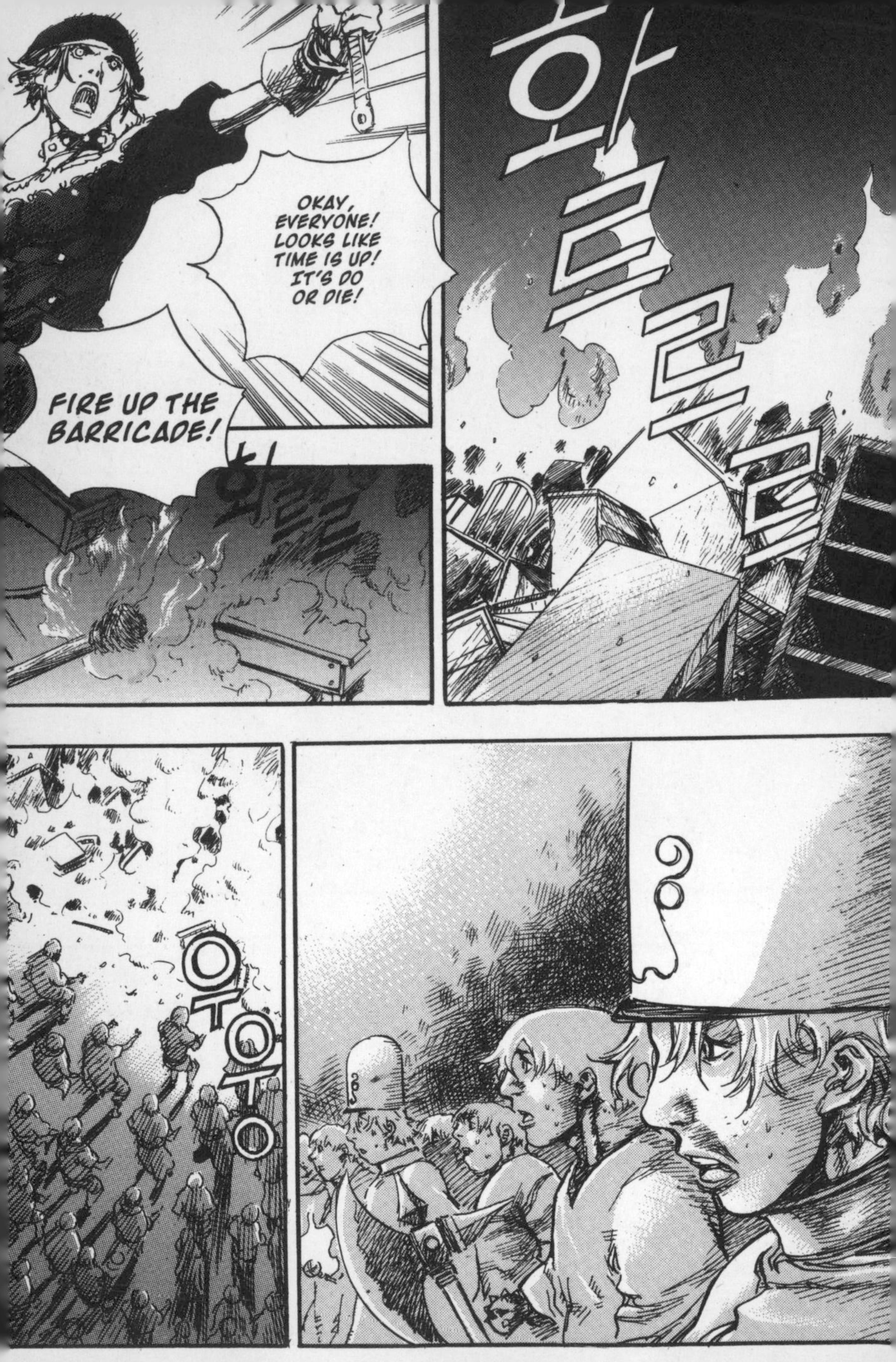
OKAY, EVERYONE! LOOKS LIKE TIME IS UP! IT'S DO OR DIE!
FIRE UP THE BARRICADE!

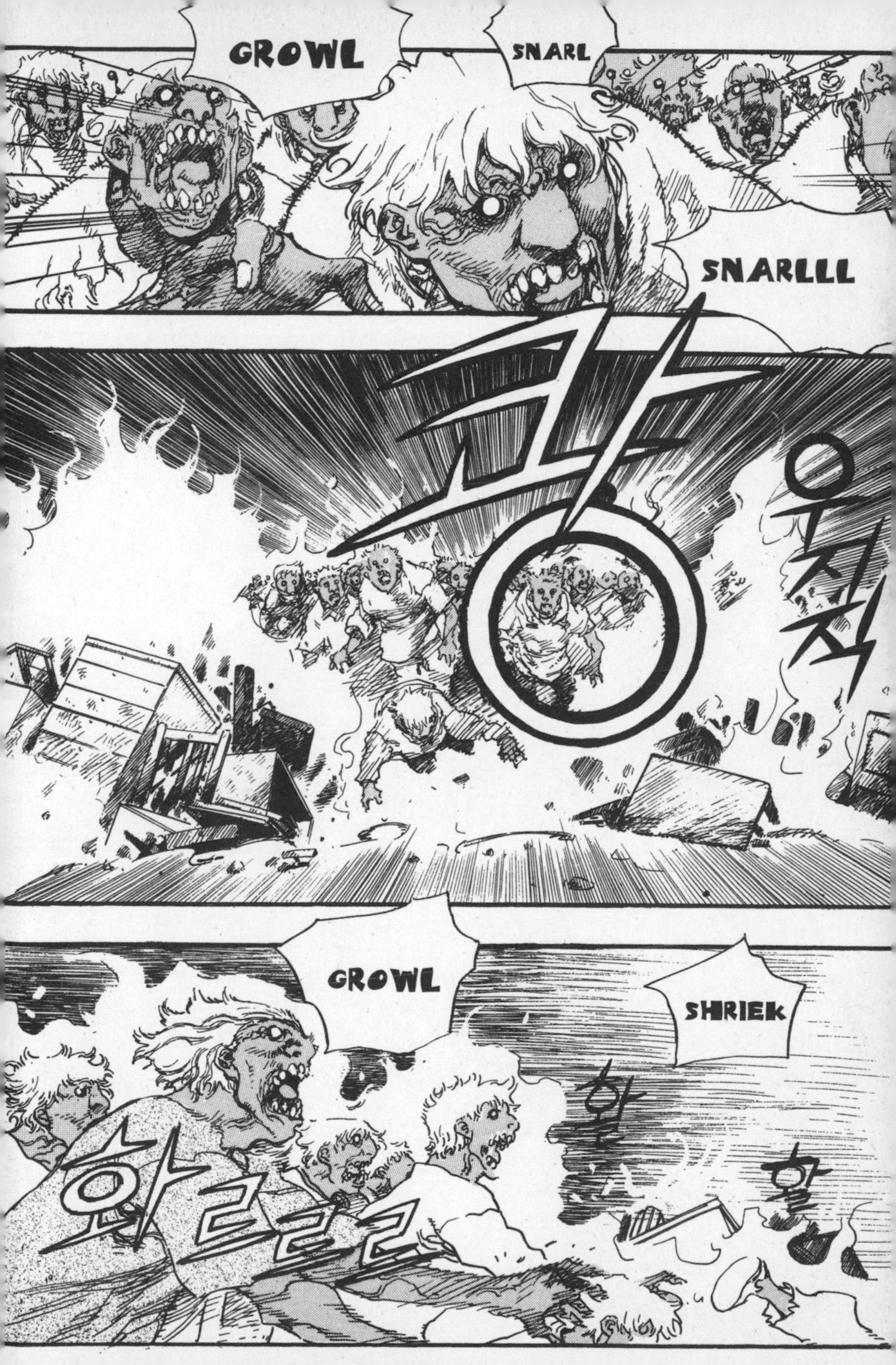
GROWL
SNARL
SNARLLL
쾅
우지직
GROWL
SHRIEK

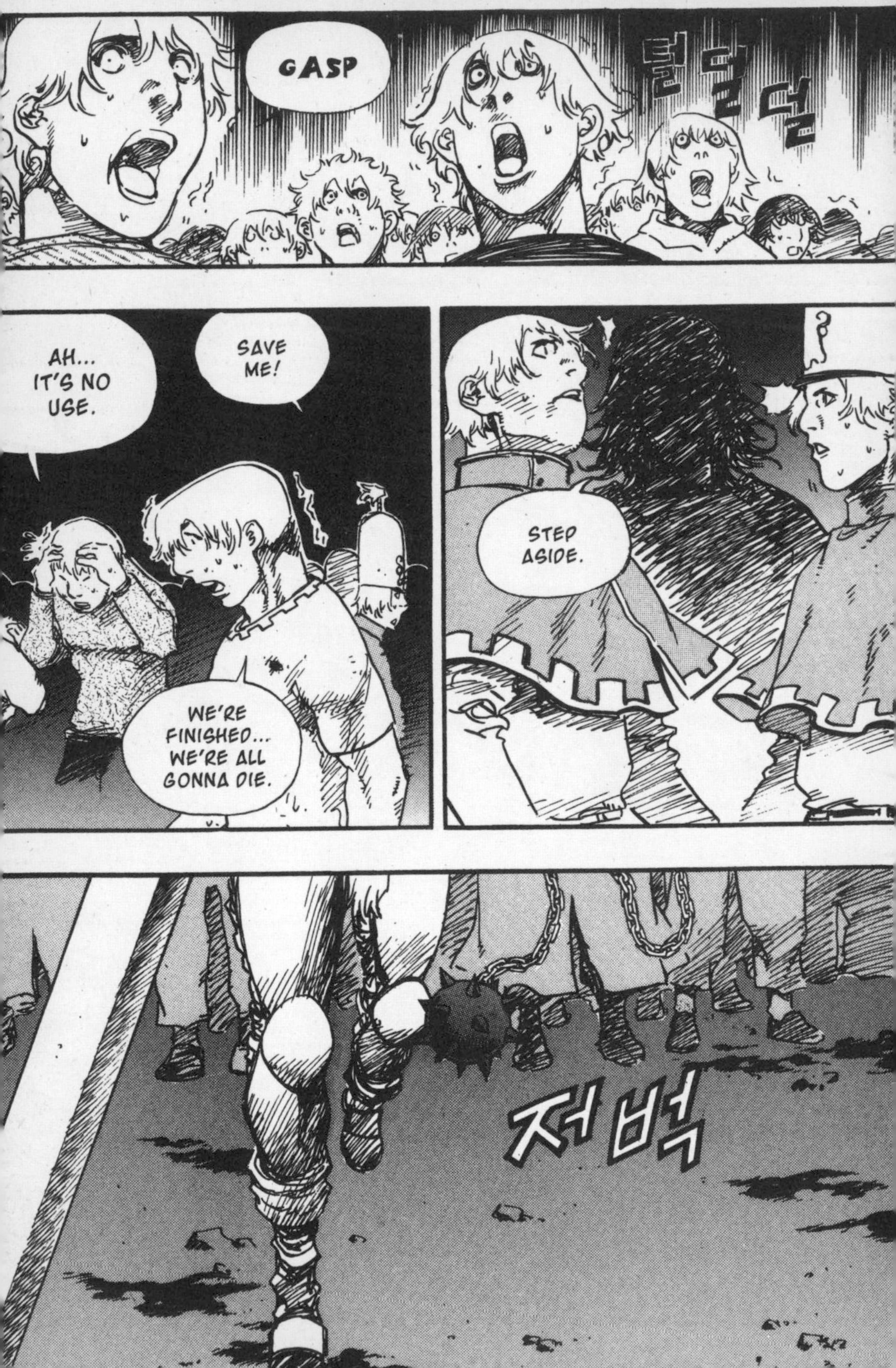
GASP
털덜덜
SAVE ME!
AH... IT'S NO USE.
WE'RE FINISHED... WE'RE ALL GONNA DIE.
STEP ASIDE.
저벅

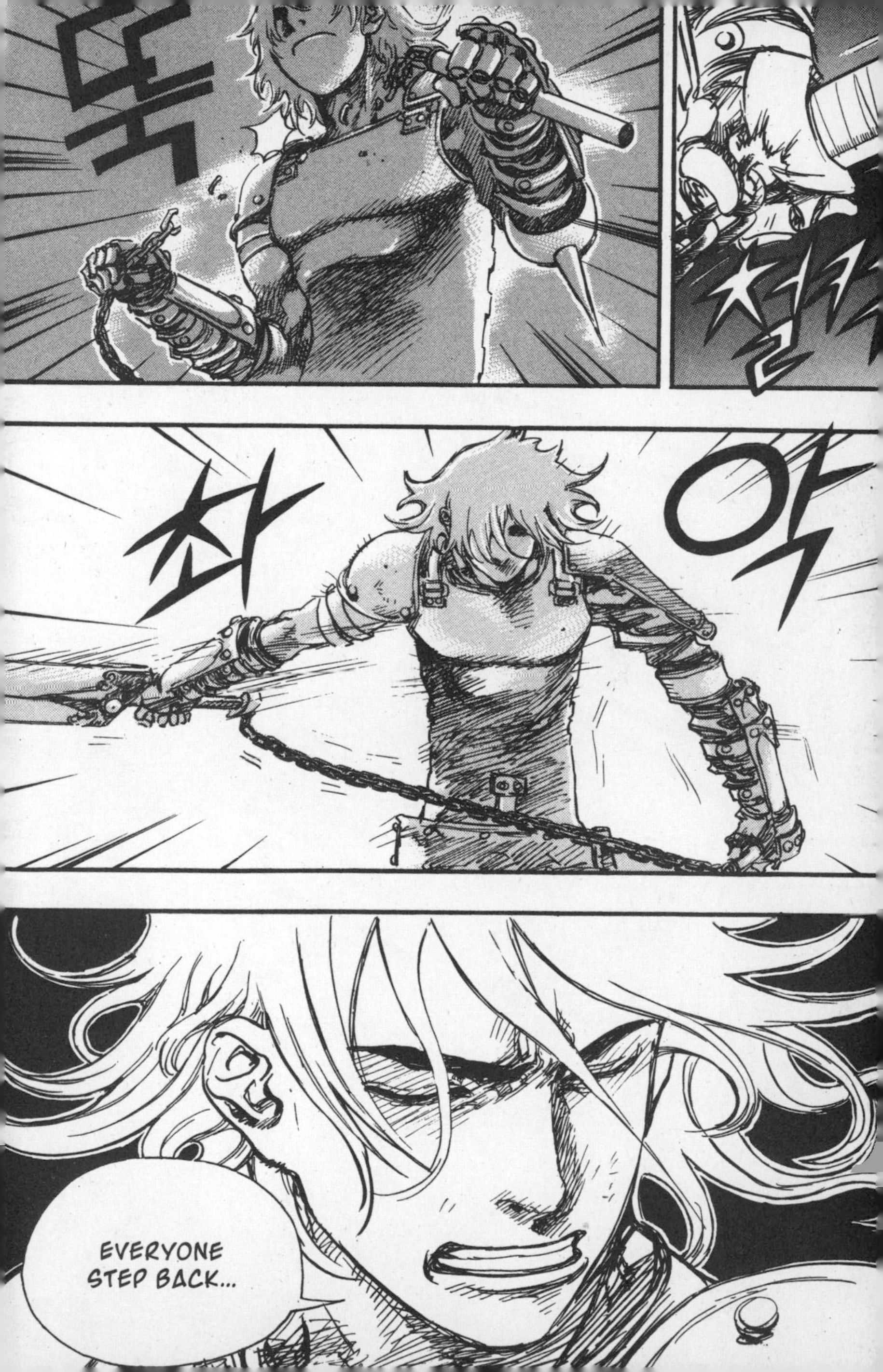
촤악
EVERYONE STEP BACK...

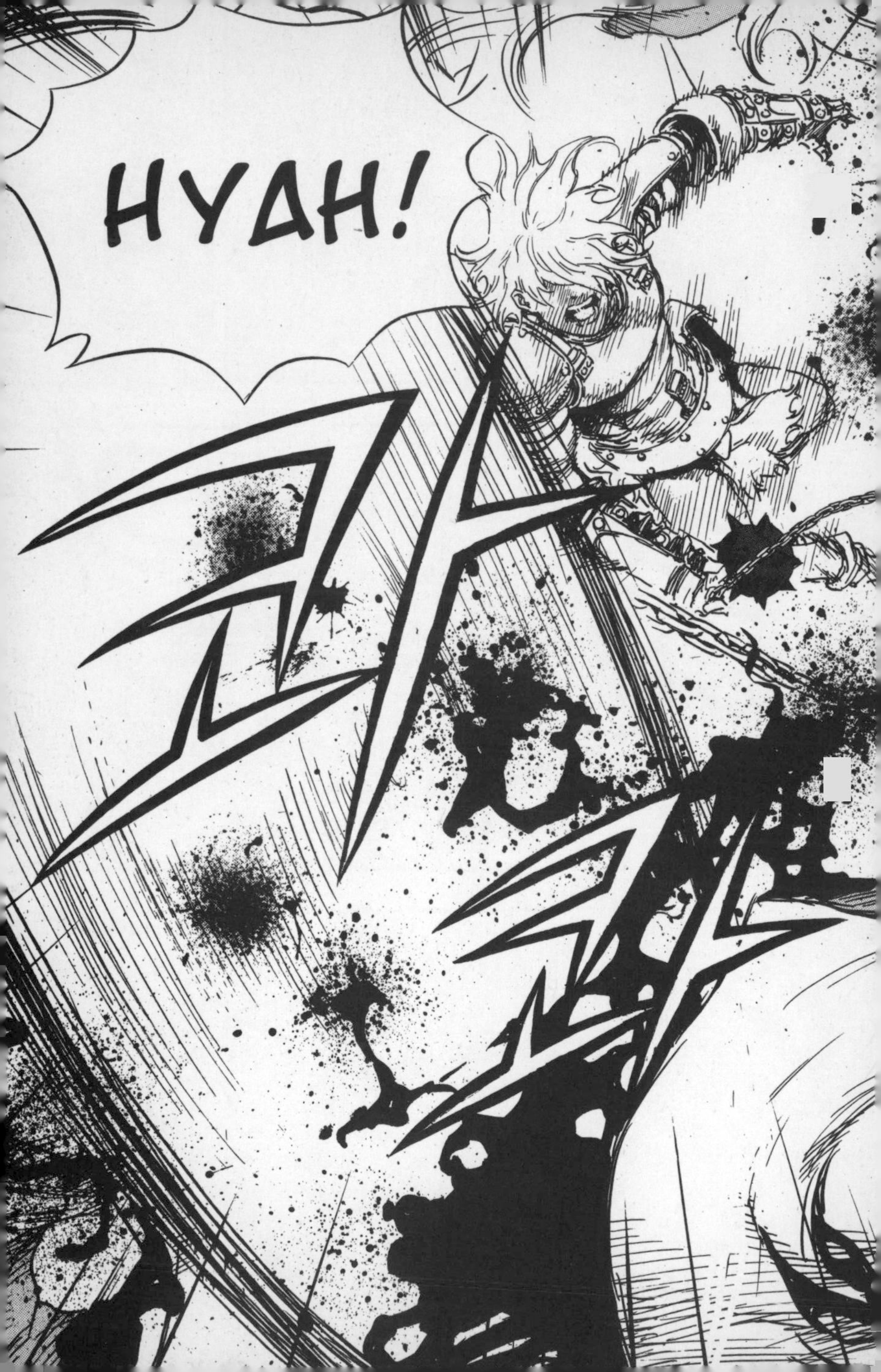
HYAH!

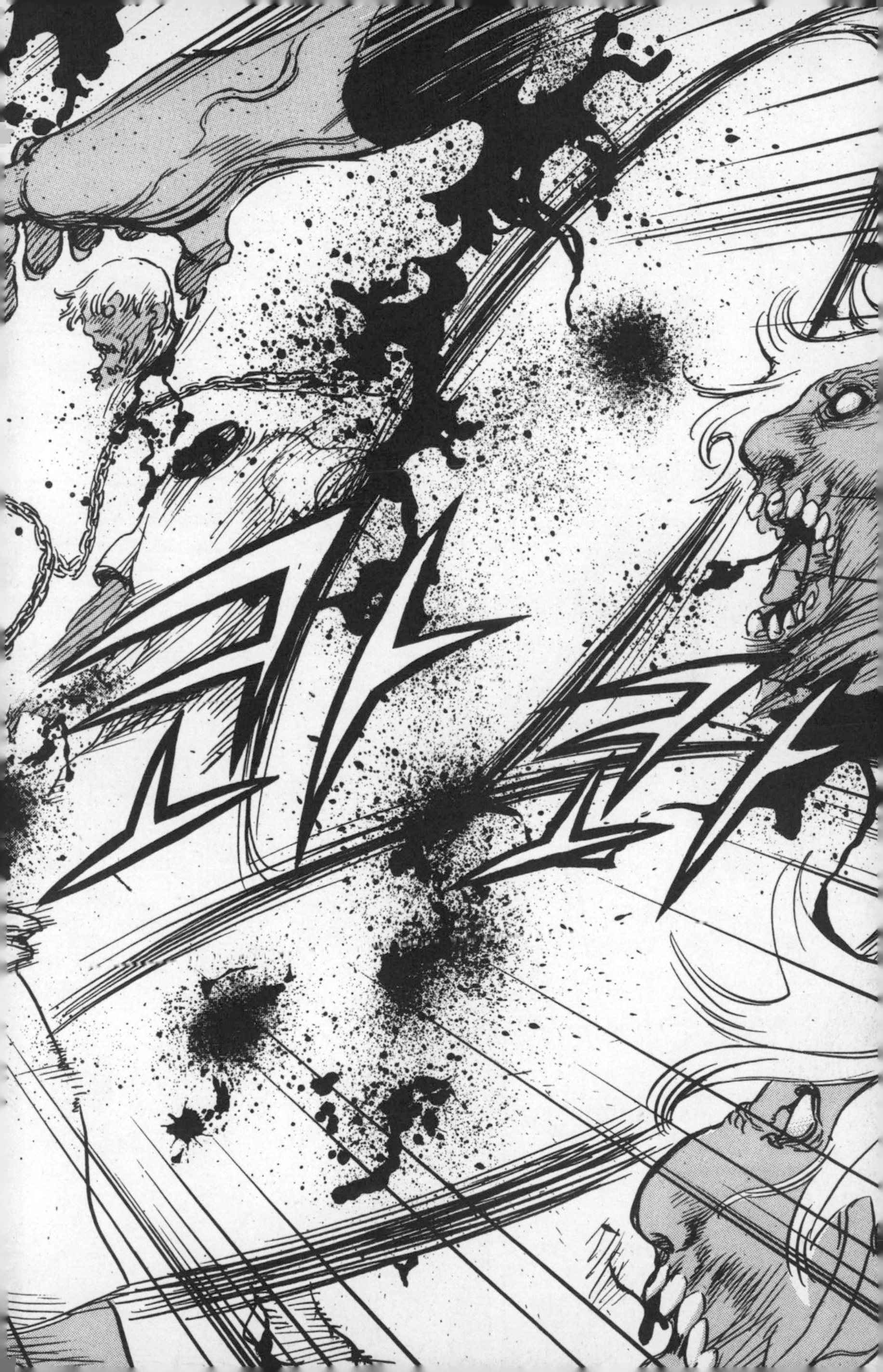

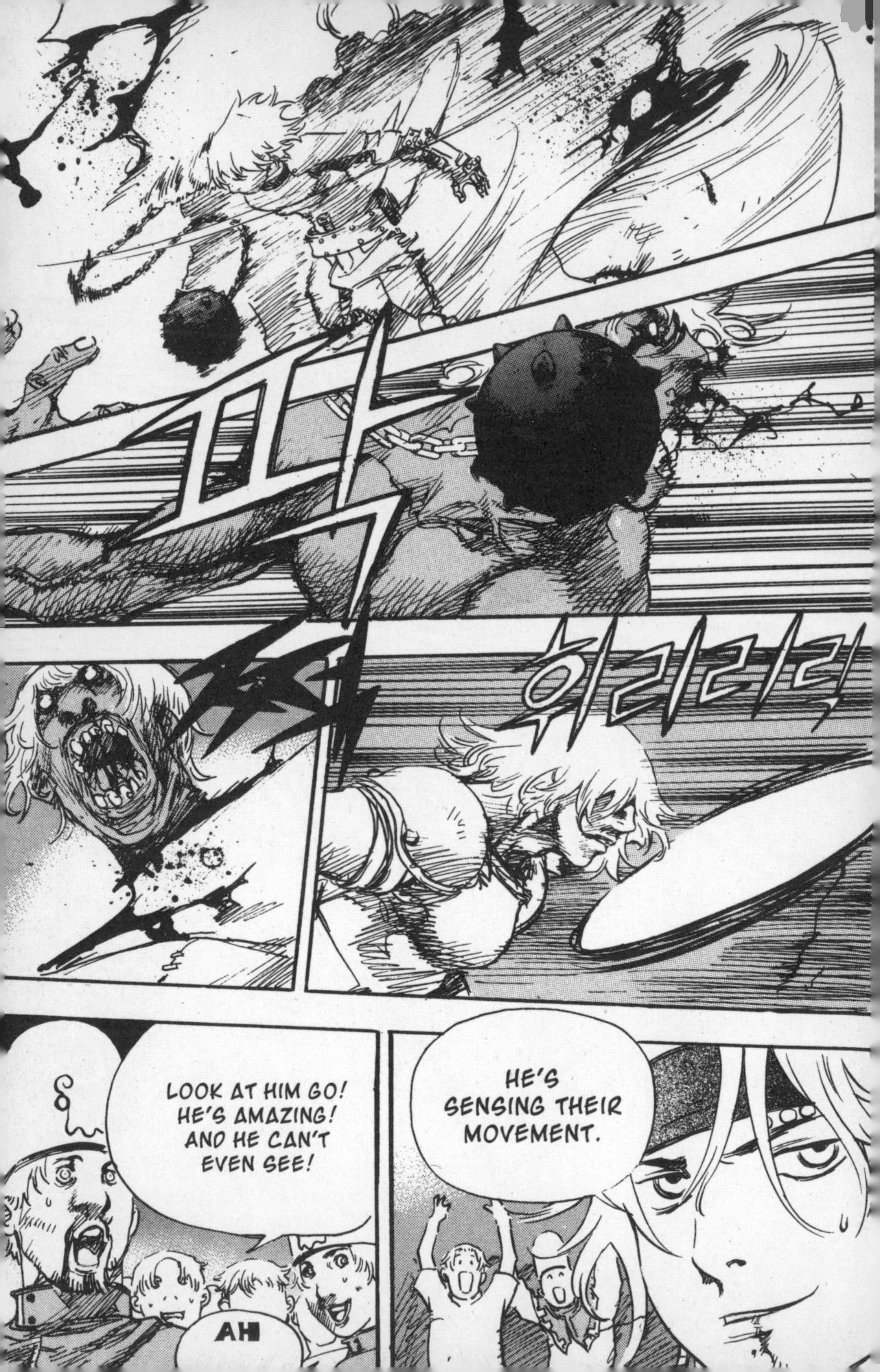

LOOK AT HIM GO! HE'S AMAZING! AND HE CAN'T EVEN SEE!
HE'S SENSING THEIR MOVEMENT.
AH

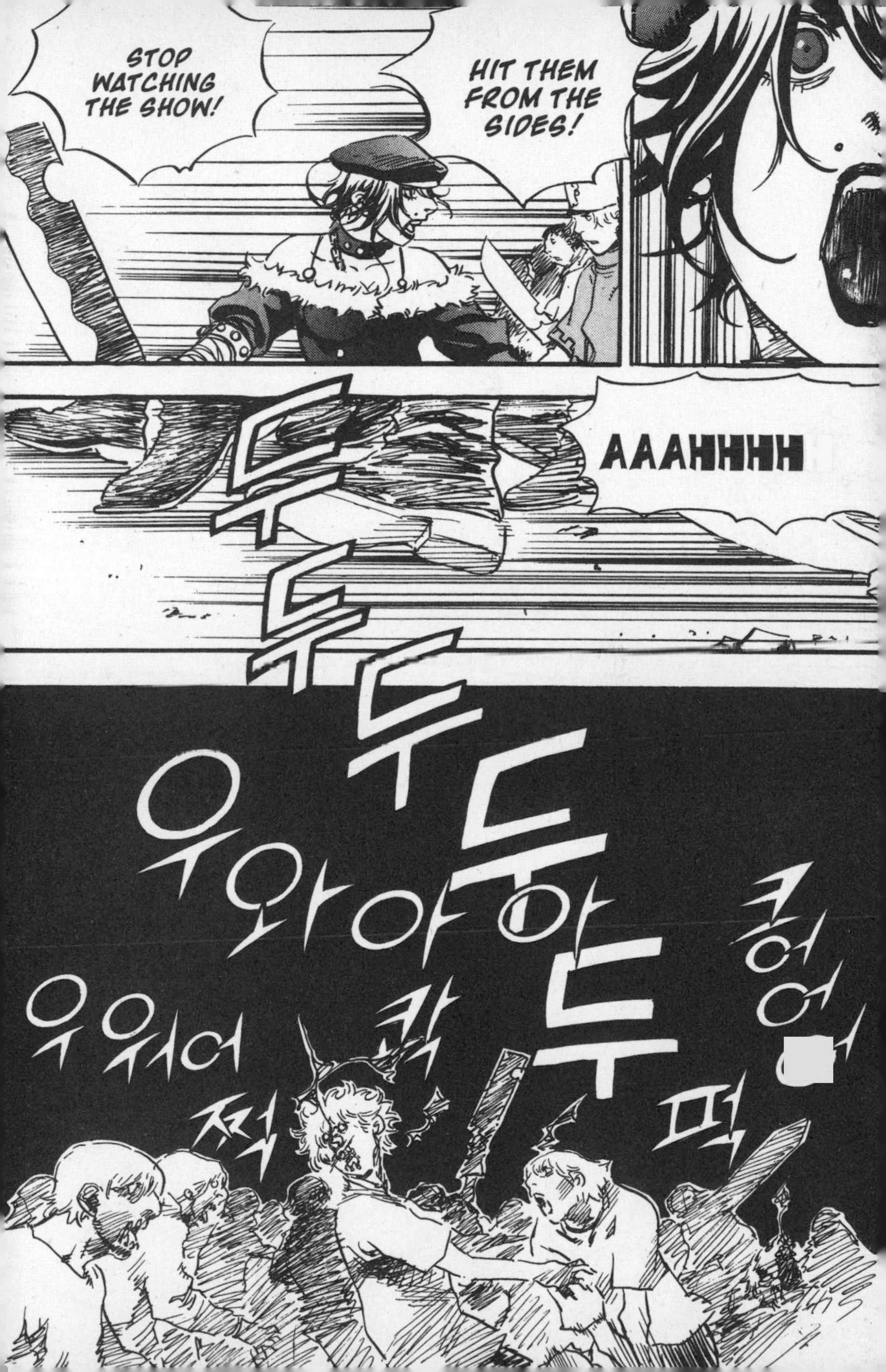
STOP WATCHING THE SHOW!
HIT THEM FROM THE SIDES!
AAAHHHH

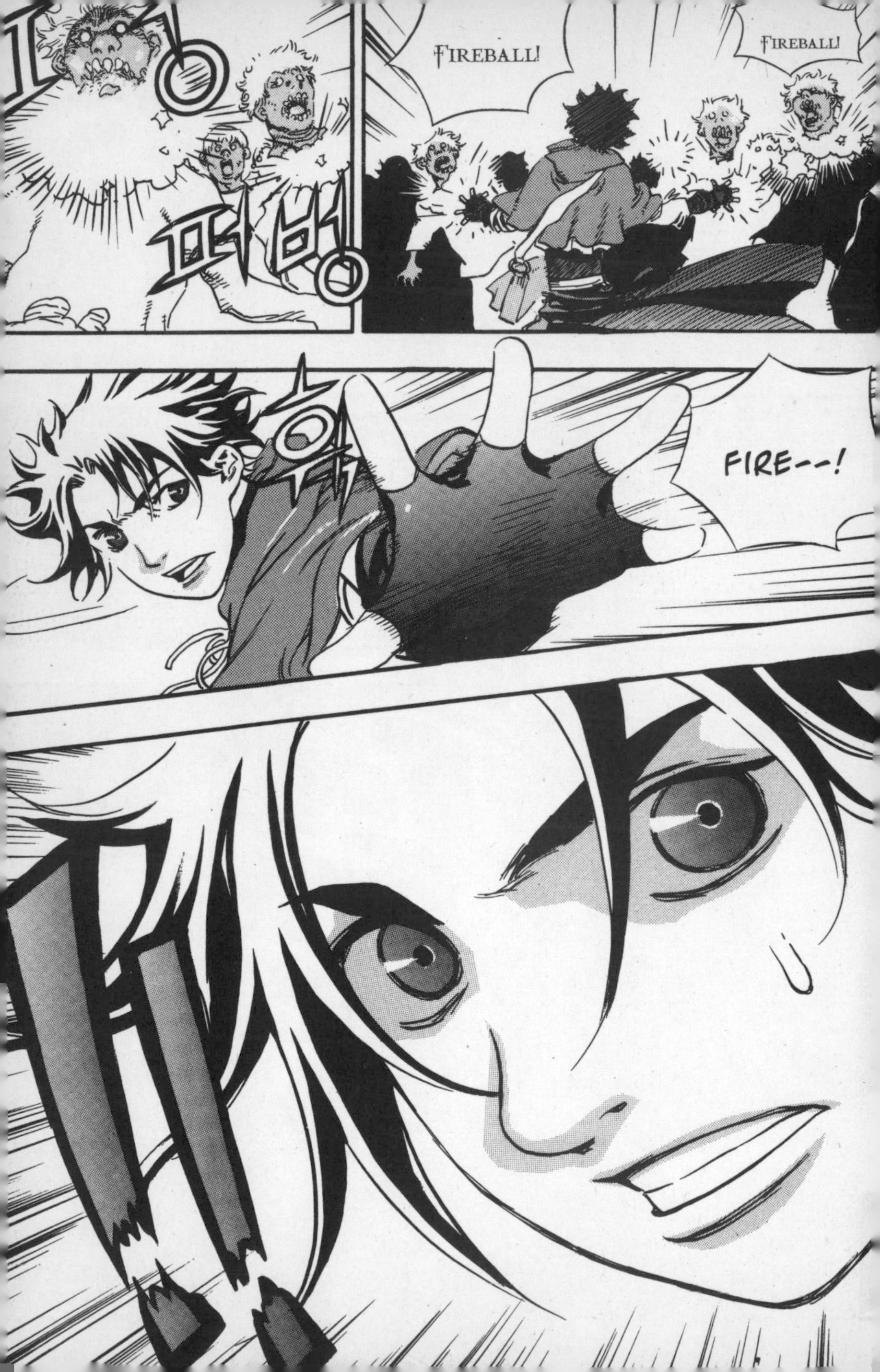
FIREBALL!
FIREBALL!
FIRE--!

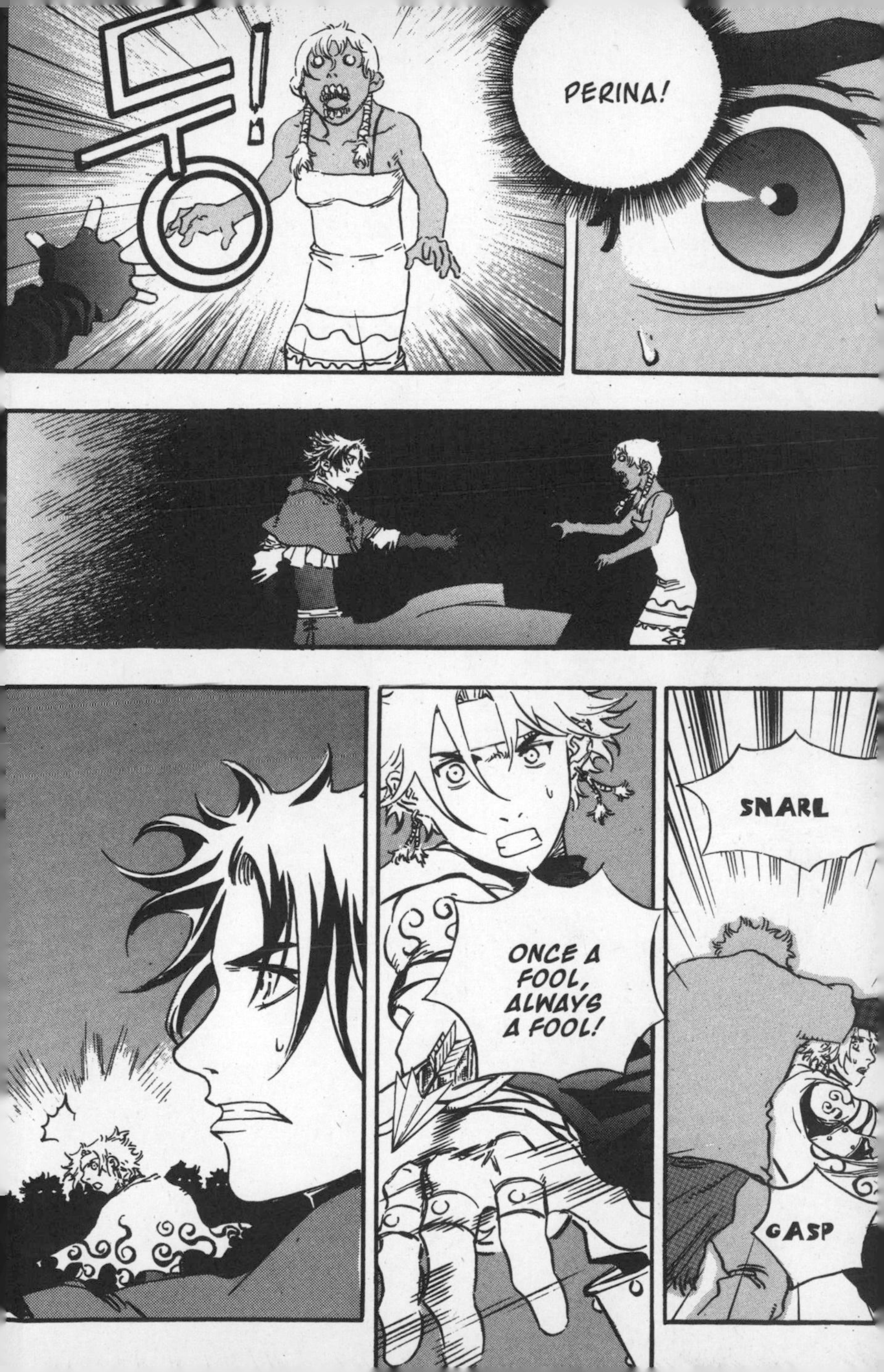
PERINA!
ONCE A FOOL, ALWAYS A FOOL!
SNARL
GASP

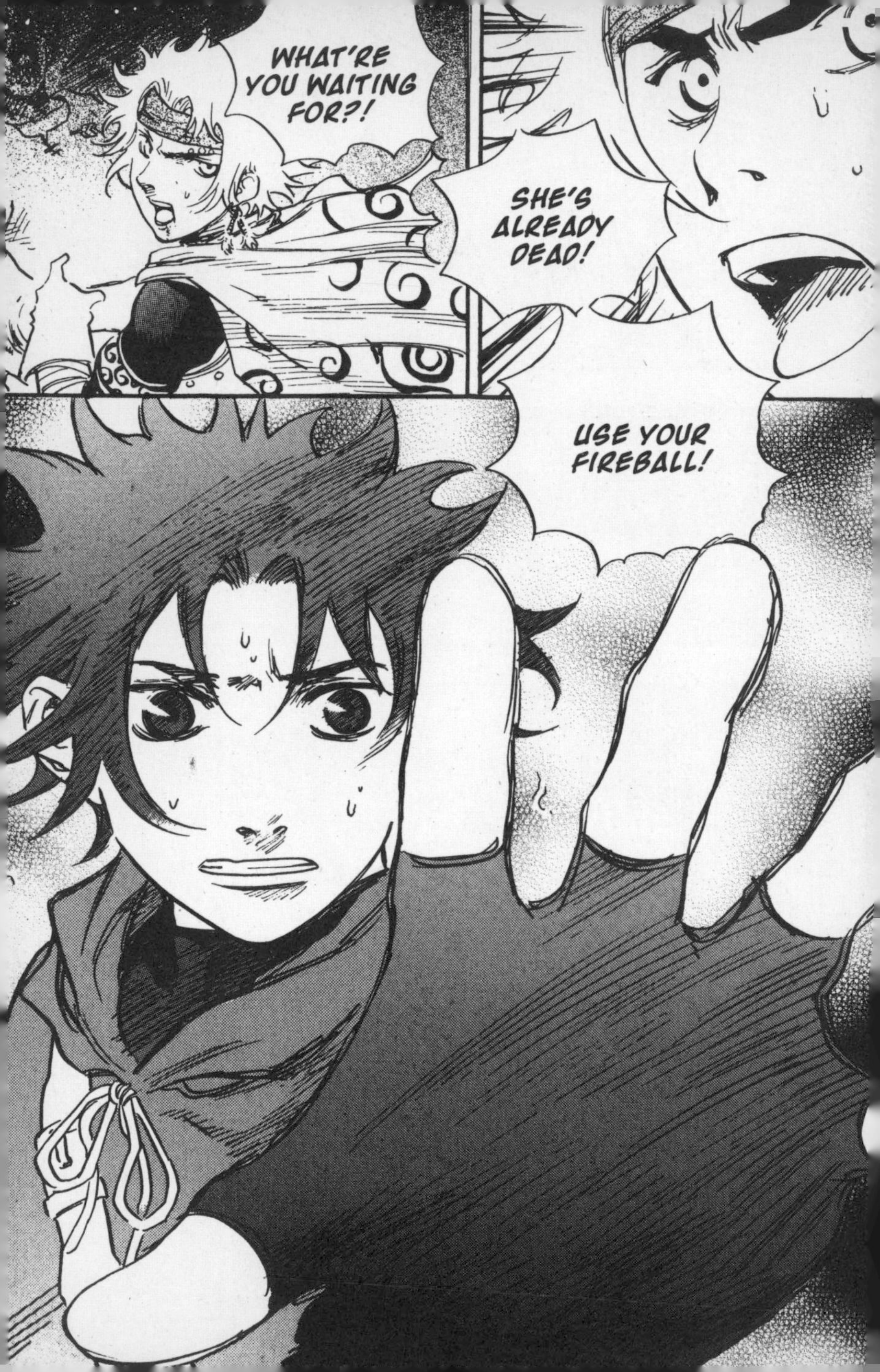
SHE'S ALREADY DEAD!
WHAT'RE YOU WAITING FOR?!
USE YOUR FIREBALL!

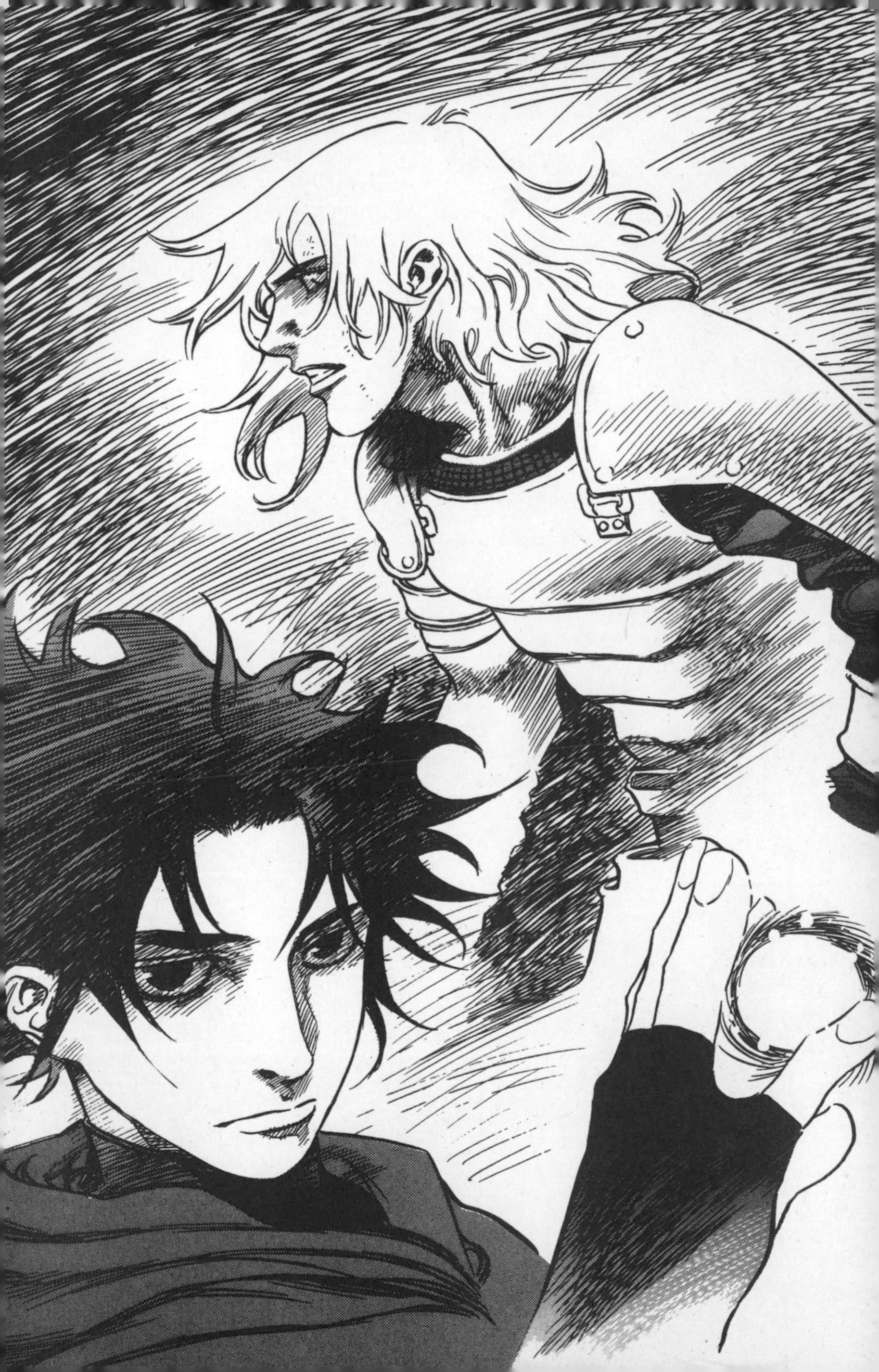

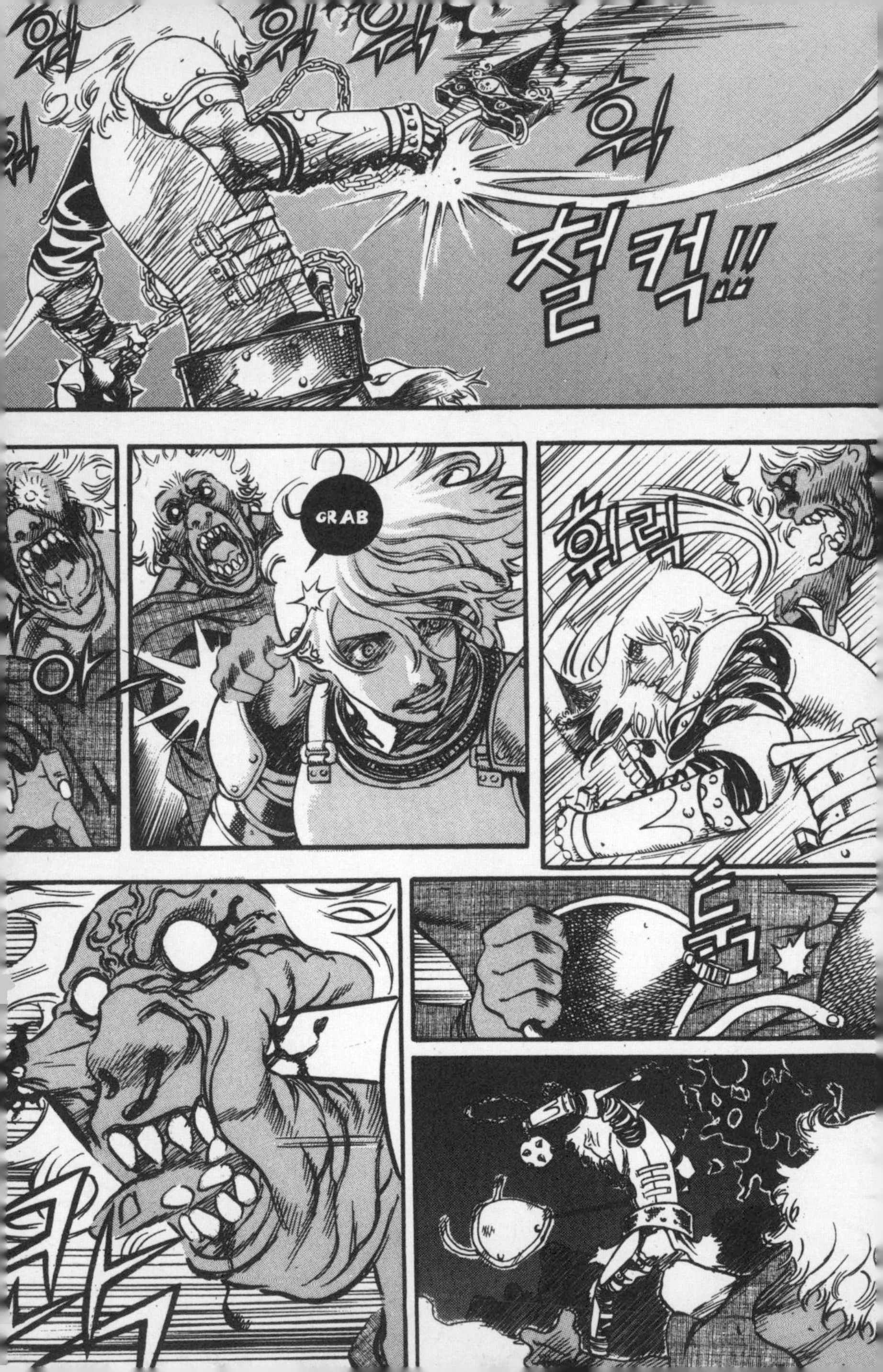
워 워 워
철컥!!
GRAB
휘릭
둑

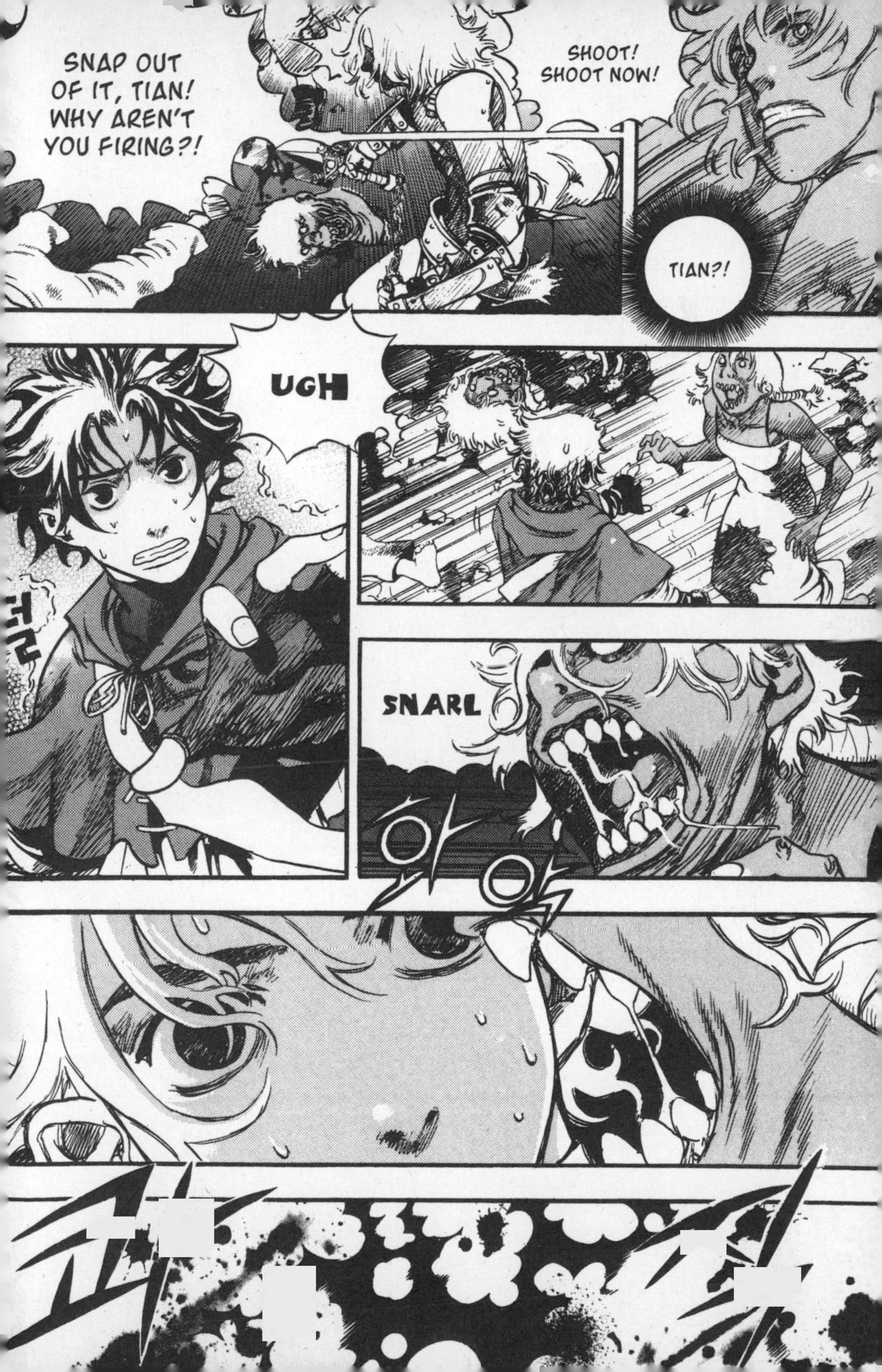
SNAP OUT OF IT, TIAN! WHY AREN'T YOU FIRING?!
SHOOT! SHOOT NOW!
TIAN?!
UGH
SNARL

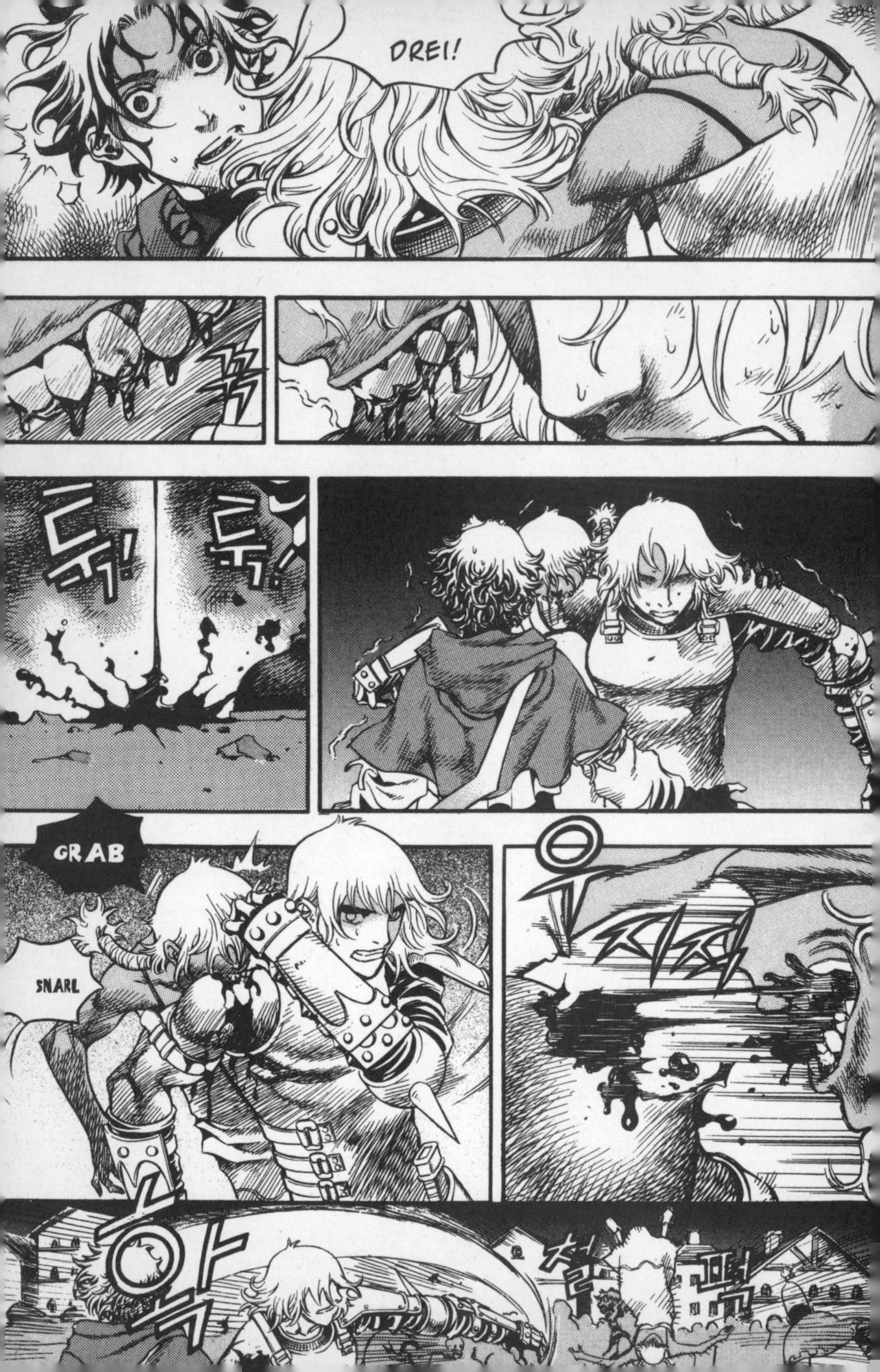
DREI!
GRAB
SNARL

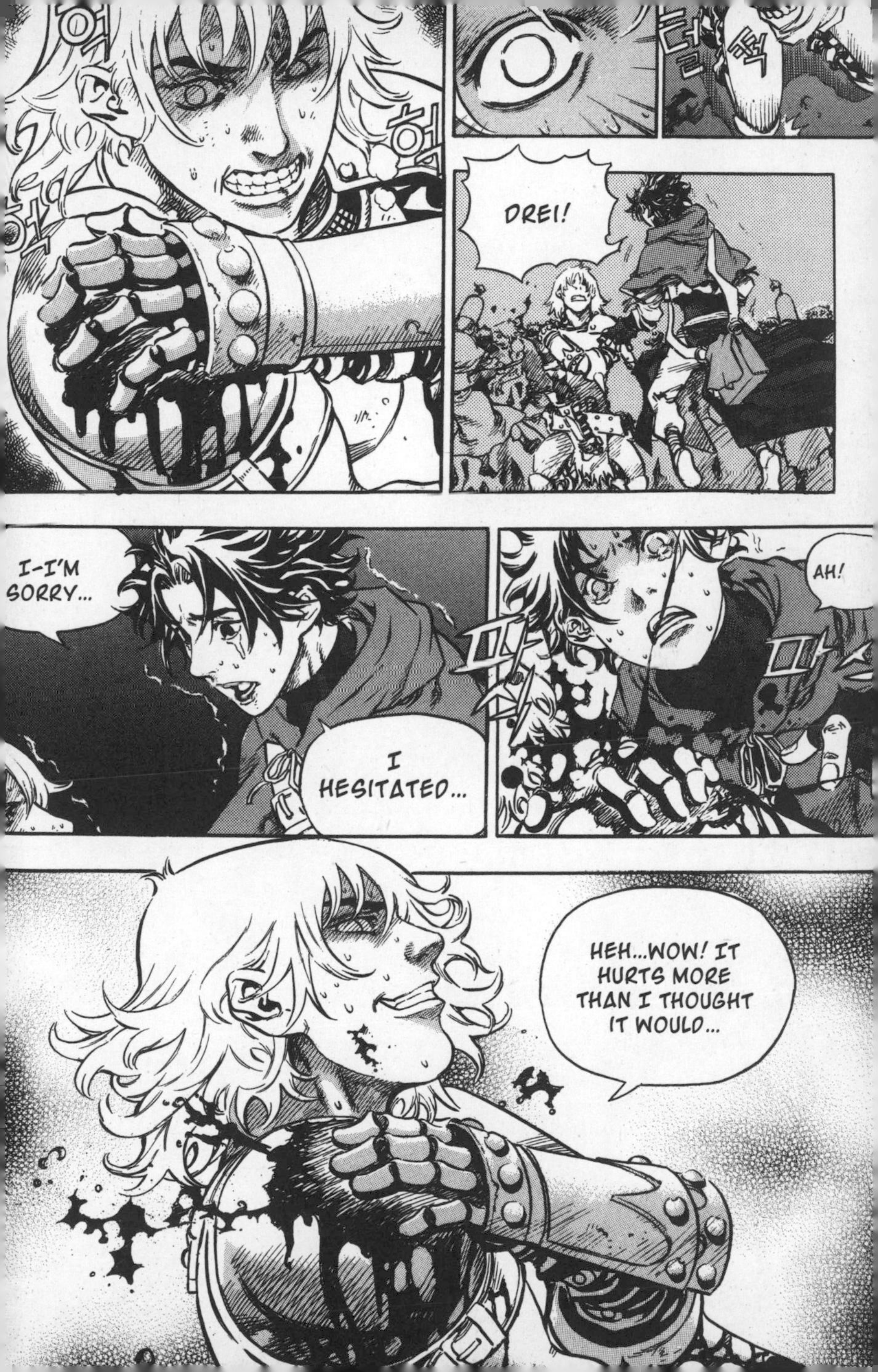

DREI!
I-I'M SORRY...
I HESITATED...
AH!
HEH...WOW! IT HURTS MORE THAN I THOUGHT IT WOULD...

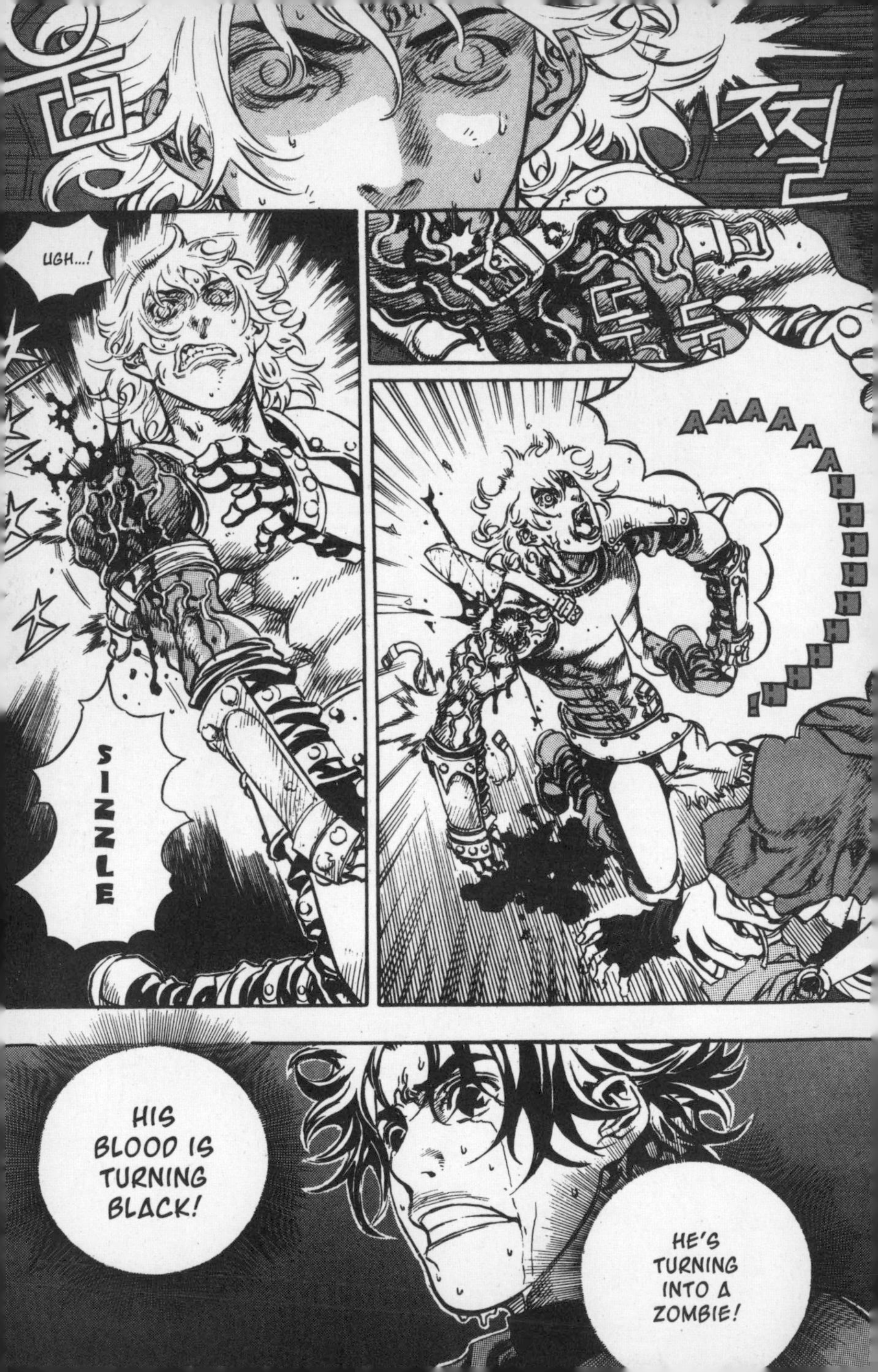
UGH...!
SIZZLE
AAAAAAAHHHHHHHHH!
HIS BLOOD IS TURNING BLACK!
HE'S TURNING INTO A ZOMBIE!

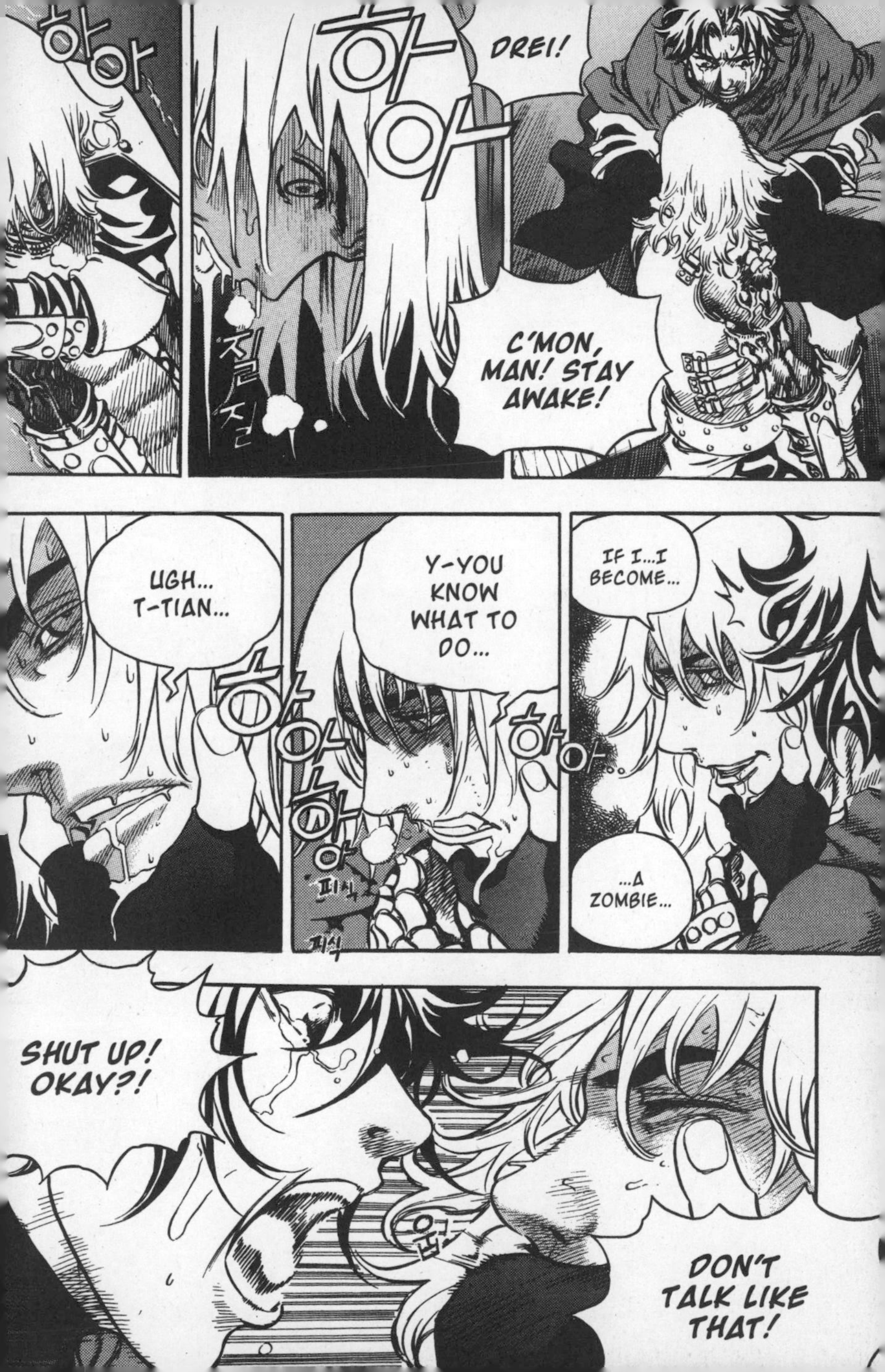

하아
하아
DREI!
C'MON, MAN! STAY AWAKE!
UGH... T-TIAN...
Y-YOU KNOW WHAT TO DO...
IF I...I BECOME...
...A ZOMBIE...
SHUT UP! OKAY?!
DON'T TALK LIKE THAT!

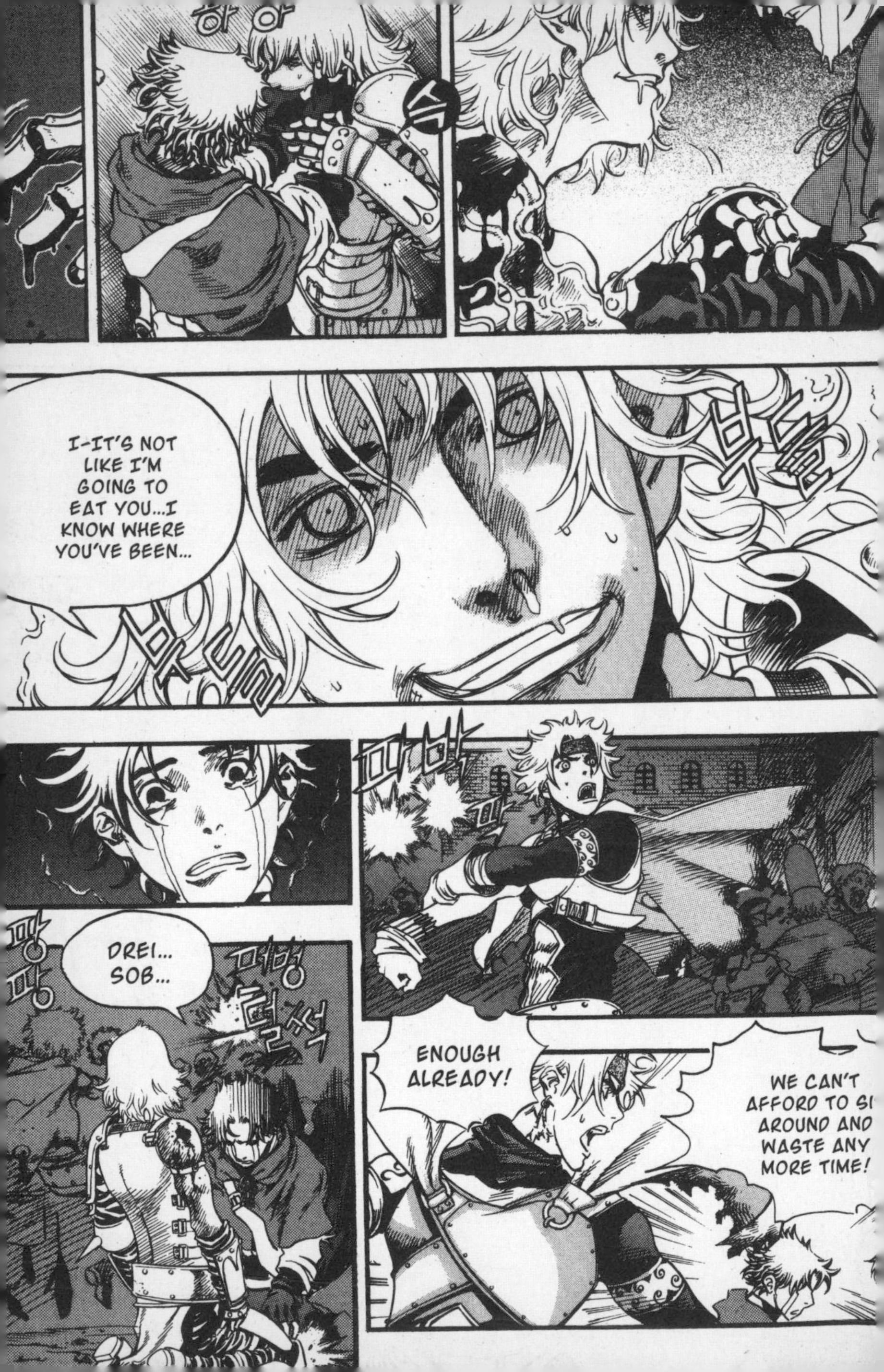

I-IT'S NOT LIKE I'M GOING TO EAT YOU...I KNOW WHERE YOU'VE BEEN...
DREI... SOB...
ENOUGH ALREADY!
WE CAN'T AFFORD TO SI AROUND AND WASTE ANY MORE TIME!

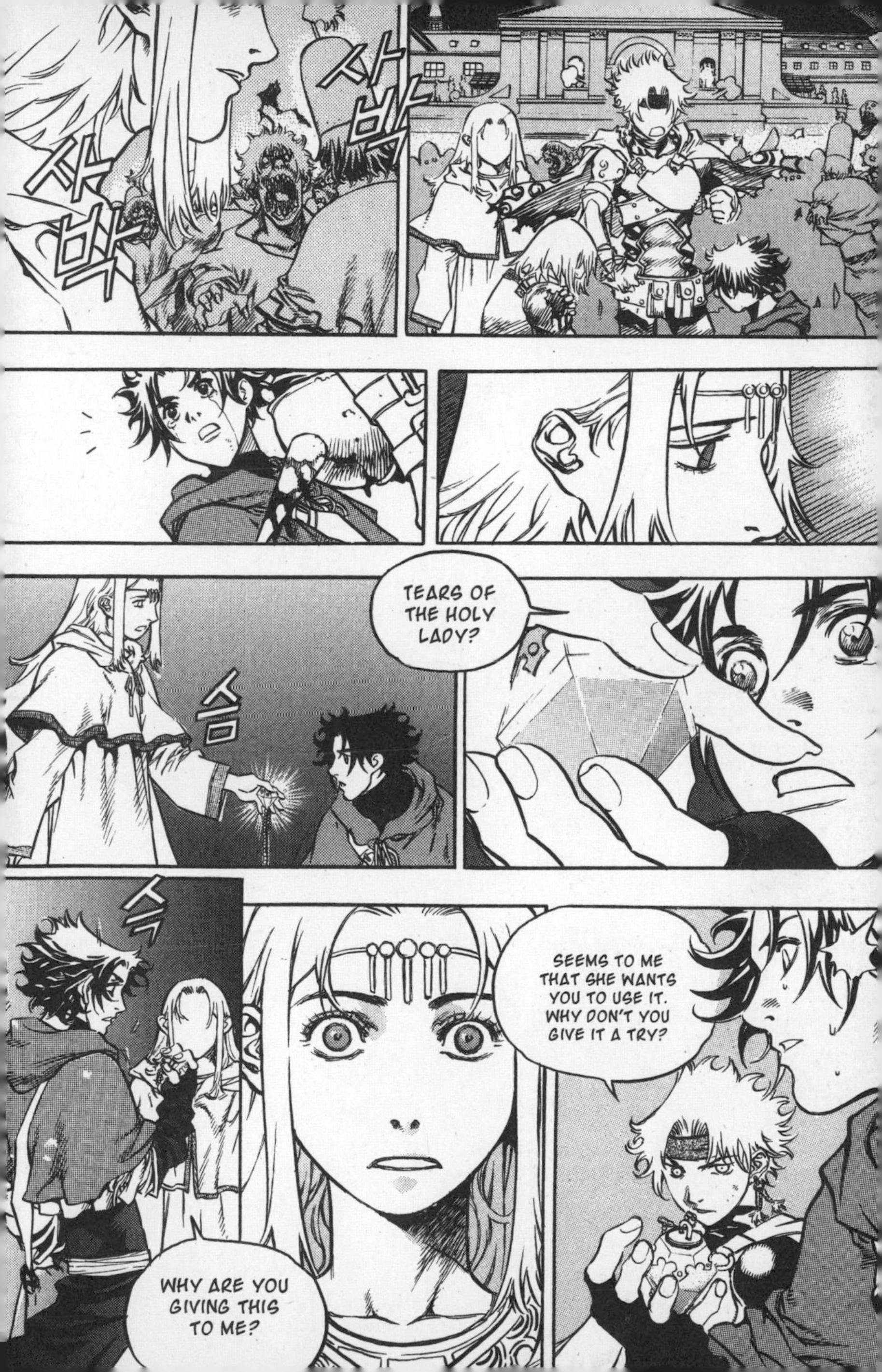
TEARS OF THE HOLY LADY?
WHY ARE YOU GIVING THIS TO ME?
SEEMS TO ME THAT SHE WANTS YOU TO USE IT. WHY DON'T YOU GIVE IT A TRY?

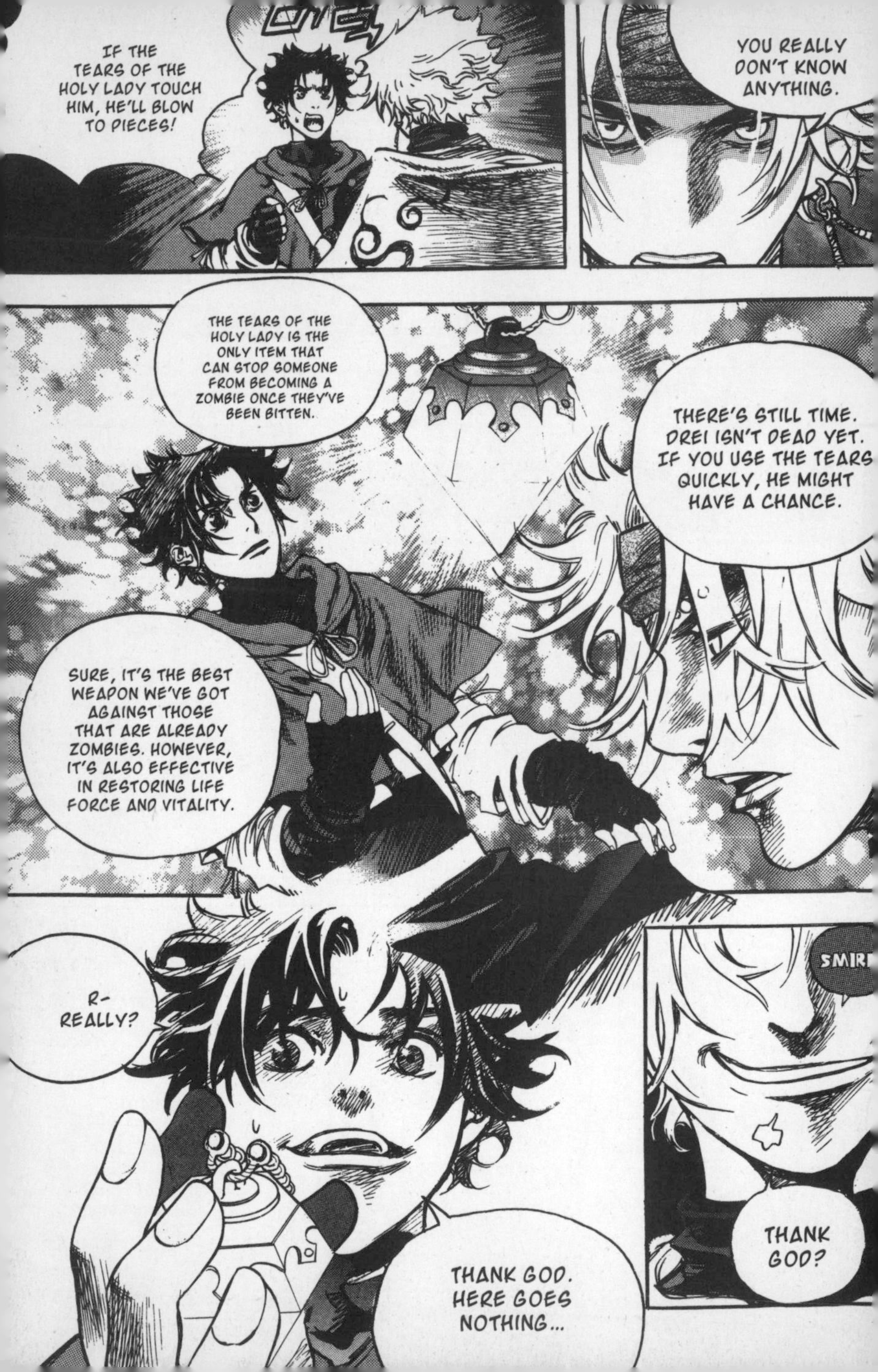
IF THE TEARS OF THE HOLY LADY TOUCH HIM, HE'LL BLOW TO PIECES!
YOU REALLY DON'T KNOW ANYTHING.
THE TEARS OF THE HOLY LADY IS THE ONLY ITEM THAT CAN STOP SOMEONE FROM BECOMING A ZOMBIE ONCE THEY'VE BEEN BITTEN.
THERE'S STILL TIME. DREI ISN'T DEAD YET. IF YOU USE THE TEARS QUICKLY, HE MIGHT HAVE A CHANCE.
SURE, IT'S THE BEST WEAPON WE'VE GOT AGAINST THOSE THAT ARE ALREADY ZOMBIES. HOWEVER, IT'S ALSO EFFECTIVE IN RESTORING LIFE FORCE AND VITALITY.
R-REALLY?
THANK GOD. HERE GOES NOTHING...
THANK GOD?

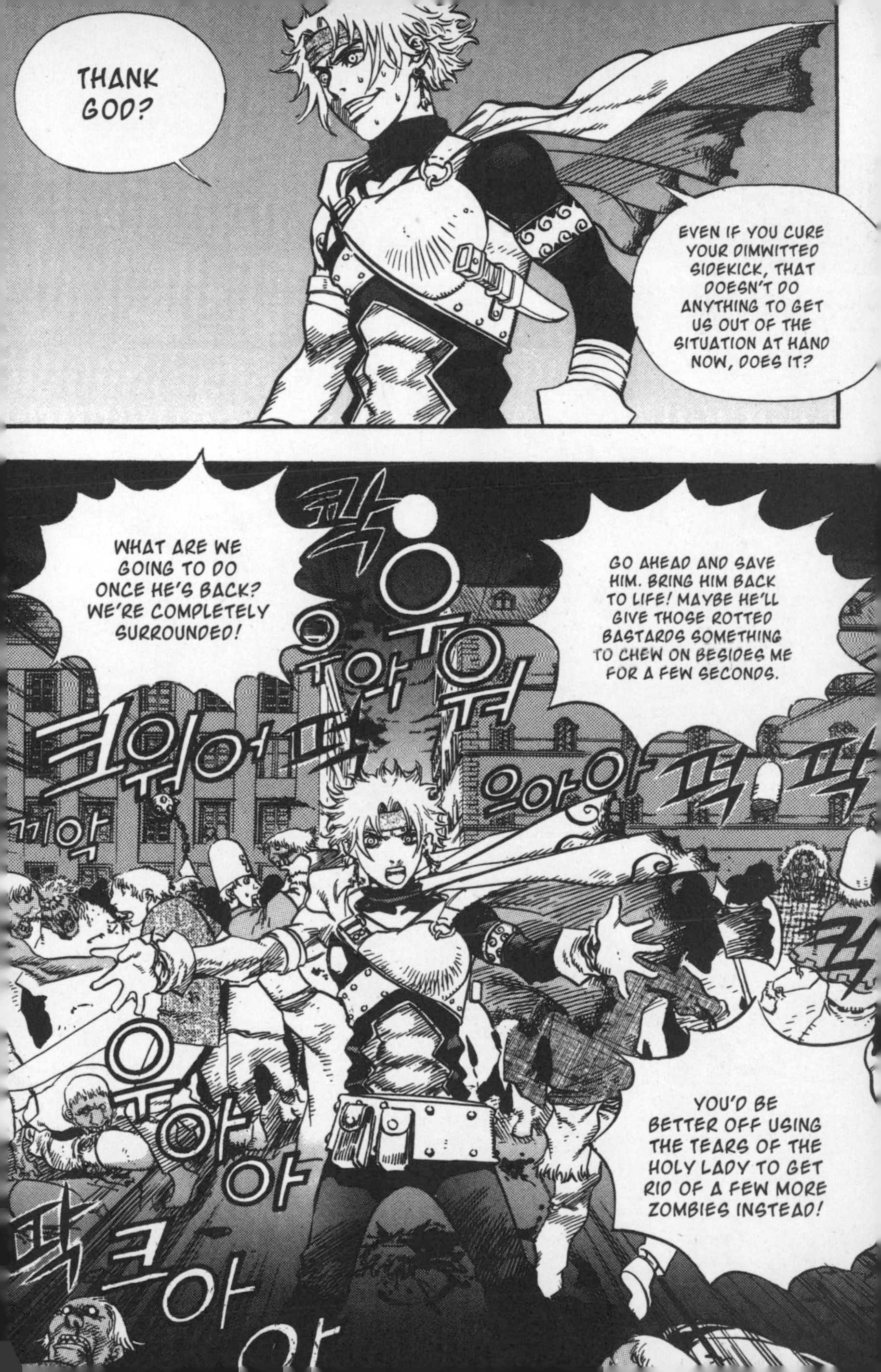
THANK GOD?
EVEN IF YOU CURE YOUR DIMWITTED SIDEKICK, THAT DOESN'T DO ANYTHING TO GET US OUT OF THE SITUATION AT HAND NOW, DOES IT?
GO AHEAD AND SAVE HIM. BRING HIM BACK TO LIFE! MAYBE HE'LL GIVE THOSE ROTTED BASTARDS SOMETHING TO CHEW ON BESIDES ME FOR A FEW SECONDS.
WHAT ARE WE GOING TO DO ONCE HE'S BACK? WE'RE COMPLETELY SURROUNDED!
YOU'D BE BETTER OFF USING THE TEARS OF THE HOLY LADY TO GET RID OF A FEW MORE ZOMBIES INSTEAD!

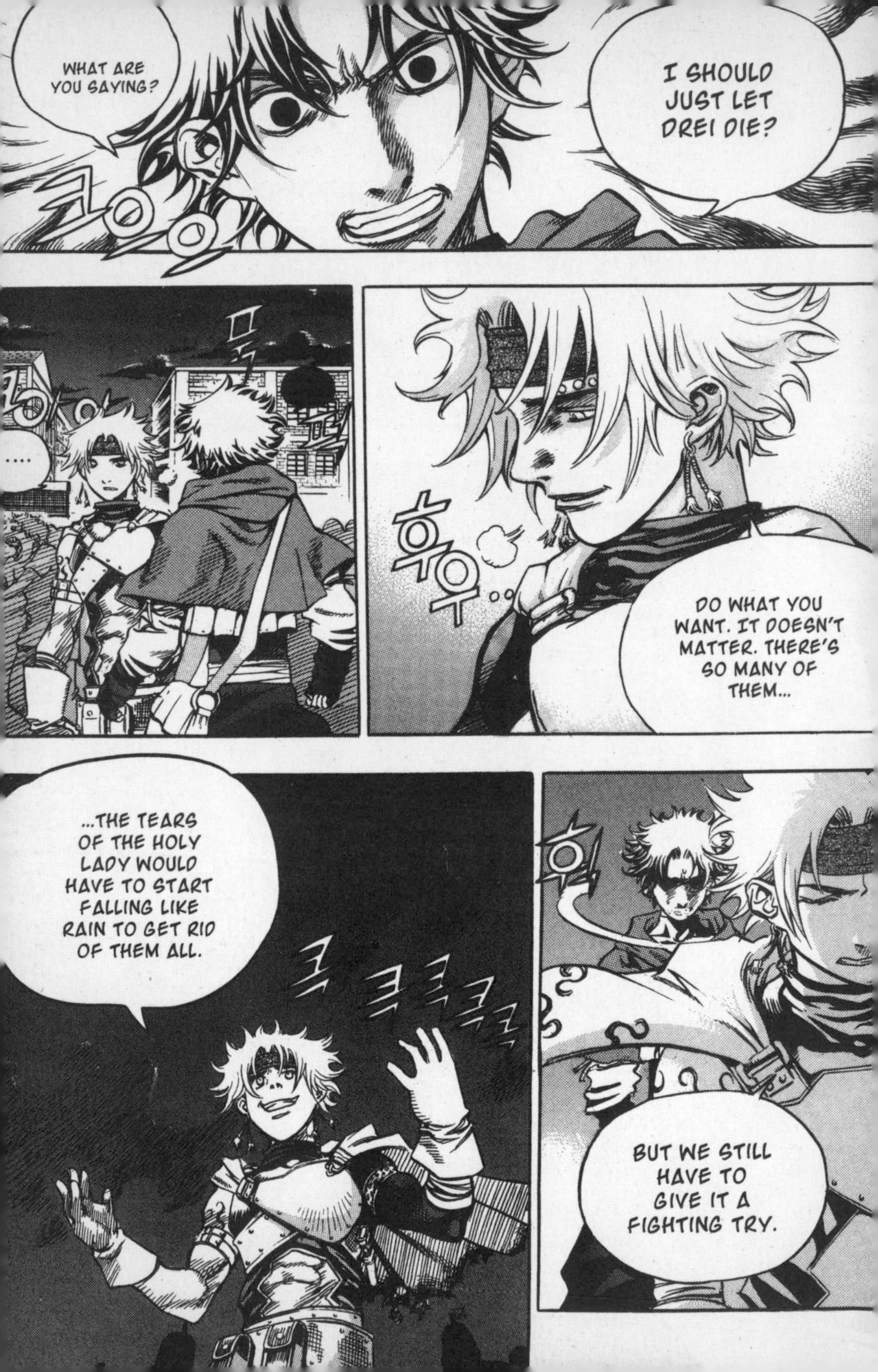
WHAT ARE YOU SAYING?
I SHOULD JUST LET DREI DIE?
.....
DO WHAT YOU WANT. IT DOESN'T MATTER. THERE'S SO MANY OF THEM...
...THE TEARS OF THE HOLY LADY WOULD HAVE TO START FALLING LIKE RAIN TO GET RID OF THEM ALL.
BUT WE STILL HAVE TO GIVE IT A FIGHTING TRY.

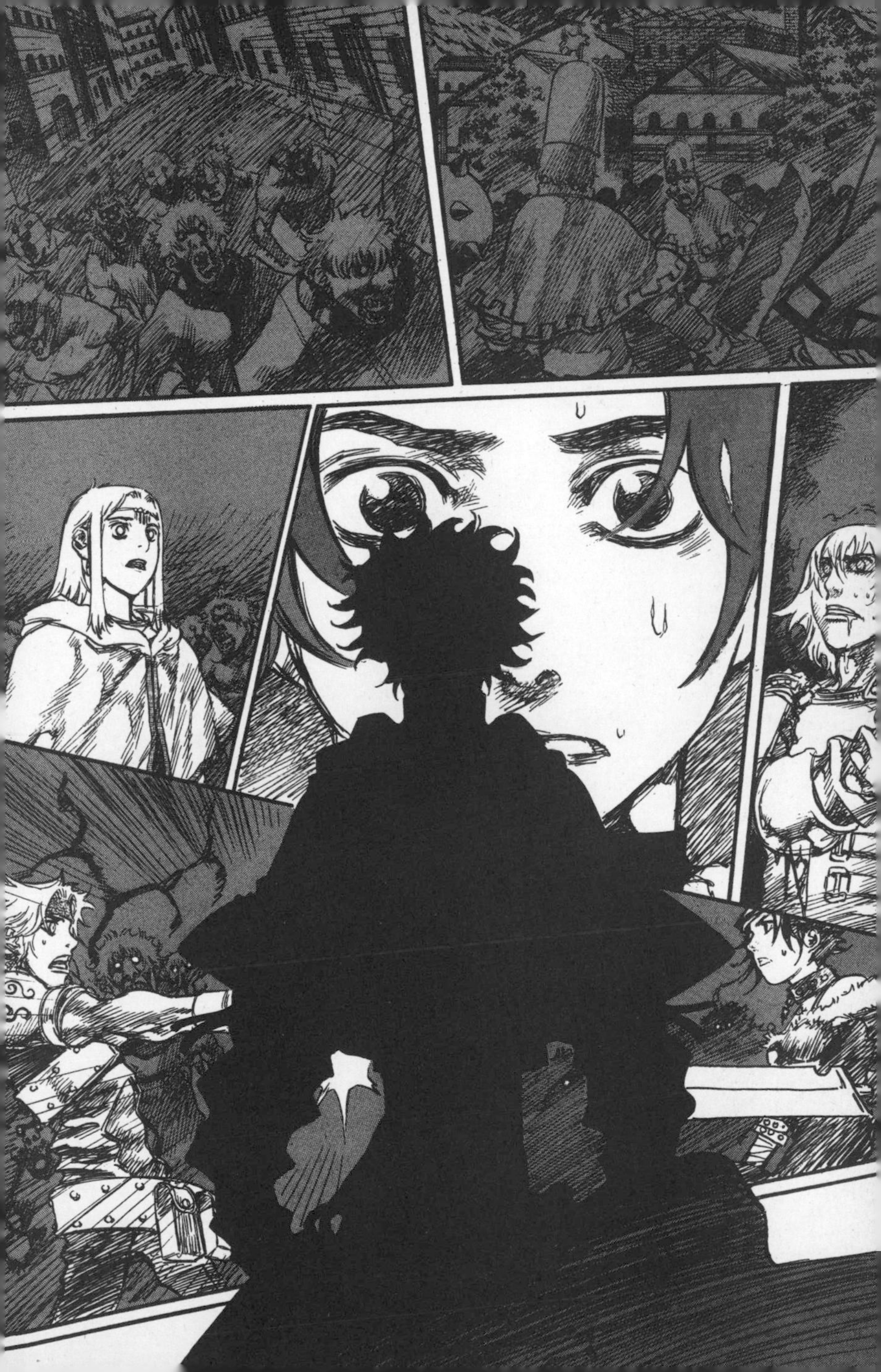

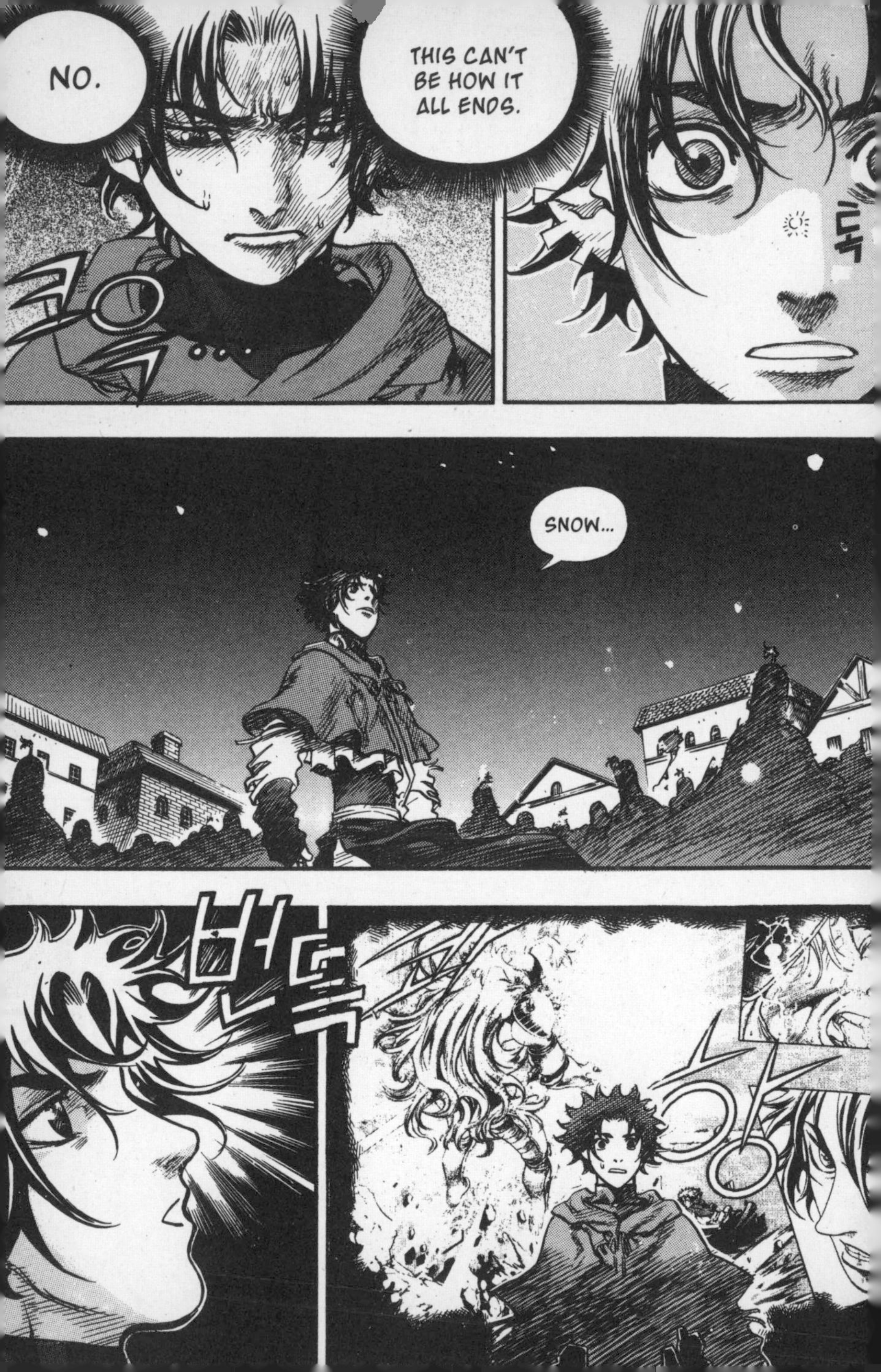
NO.
THIS CAN'T BE HOW IT ALL ENDS.
SNOW...

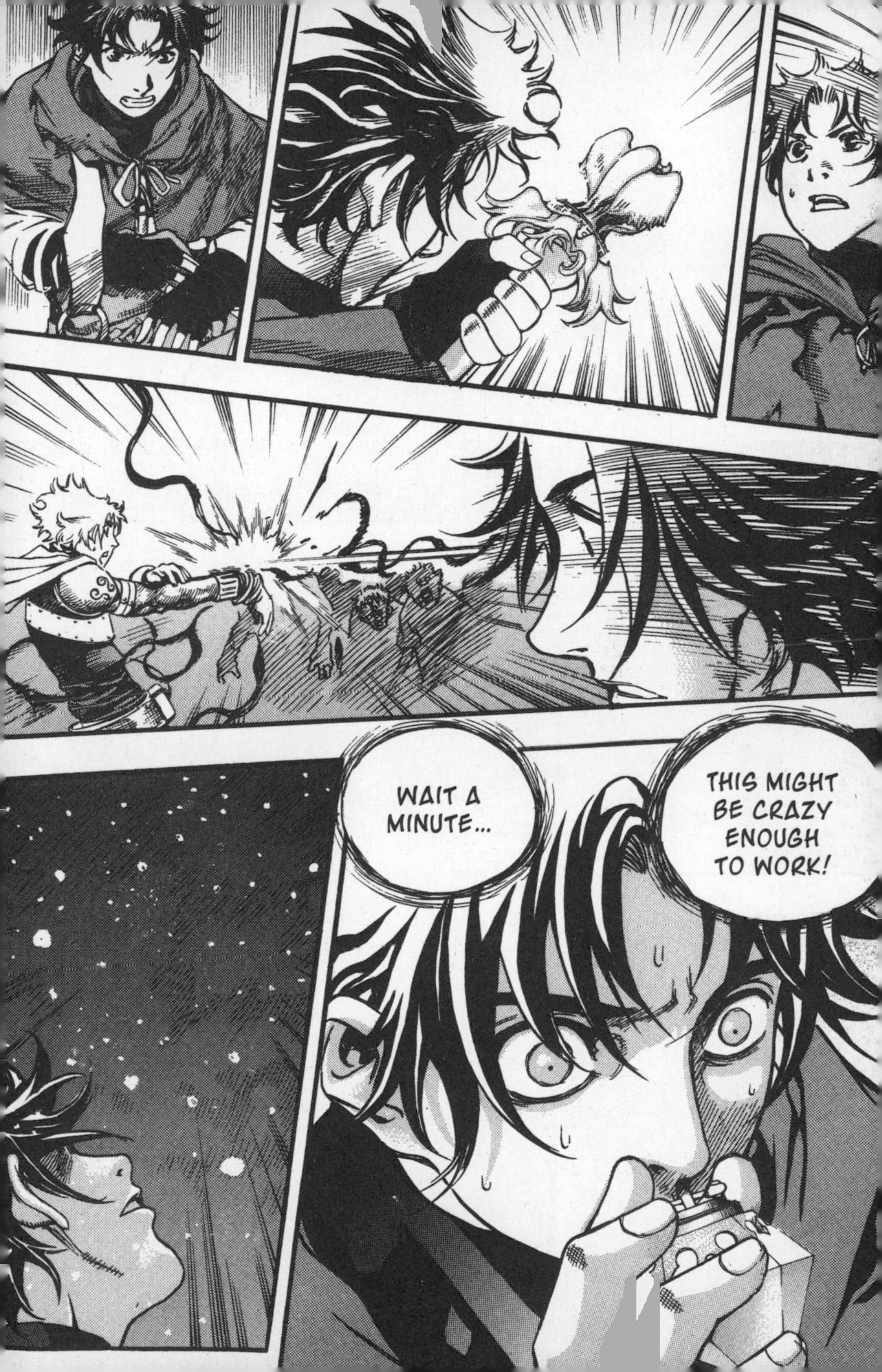
WAIT A MINUTE...
THIS MIGHT BE CRAZY ENOUGH TO WORK!

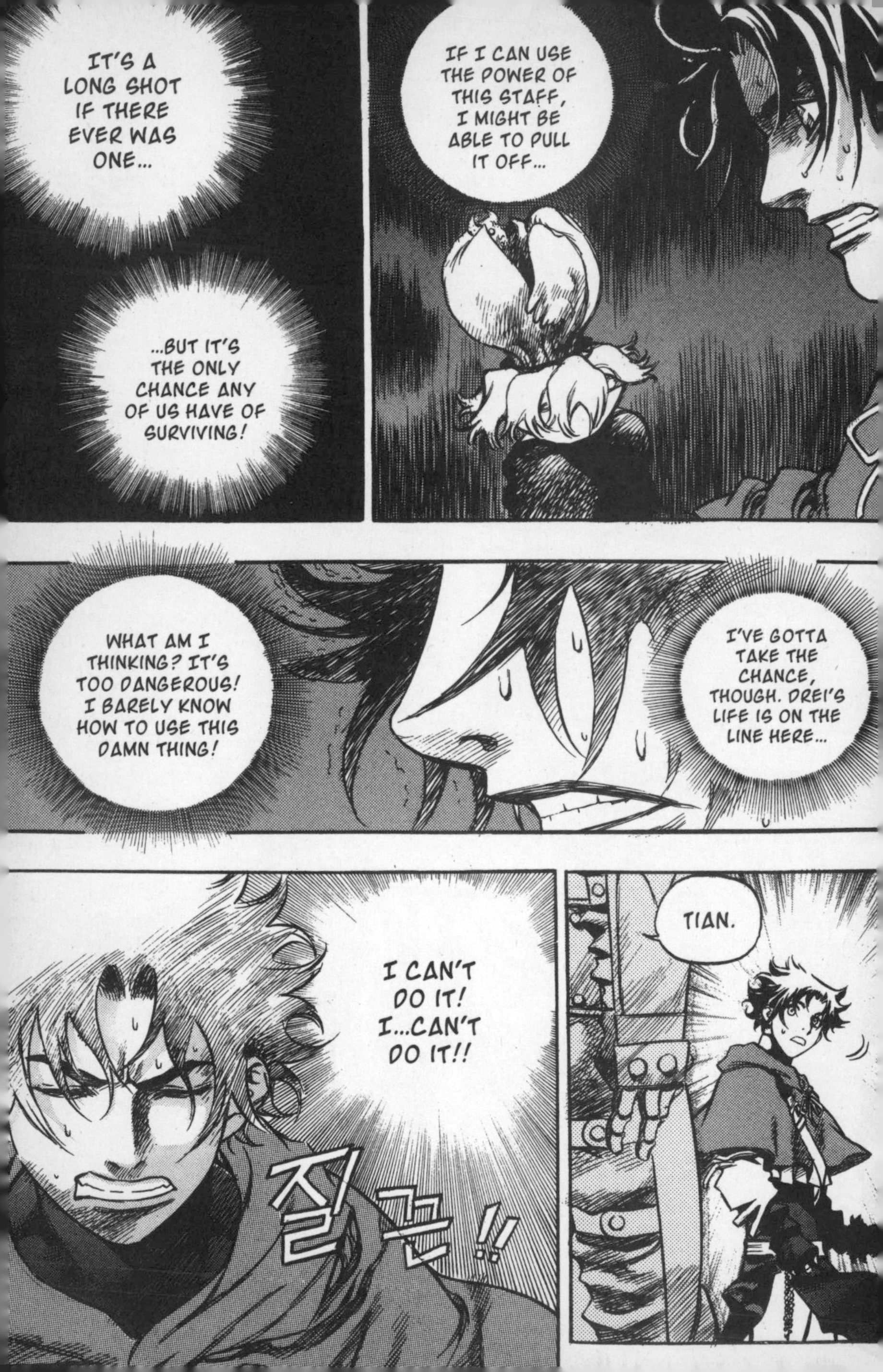
IT'S A LONG SHOT IF THERE EVER WAS ONE...
...BUT IT'S THE ONLY CHANCE ANY OF US HAVE OF SURVIVING!
IF I CAN USE THE POWER OF THIS STAFF, I MIGHT BE ABLE TO PULL IT OFF...
WHAT AM I THINKING? IT'S TOO DANGEROUS! I BARELY KNOW HOW TO USE THIS DAMN THING!
I'VE GOTTA TAKE THE CHANCE, THOUGH. DREI'S LIFE IS ON THE LINE HERE...
I CAN'T DO IT! I...CAN'T DO IT!!
질끈!!
TIAN.

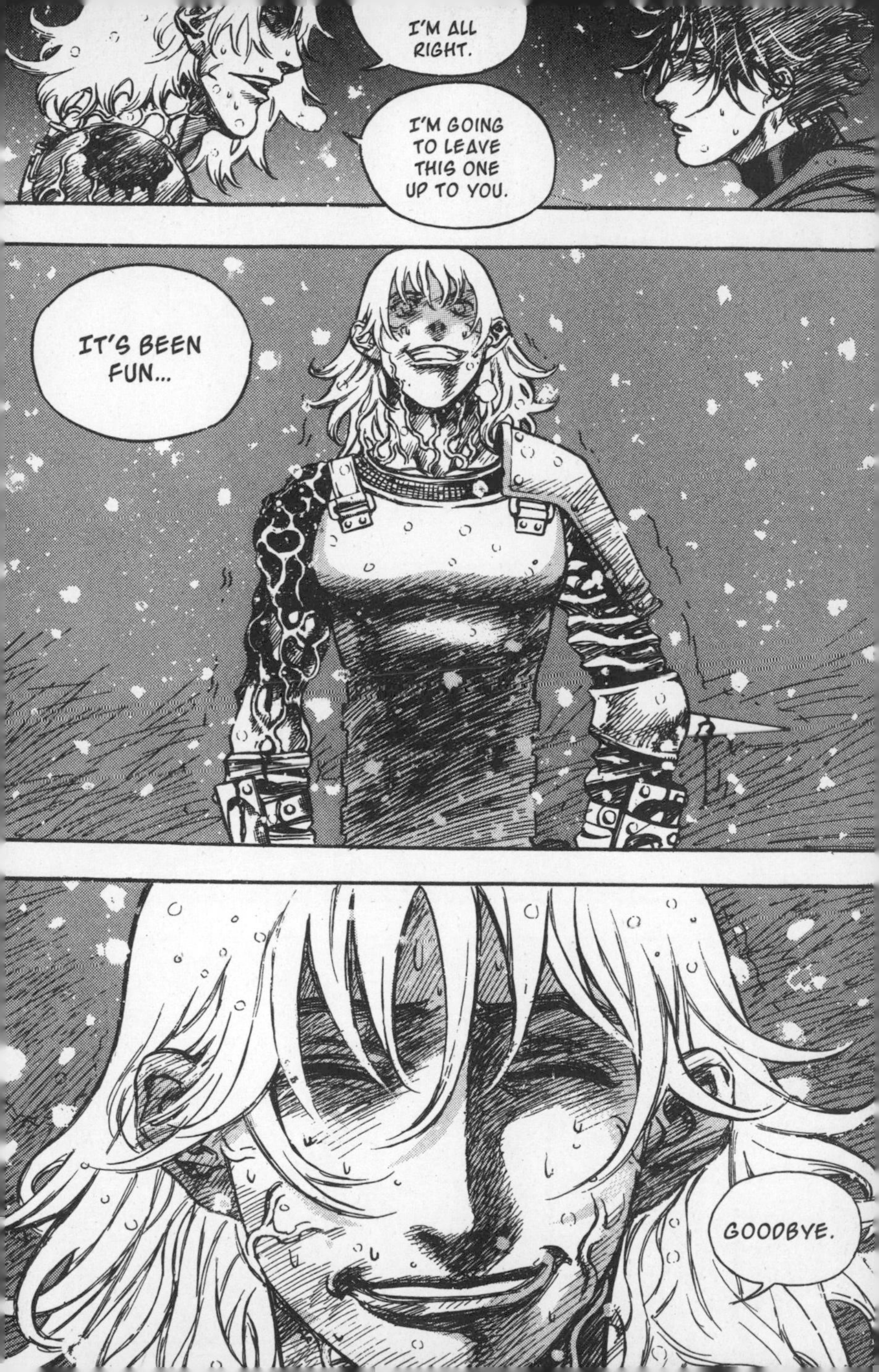
I'M ALL RIGHT.
I'M GOING TO LEAVE THIS ONE UP TO YOU.
IT'S BEEN FUN...
GOODBYE.

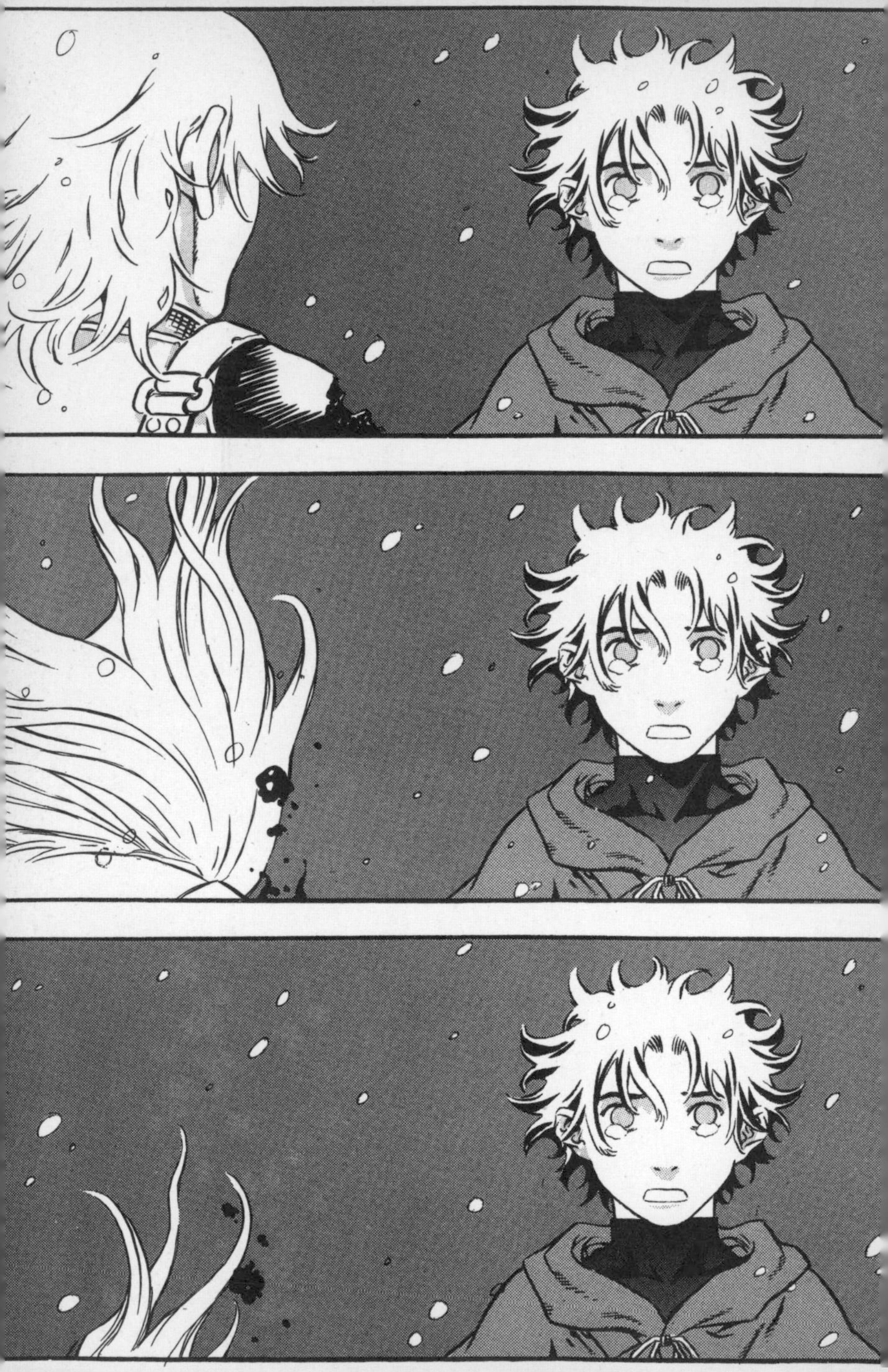

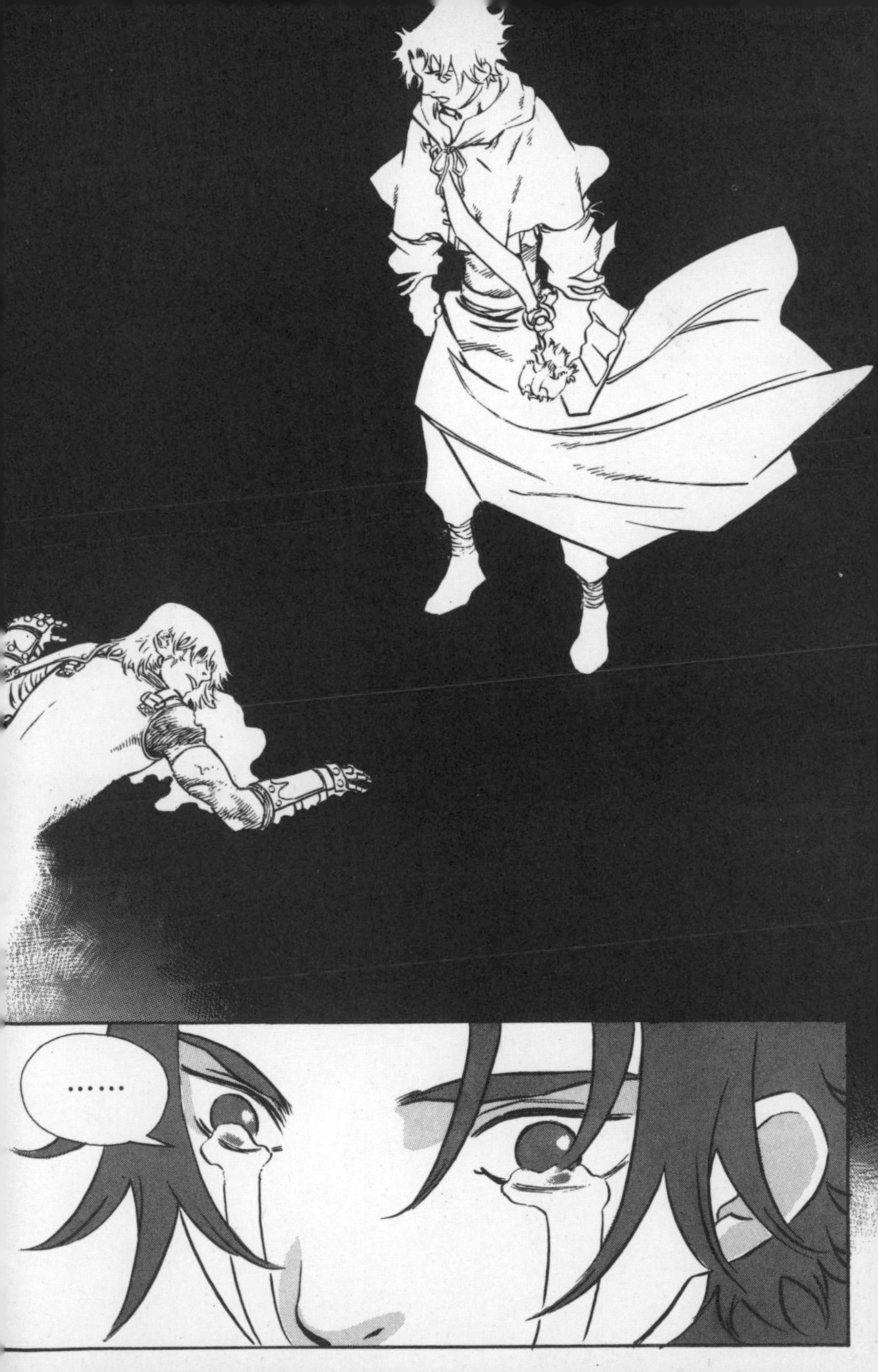
......

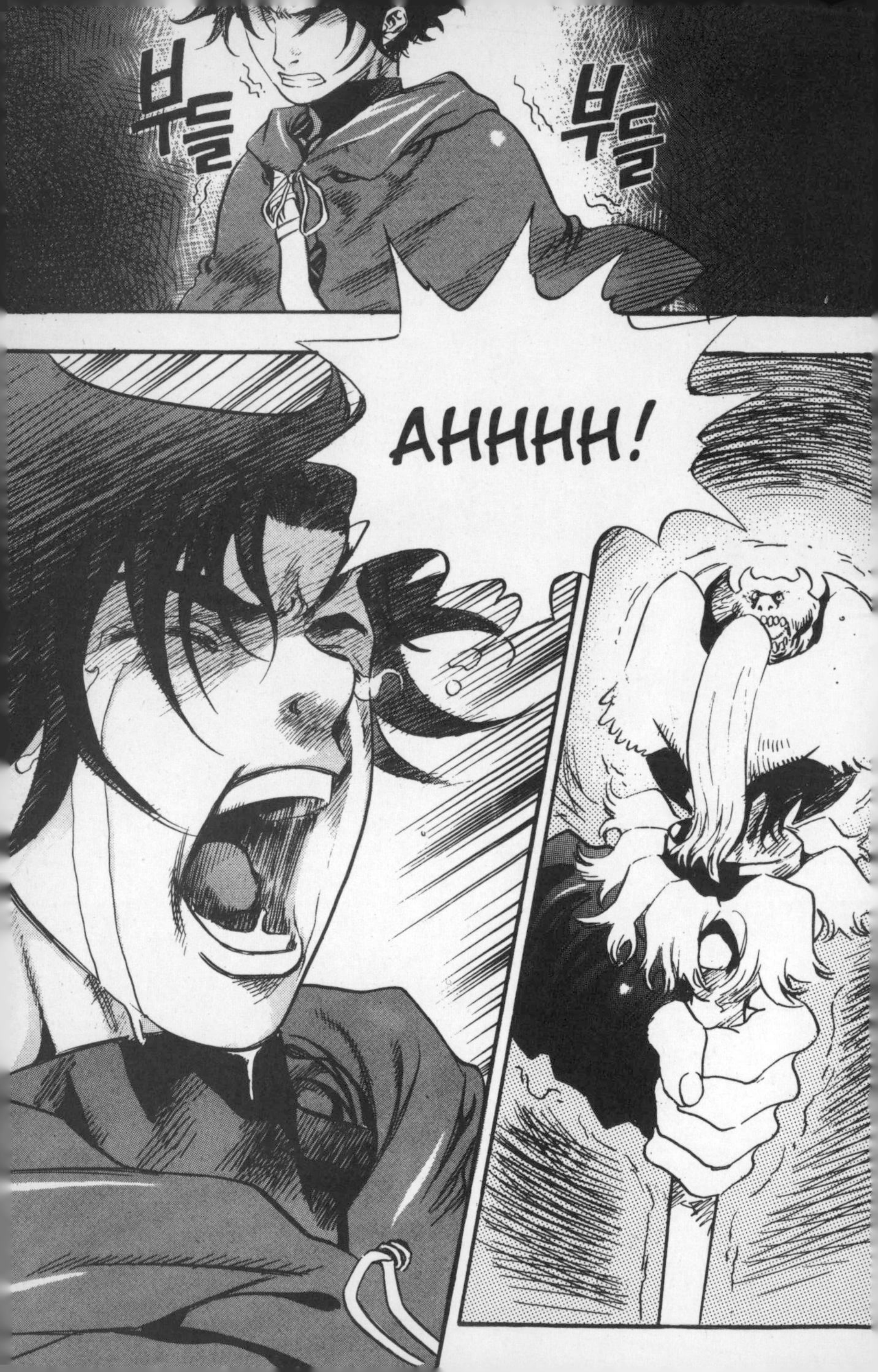
부들
부들
AHHHH!

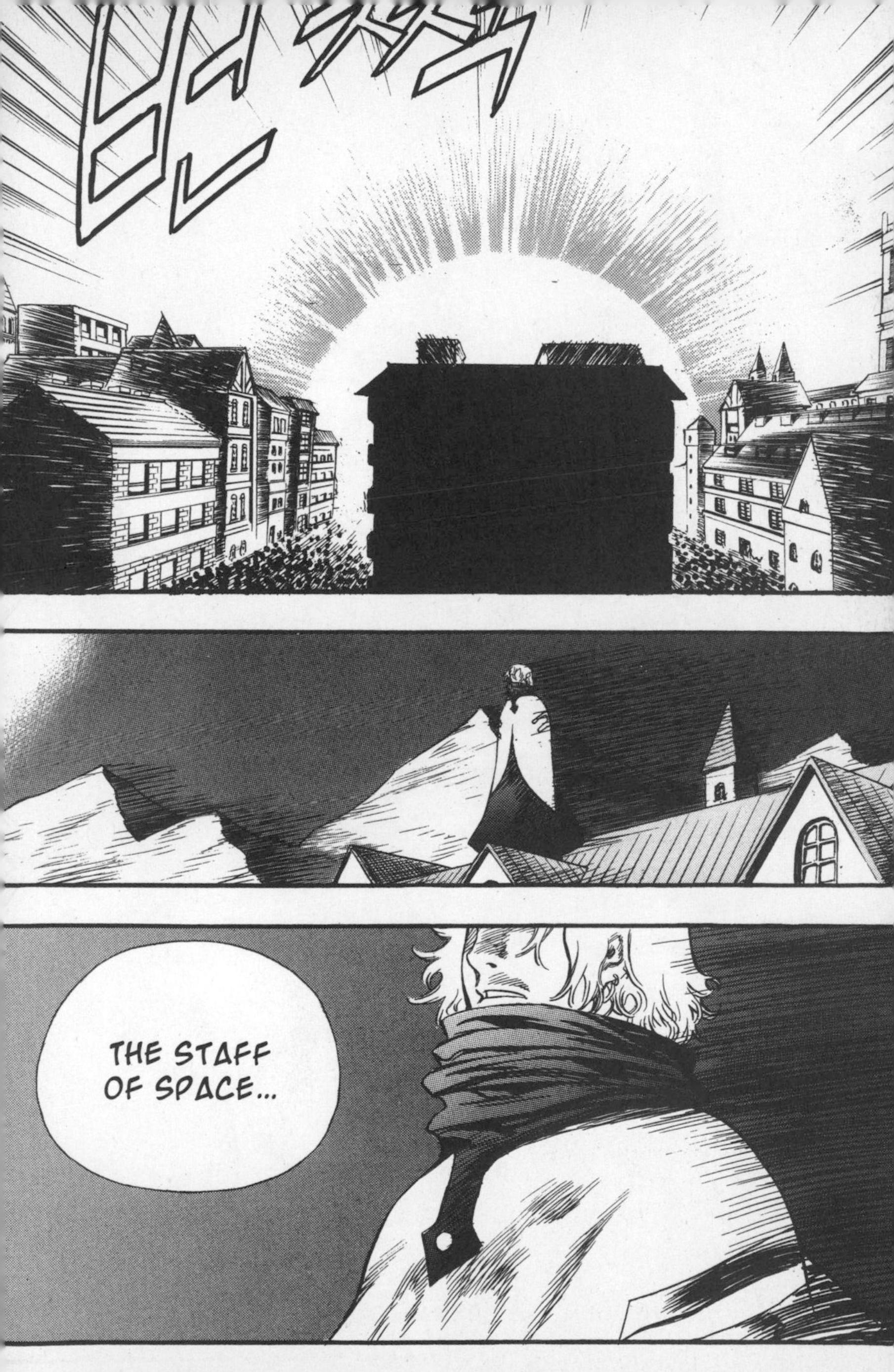
THE STAFF OF SPACE...

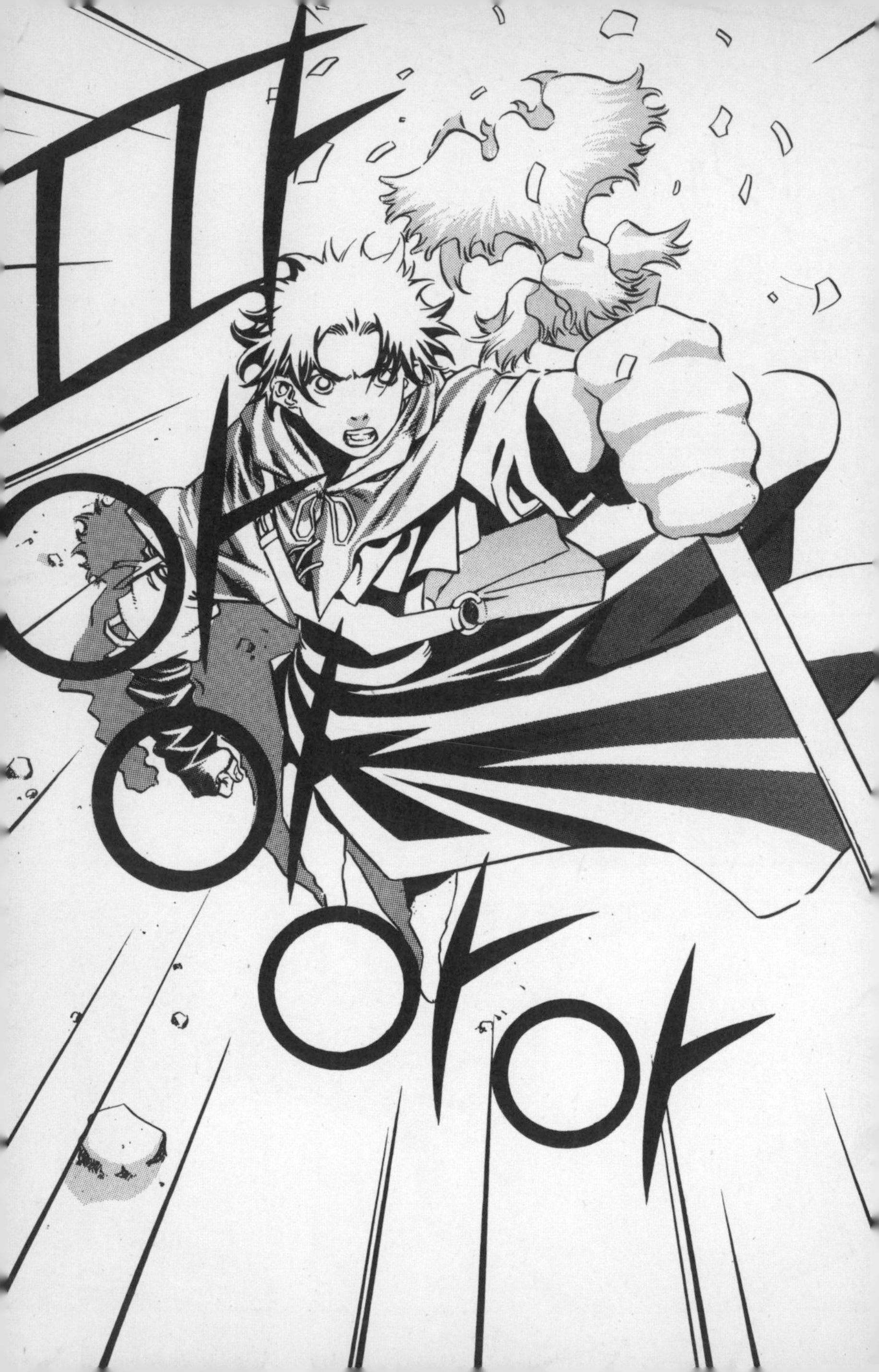

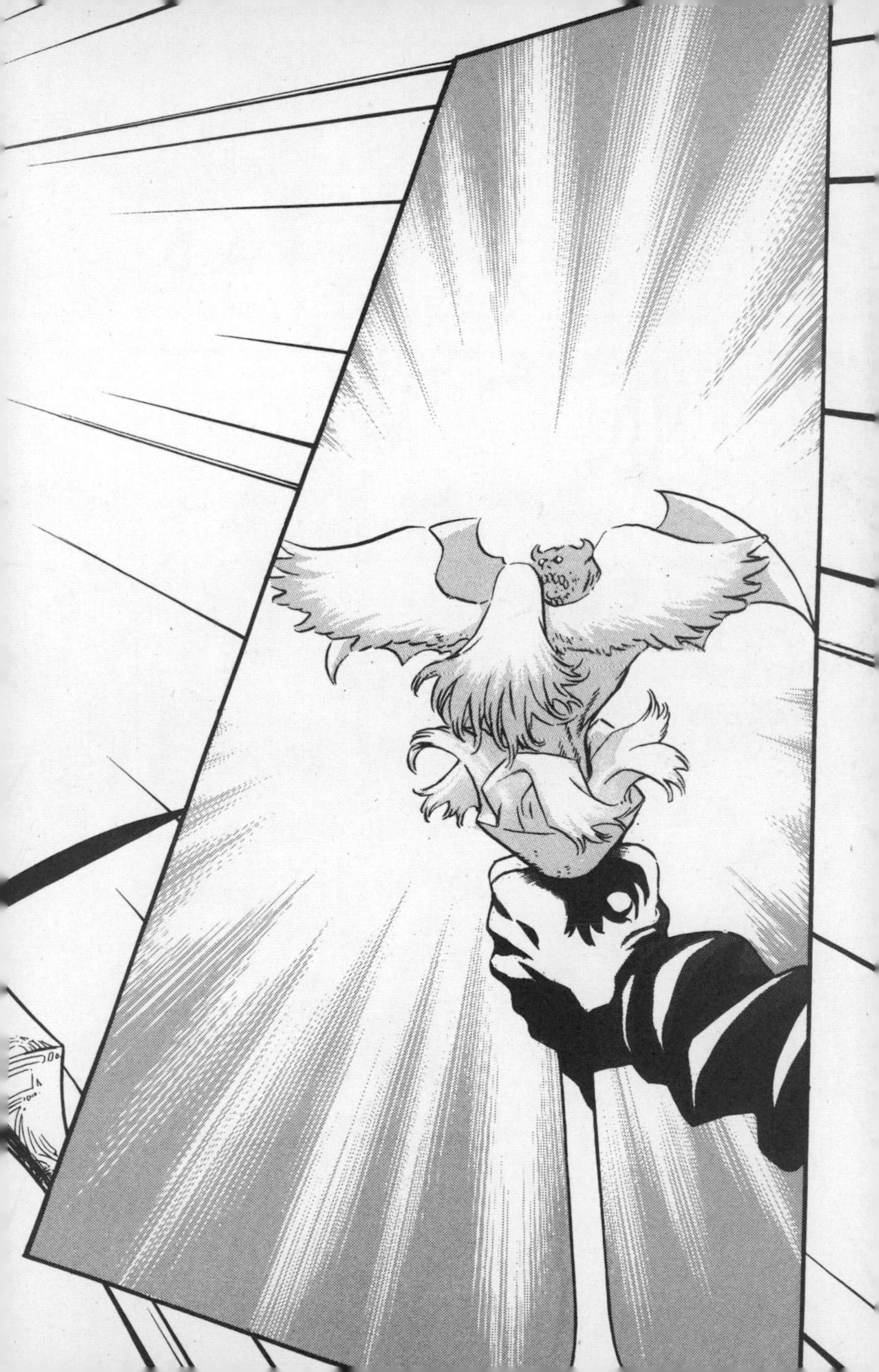

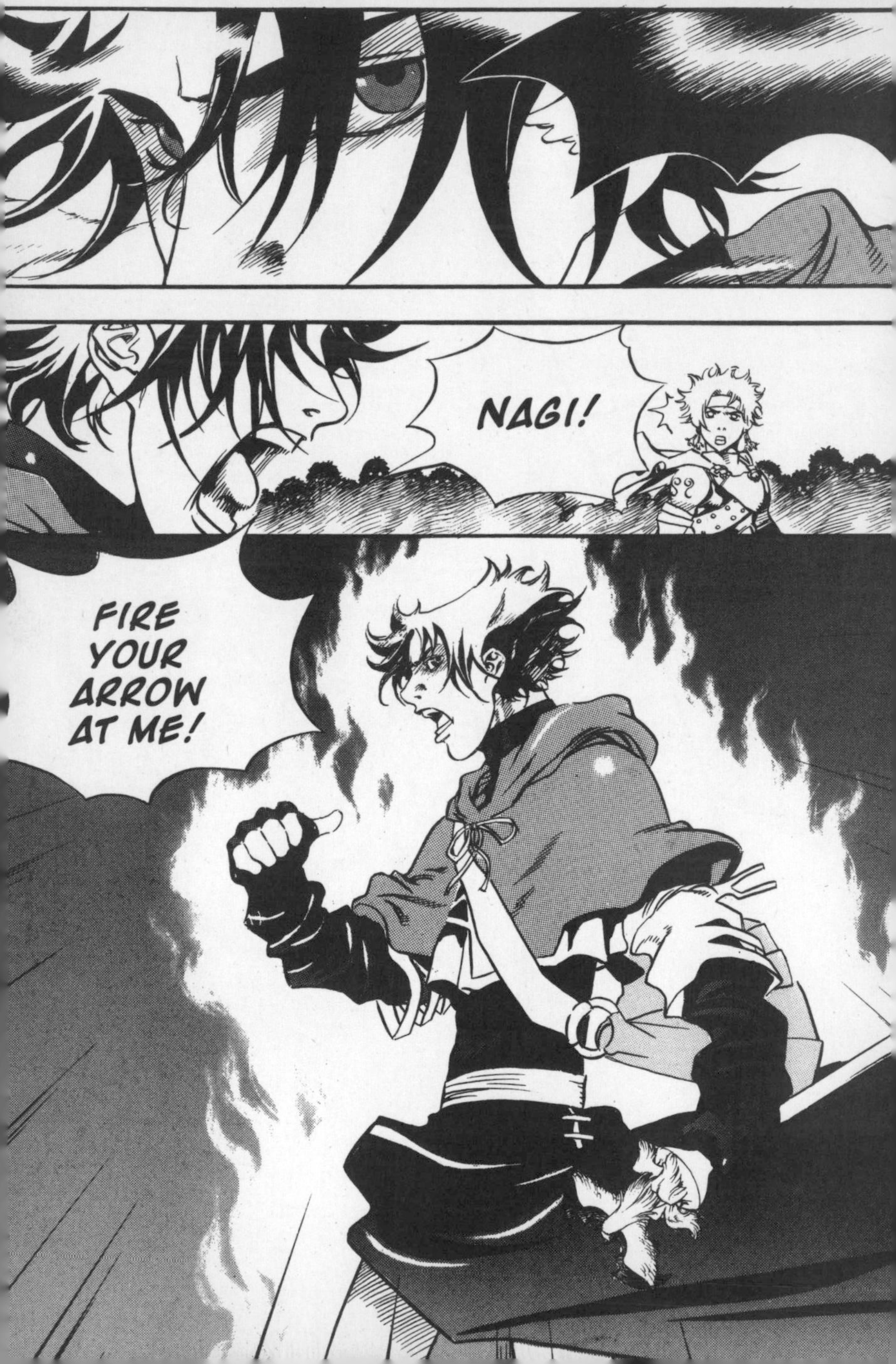
NAGI!
FIRE YOUR ARROW AT ME!

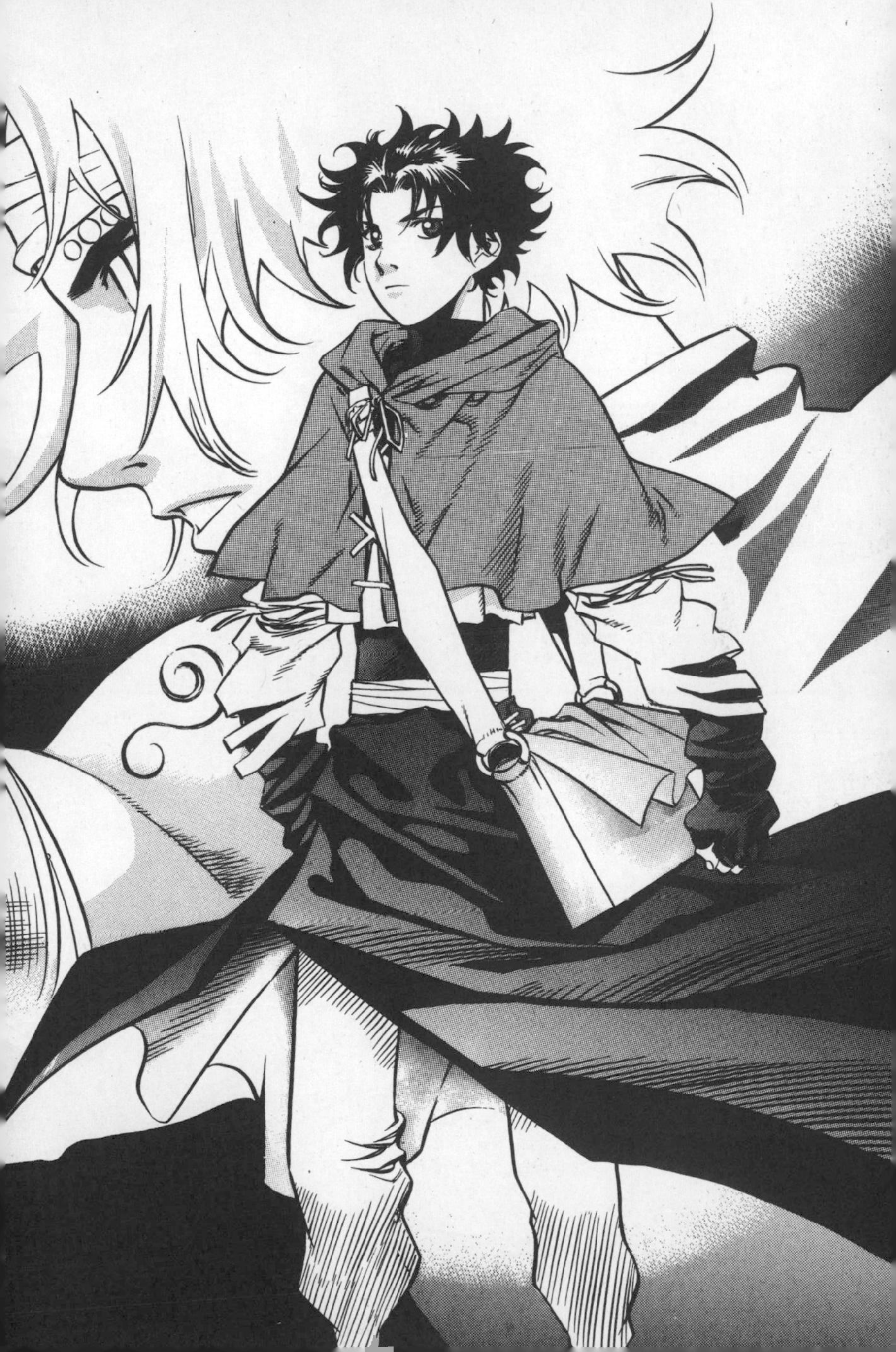

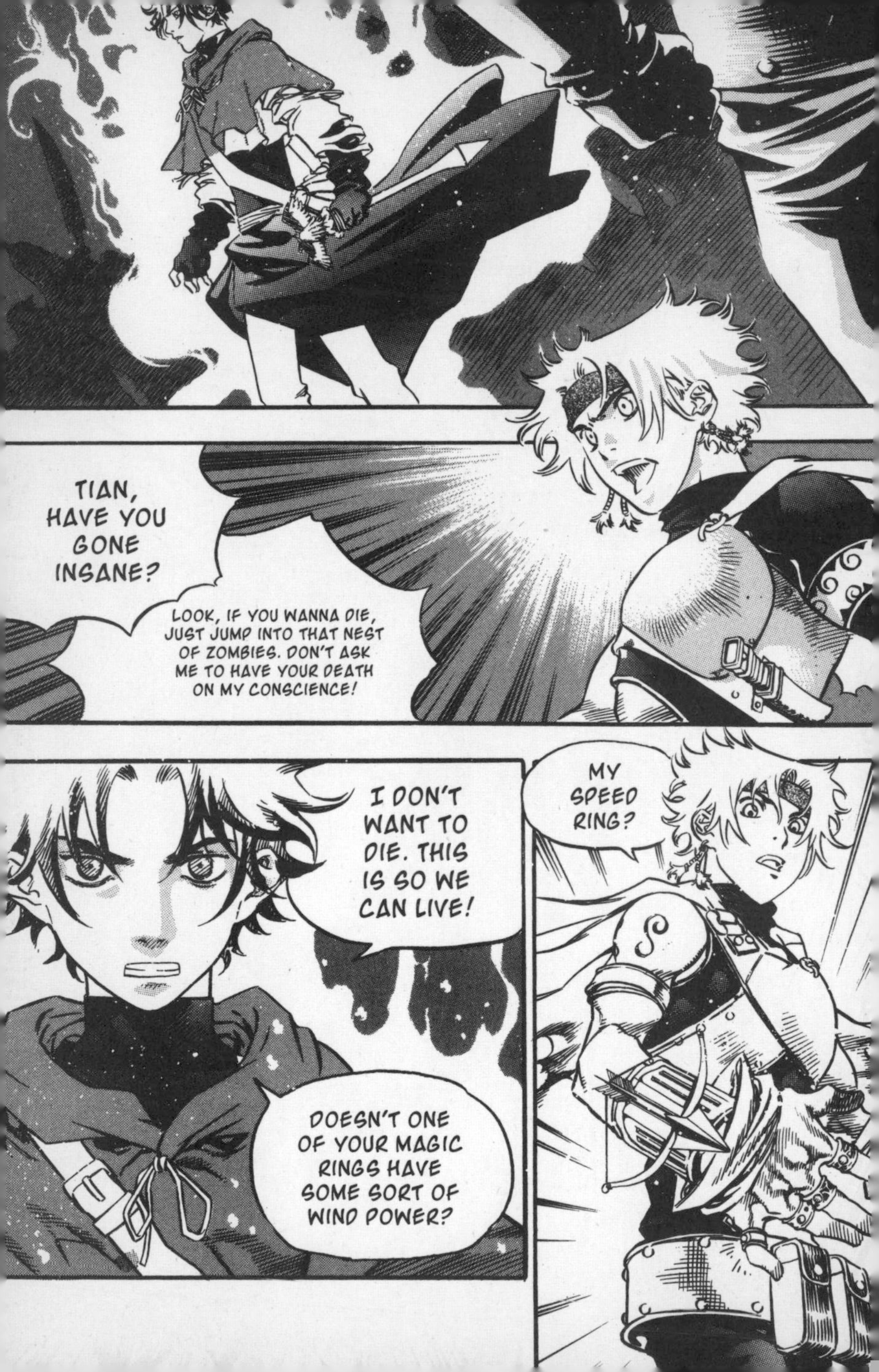

TIAN, HAVE YOU GONE INSANE?
LOOK, IF YOU WANNA DIE, JUST JUMP INTO THAT NEST OF ZOMBIES. DON'T ASK ME TO HAVE YOUR DEATH ON MY CONSCIENCE!
I DON'T WANT TO DIE. THIS IS SO WE CAN LIVE!
DOESN'T ONE OF YOUR MAGIC RINGS HAVE SOME SORT OF WIND POWER?
MY SPEED RING?

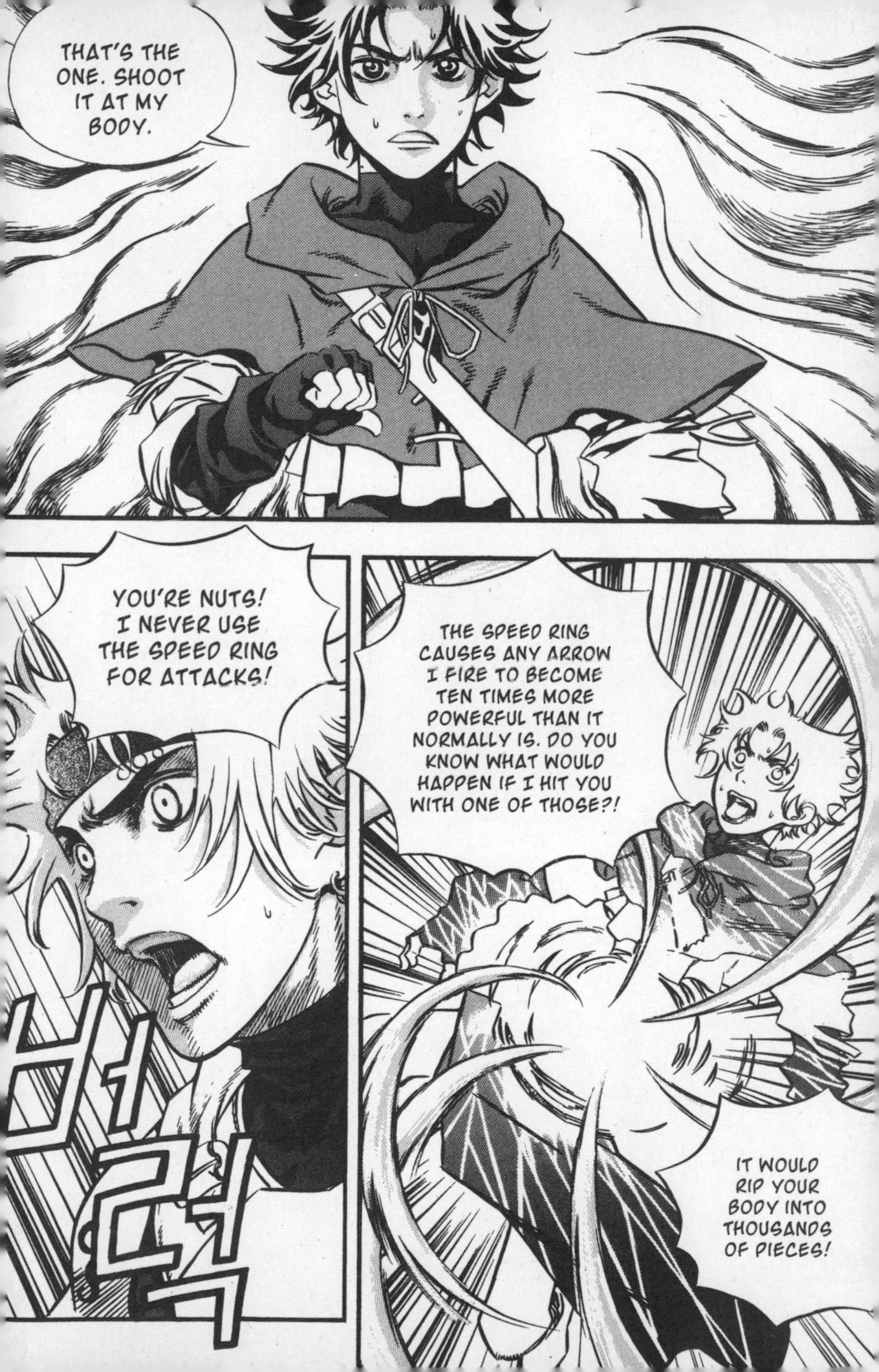
THAT'S THE ONE. SHOOT IT AT MY BODY.
YOU'RE NUTS! I NEVER USE THE SPEED RING FOR ATTACKS!
THE SPEED RING CAUSES ANY ARROW I FIRE TO BECOME TEN TIMES MORE POWERFUL THAN IT NORMALLY IS. DO YOU KNOW WHAT WOULD HAPPEN IF I HIT YOU WITH ONE OF THOSE?!
IT WOULD RIP YOUR BODY INTO THOUSANDS OF PIECES!

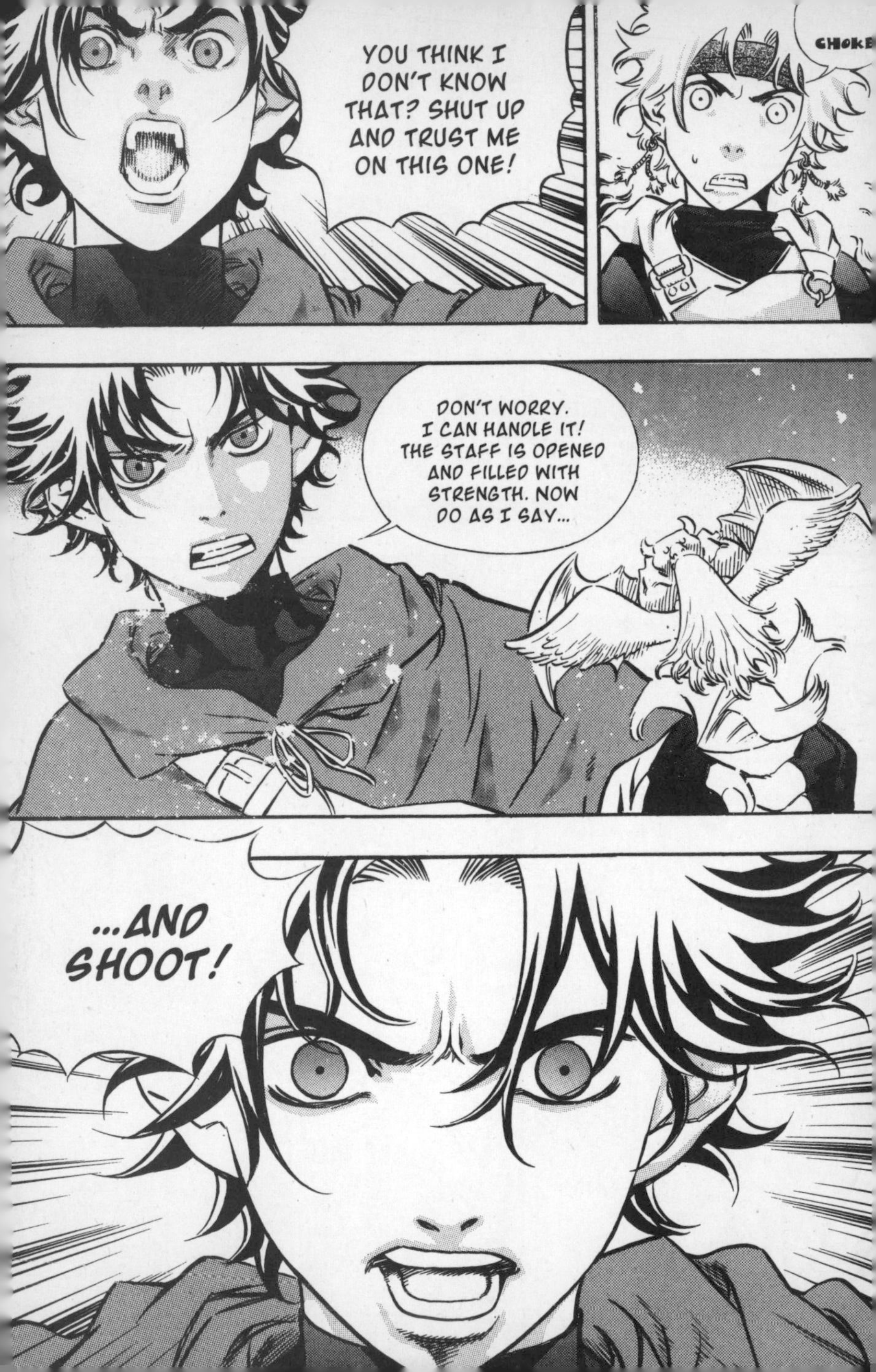
YOU THINK I DON'T KNOW THAT? SHUT UP AND TRUST ME ON THIS ONE!
CHOKE
DON'T WORRY. I CAN HANDLE IT! THE STAFF IS OPENED AND FILLED WITH STRENGTH. NOW DO AS I SAY...
...AND SHOOT!

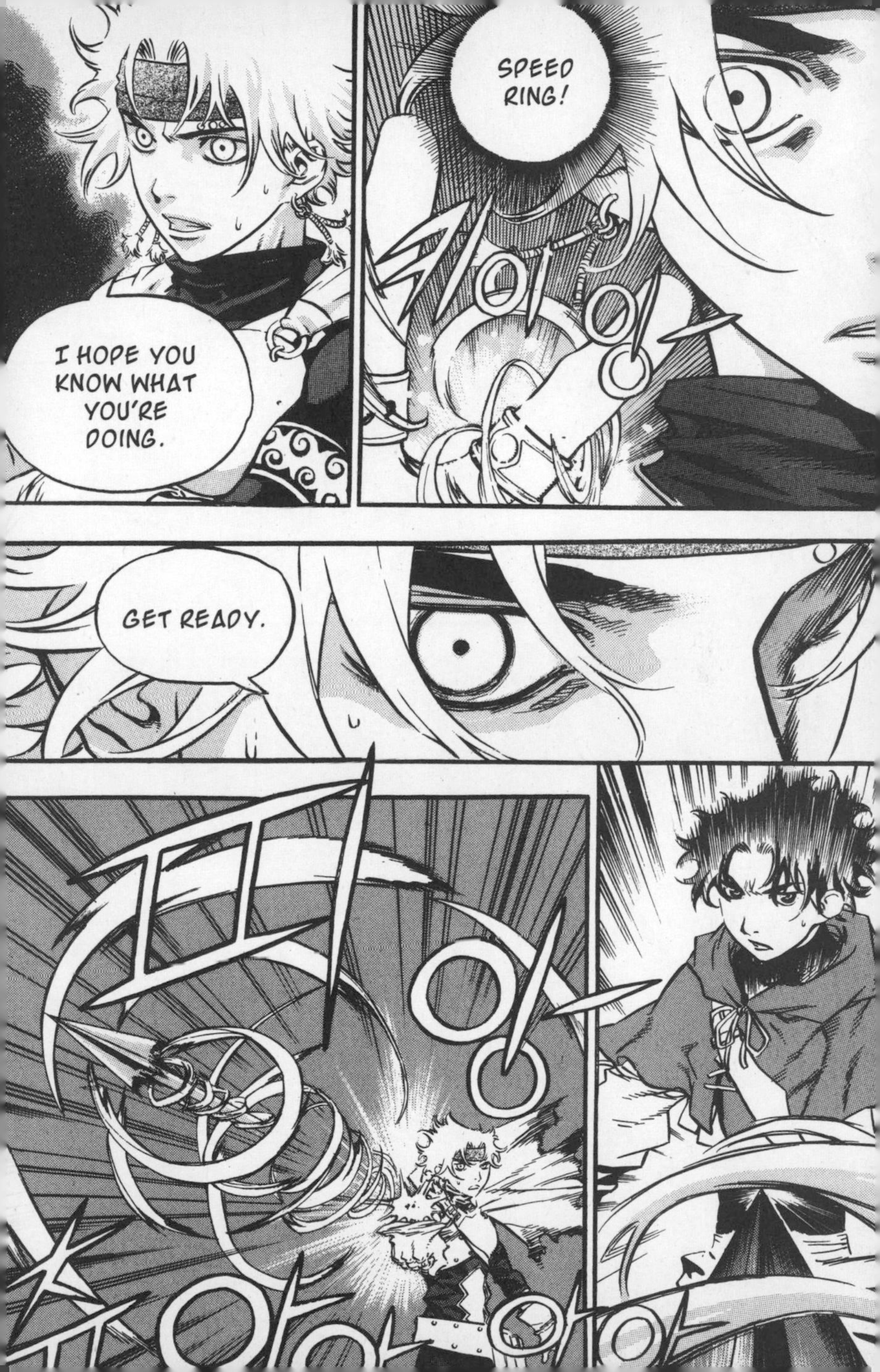
I HOPE YOU KNOW WHAT YOU'RE DOING.
SPEED RING!
GET READY.

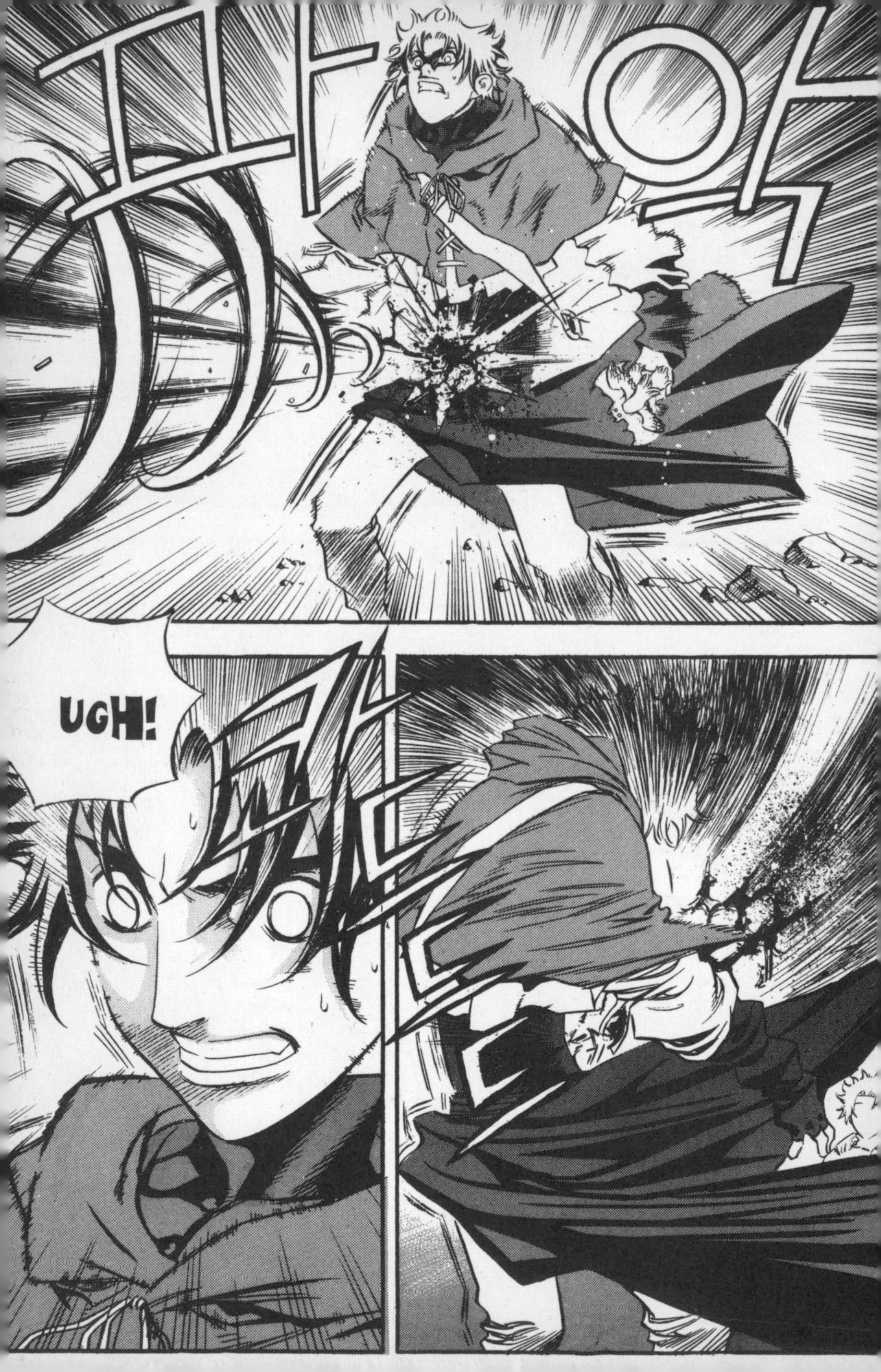
UGH!

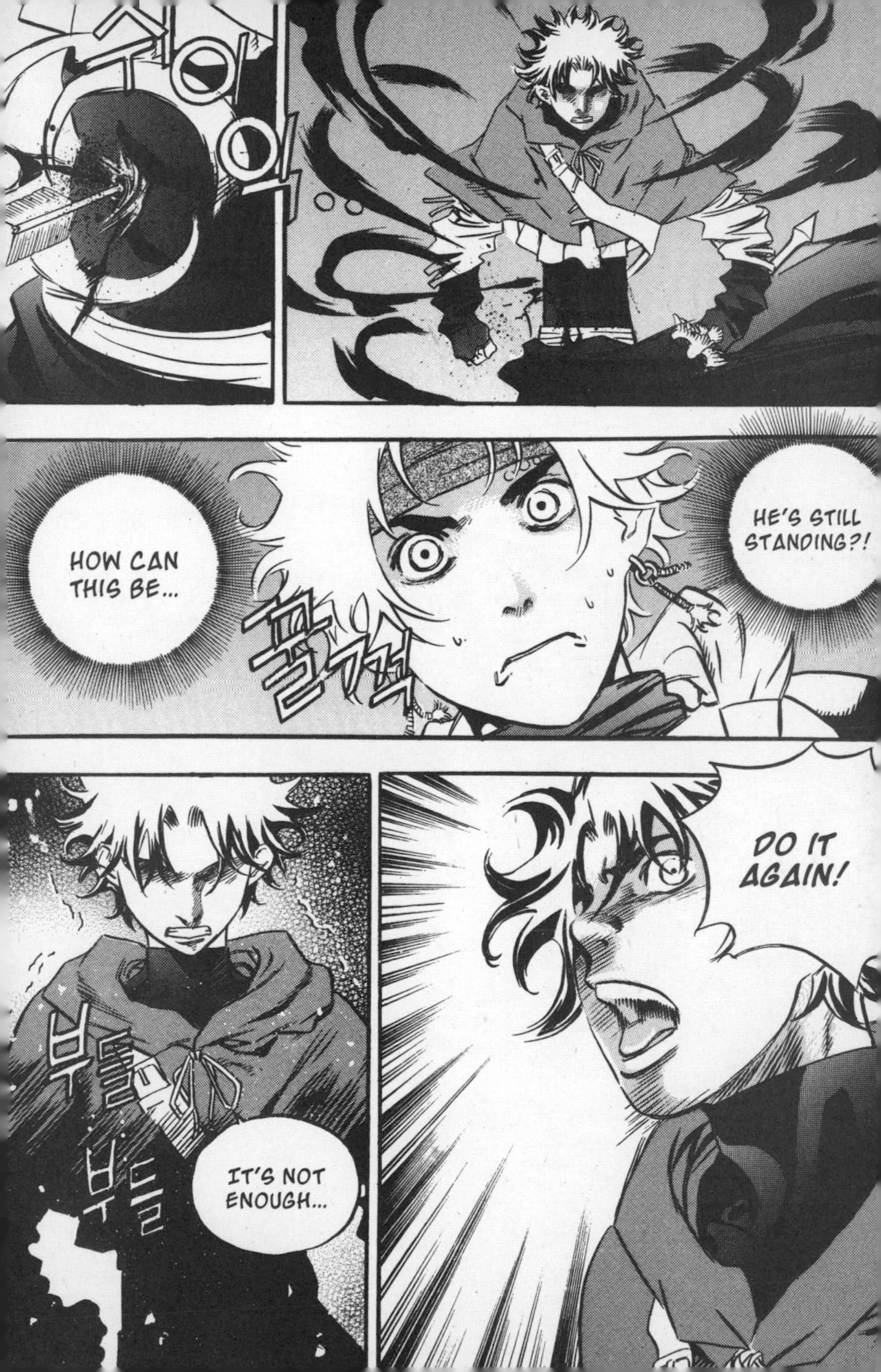
HOW CAN THIS BE...
HE'S STILL STANDING?!
부들부들
IT'S NOT ENOUGH...
DO IT AGAIN!

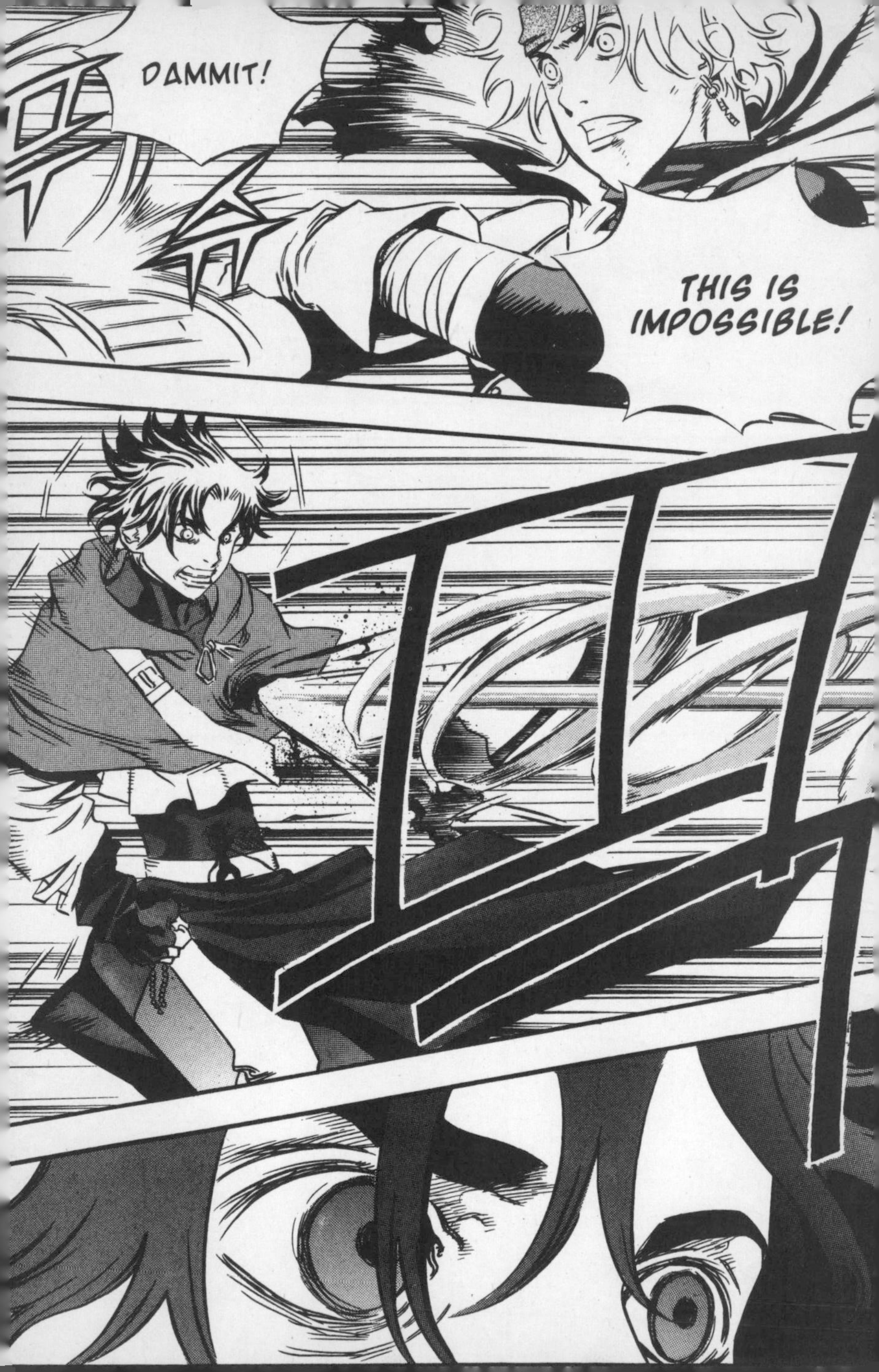
DAMMIT!
THIS IS IMPOSSIBLE!

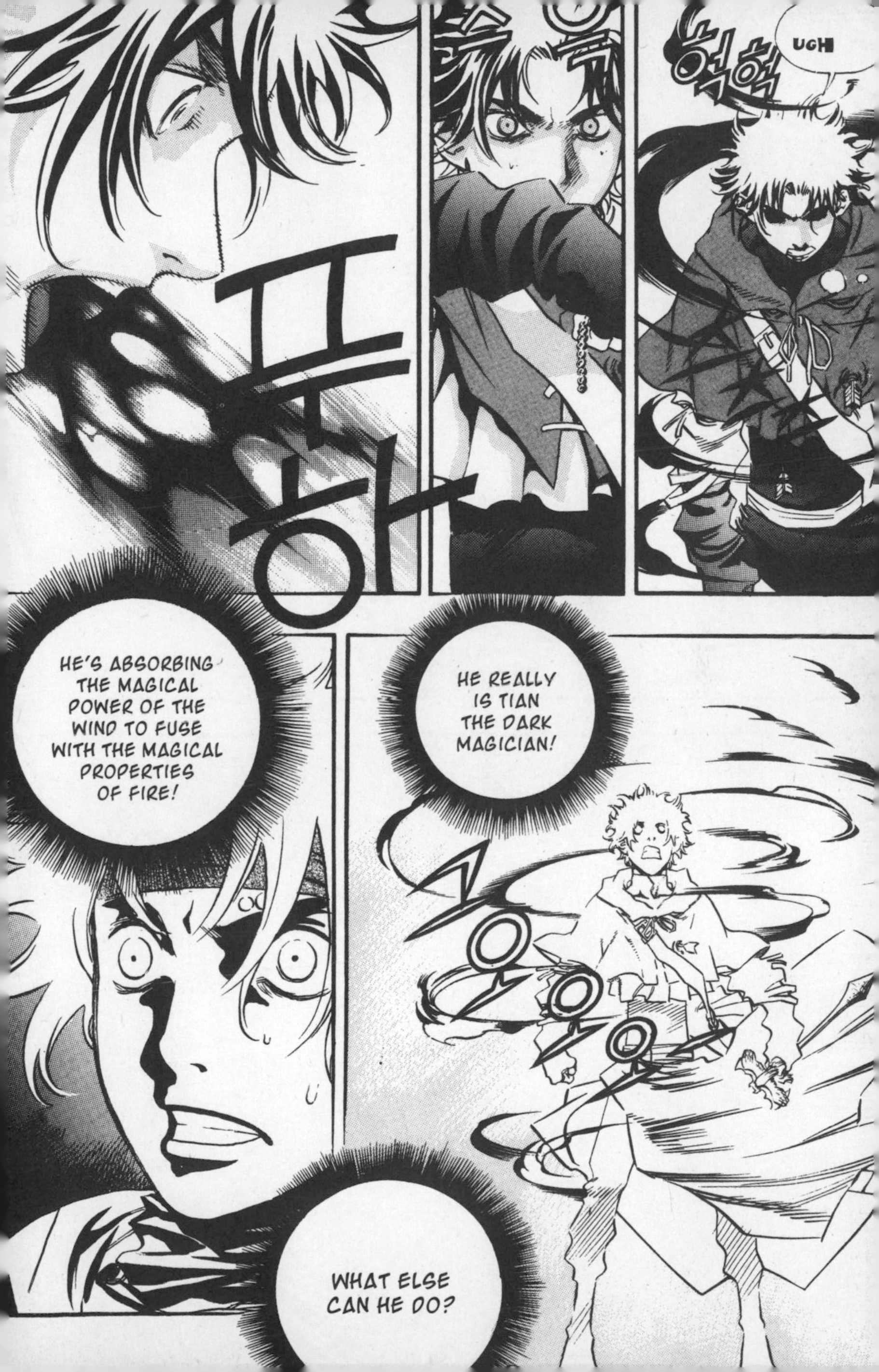
UGH
HE'S ABSORBING THE MAGICAL POWER OF THE WIND TO FUSE WITH THE MAGICAL PROPERTIES OF FIRE!
HE REALLY IS TIAN THE DARK MAGICIAN!
WHAT ELSE CAN HE DO?

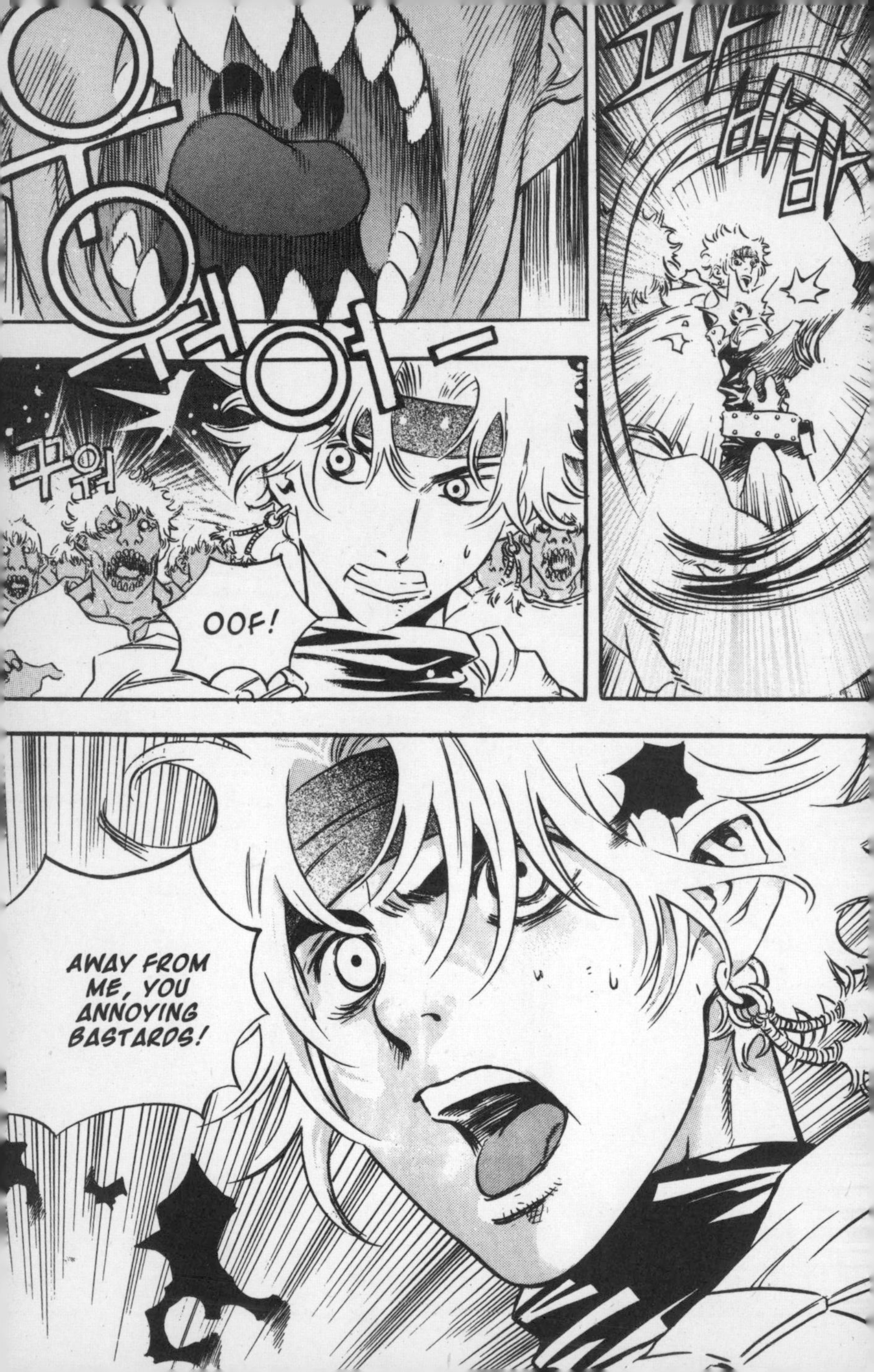
OOF!
AWAY FROM ME, YOU ANNOYING BASTARDS!

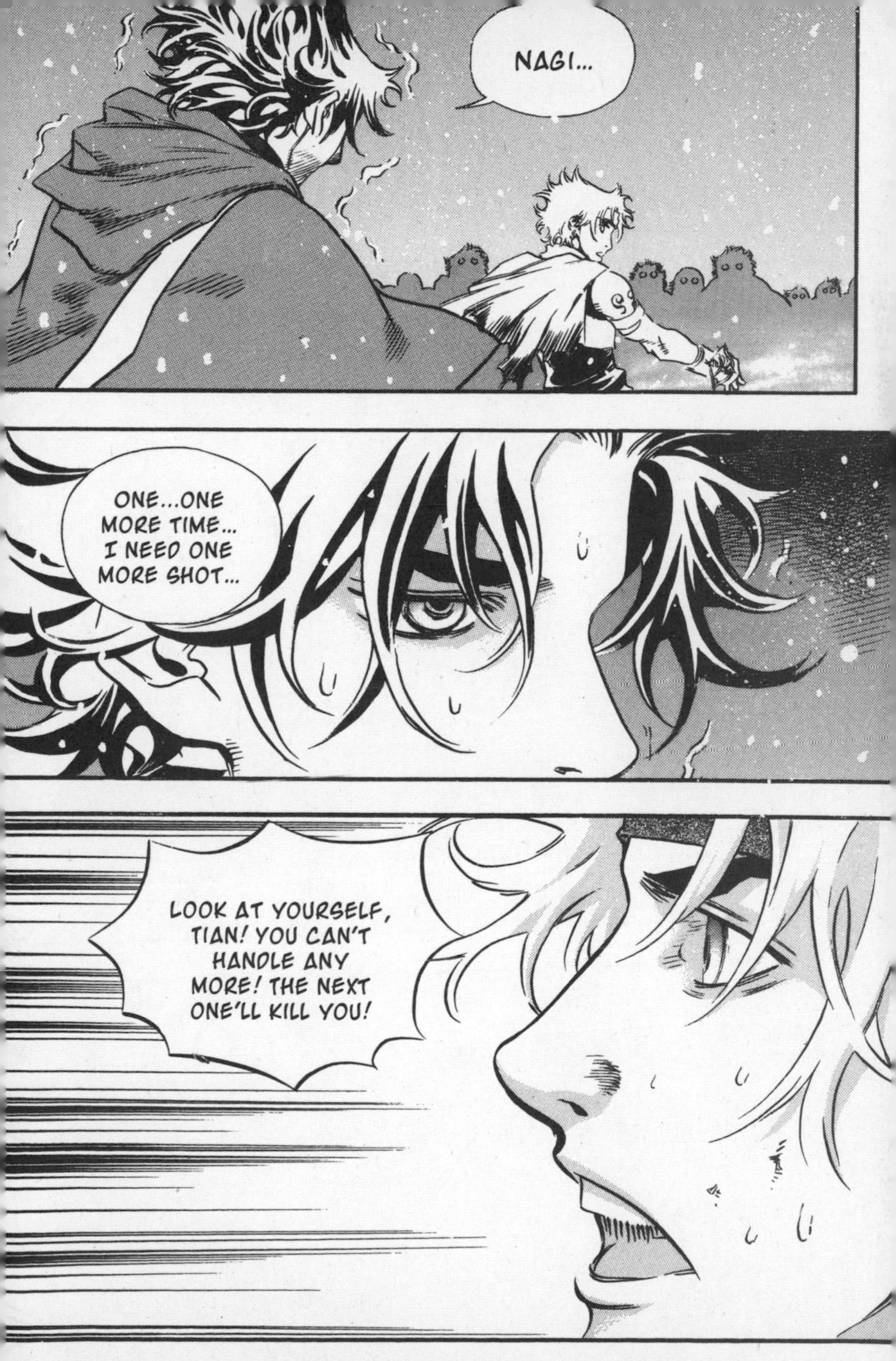
NAGI...
ONE...ONE MORE TIME... I NEED ONE MORE SHOT...
LOOK AT YOURSELF, TIAN! YOU CAN'T HANDLE ANY MORE! THE NEXT ONE'LL KILL YOU!

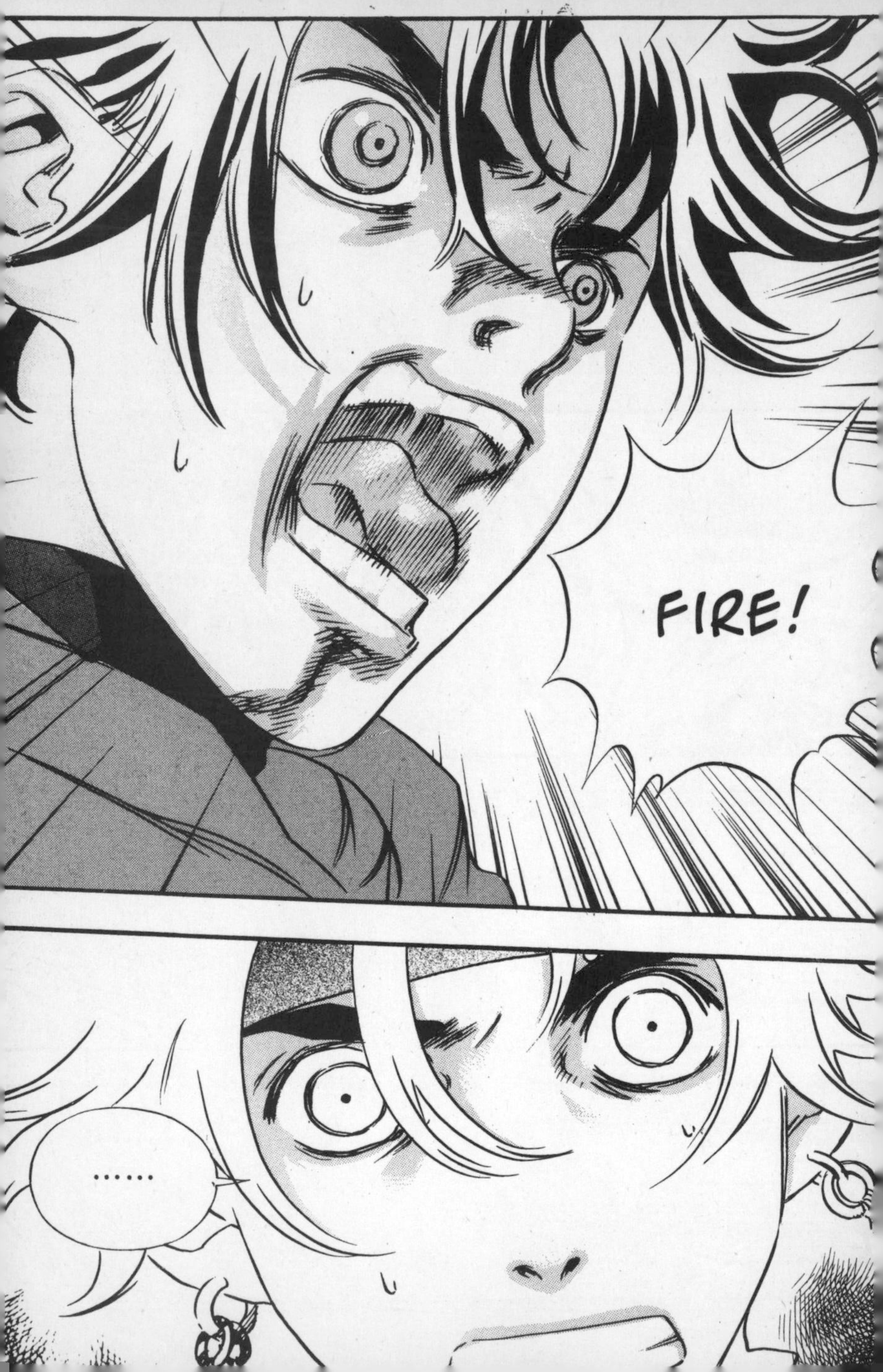
FIRE!
......

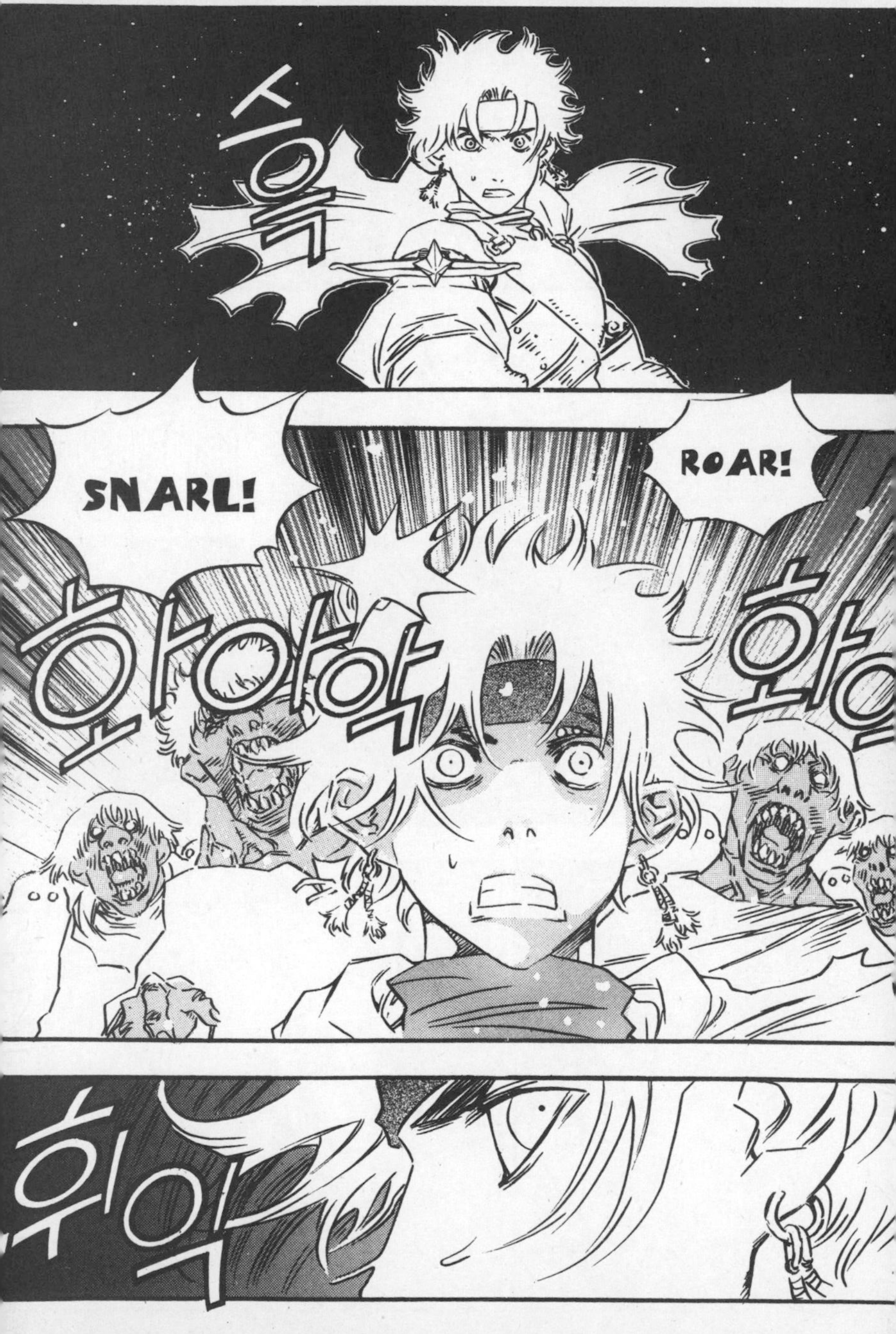
SNARL!
ROAR!

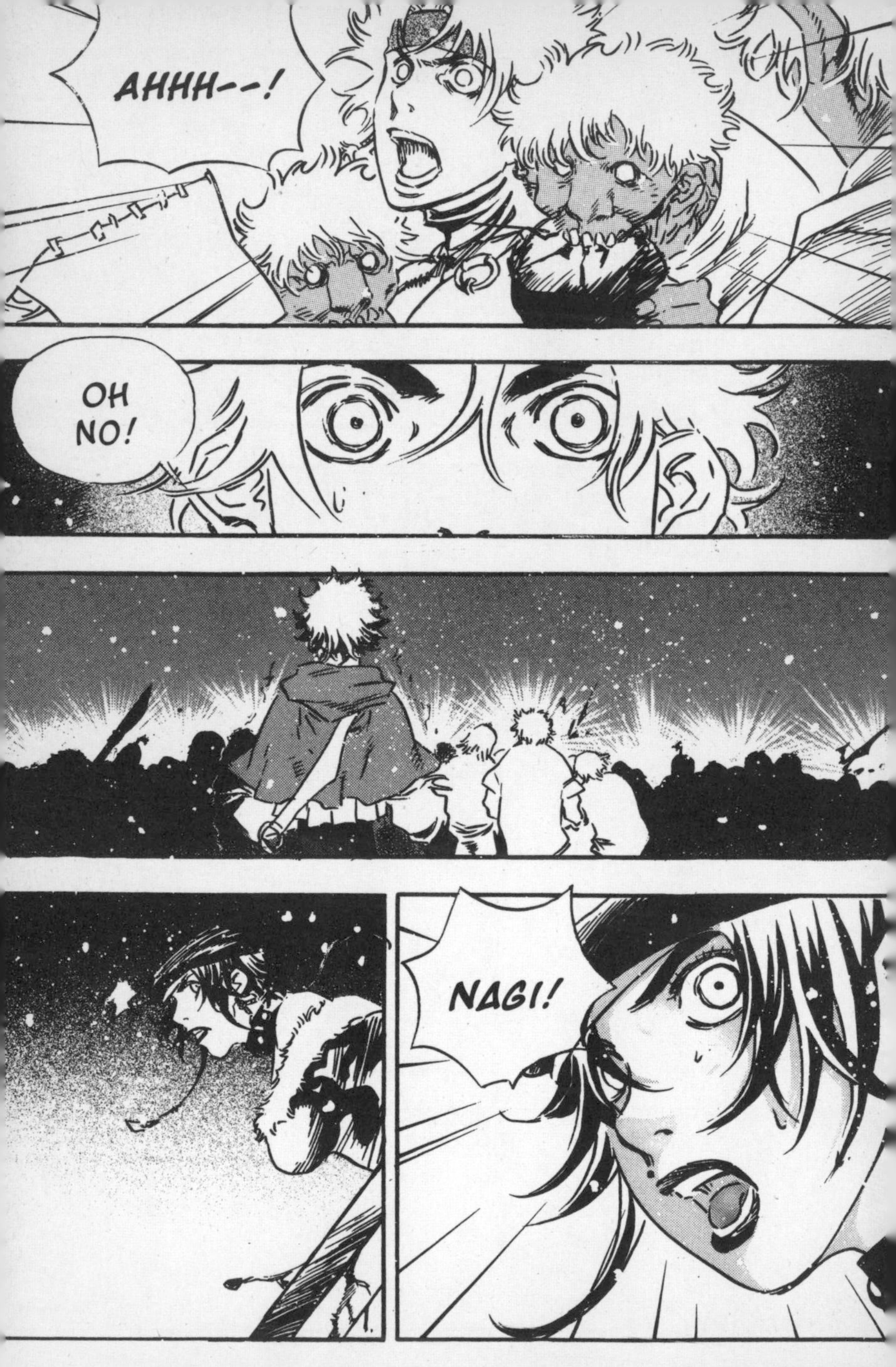
AHHH--!
OH NO!
NAGI!

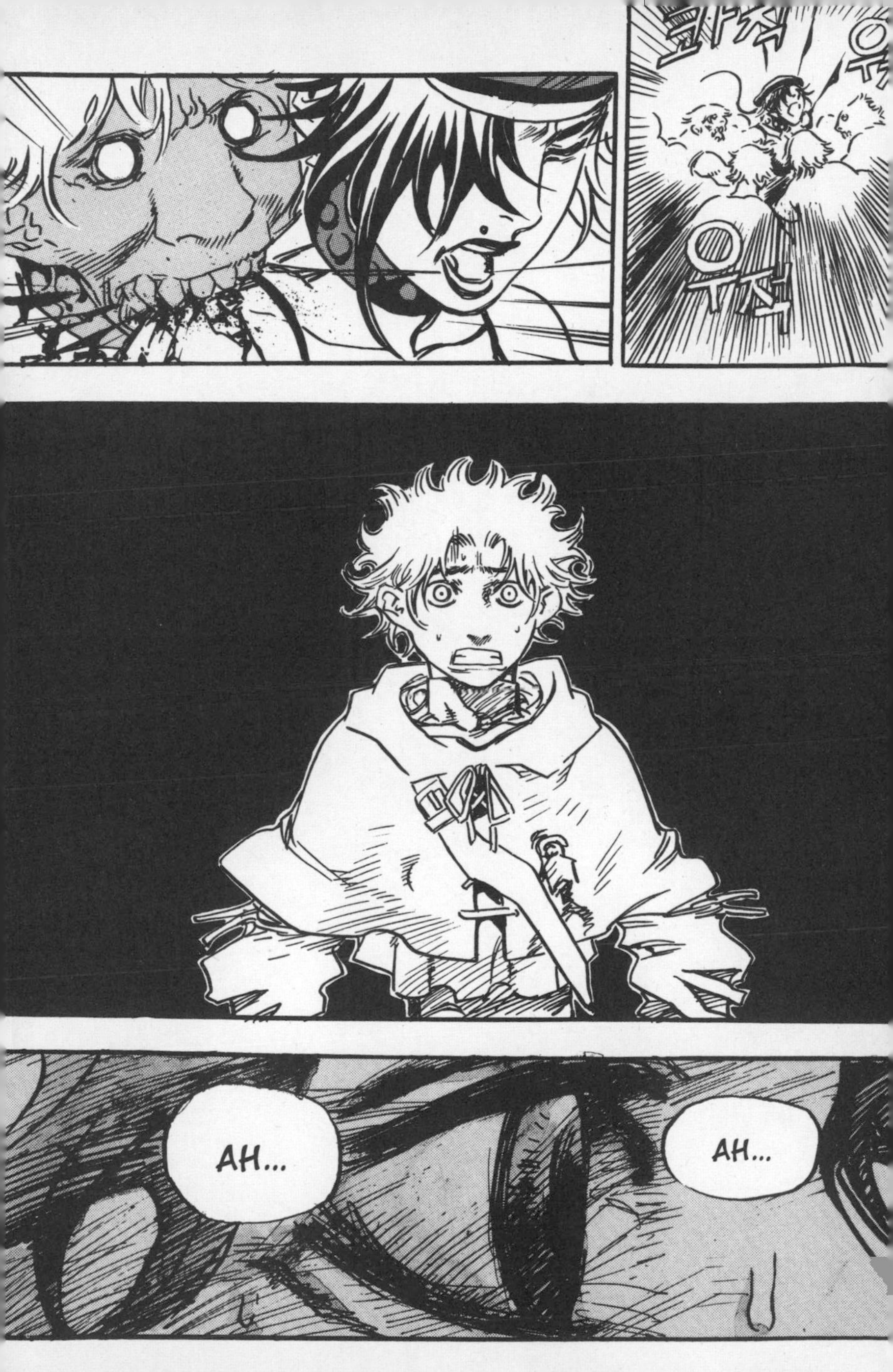
콰직
우적
AH...
AH...

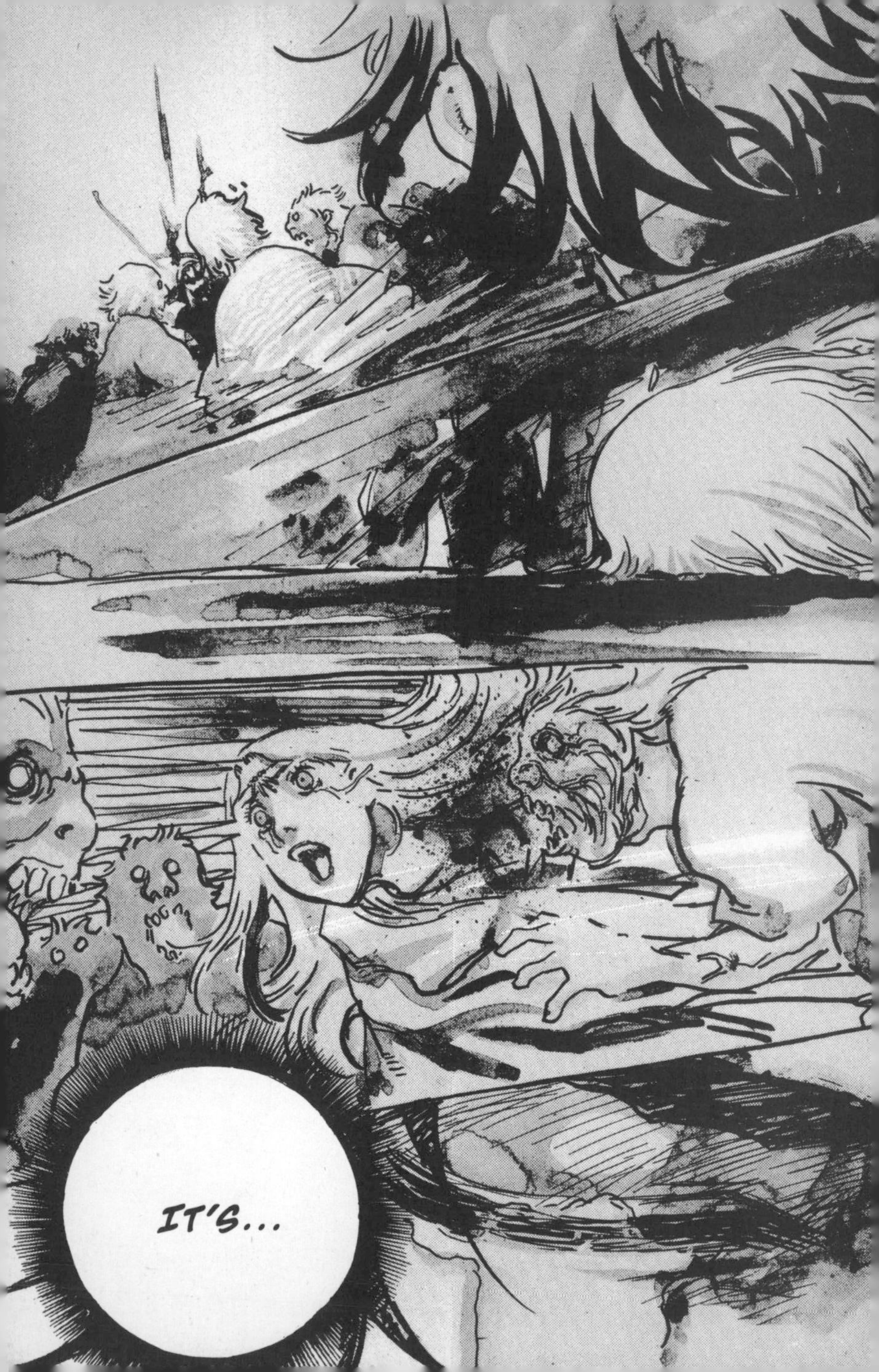
IT'S...

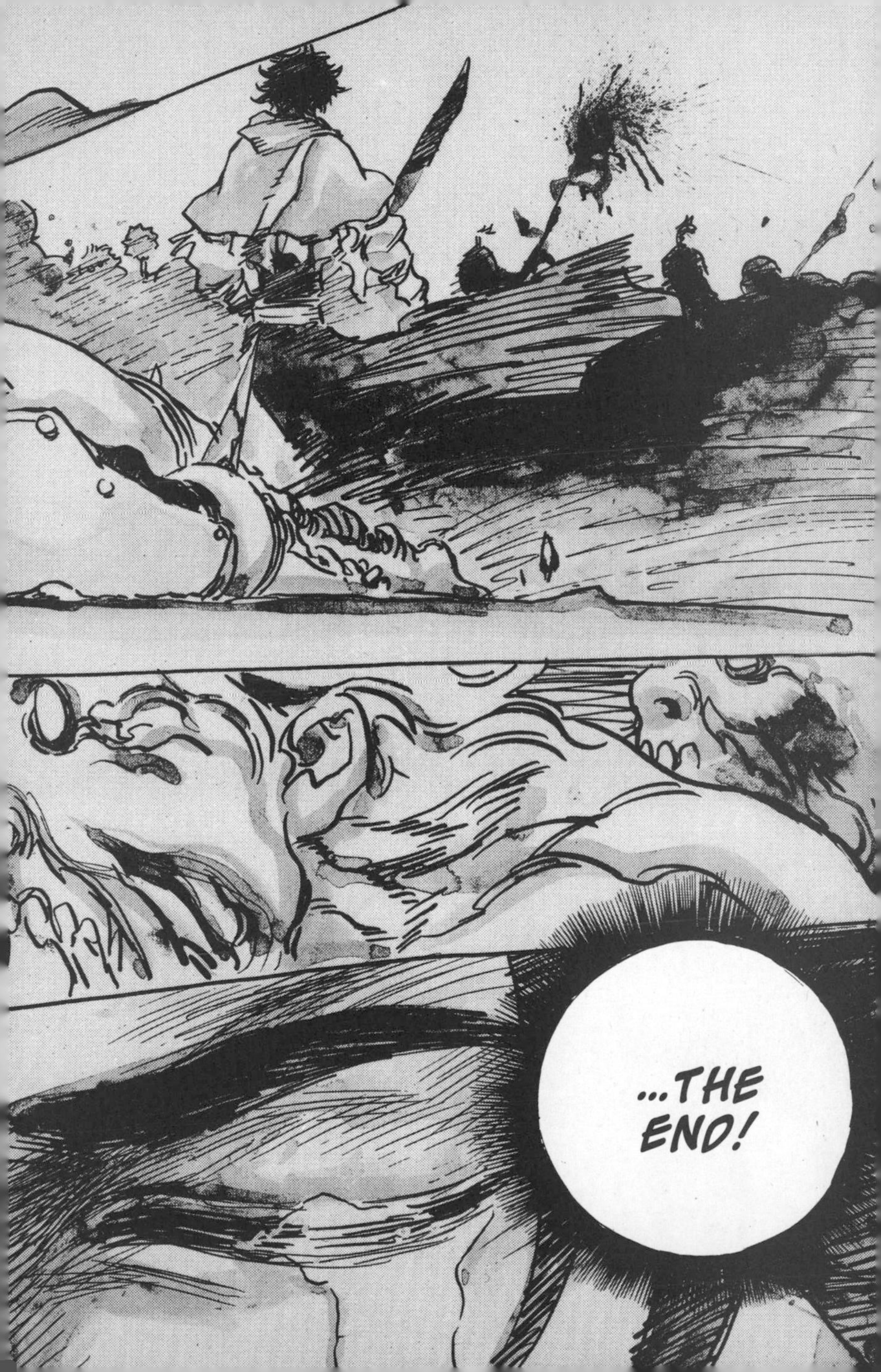
...THE END!

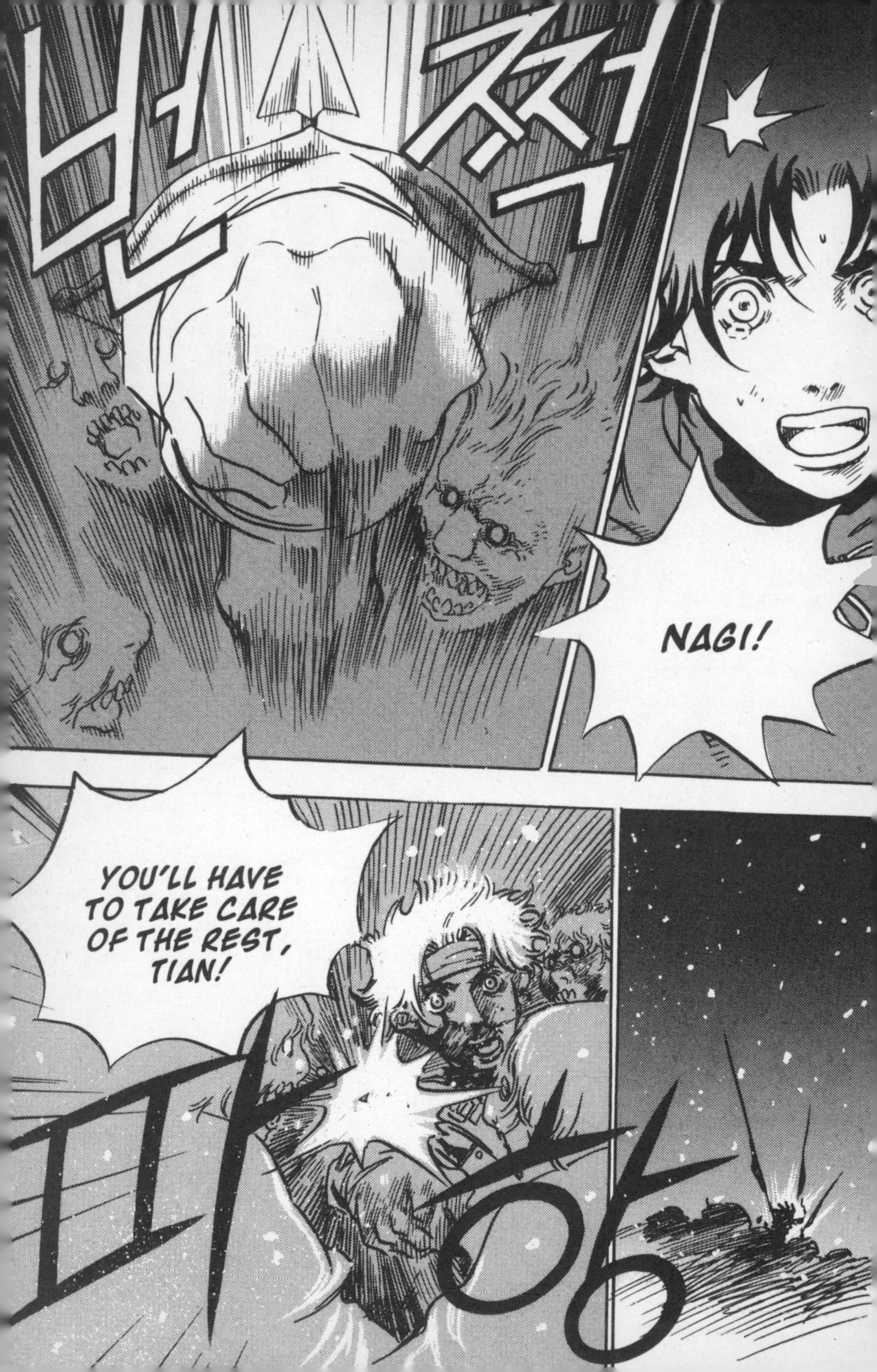
NAGI!
YOU'LL HAVE TO TAKE CARE OF THE REST, TIAN!

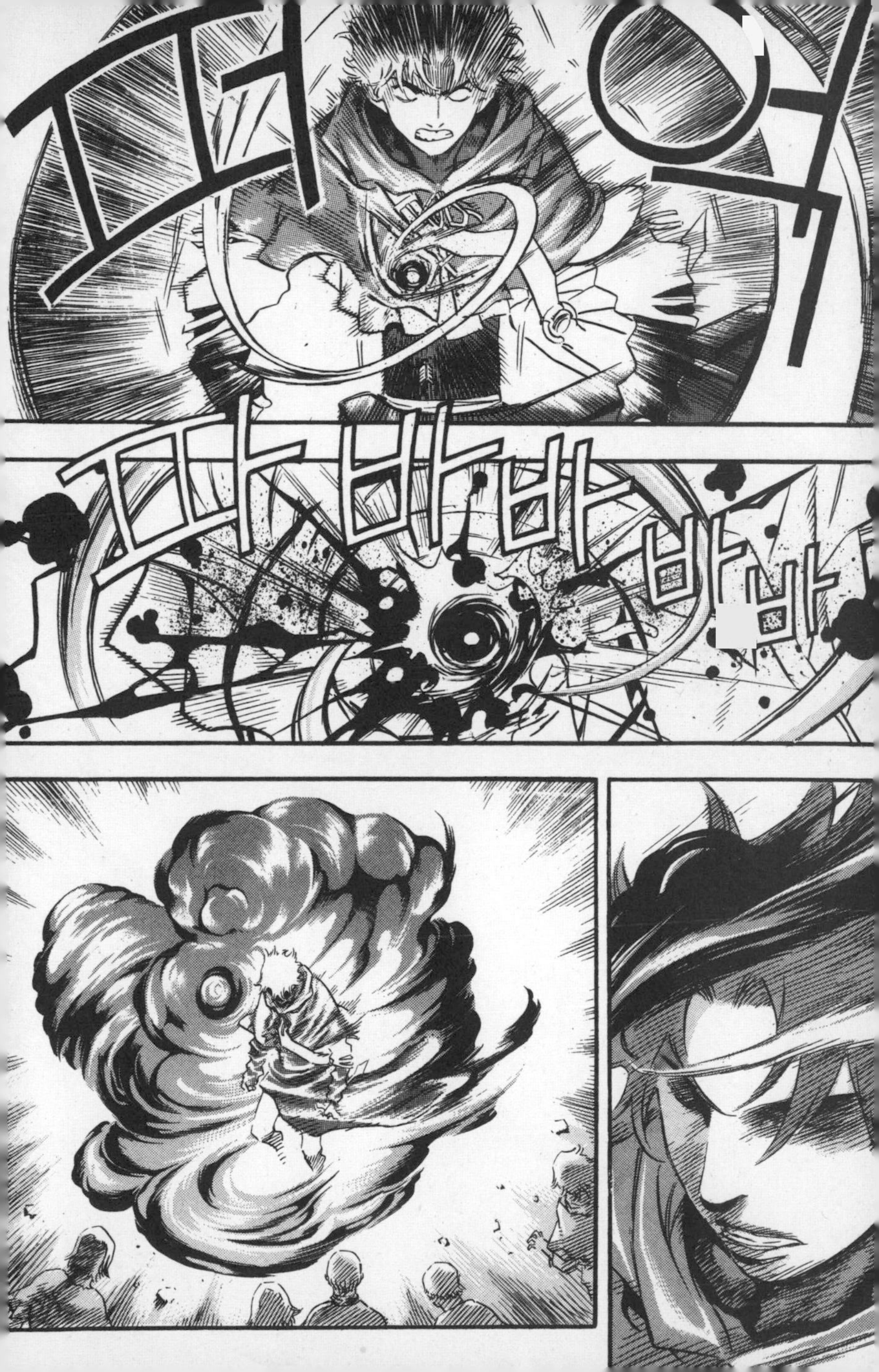
퍼어
파바바바바

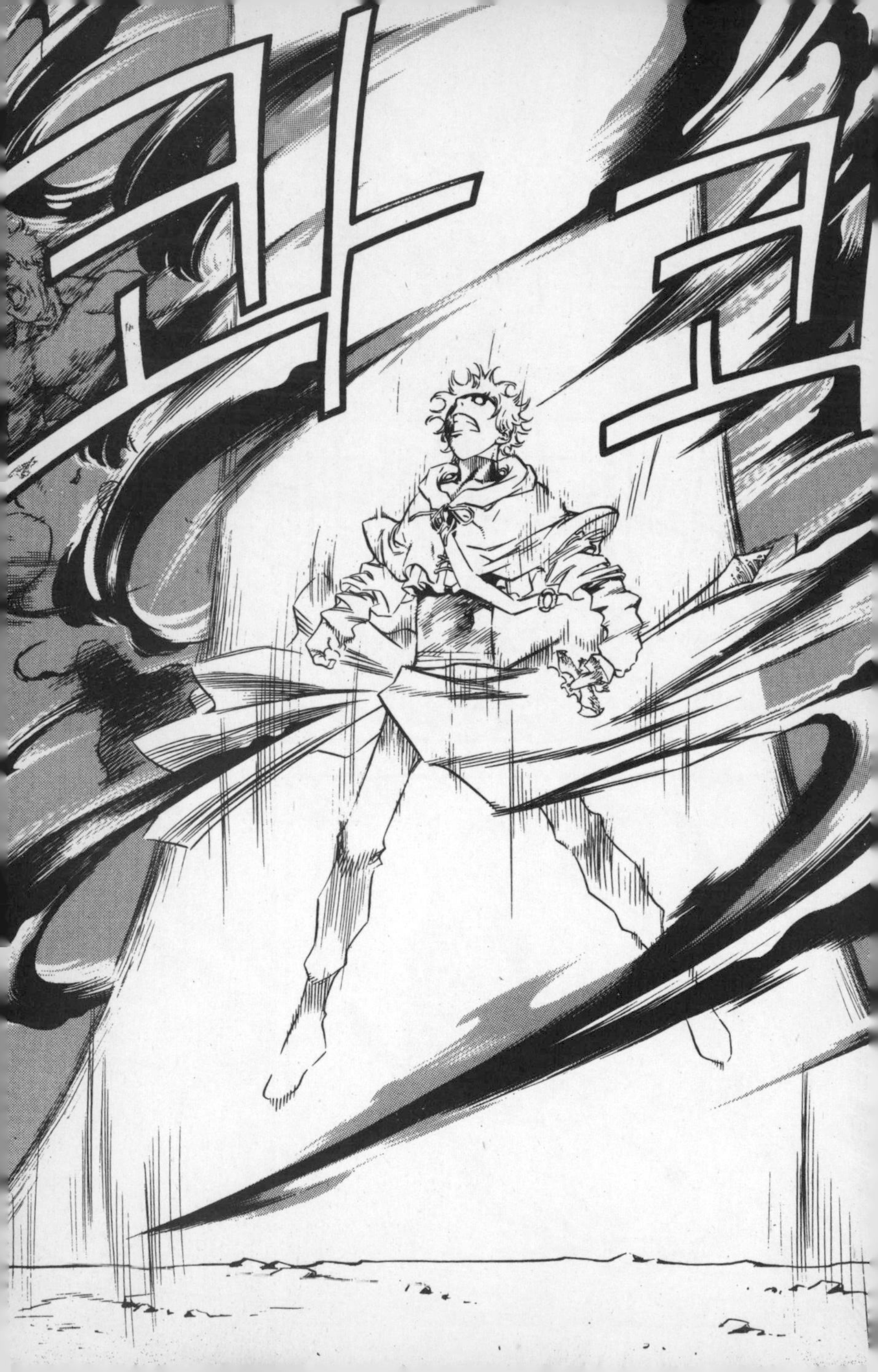

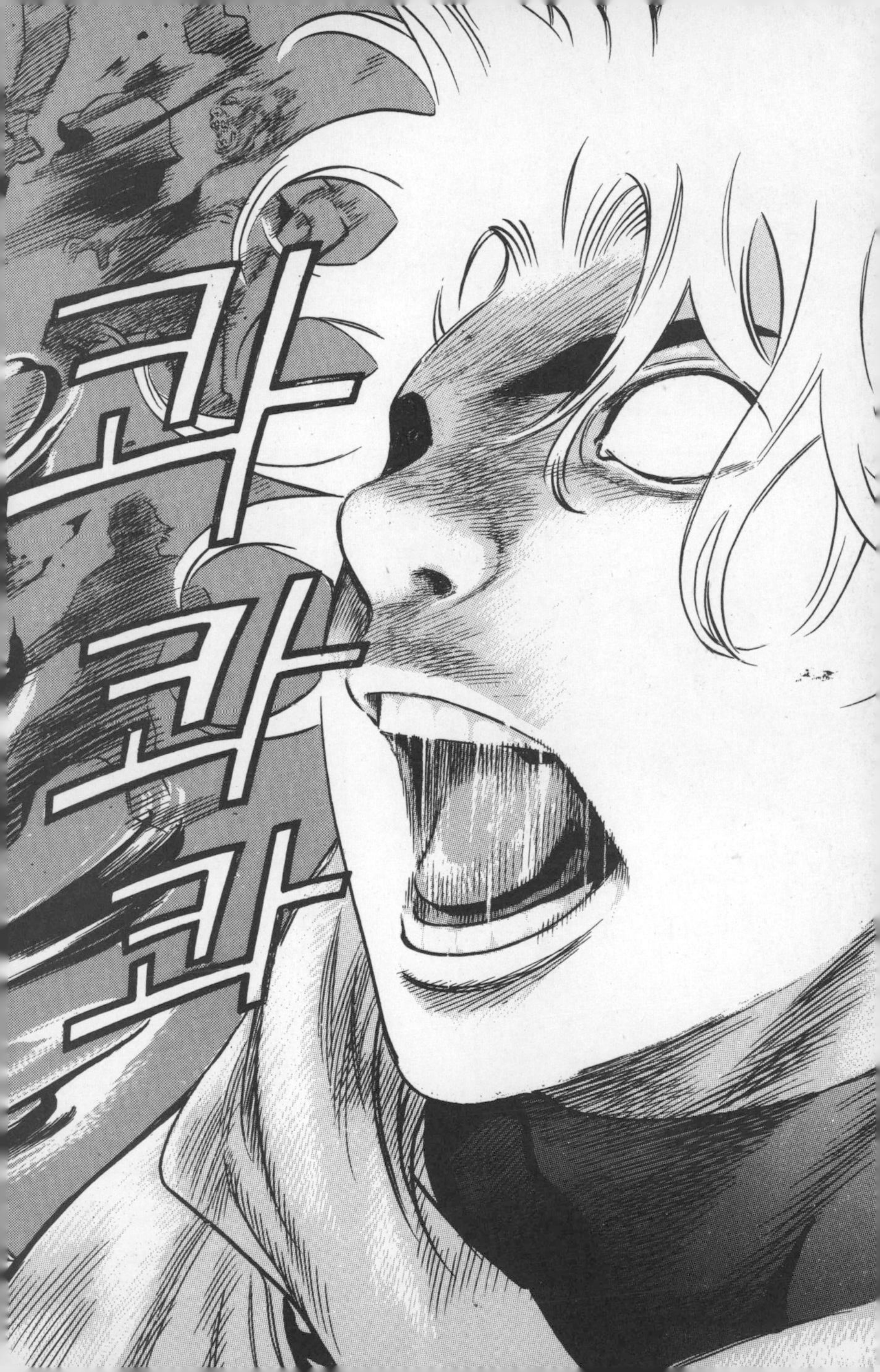
콰콰콰

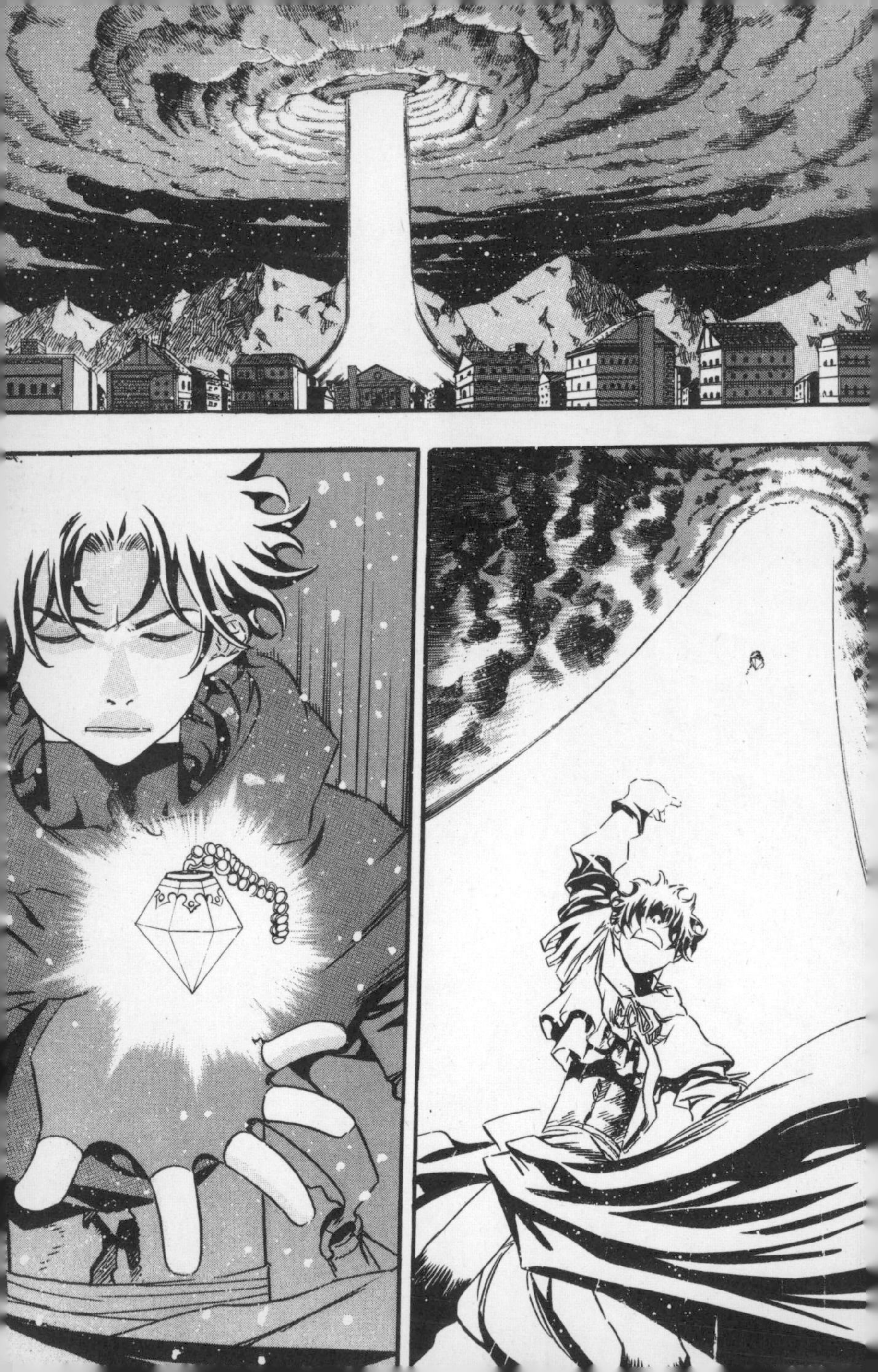

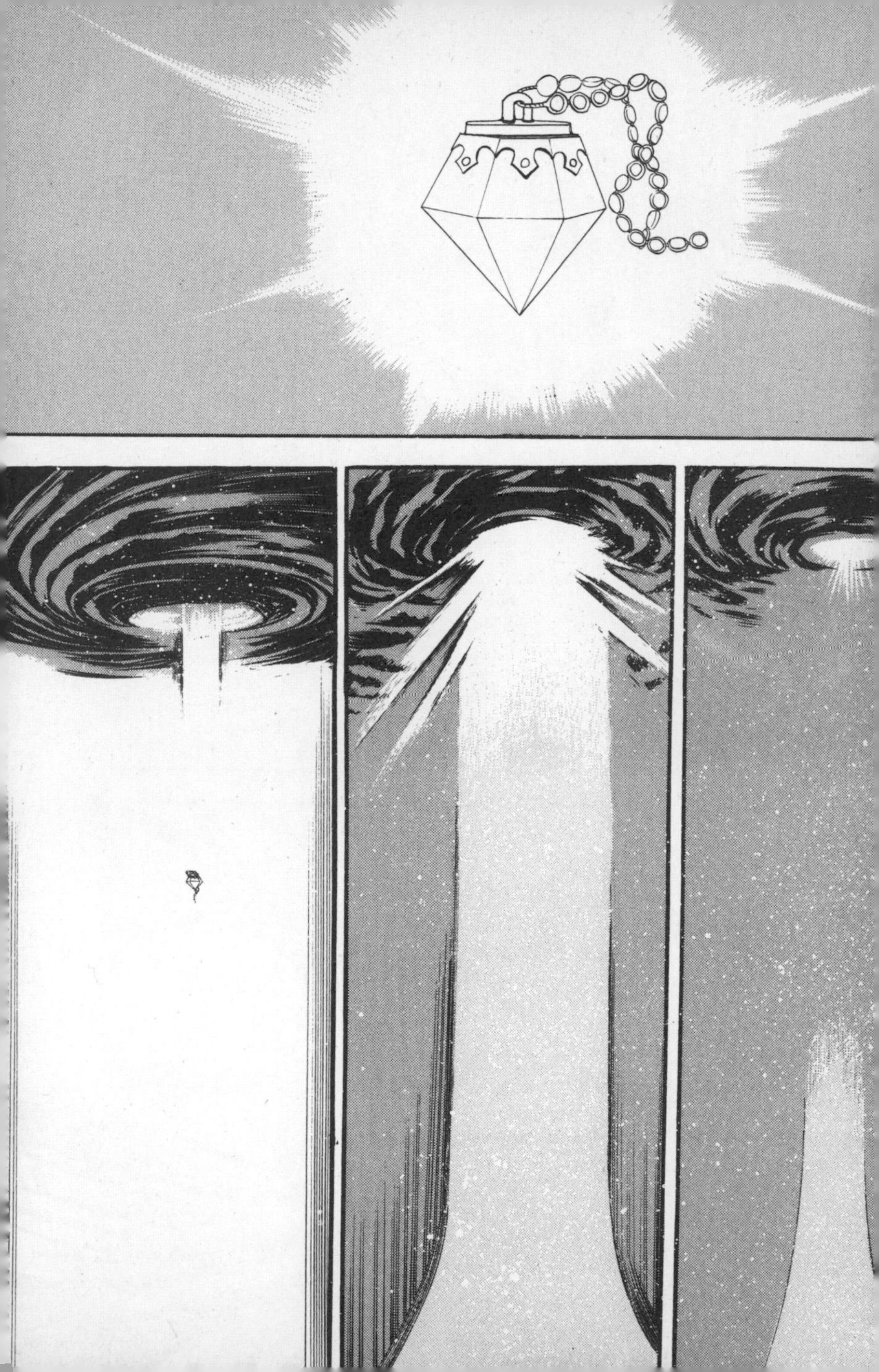

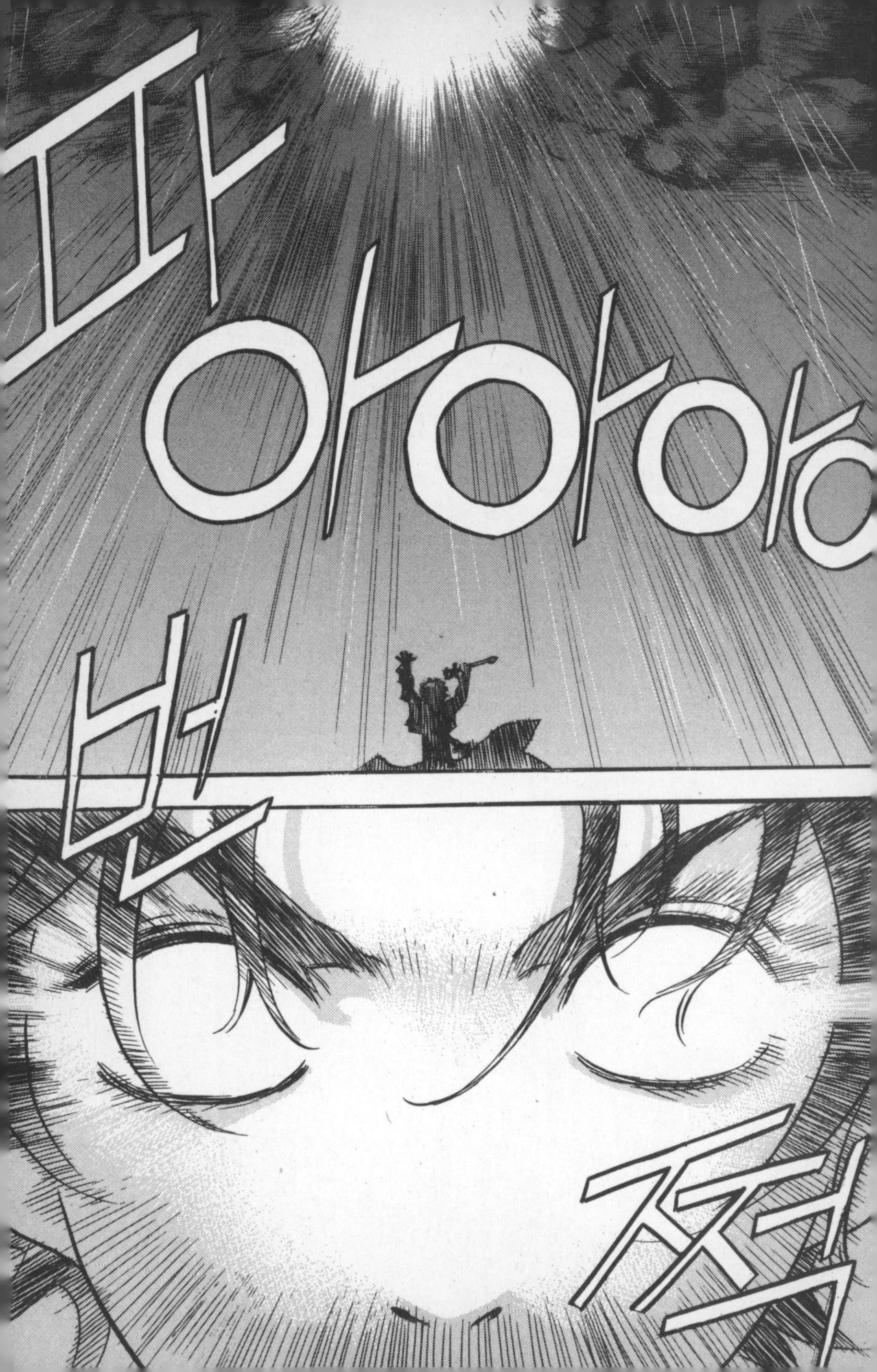
파아아아아
번쩍

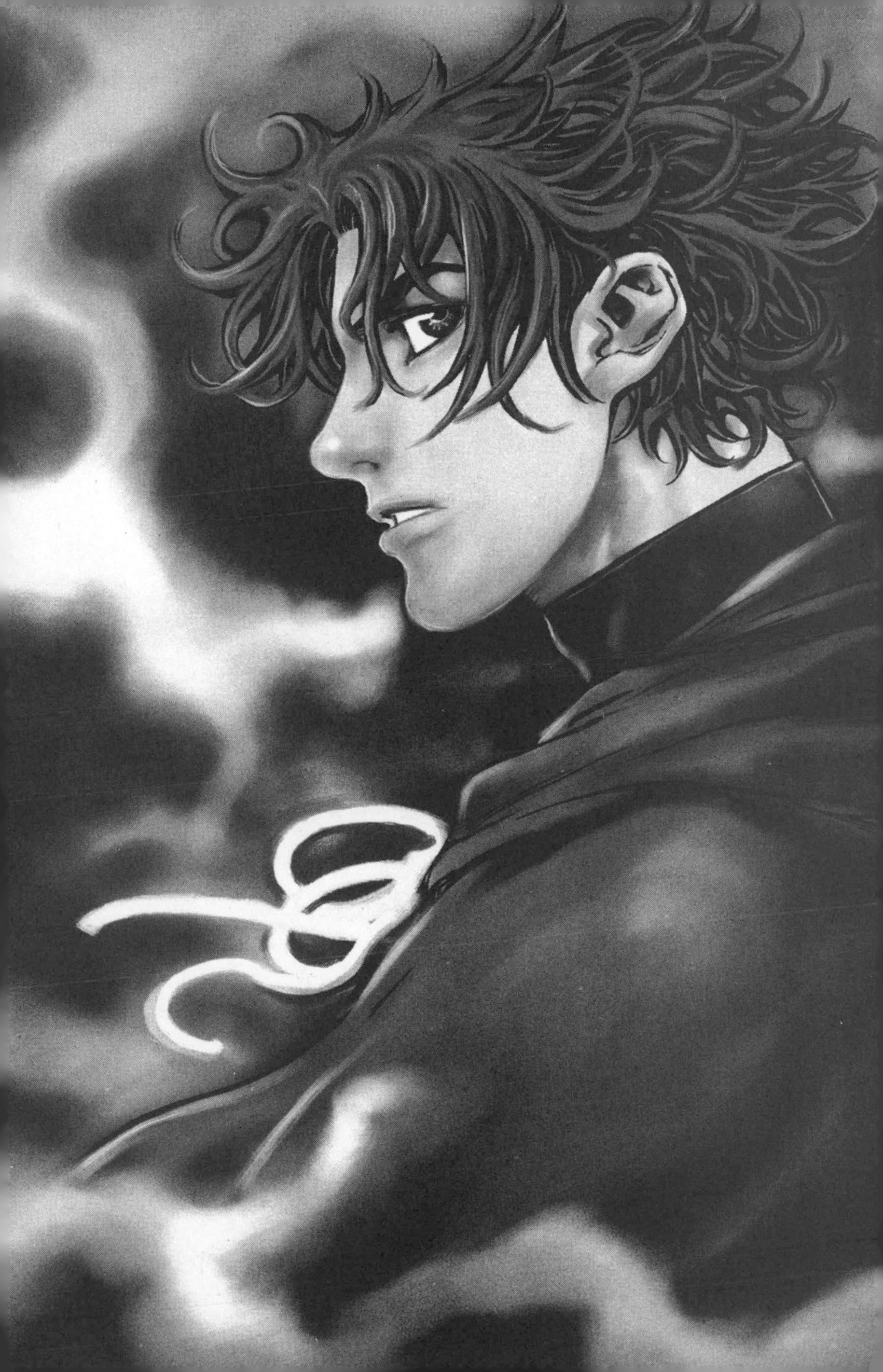

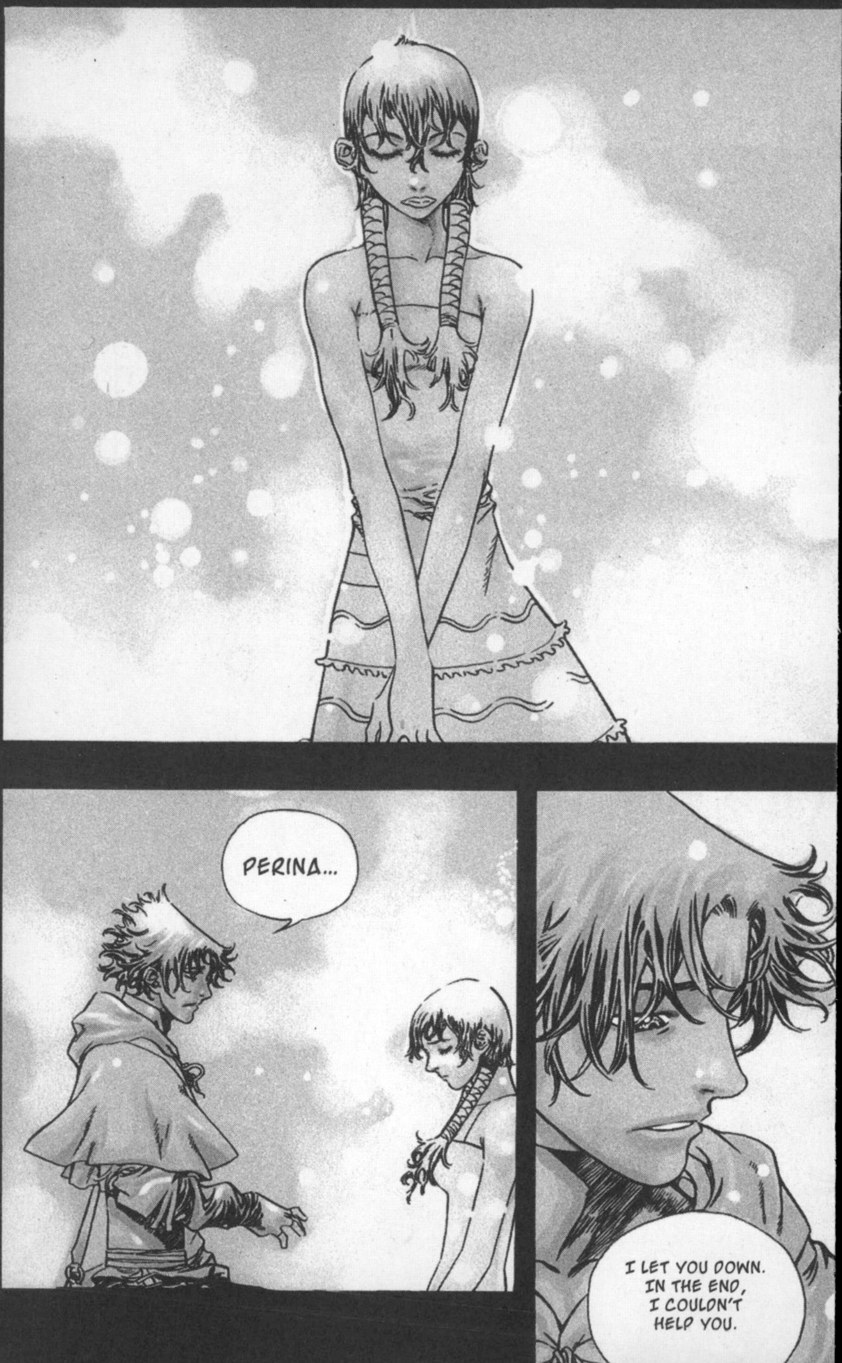
PERINA...
I LET YOU DOWN. IN THE END, I COULDN'T HELP YOU.

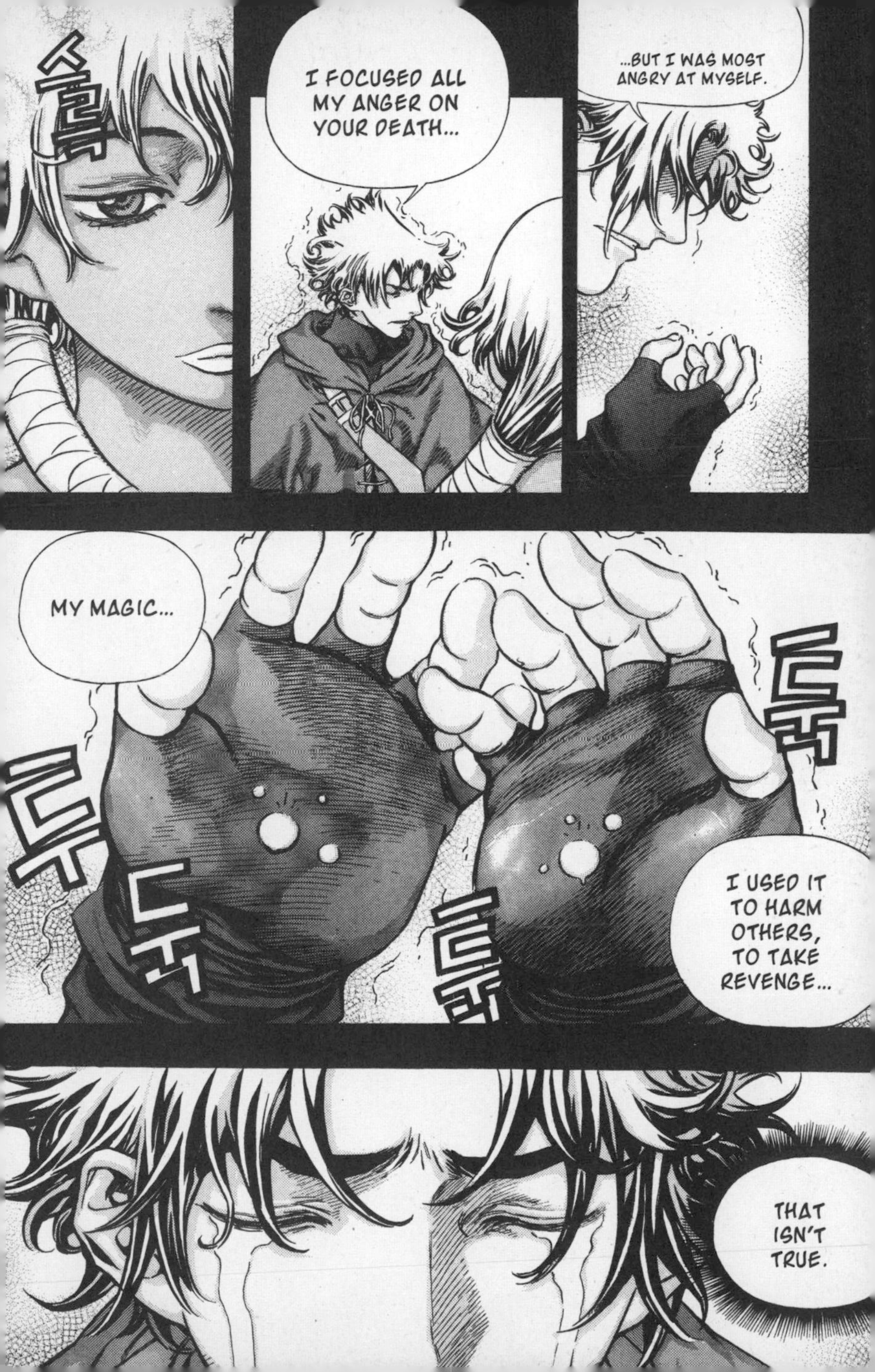
I FOCUSED ALL MY ANGER ON YOUR DEATH...
...BUT I WAS MOST ANGRY AT MYSELF.
MY MAGIC...
I USED IT TO HARM OTHERS, TO TAKE REVENGE...
THAT ISN'T TRUE.

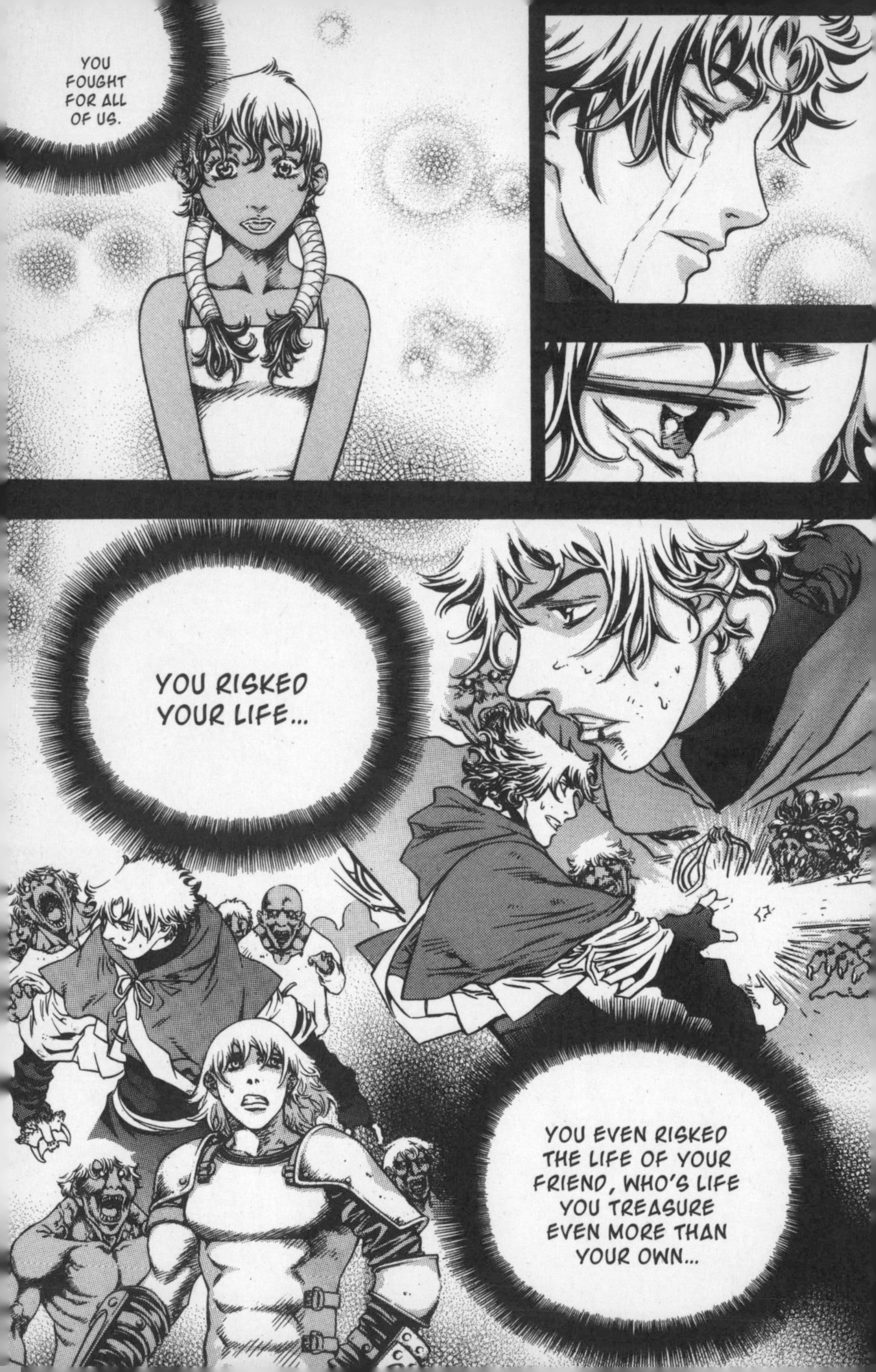
YOU FOUGHT FOR ALL OF US.
YOU RISKED YOUR LIFE...
YOU EVEN RISKED THE LIFE OF YOUR FRIEND, WHO'S LIFE YOU TREASURE EVEN MORE THAN YOUR OWN...

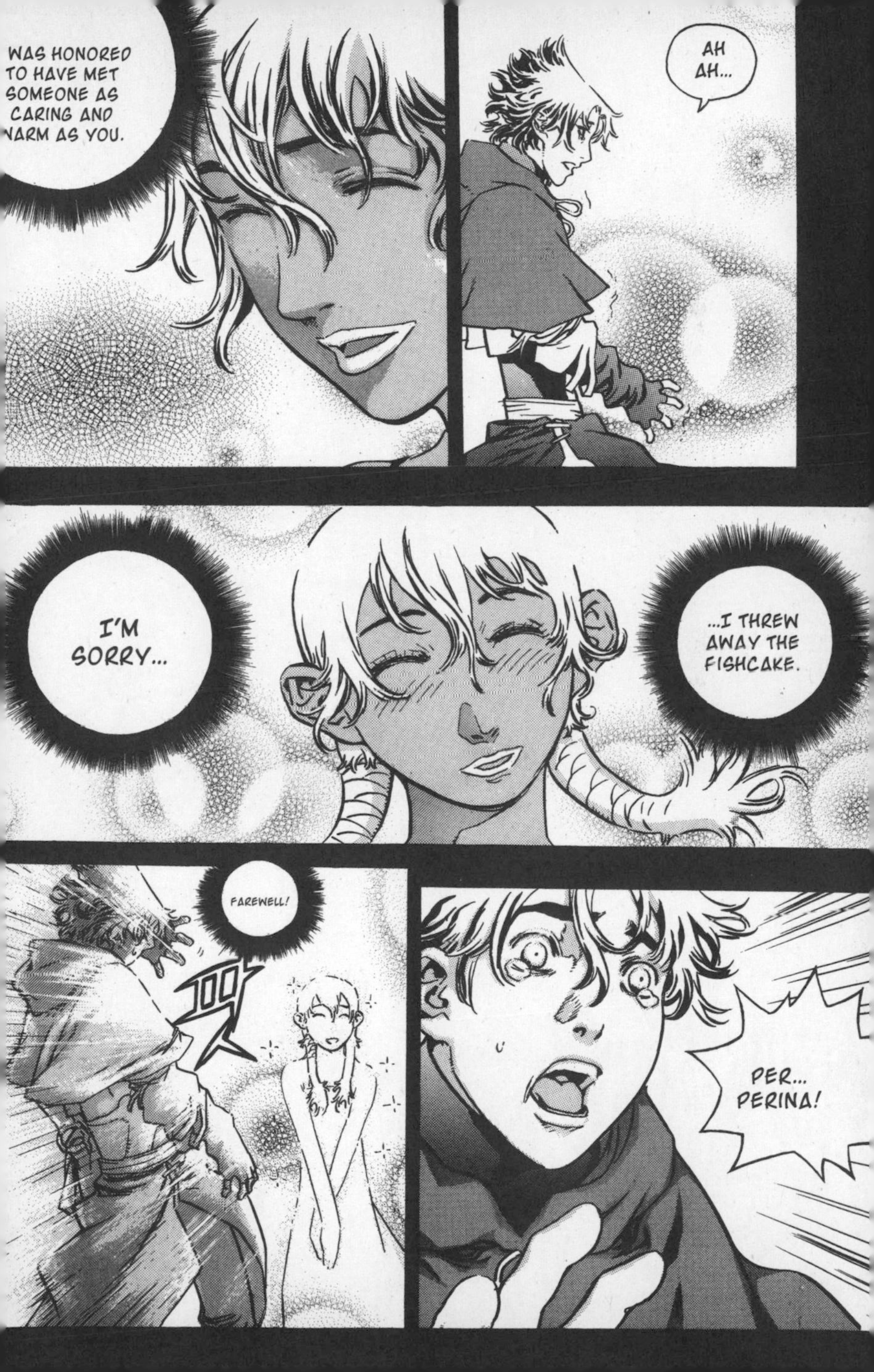
WAS HONORED TO HAVE MET SOMEONE AS CARING AND WARM AS YOU.
AH AH...
I'M SORRY...
...I THREW AWAY THE FISHCAKE.
FAREWELL!
PER... PERINA!

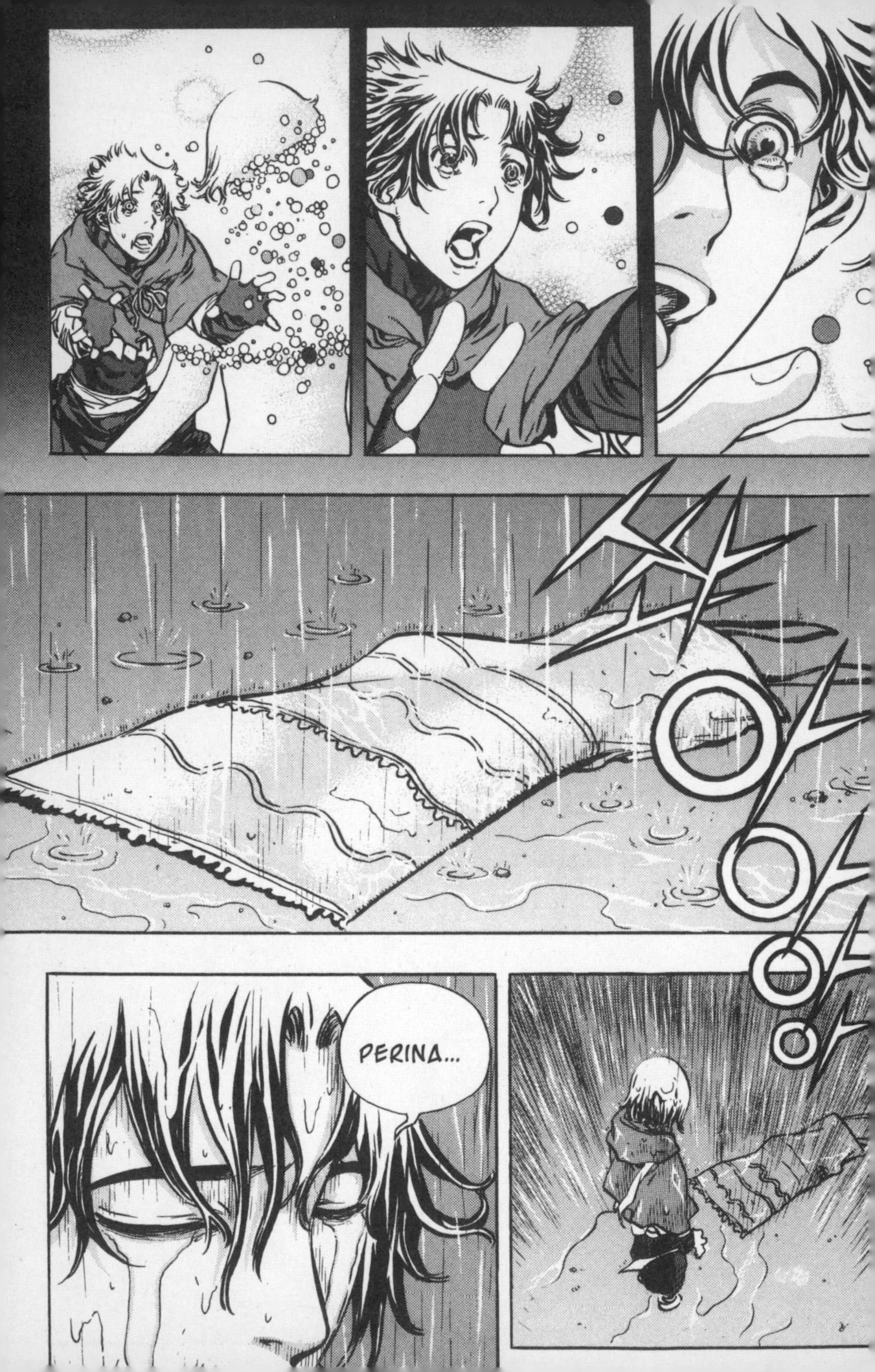
PERINA...

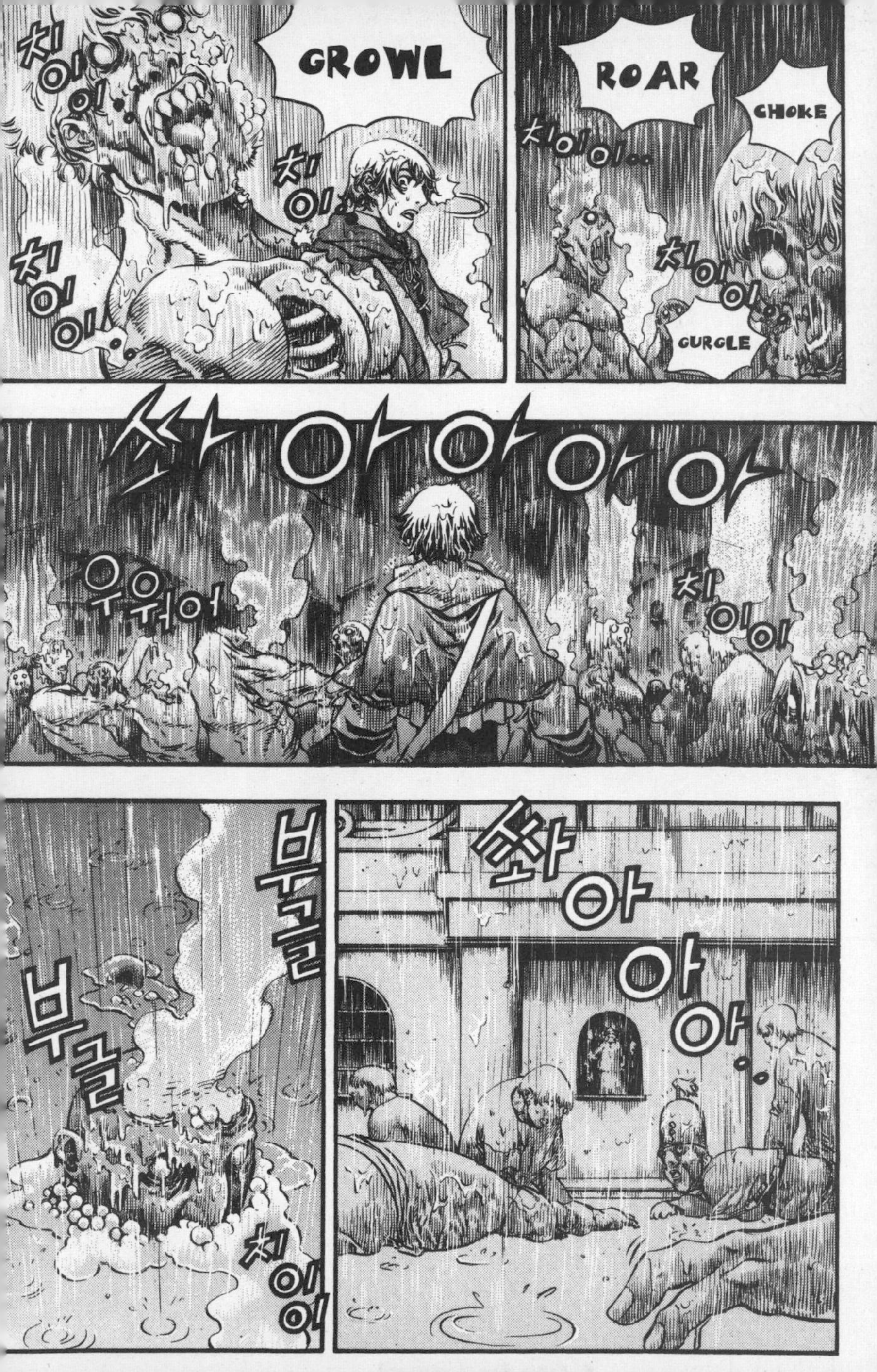

치이이..
GROWL
치이
치이이..
ROAR
CHOKE
치이이이..
치이이이..
GURGLE
쏴아아아아아
치이이
부글
부글
치이이
쏴아아아.

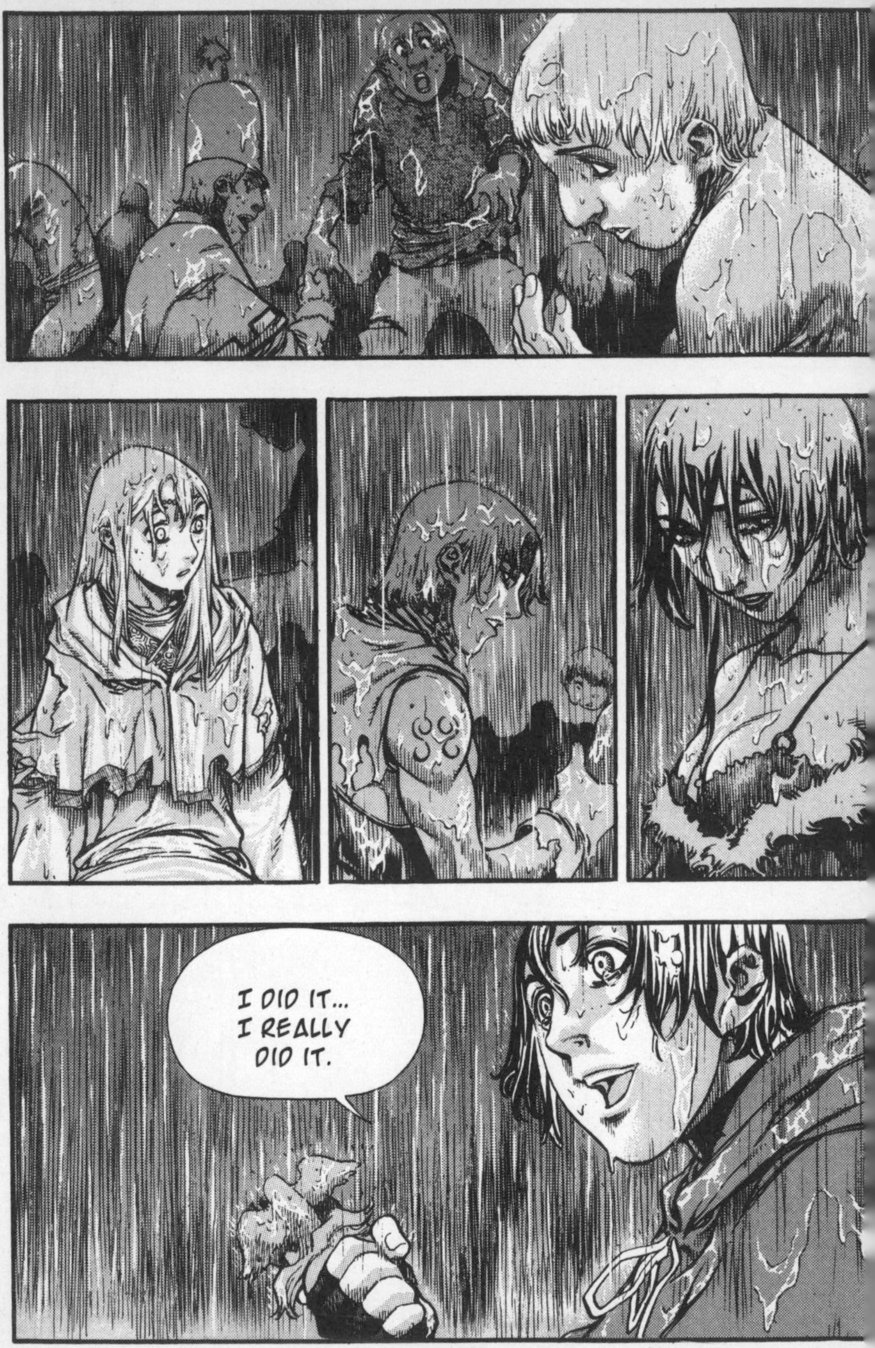
I DID IT... I REALLY DID IT.

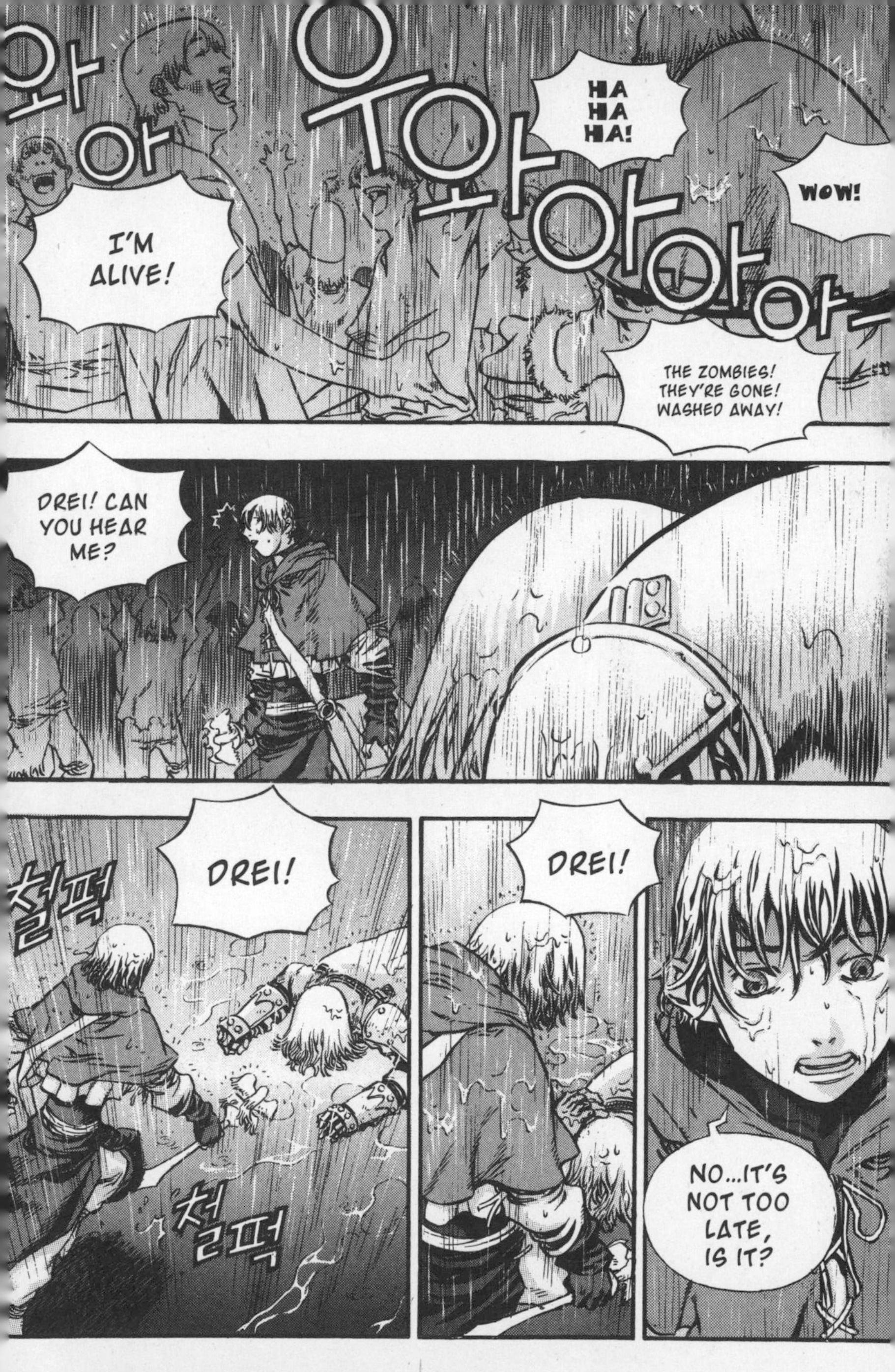
와아 우와아아아아—
HA HA HA HA!
WOW!
I'M ALIVE!
THE ZOMBIES! THEY'RE GONE! WASHED AWAY!
DREI! CAN YOU HEAR ME?
철퍽
DREI!
철퍽
DREI!
NO...IT'S NOT TOO LATE, IS IT?

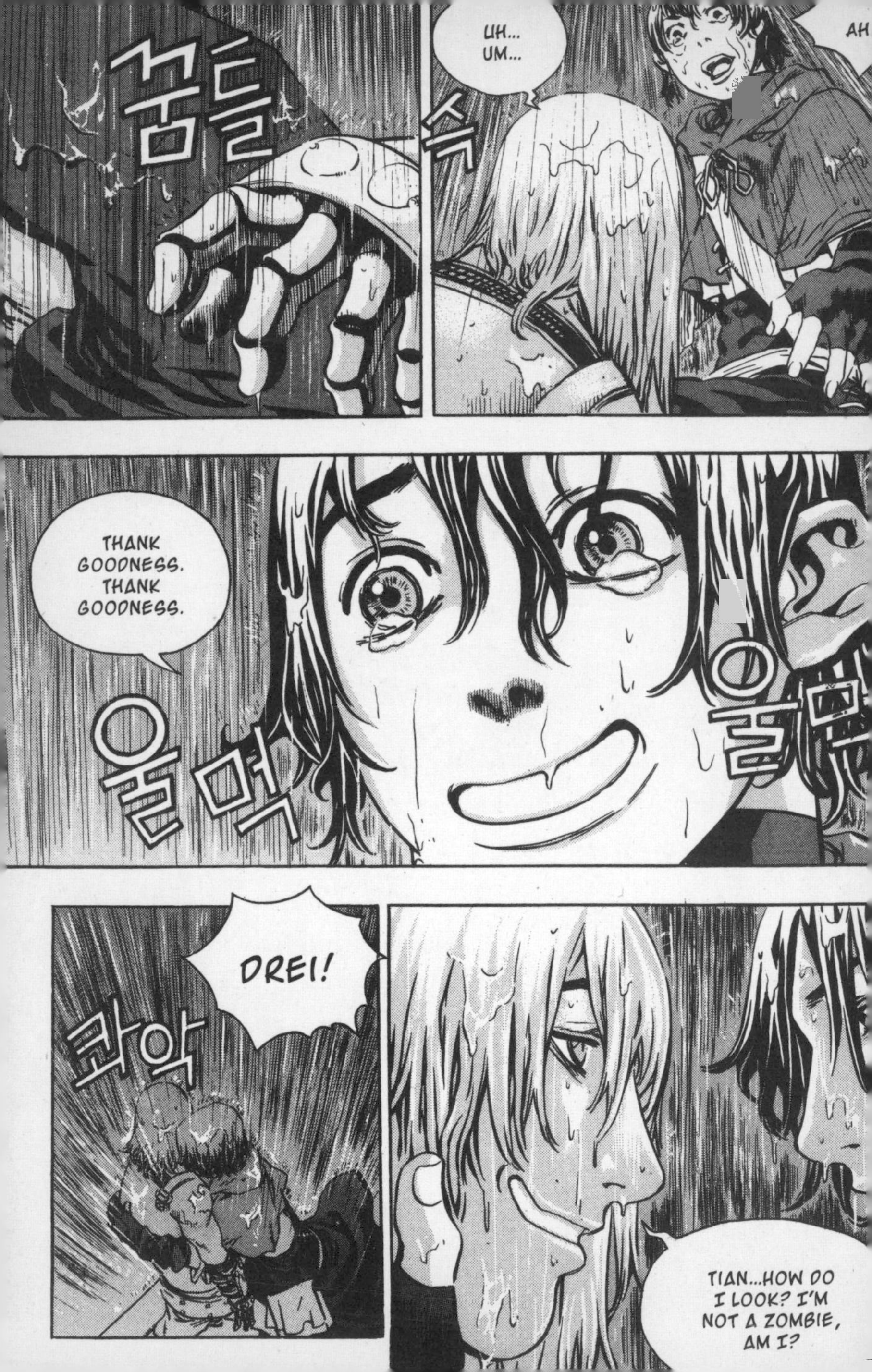
AH
UH... UM...
쓱
꿈틀
울먹
THANK GOODNESS. THANK GOODNESS.
울먹
TIAN...HOW DO I LOOK? I'M NOT A ZOMBIE, AM I?
DREI!
콰악

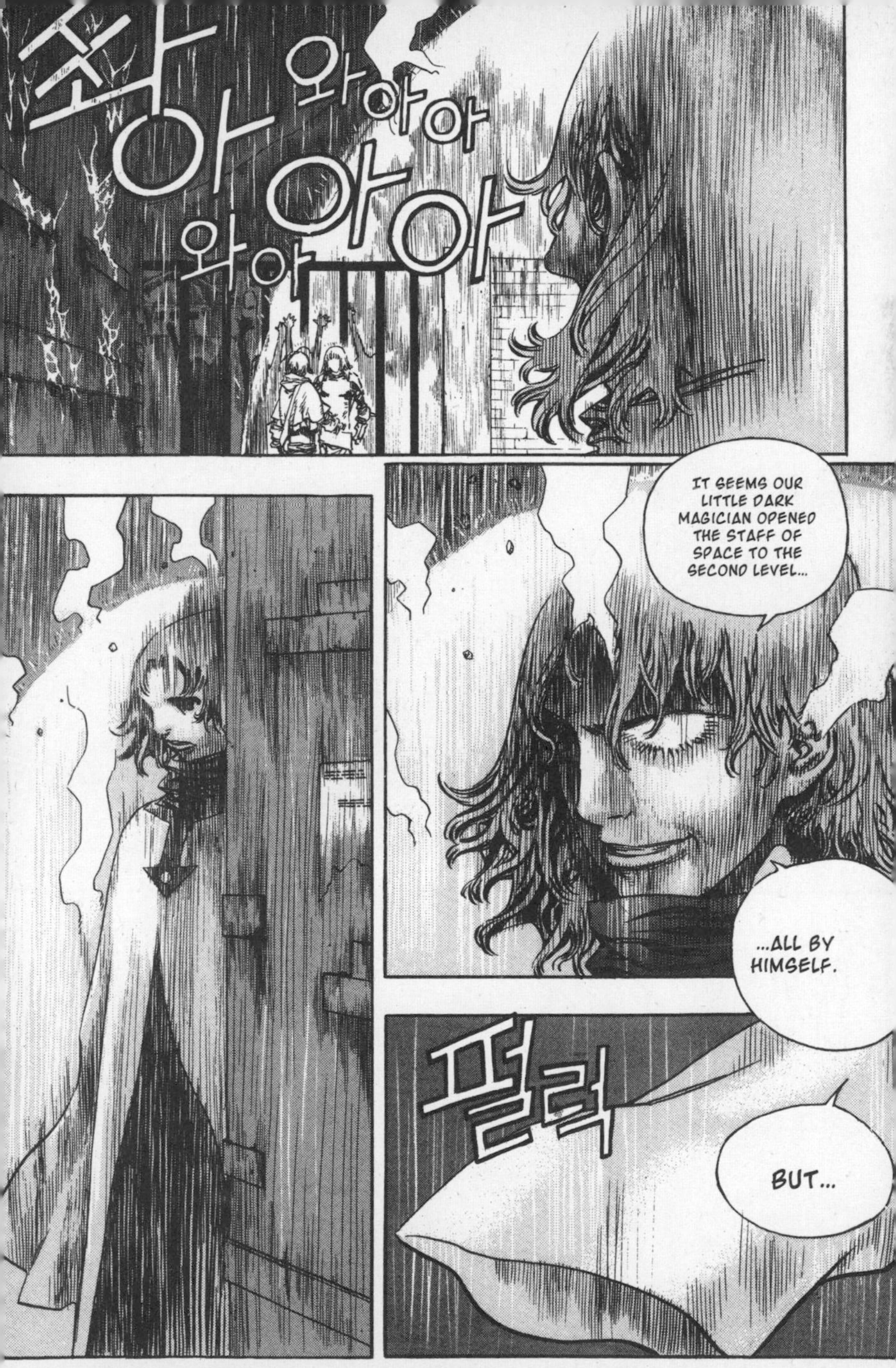

좌아아아
와아아아
와아
IT SEEMS OUR LITTLE DARK MAGICIAN OPENED THE STAFF OF SPACE TO THE SECOND LEVEL...
...ALL BY HIMSELF.
펄럭
BUT...

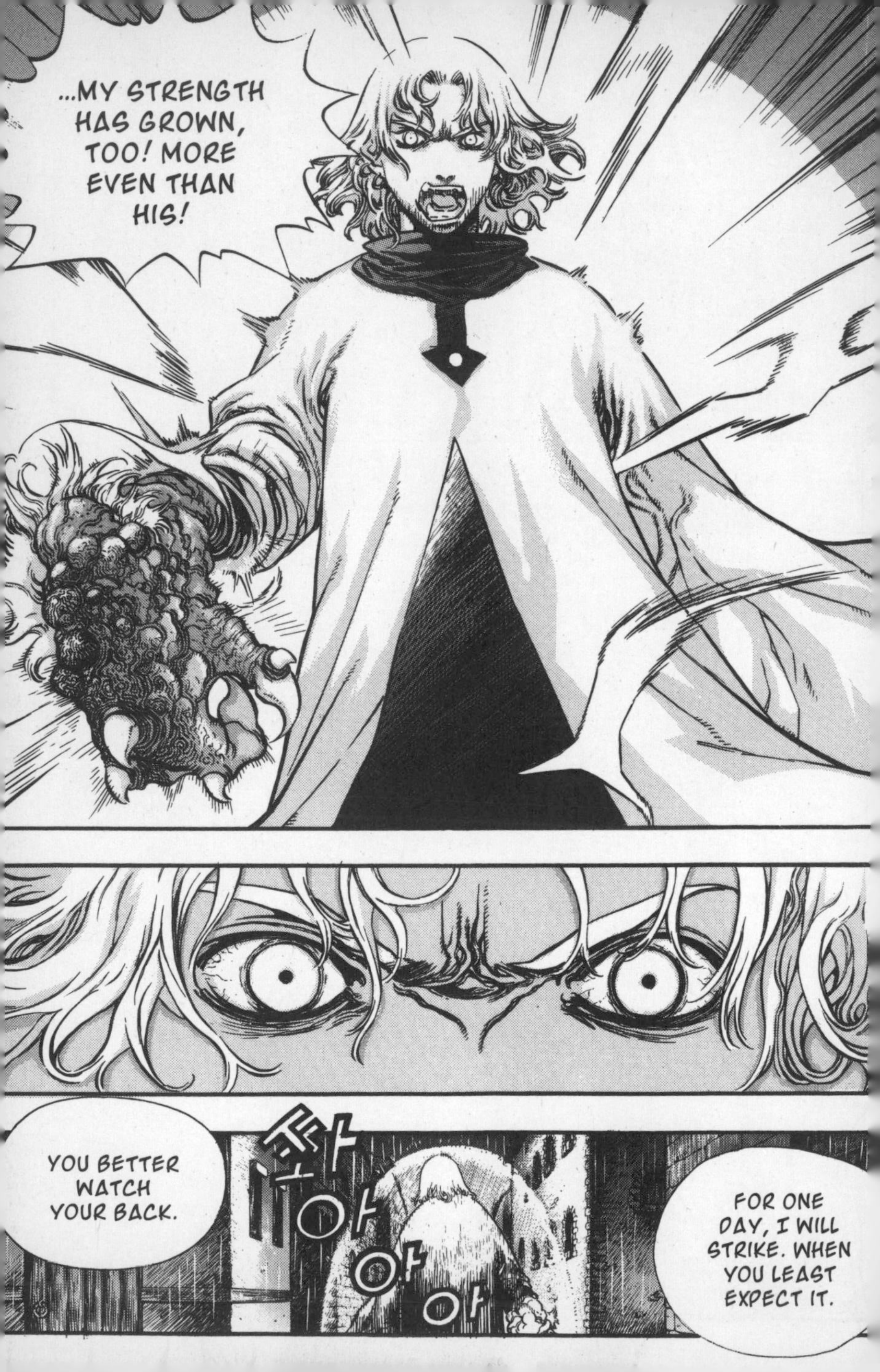
...MY STRENGTH HAS GROWN, TOO! MORE EVEN THAN HIS!
YOU BETTER WATCH YOUR BACK.
FOR ONE DAY, I WILL STRIKE. WHEN YOU LEAST EXPECT IT.

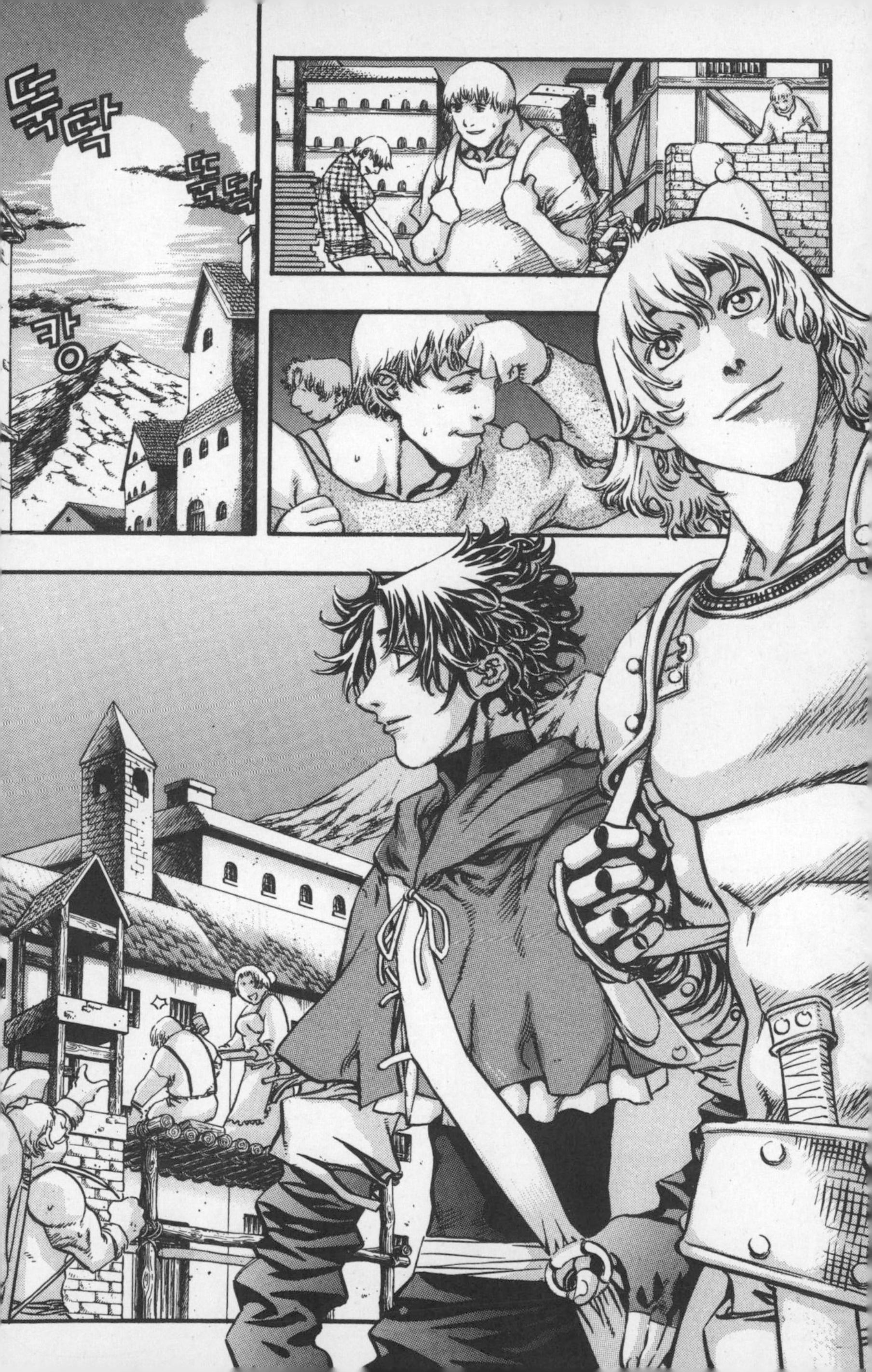
뚝딱
뚝딱
캉

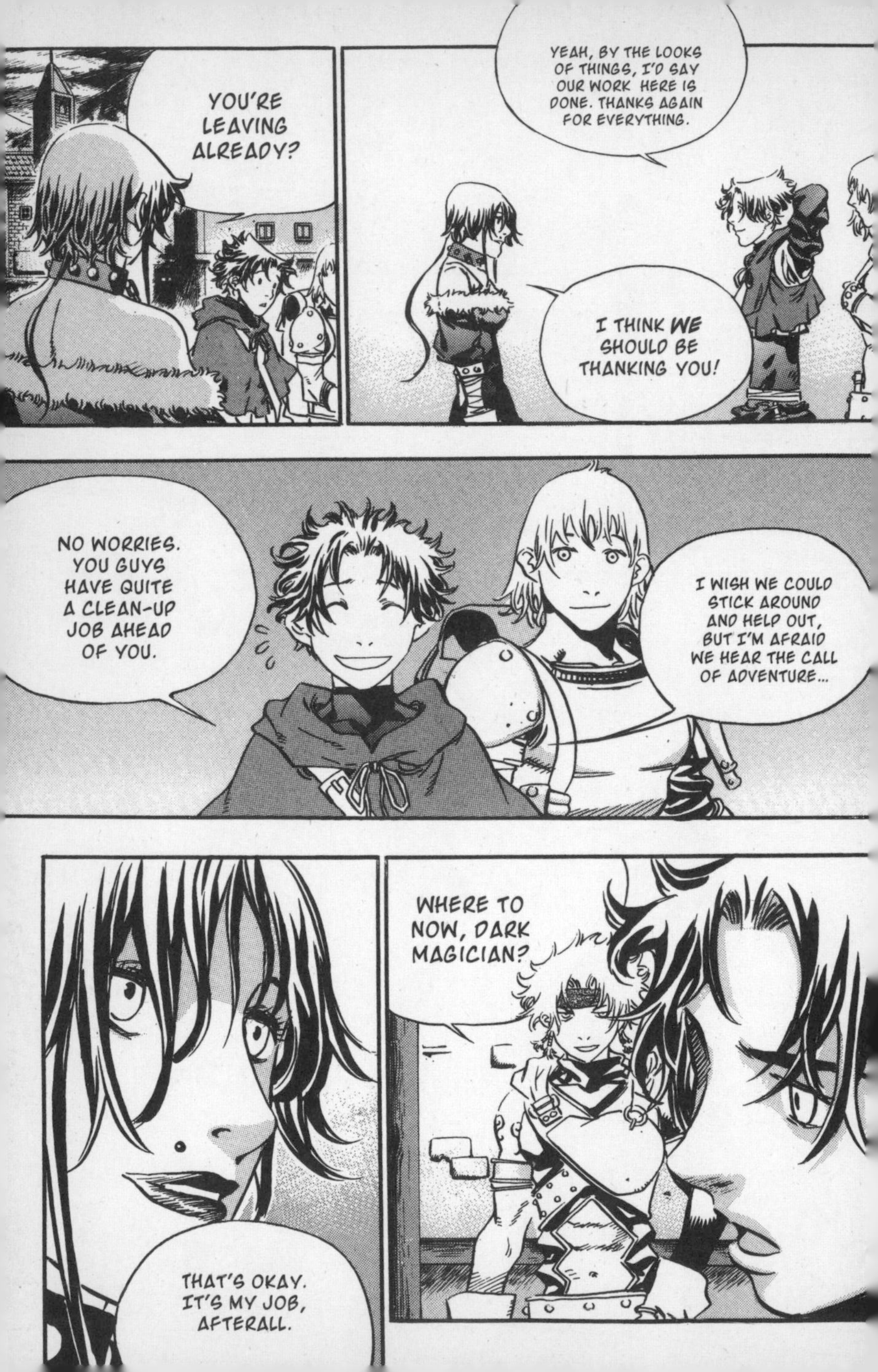
YOU'RE LEAVING ALREADY?
YEAH, BY THE LOOKS OF THINGS, I'D SAY OUR WORK HERE IS DONE. THANKS AGAIN FOR EVERYTHING.
I THINK WE SHOULD BE THANKING YOU!
NO WORRIES. YOU GUYS HAVE QUITE A CLEAN-UP JOB AHEAD OF YOU.
I WISH WE COULD STICK AROUND AND HELP OUT, BUT I'M AFRAID WE HEAR THE CALL OF ADVENTURE...
THAT'S OKAY. IT'S MY JOB, AFTERALL.
WHERE TO NOW, DARK MAGICIAN?

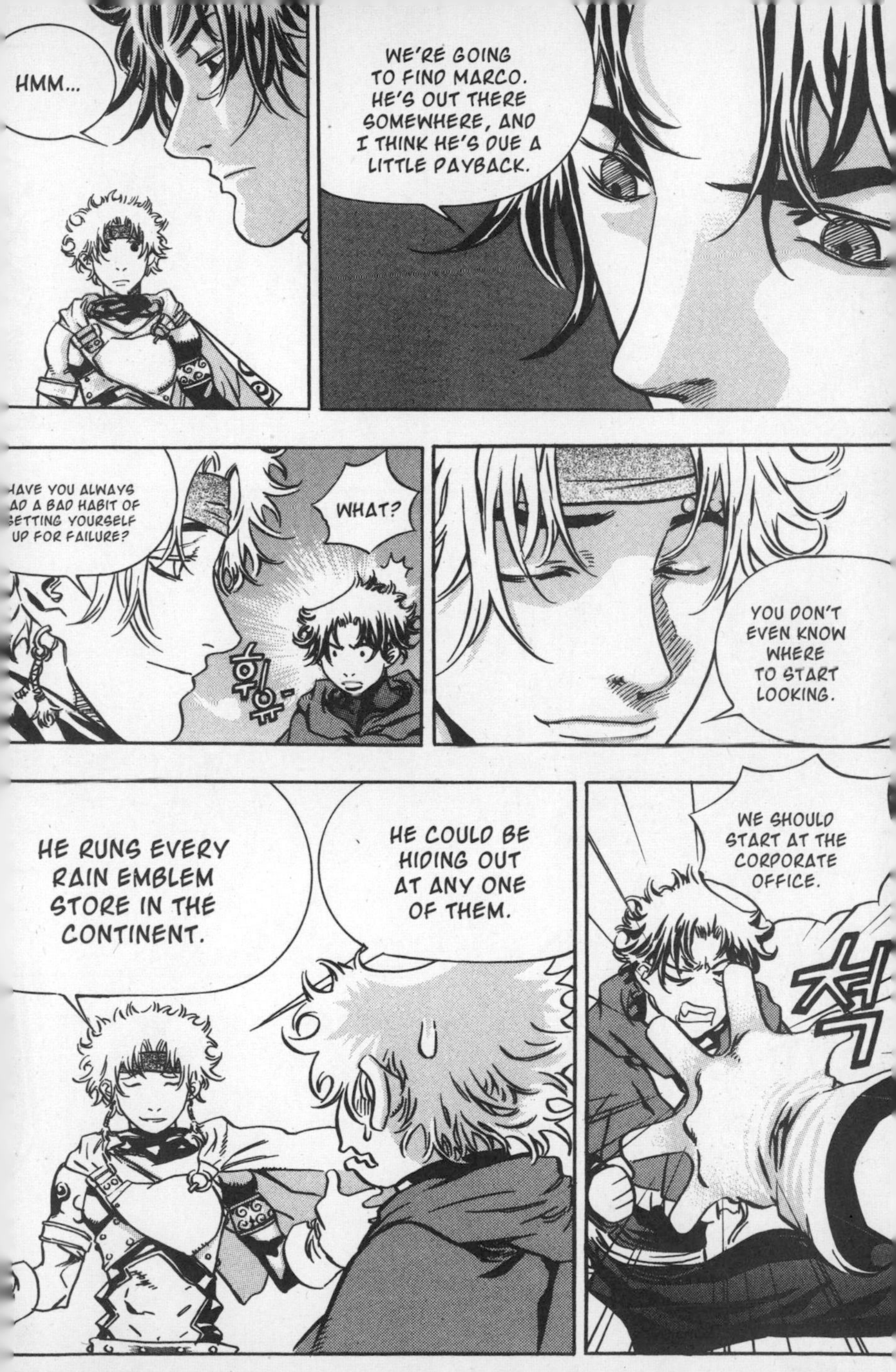
HMM...
WE'RE GOING TO FIND MARCO. HE'S OUT THERE SOMEWHERE, AND I THINK HE'S DUE A LITTLE PAYBACK.
HAVE YOU ALWAYS AD A BAD HABIT OF ETTING YOURSELF UP FOR FAILURE?
WHAT?
YOU DON'T EVEN KNOW WHERE TO START LOOKING.
HE RUNS EVERY RAIN EMBLEM STORE IN THE CONTINENT.
HE COULD BE HIDING OUT AT ANY ONE OF THEM.
WE SHOULD START AT THE CORPORATE OFFICE.

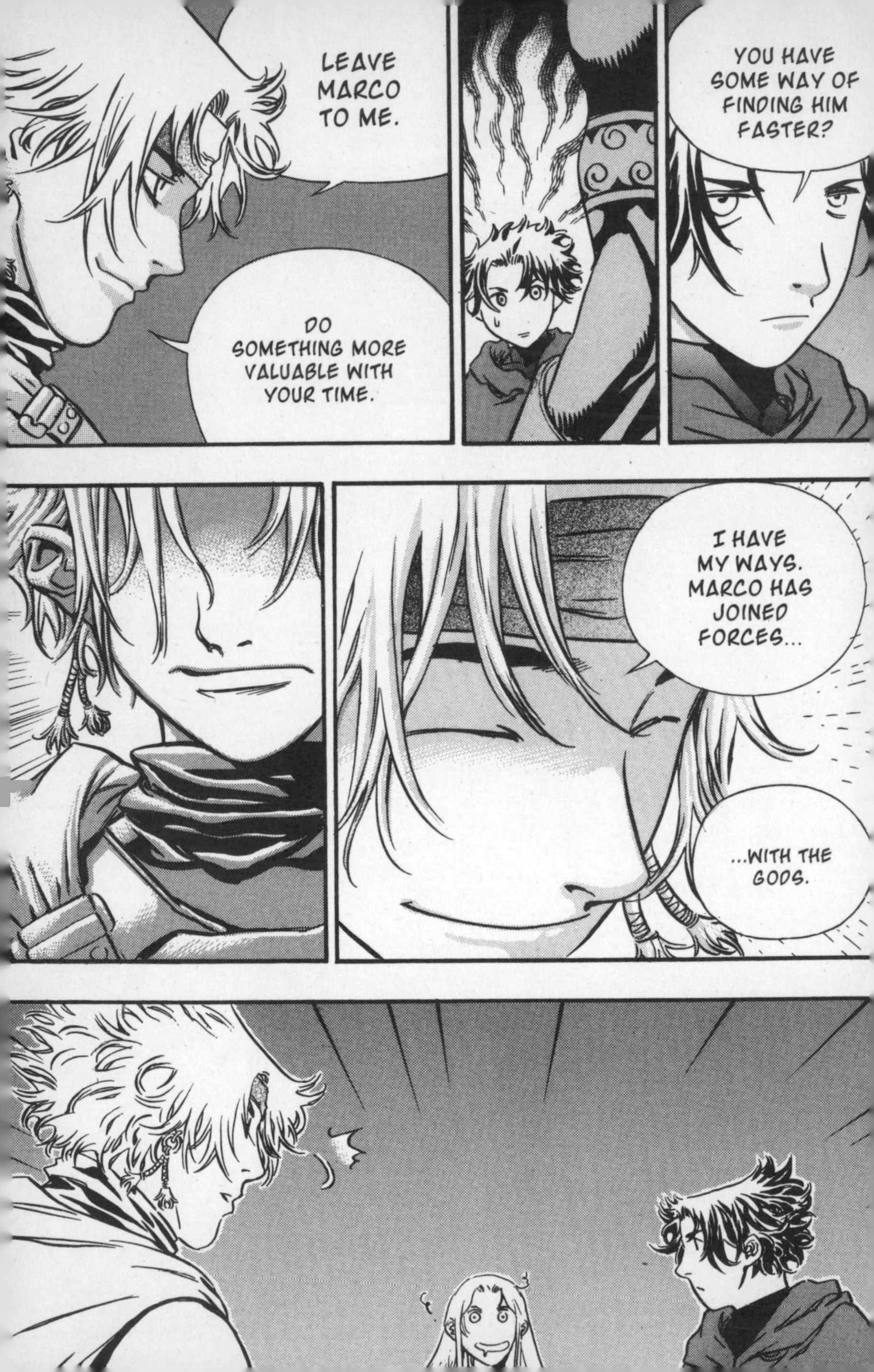
LEAVE MARCO TO ME.
DO SOMETHING MORE VALUABLE WITH YOUR TIME.
YOU HAVE SOME WAY OF FINDING HIM FASTER?
I HAVE MY WAYS. MARCO HAS JOINED FORCES...
...WITH THE GODS.

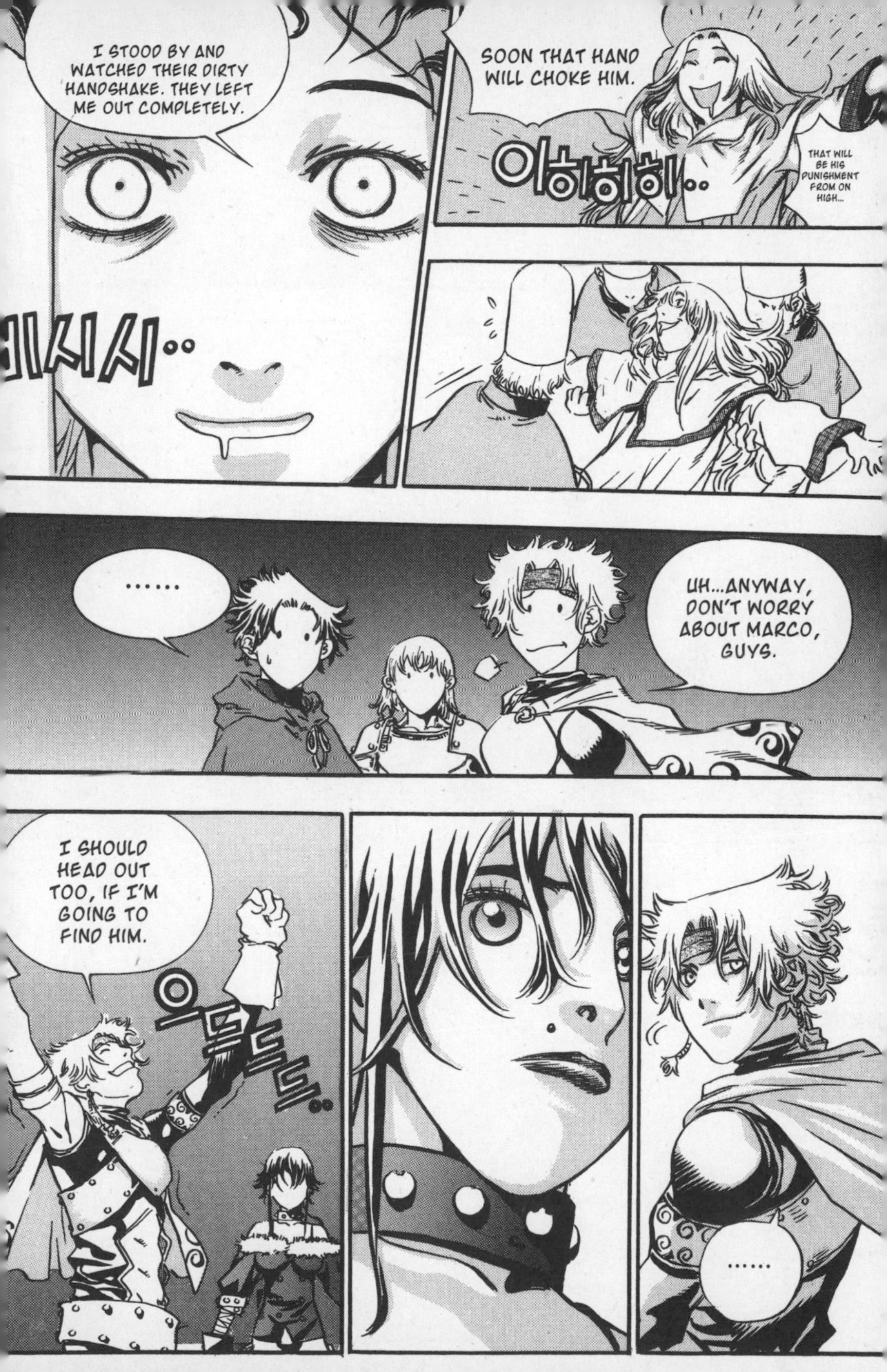
I STOOD BY AND WATCHED THEIR DIRTY HANDSHAKE. THEY LEFT ME OUT COMPLETELY.
SOON THAT HAND WILL CHOKE HIM.
THAT WILL BE HIS PUNISHMENT FROM ON HIGH...
......
UH...ANYWAY, DON'T WORRY ABOUT MARCO, GUYS.
I SHOULD HEAD OUT TOO, IF I'M GOING TO FIND HIM.
......

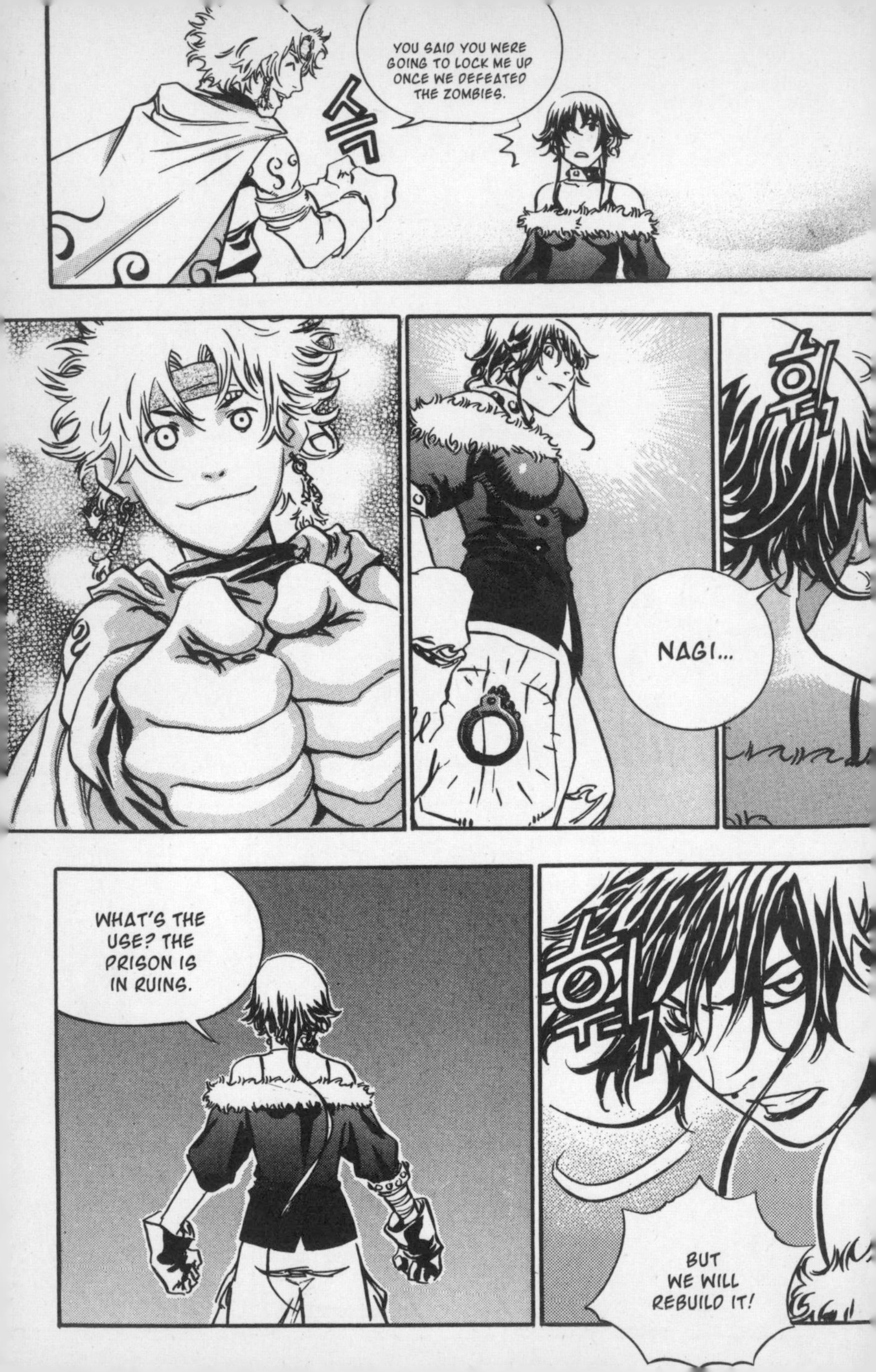

YOU SAID YOU WERE GOING TO LOCK ME UP ONCE WE DEFEATED THE ZOMBIES.
NAGI...
WHAT'S THE USE? THE PRISON IS IN RUINS.
BUT WE WILL REBUILD IT!

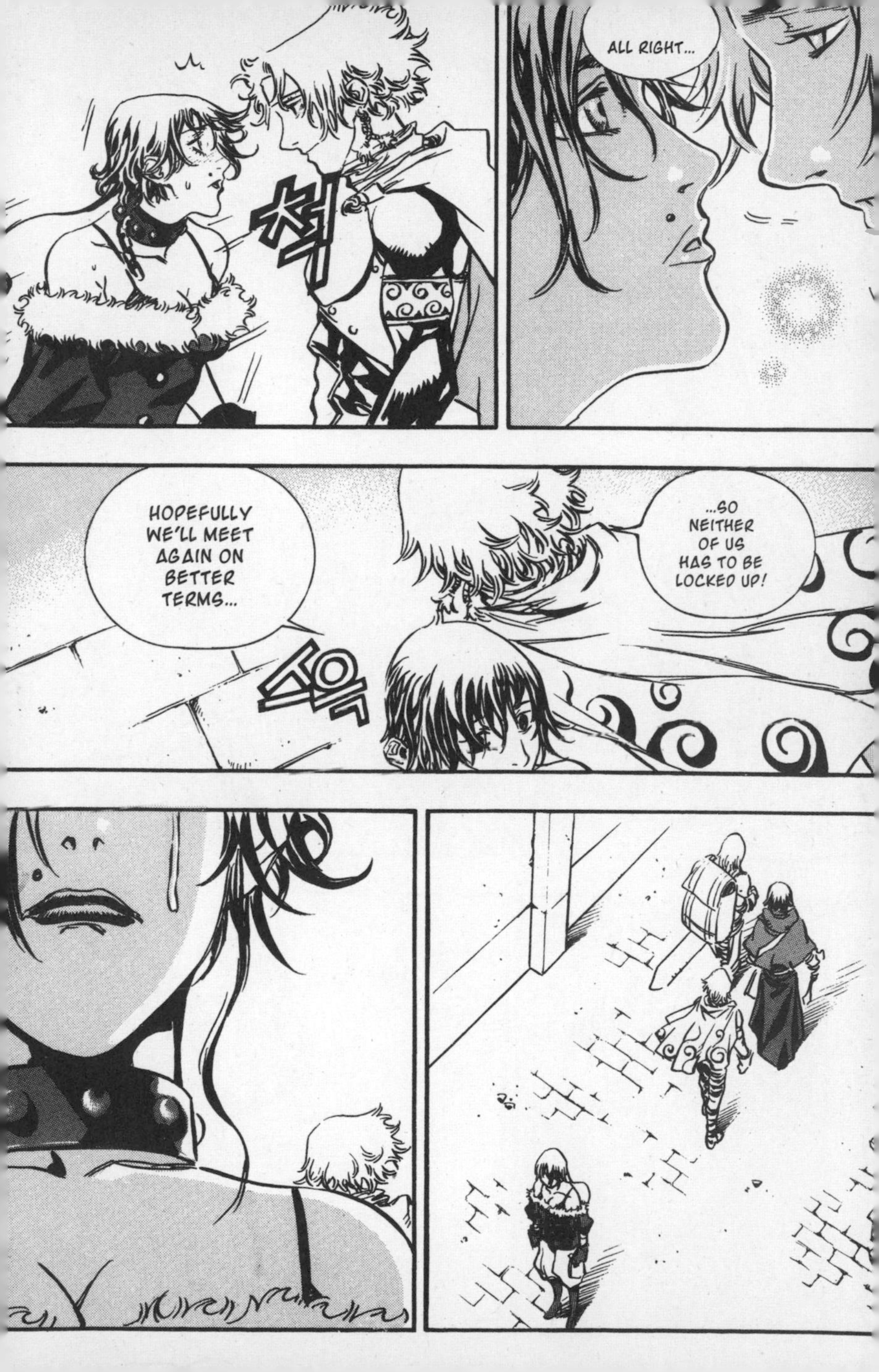

ALL RIGHT...
HOPEFULLY WE'LL MEET AGAIN ON BETTER TERMS...
...SO NEITHER OF US HAS TO BE LOCKED UP!

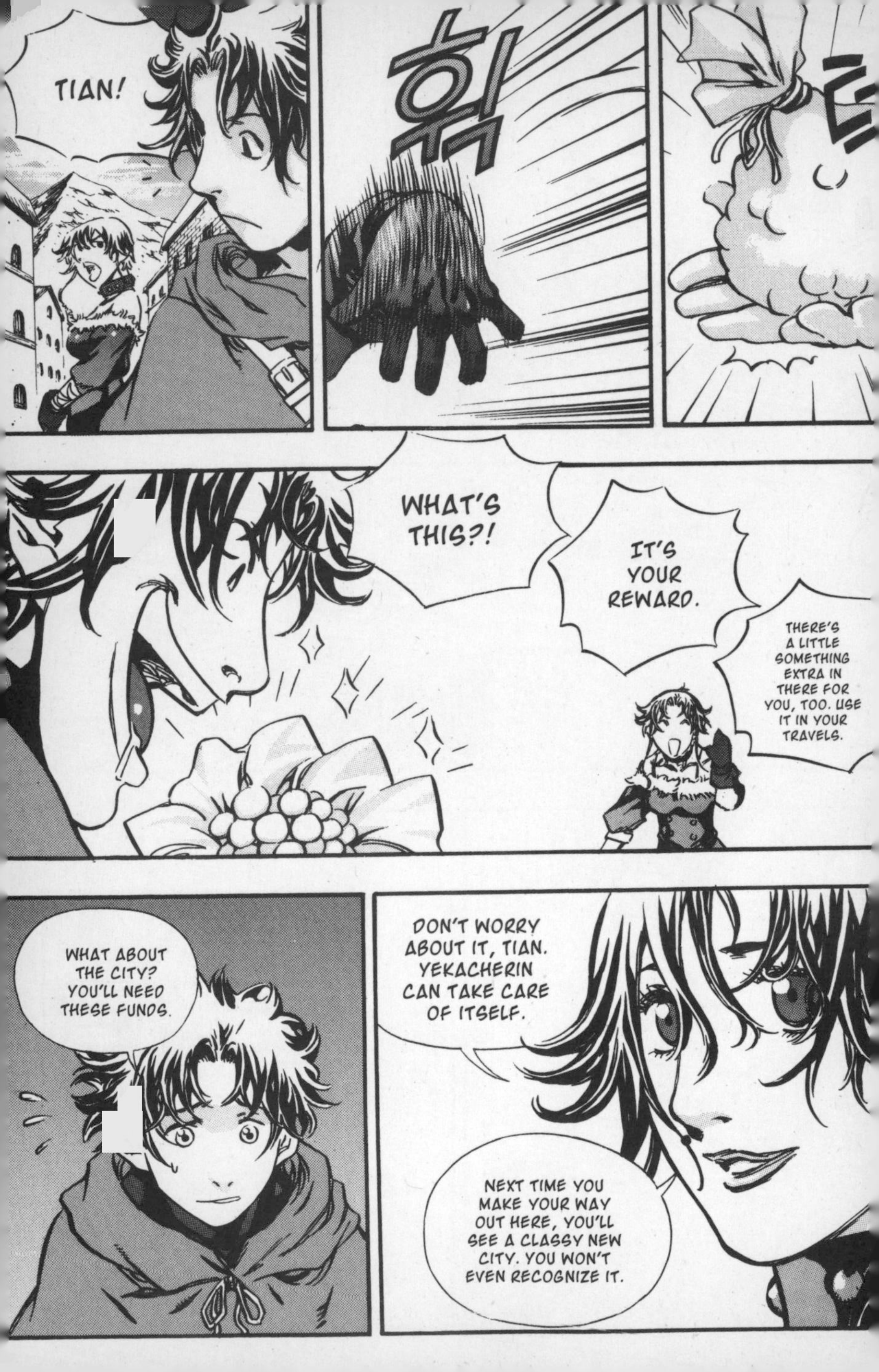
TIAN!
WHAT'S THIS?!
IT'S YOUR REWARD.
THERE'S A LITTLE SOMETHING EXTRA IN THERE FOR YOU, TOO. USE IT IN YOUR TRAVELS.
WHAT ABOUT THE CITY? YOU'LL NEED THESE FUNDS.
DON'T WORRY ABOUT IT, TIAN. YEKACHERIN CAN TAKE CARE OF ITSELF.
NEXT TIME YOU MAKE YOUR WAY OUT HERE, YOU'LL SEE A CLASSY NEW CITY. YOU WON'T EVEN RECOGNIZE IT.

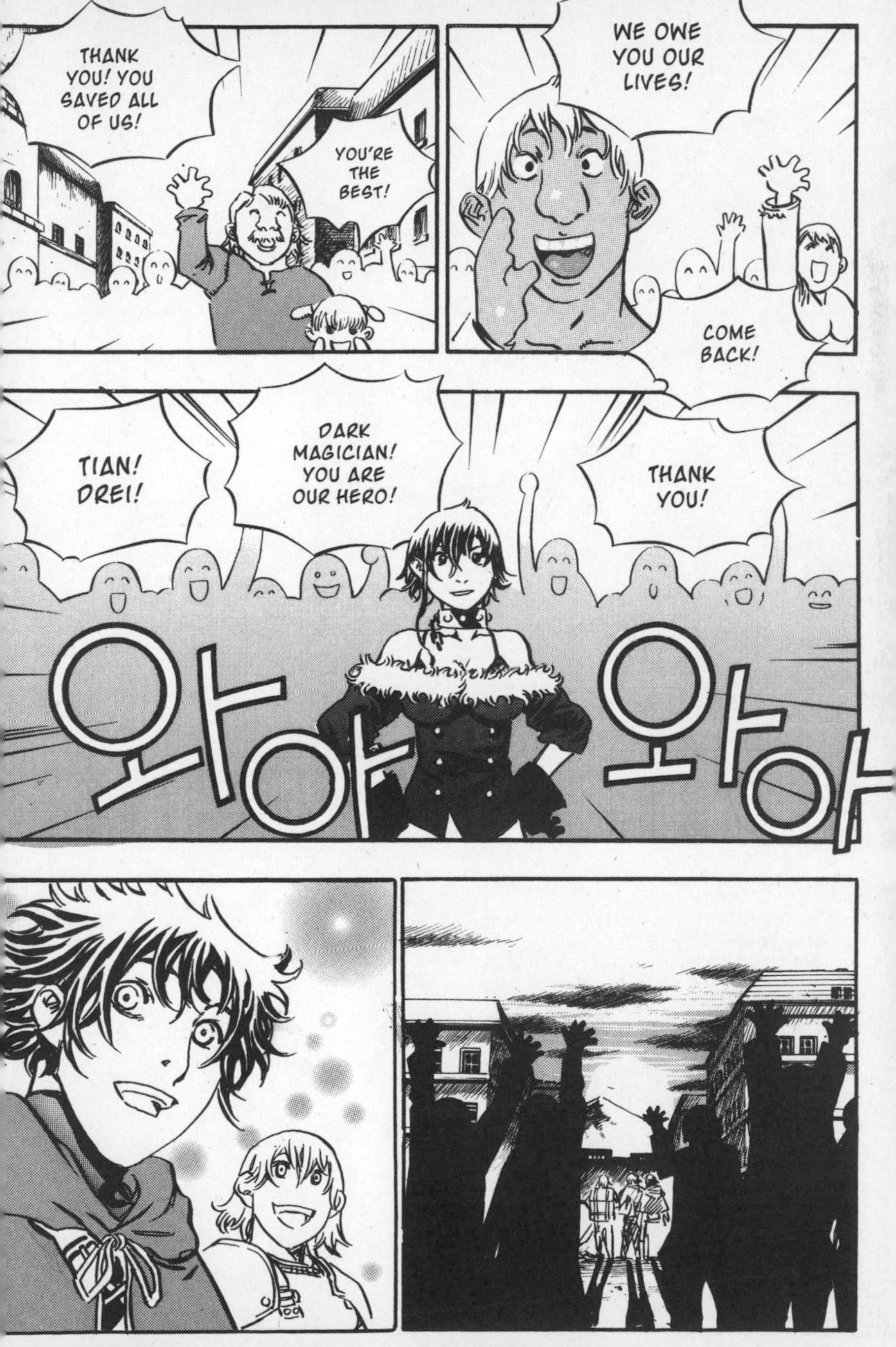

THANK YOU! YOU SAVED ALL OF US!
YOU'RE THE BEST!
WE OWE YOU OUR LIVES!
COME BACK!
TIAN! DREI!
DARK MAGICIAN! YOU ARE OUR HERO!
THANK YOU!
와아 와아

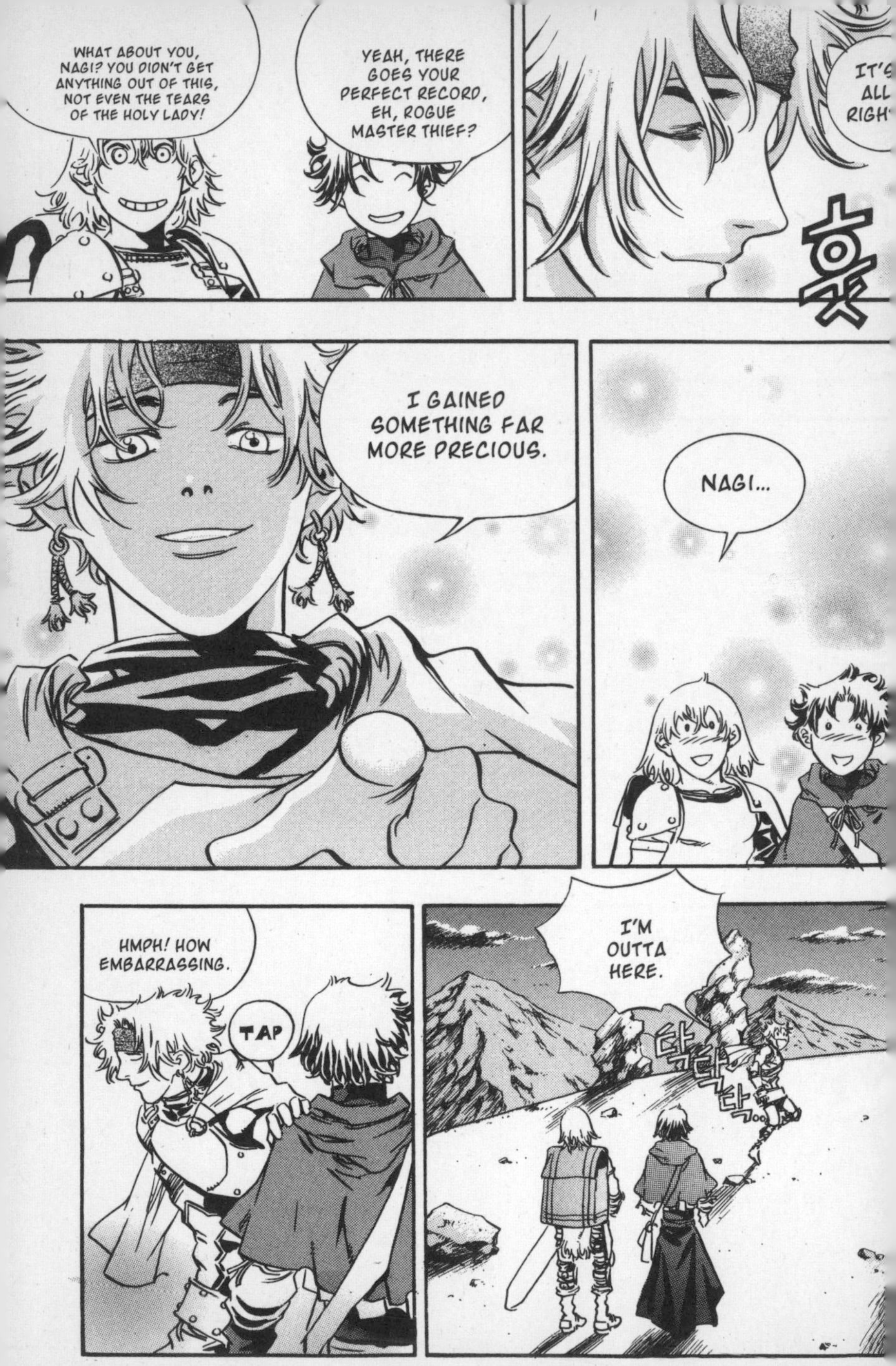
WHAT ABOUT YOU, NAGI? YOU DIDN'T GET ANYTHING OUT OF THIS, NOT EVEN THE TEARS OF THE HOLY LADY!
YEAH, THERE GOES YOUR PERFECT RECORD, EH, ROGUE MASTER THIEF?
IT'S ALL RIGH
후
I GAINED SOMETHING FAR MORE PRECIOUS.
NAGI...
HMPH! HOW EMBARRASSING.
TAP
I'M OUTTA HERE.

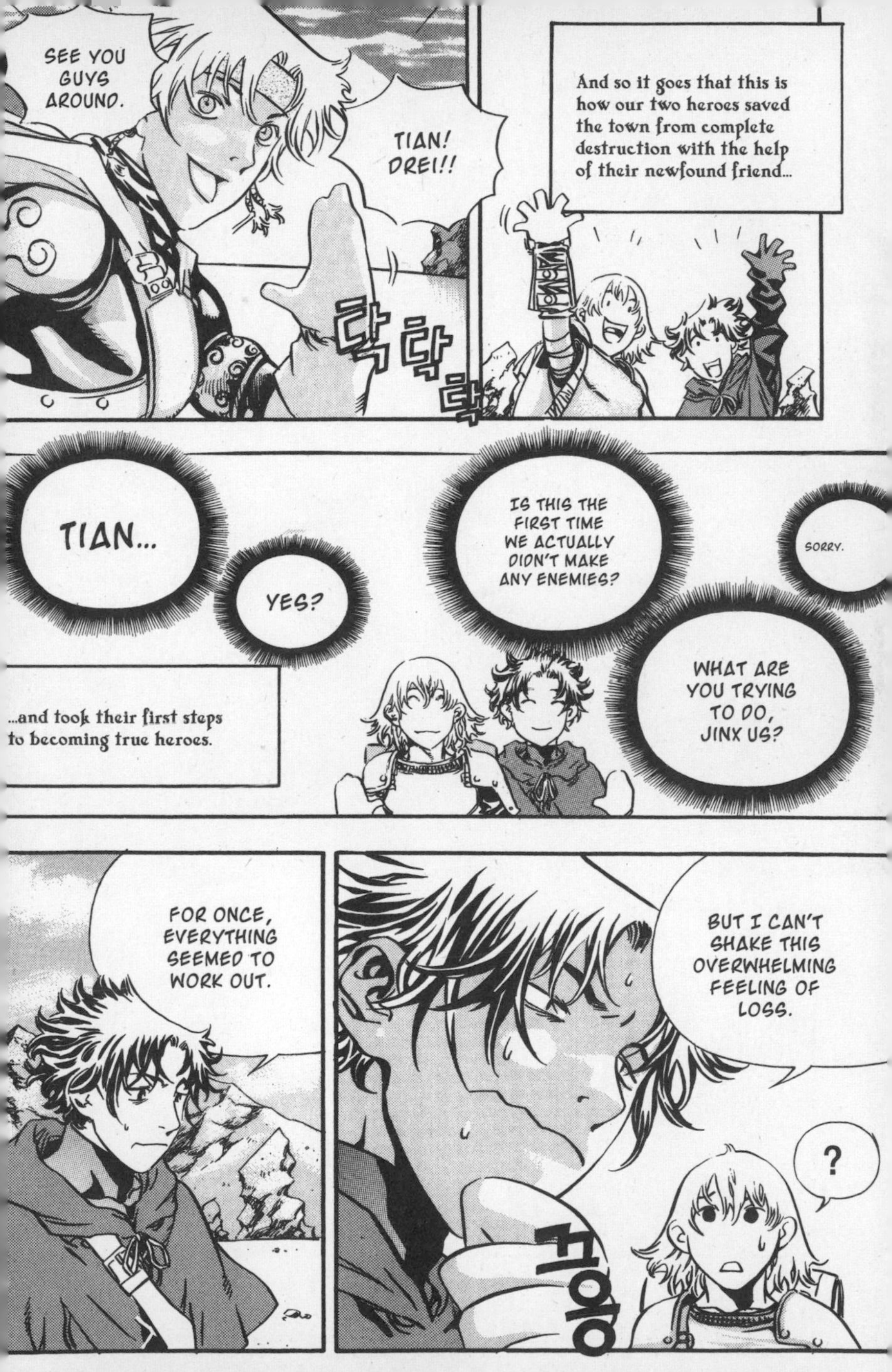
SEE YOU GUYS AROUND.
TIAN! DREI!!
닥 닥 닥
And so it goes that this is how our two heroes saved the town from complete destruction with the help of their newfound friend...
TIAN...
YES?
IS THIS THE FIRST TIME WE ACTUALLY DIDN'T MAKE ANY ENEMIES?
SORRY.
WHAT ARE YOU TRYING TO DO, JINX US?
...and took their first steps to becoming true heroes.
FOR ONCE, EVERYTHING SEEMED TO WORK OUT.
BUT I CAN'T SHAKE THIS OVERWHELMING FEELING OF LOSS.
?

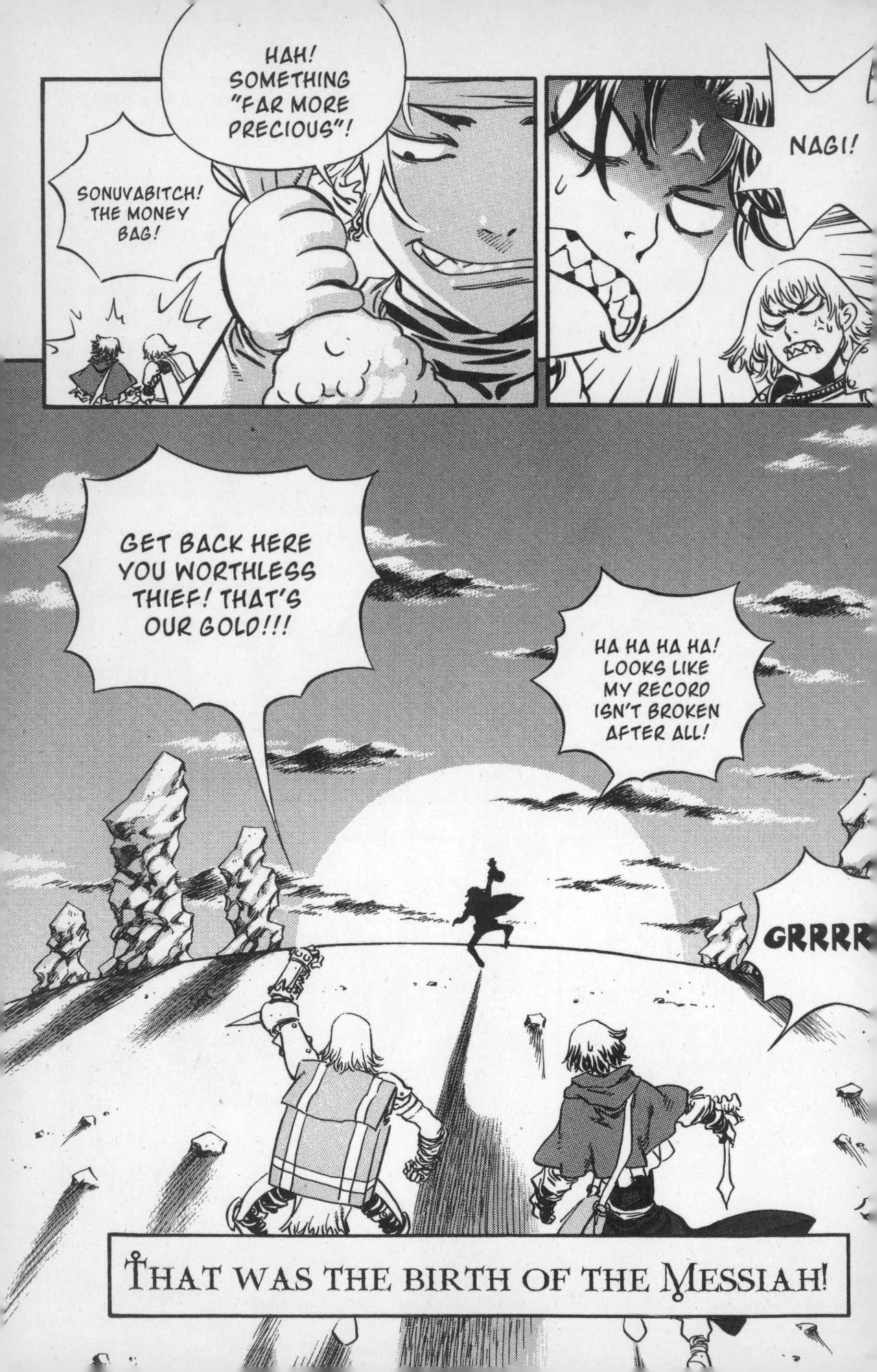
HAH! SOMETHING "FAR MORE PRECIOUS"!
SONUVABITCH! THE MONEY BAG!
NAGI!
GET BACK HERE YOU WORTHLESS THIEF! THAT'S OUR GOLD!!!
HA HA HA HA! LOOKS LIKE MY RECORD ISN'T BROKEN AFTER ALL!
GRRRR
THAT WAS THE BIRTH OF THE MESSIAH!

CHAPTER 7

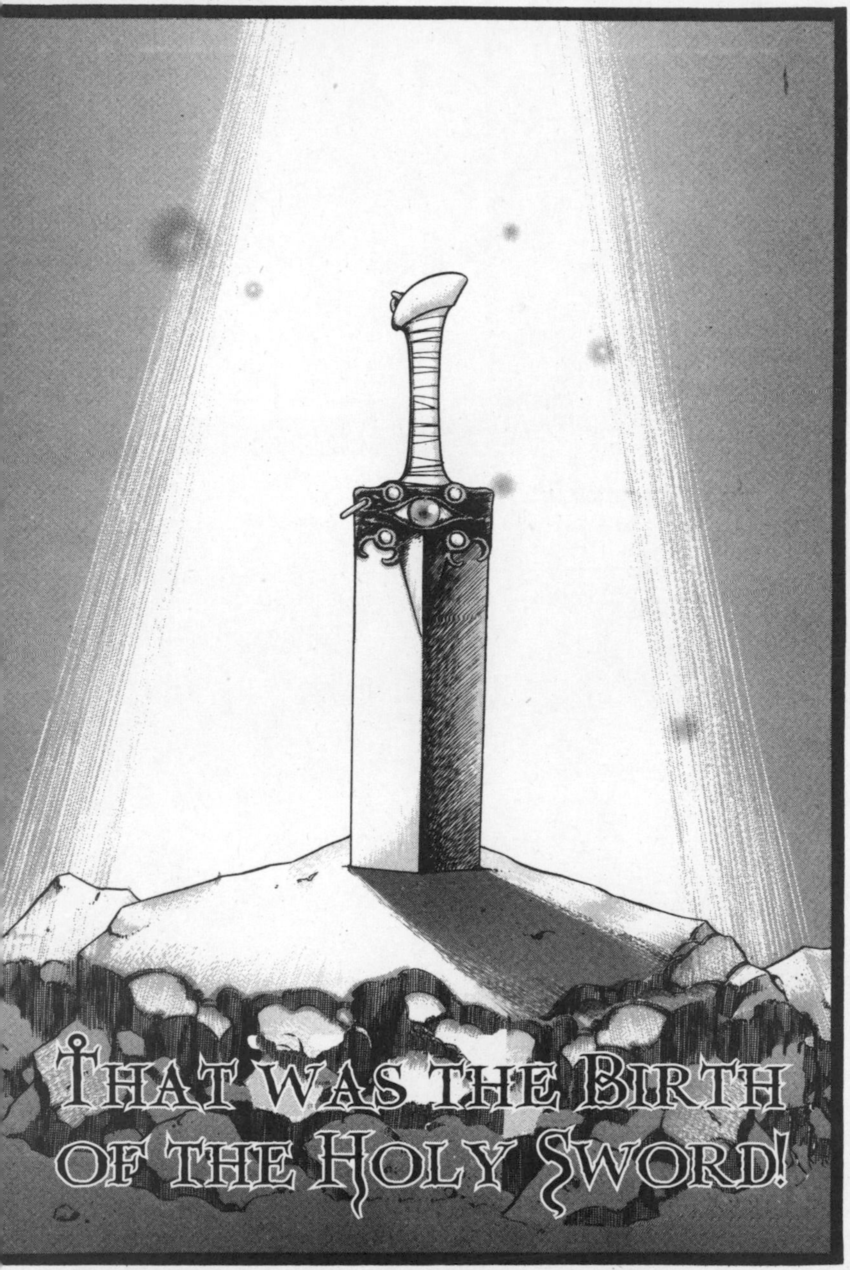
THAT WAS THE BIRTH
OF THE HOLY SWORD!

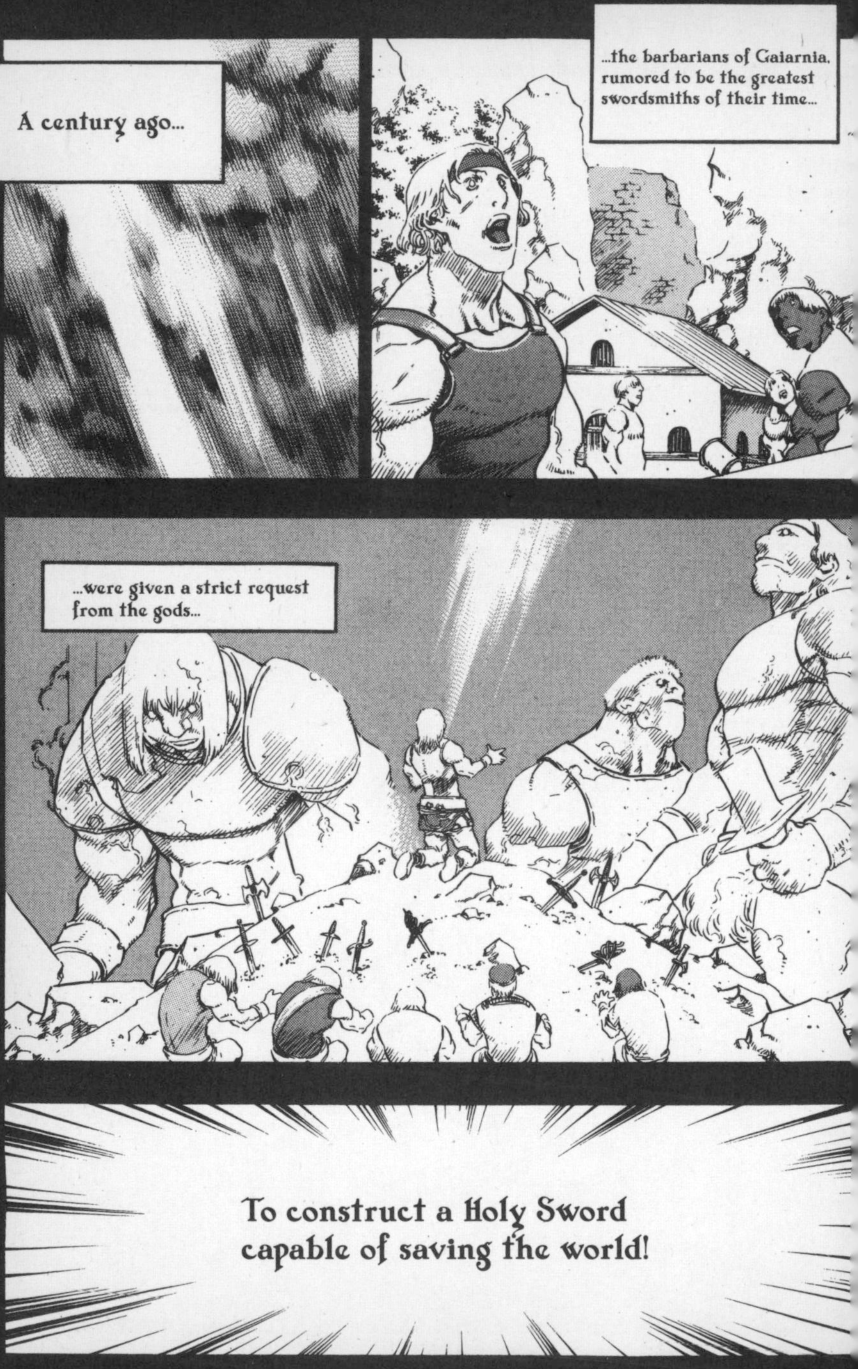
A century ago...
...the barbarians of Gaiarnia, rumored to be the greatest swordsmiths of their time...
...were given a strict request from the gods...
To construct a Holy Sword capable of saving the world!

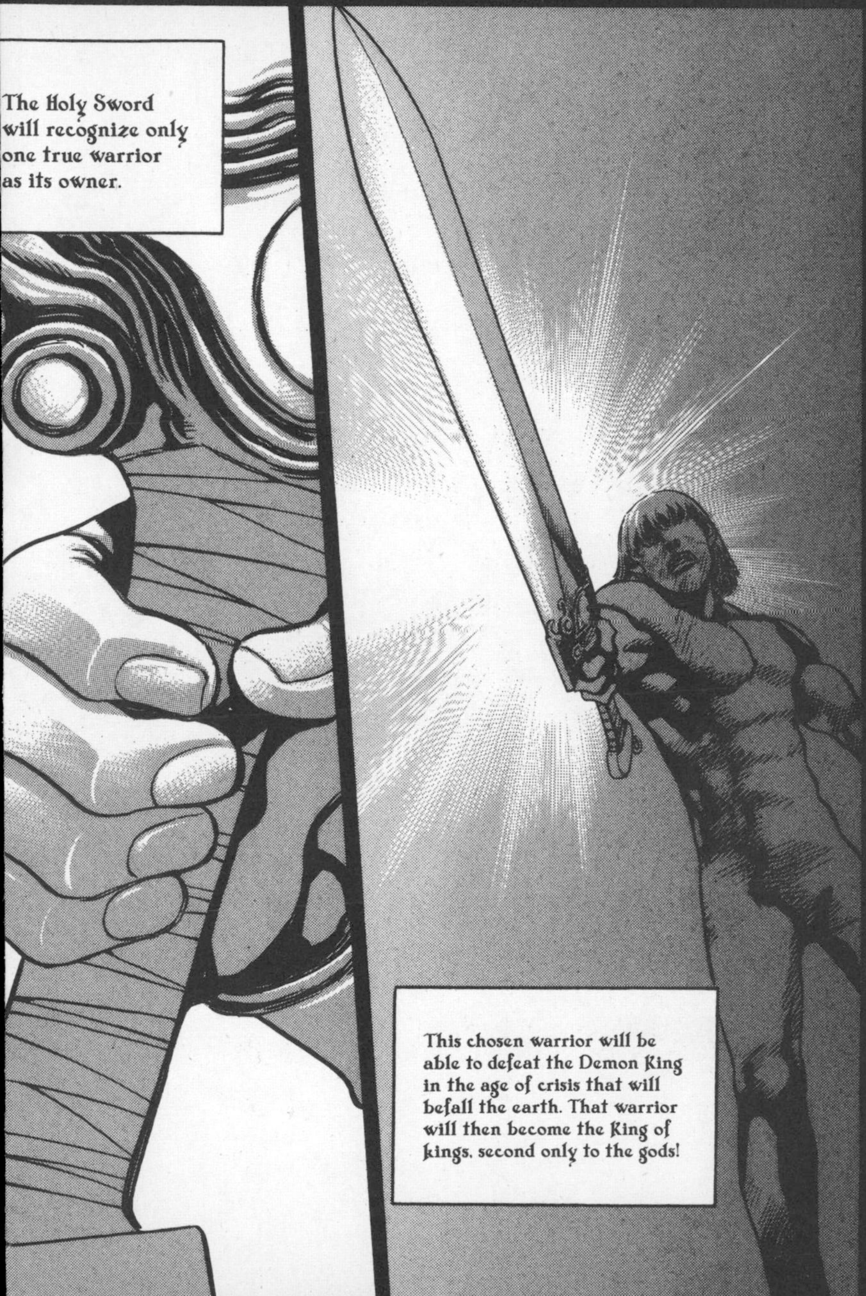
The Holy Sword will recognize only one true warrior as its owner.
This chosen warrior will be able to defeat the Demon King in the age of crisis that will befall the earth. That warrior will then become the King of kings, second only to the gods!

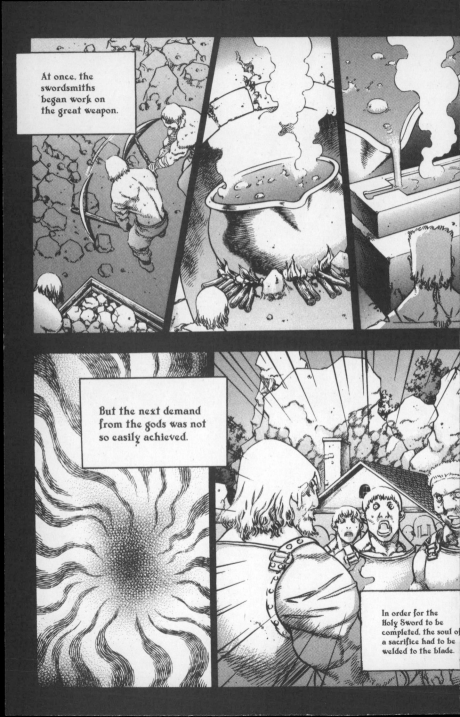

At once, the swordsmiths began work on the great weapon.

But the next demand from the gods was not so easily achieved.

In order for the Holy Sword to be completed, the soul of a sacrifice had to be welded to the blade.

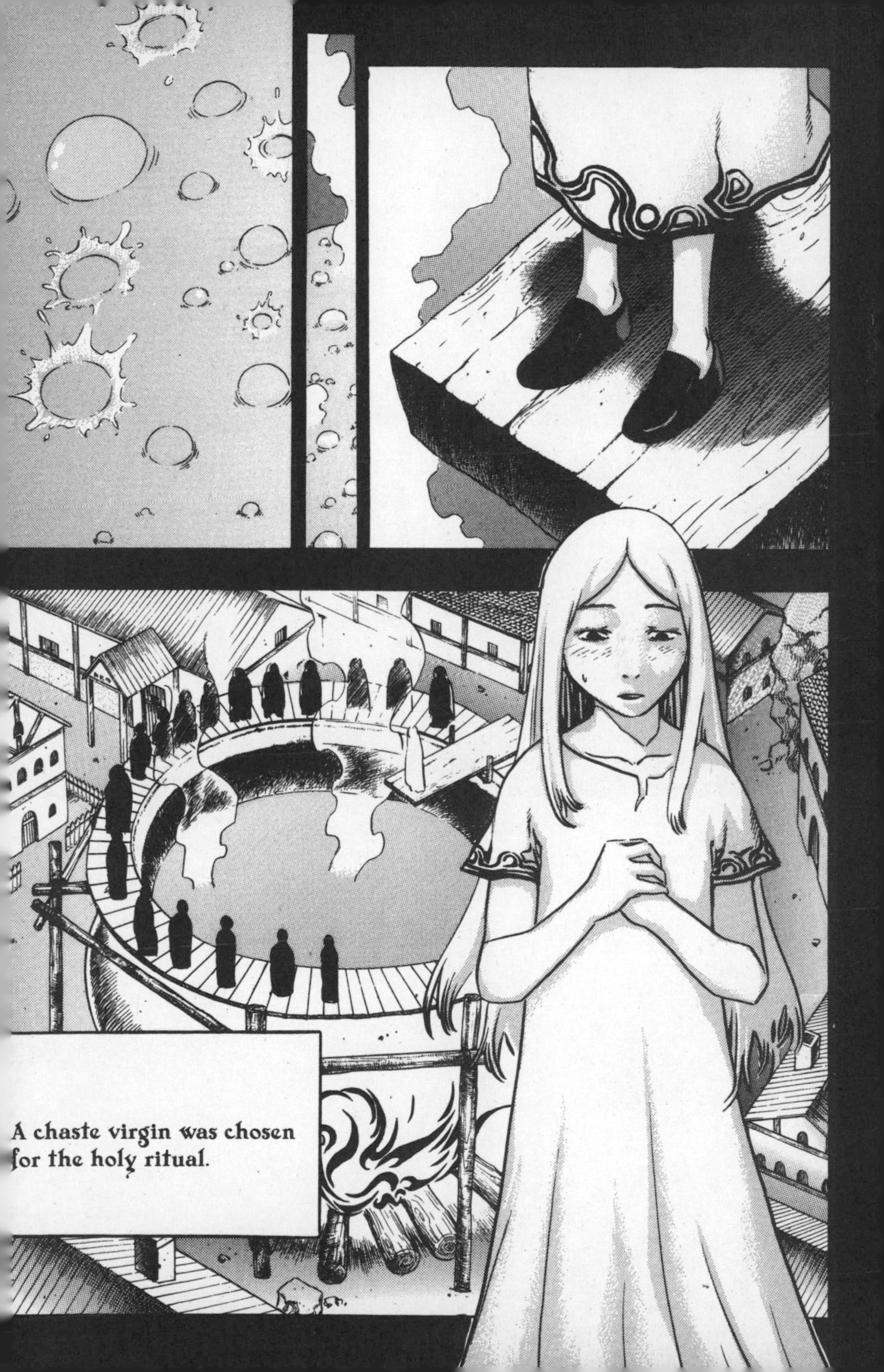
A chaste virgin was chosen for the holy ritual.

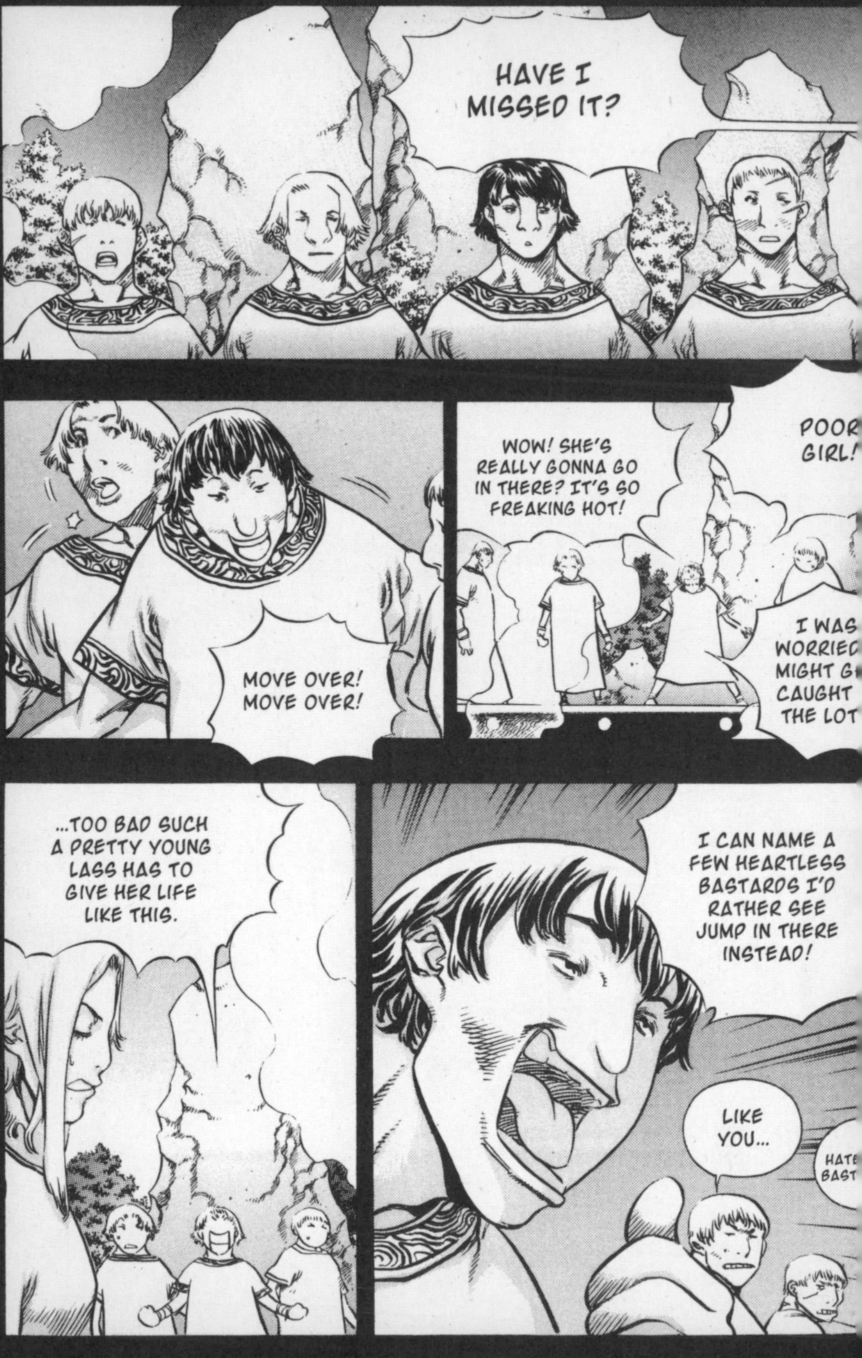
HAVE I MISSED IT?
MOVE OVER! MOVE OVER!
WOW! SHE'S REALLY GONNA GO IN THERE? IT'S SO FREAKING HOT!
POOR GIRL!
I WAS WORRIED MIGHT G CAUGHT THE LOT
...TOO BAD SUCH A PRETTY YOUNG LASS HAS TO GIVE HER LIFE LIKE THIS.
I CAN NAME A FEW HEARTLESS BASTARDS I'D RATHER SEE JUMP IN THERE INSTEAD!
LIKE YOU...

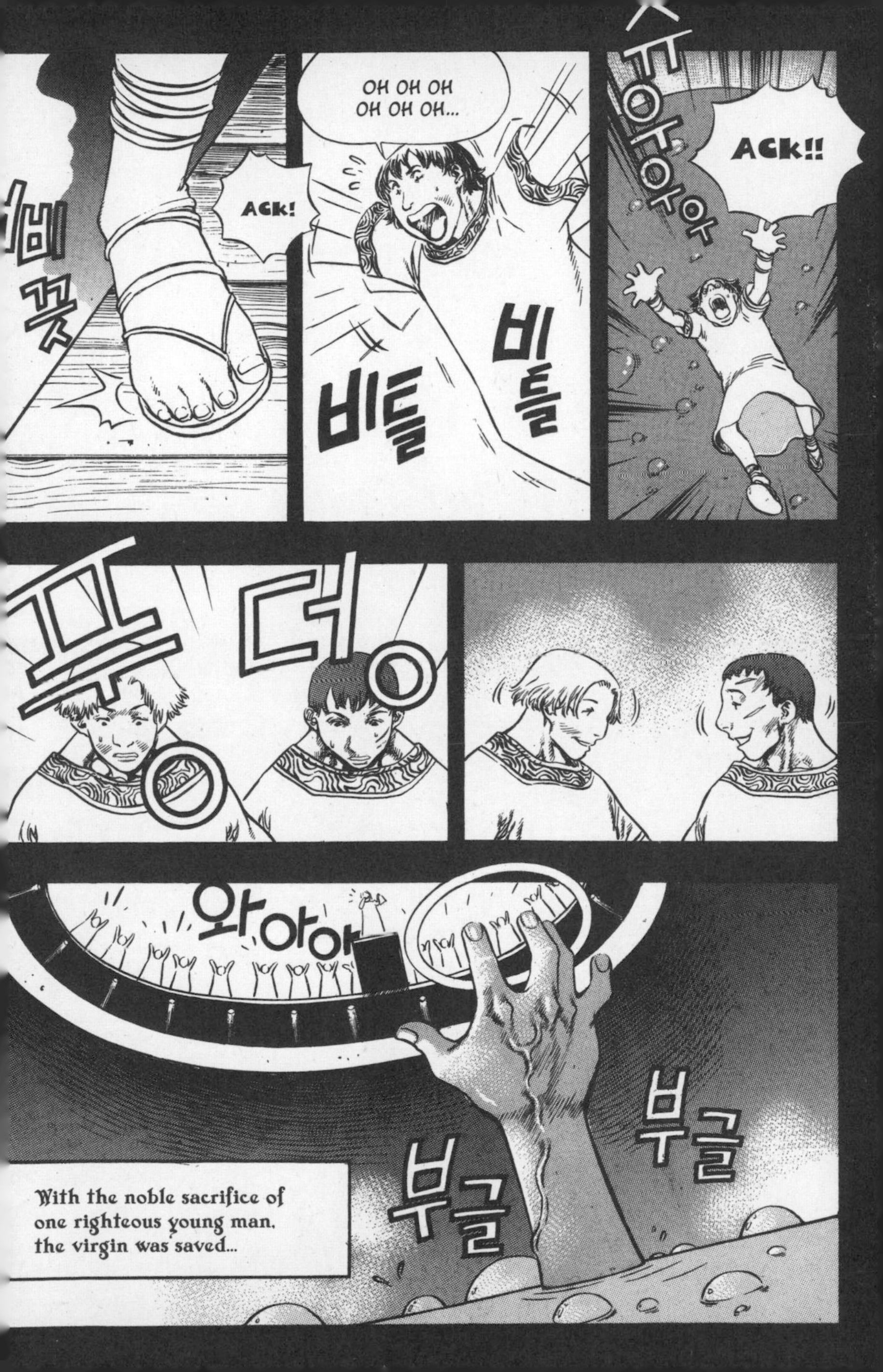
삐끗
ACK!
OH OH OH
OH OH OH...
비틀 비틀
ACK!!
풍덩
와아아
부글 부글
With the noble sacrifice of
one righteous young man,
the virgin was saved...

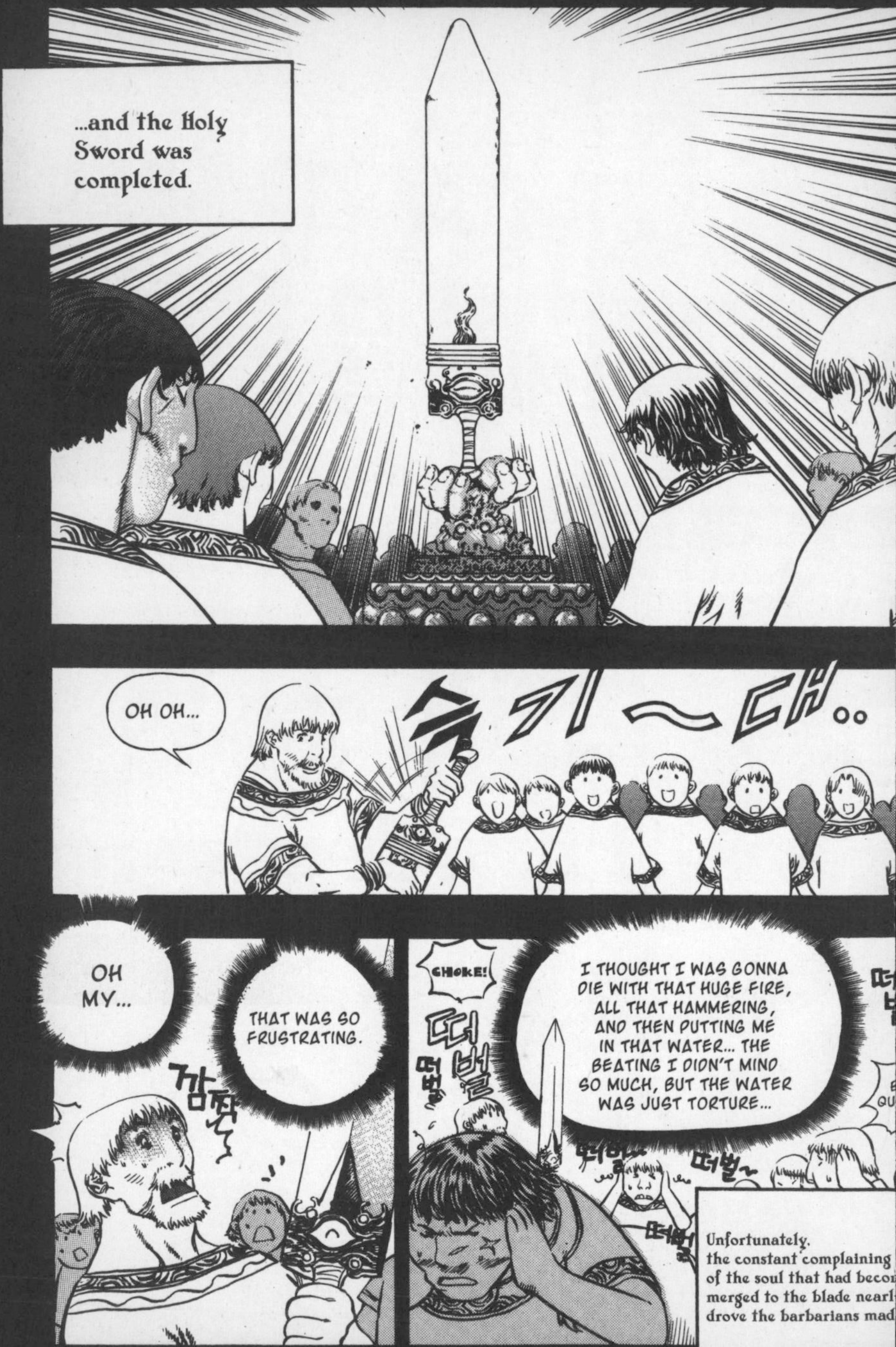
...and the Holy Sword was completed.
OH OH...
OH MY...
깜짝
THAT WAS SO FRUSTRATING.
CHOKE!
떠벌
I THOUGHT I WAS GONNA DIE WITH THAT HUGE FIRE, ALL THAT HAMMERING, AND THEN PUTTING ME IN THAT WATER... THE BEATING I DIDN'T MIND SO MUCH, BUT THE WATER WAS JUST TORTURE...
떠벌~
Unfortunately, the constant complaining of the soul that had becon merged to the blade nearl drove the barbarians mad

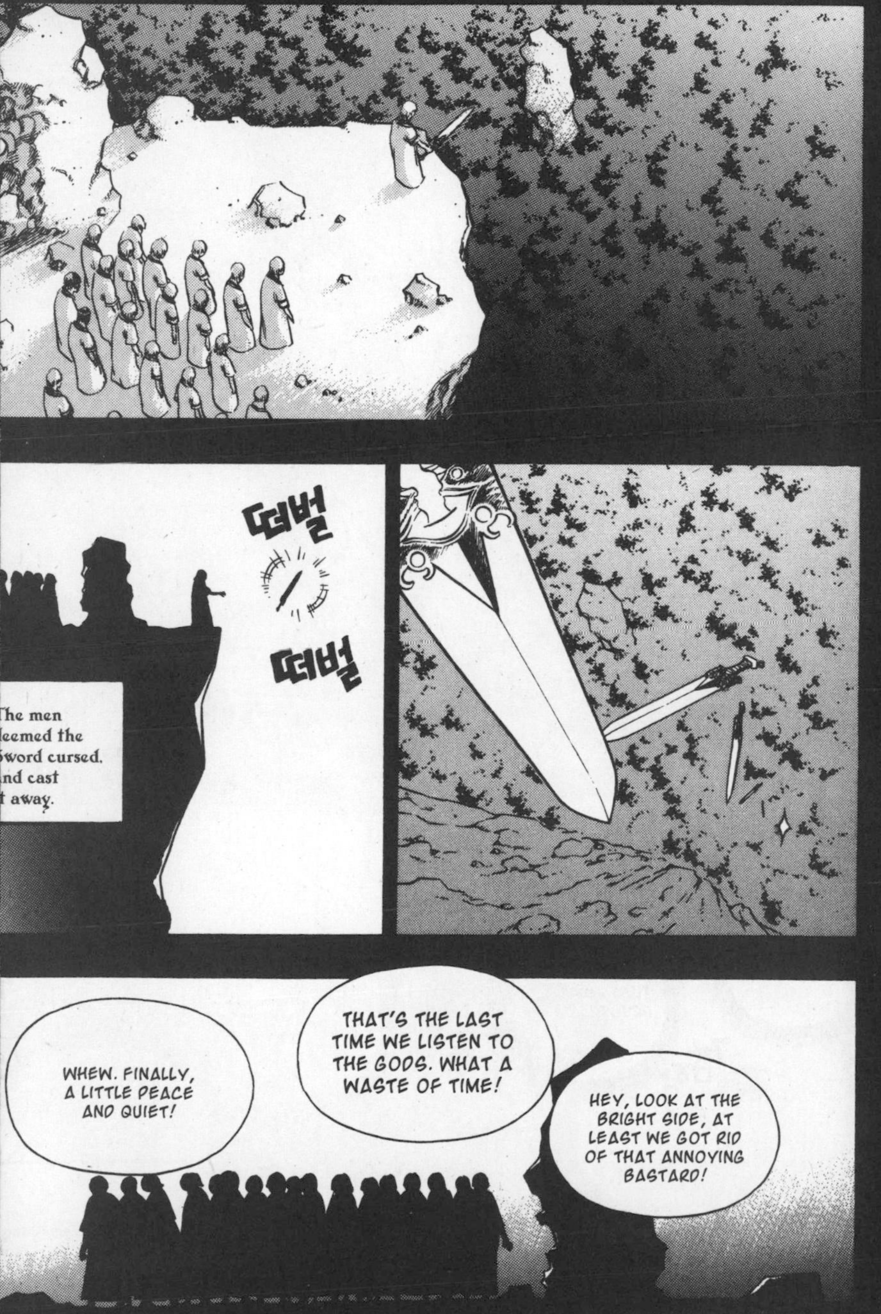
떠벌
떠벌
The men
leemed the
Sword cursed,
nd cast
t away.
WHEW. FINALLY, A LITTLE PEACE AND QUIET!
THAT'S THE LAST TIME WE LISTEN TO THE GODS. WHAT A WASTE OF TIME!
HEY, LOOK AT THE BRIGHT SIDE, AT LEAST WE GOT RID OF THAT ANNOYING BASTARD!

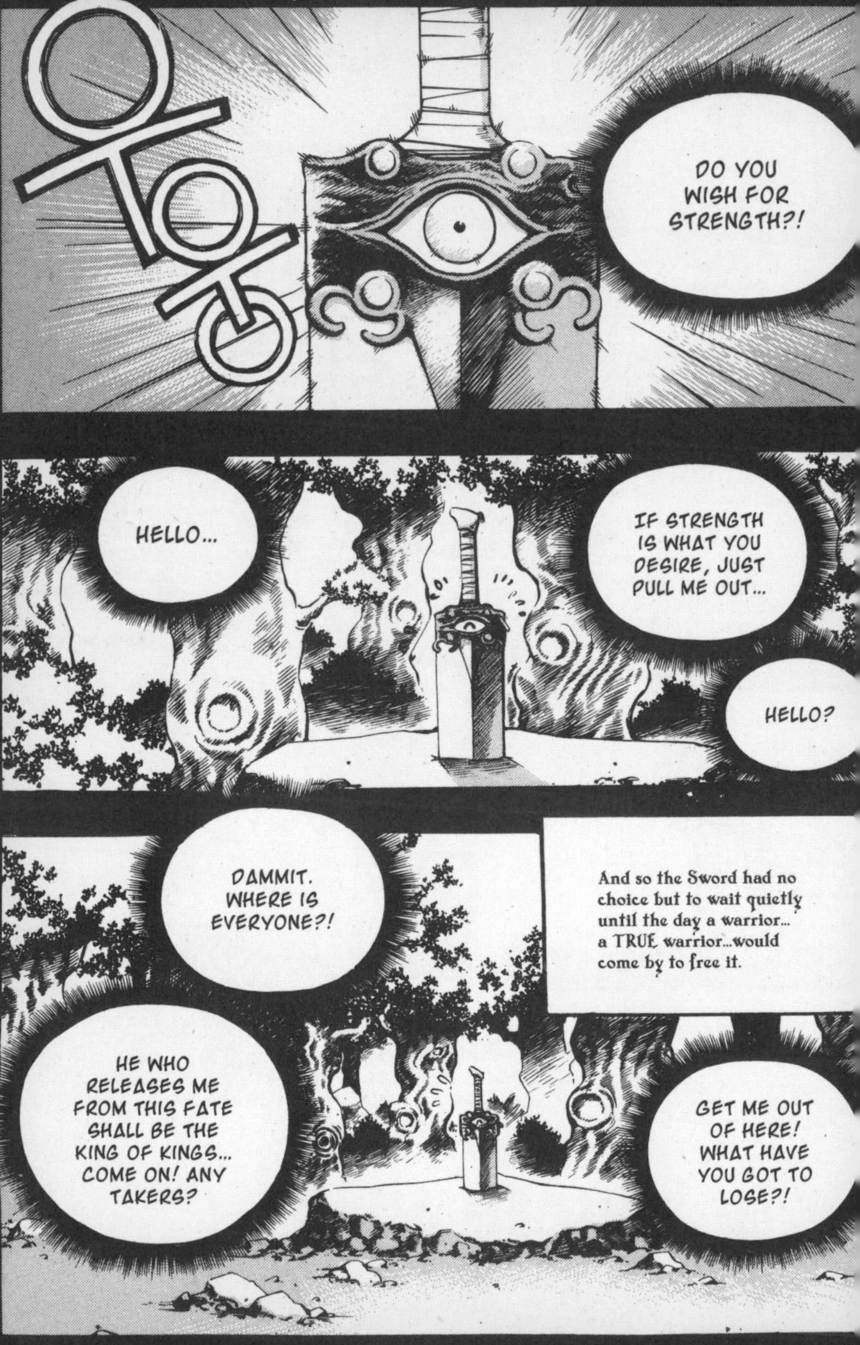
DO YOU WISH FOR STRENGTH?!
HELLO...
IF STRENGTH IS WHAT YOU DESIRE, JUST PULL ME OUT...
HELLO?
DAMMIT. WHERE IS EVERYONE?!
And so the Sword had no choice but to wait quietly until the day a warrior... a TRUE warrior...would come by to free it.
HE WHO RELEASES ME FROM THIS FATE SHALL BE THE KING OF KINGS... COME ON! ANY TAKERS?
GET ME OUT OF HERE! WHAT HAVE YOU GOT TO LOSE?!

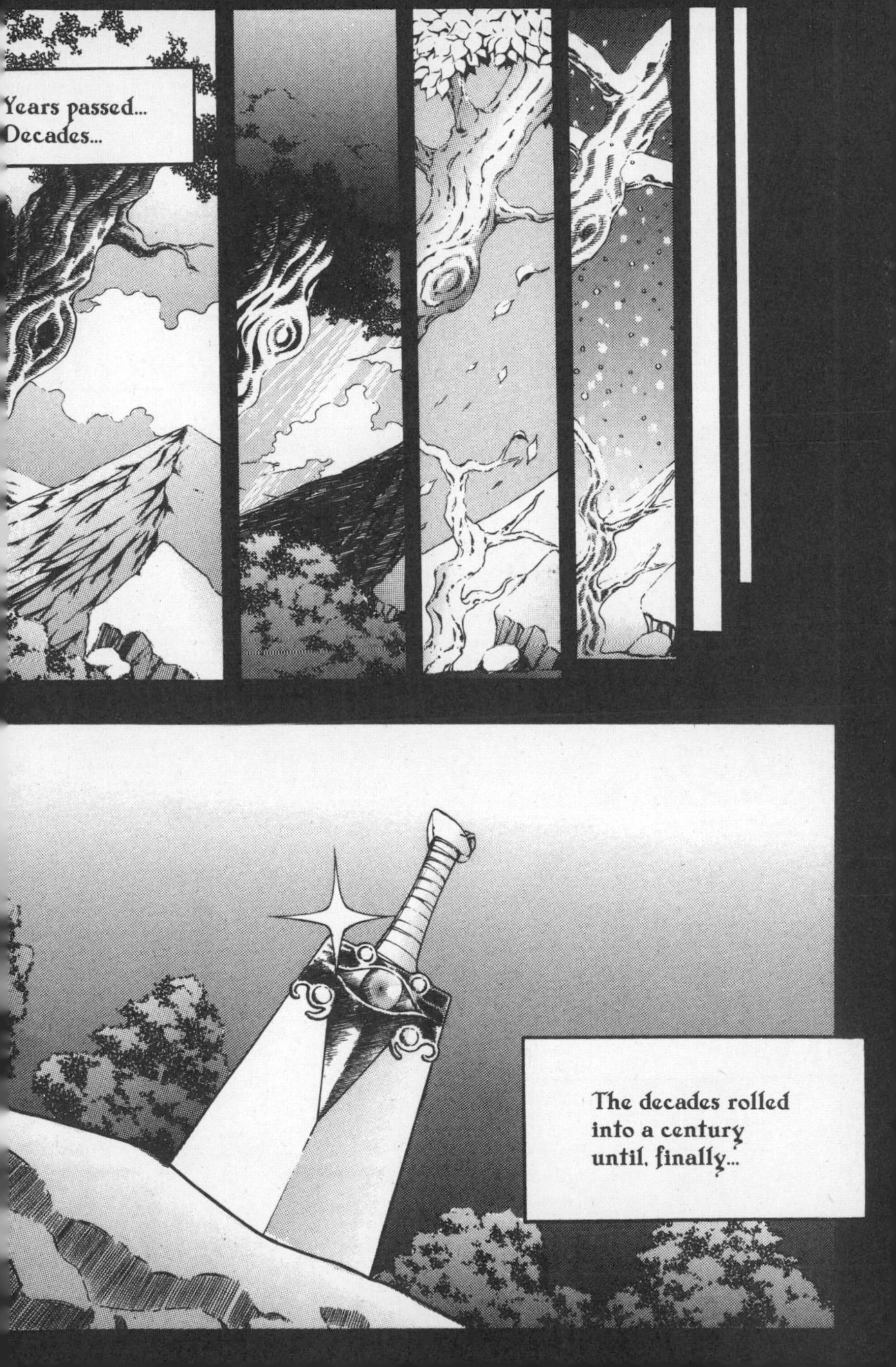
Years passed...
Decades...
The decades rolled into a century until, finally...

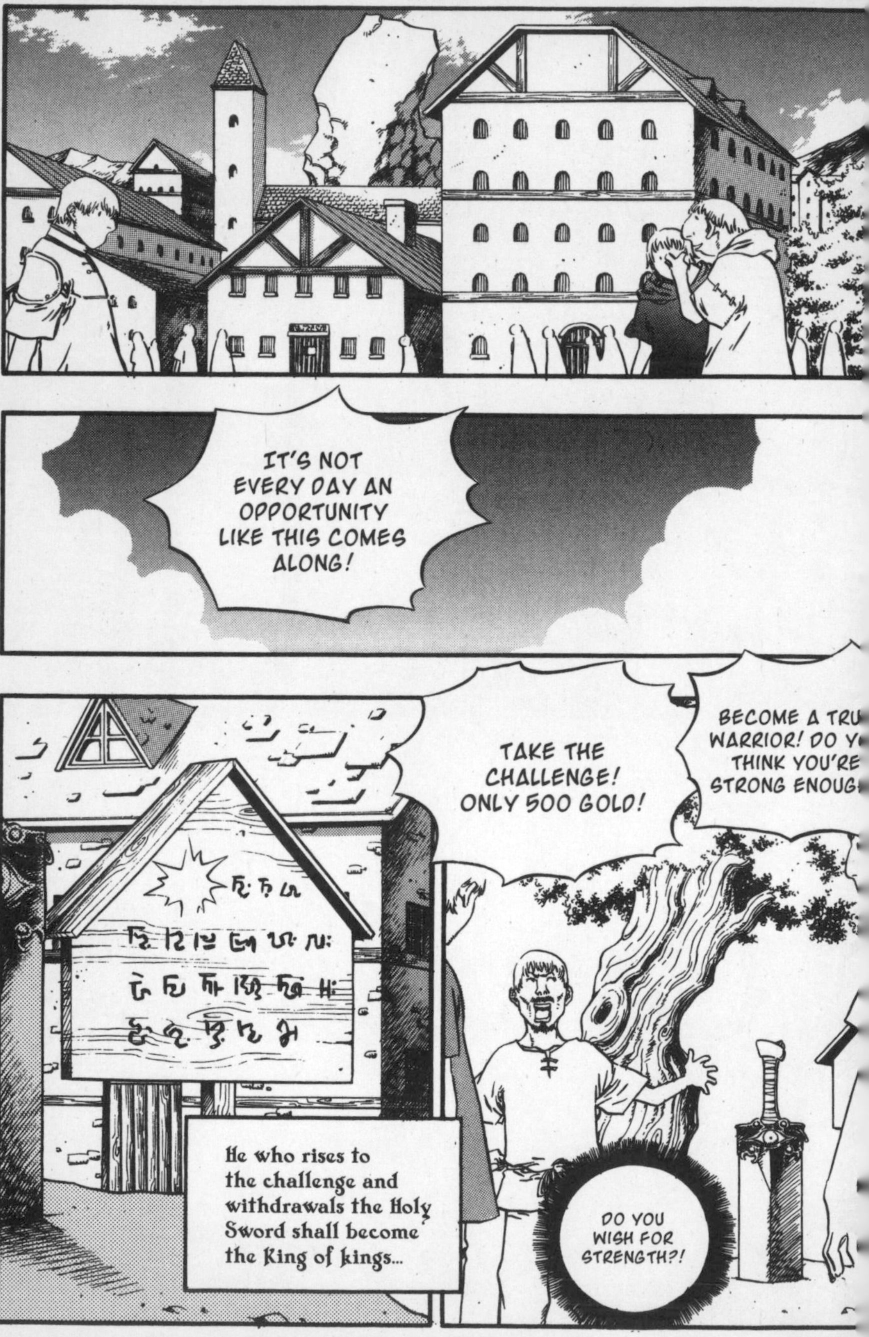
IT'S NOT EVERY DAY AN OPPORTUNITY LIKE THIS COMES ALONG!
TAKE THE CHALLENGE! ONLY 500 GOLD!
BECOME A TRU WARRIOR! DO Y THINK YOU'RE STRONG ENOUG
He who rises to the challenge and withdrawals the Holy Sword shall become the King of kings...
DO YOU WISH FOR STRENGTH?!

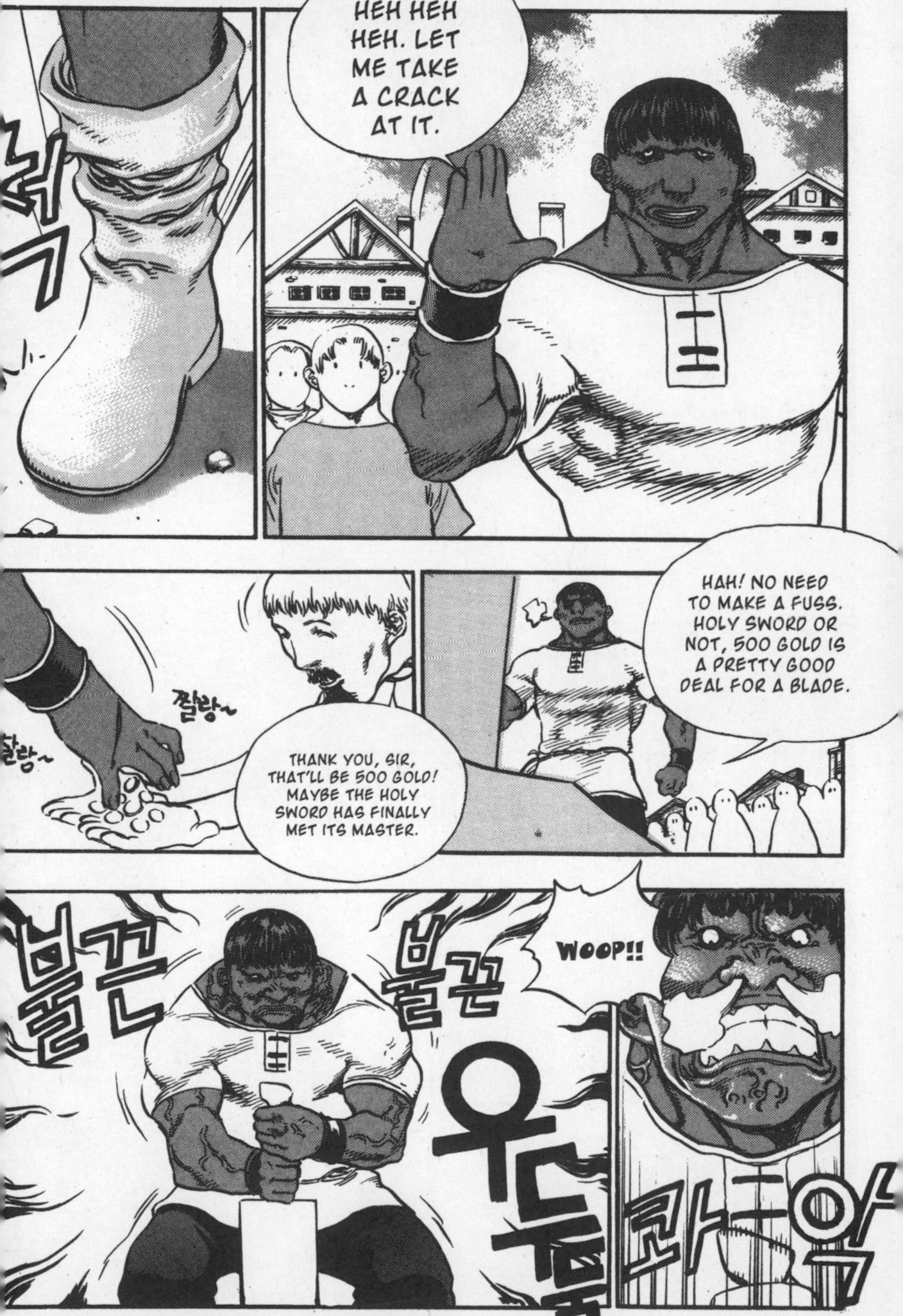
HEH HEH HEH. LET ME TAKE A CRACK AT IT.
THANK YOU, SIR, THAT'LL BE 500 GOLD! MAYBE THE HOLY SWORD HAS FINALLY MET ITS MASTER.
HAH! NO NEED TO MAKE A FUSS. HOLY SWORD OR NOT, 500 GOLD IS A PRETTY GOOD DEAL FOR A BLADE.
불끈 불끈
WOOP!!

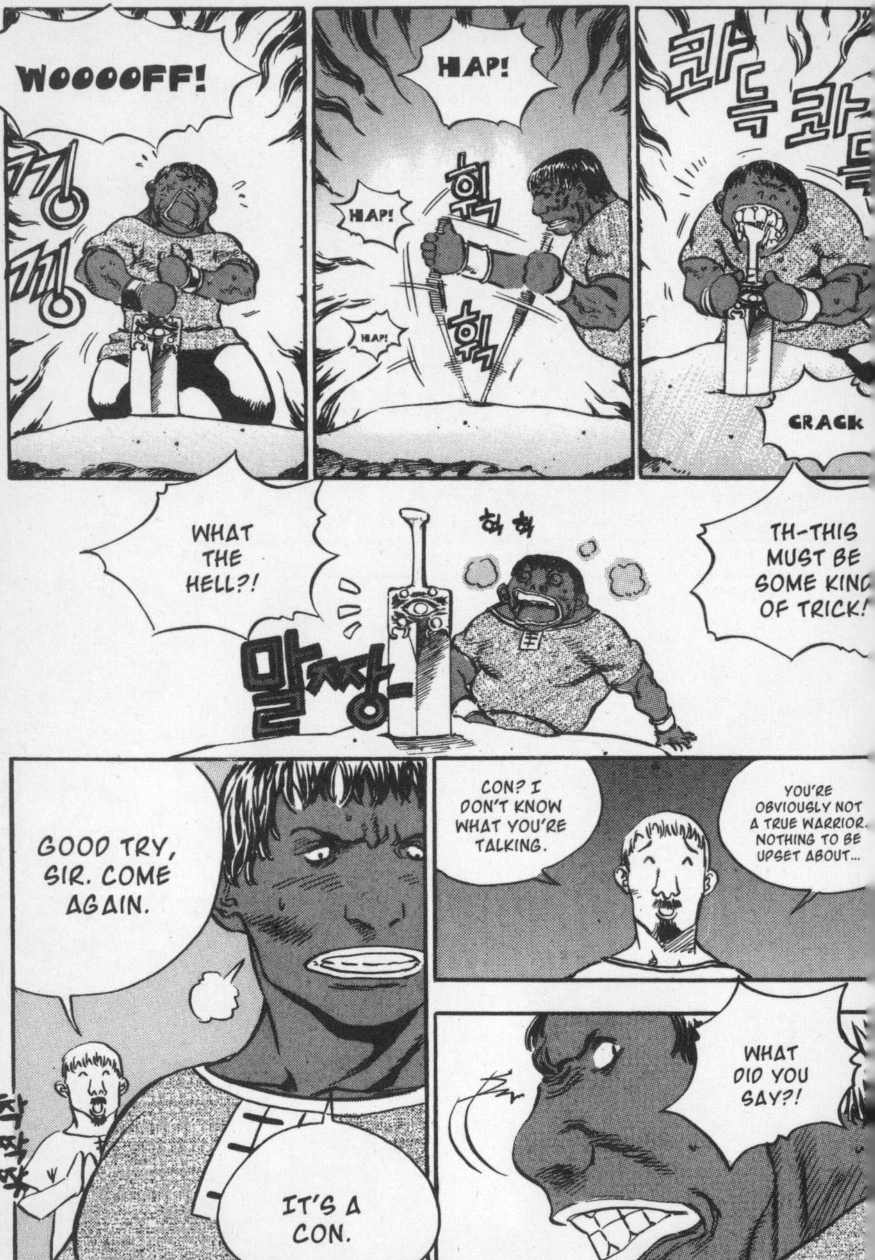
WOOOOFF!
HAP!
HAP!
휙
HAP!
휙
콰득 콰득
CRACK
WHAT THE HELL?!
말짱-
TH-THIS MUST BE SOME KIND OF TRICK!
GOOD TRY, SIR. COME AGAIN.
IT'S A CON.
CON? I DON'T KNOW WHAT YOU'RE TALKING.
YOU'RE OBVIOUSLY NOT A TRUE WARRIOR. NOTHING TO BE UPSET ABOUT...
WHAT DID YOU SAY?!

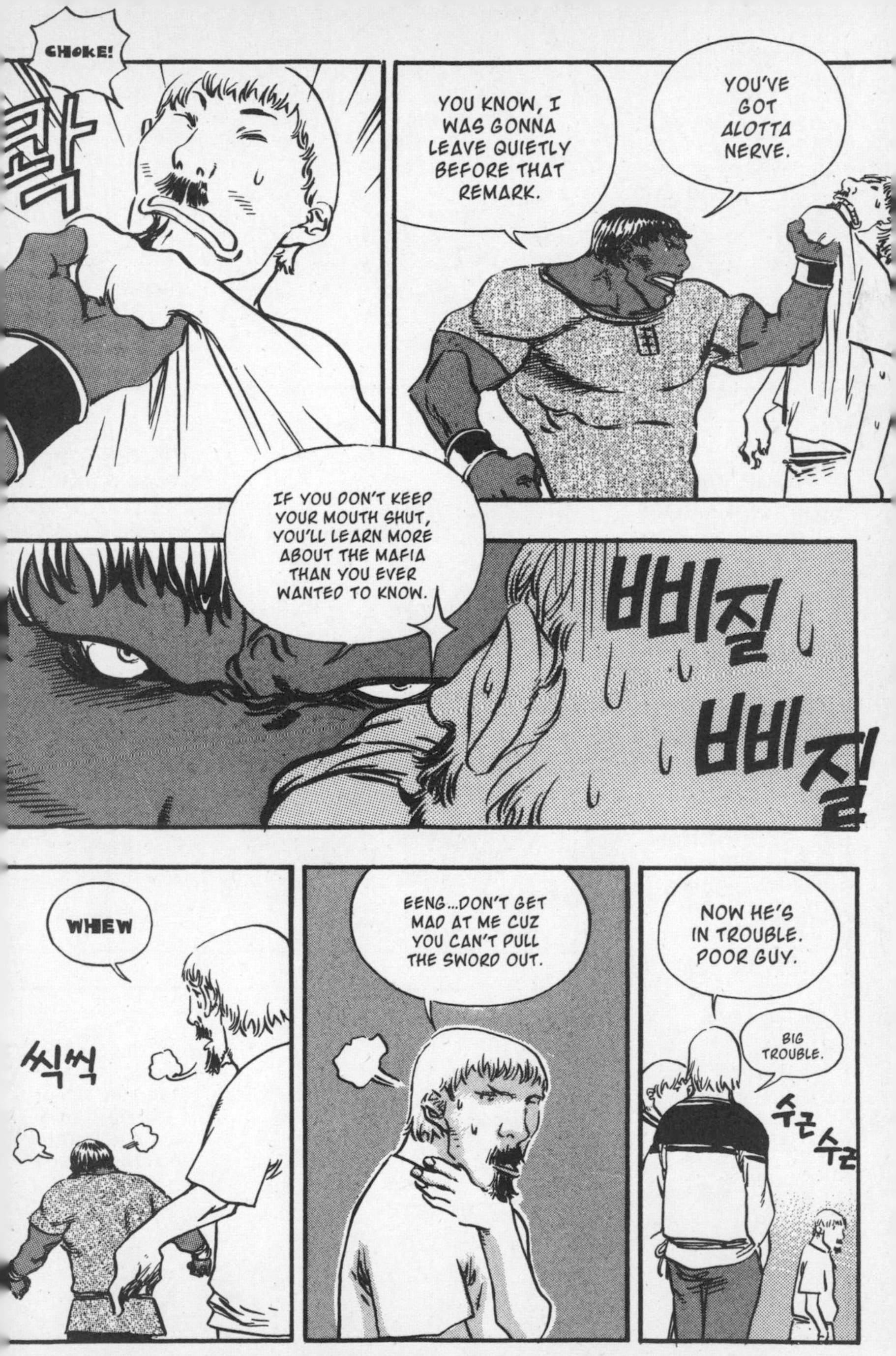

CHOKE!
YOU KNOW, I WAS GONNA LEAVE QUIETLY BEFORE THAT REMARK.
YOU'VE GOT ALOTTA NERVE.
IF YOU DON'T KEEP YOUR MOUTH SHUT, YOU'LL LEARN MORE ABOUT THE MAFIA THAN YOU EVER WANTED TO KNOW.
삐질
삐질
WHEW
씩씩
EENG...DON'T GET MAD AT ME CUZ YOU CAN'T PULL THE SWORD OUT.
NOW HE'S IN TROUBLE. POOR GUY.
BIG TROUBLE.

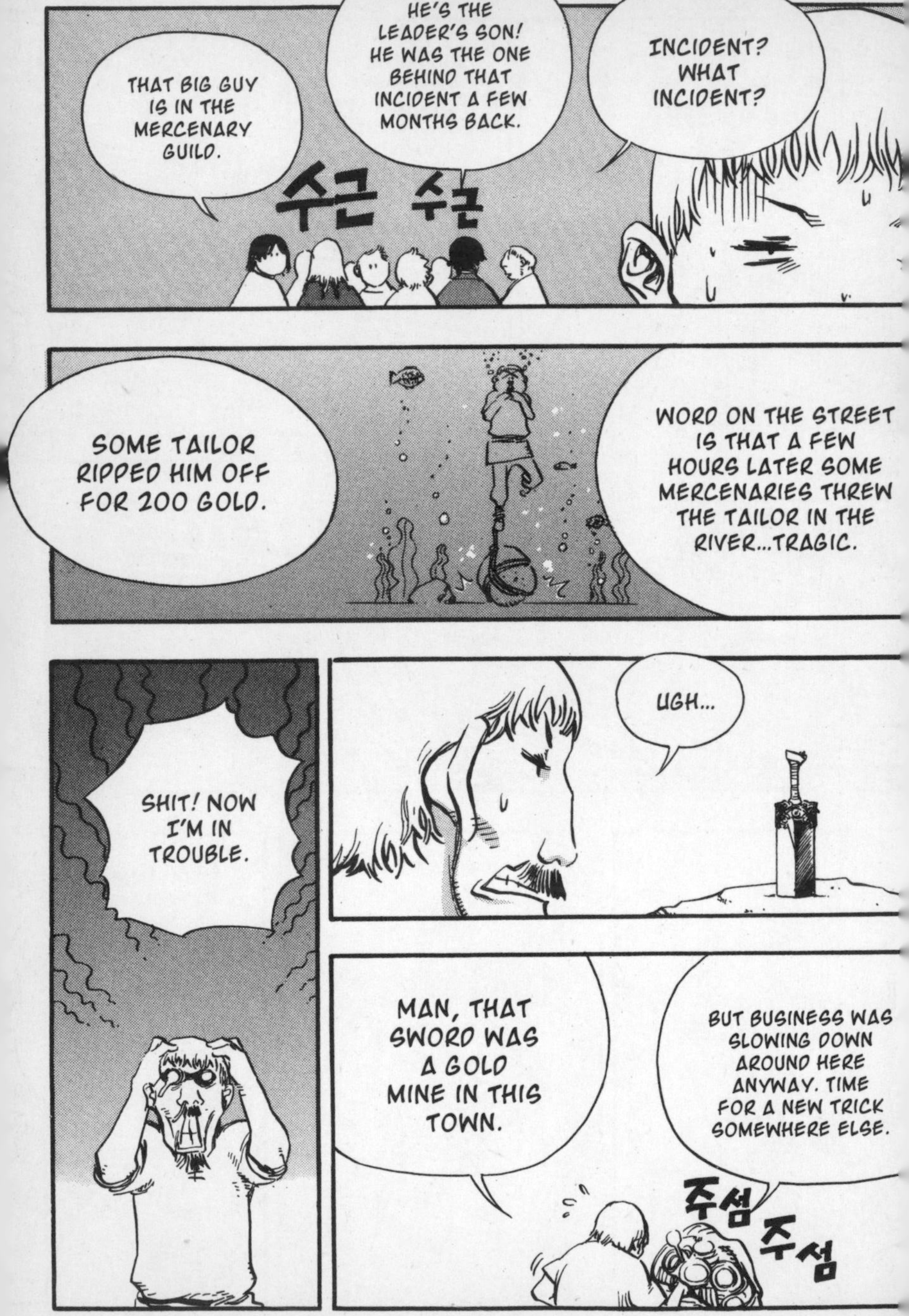
THAT BIG GUY IS IN THE MERCENARY GUILD.
HE'S THE LEADER'S SON! HE WAS THE ONE BEHIND THAT INCIDENT A FEW MONTHS BACK.
수근 수근
INCIDENT? WHAT INCIDENT?
SOME TAILOR RIPPED HIM OFF FOR 200 GOLD.
WORD ON THE STREET IS THAT A FEW HOURS LATER SOME MERCENARIES THREW THE TAILOR IN THE RIVER...TRAGIC.
SHIT! NOW I'M IN TROUBLE.
UGH...
MAN, THAT SWORD WAS A GOLD MINE IN THIS TOWN.
BUT BUSINESS WAS SLOWING DOWN AROUND HERE ANYWAY. TIME FOR A NEW TRICK SOMEWHERE ELSE.
주섬 주섬

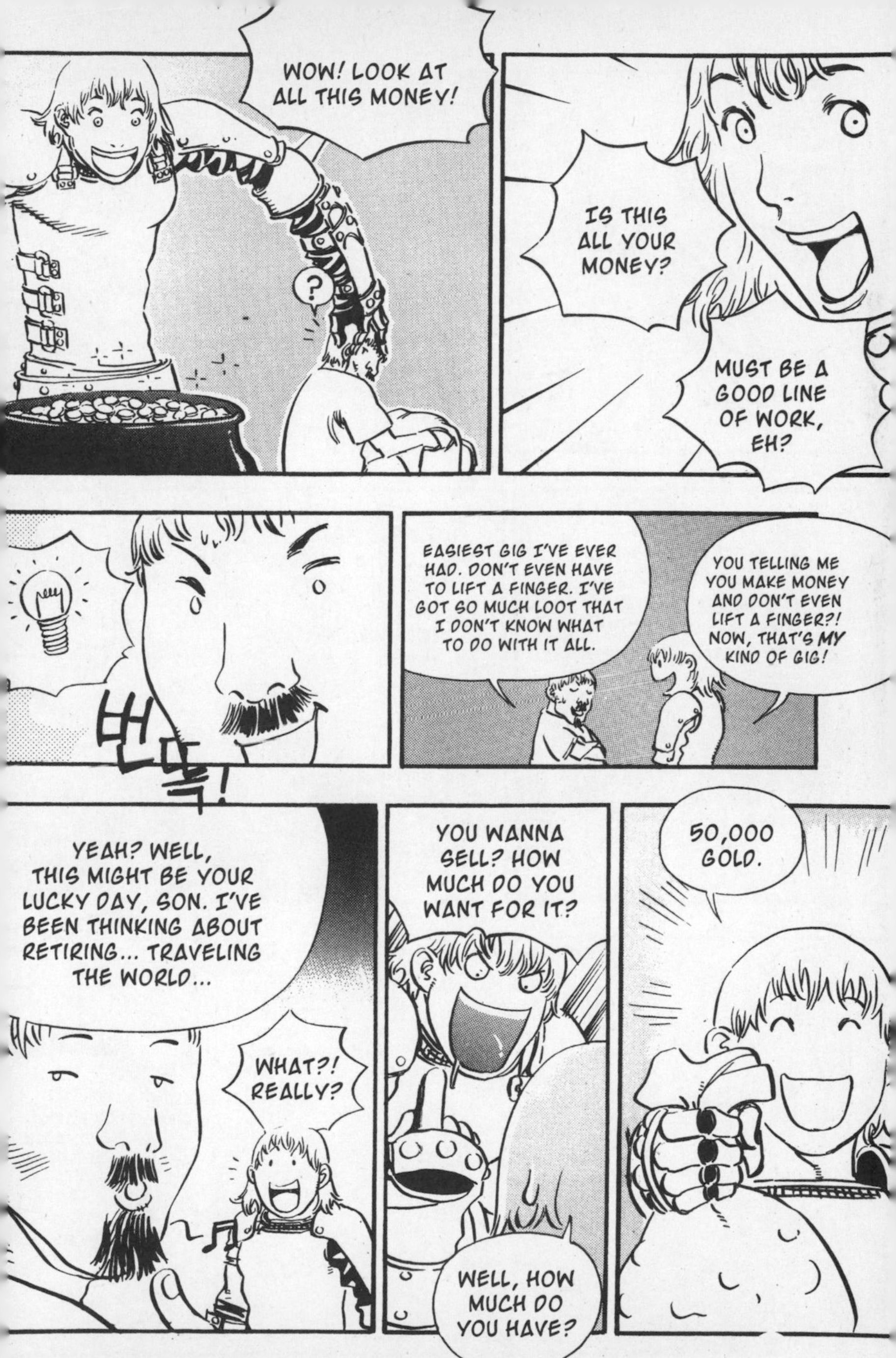
WOW! LOOK AT ALL THIS MONEY!
?
IS THIS ALL YOUR MONEY?
MUST BE A GOOD LINE OF WORK, EH?
EASIEST GIG I'VE EVER HAD. DON'T EVEN HAVE TO LIFT A FINGER. I'VE GOT SO MUCH LOOT THAT I DON'T KNOW WHAT TO DO WITH IT ALL.
YOU TELLING ME YOU MAKE MONEY AND DON'T EVEN LIFT A FINGER?! NOW, THAT'S MY KIND OF GIG!
YEAH? WELL, THIS MIGHT BE YOUR LUCKY DAY, SON. I'VE BEEN THINKING ABOUT RETIRING... TRAVELING THE WORLD...
WHAT?! REALLY?
YOU WANNA SELL? HOW MUCH DO YOU WANT FOR IT?
WELL, HOW MUCH DO YOU HAVE?
50,000 GOLD.

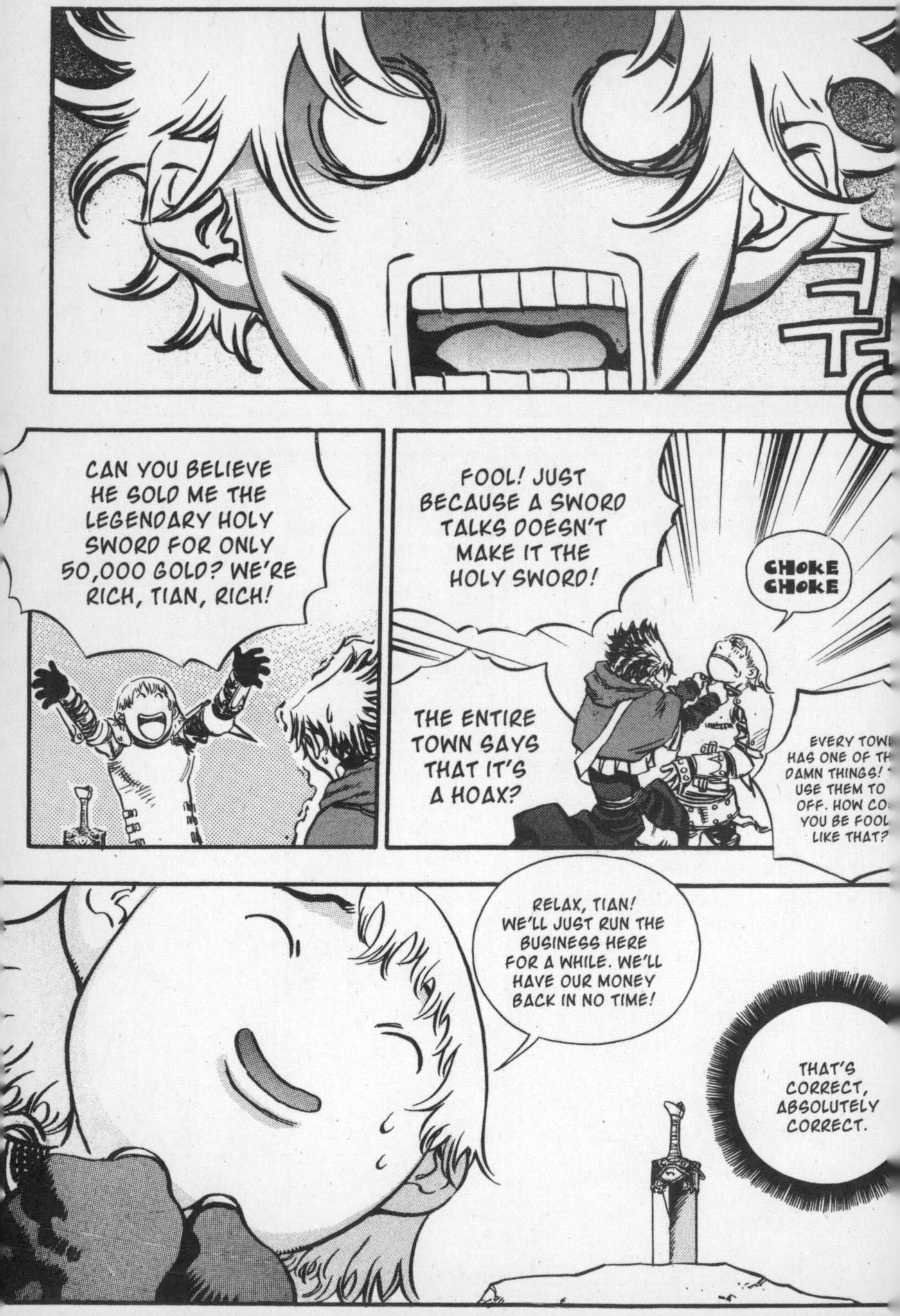
CAN YOU BELIEVE HE SOLD ME THE LEGENDARY HOLY SWORD FOR ONLY 50,000 GOLD? WE'RE RICH, TIAN, RICH!
FOOL! JUST BECAUSE A SWORD TALKS DOESN'T MAKE IT THE HOLY SWORD!
THE ENTIRE TOWN SAYS THAT IT'S A HOAX?
CHOKE CHOKE
EVERY TOW HAS ONE OF TH DAMN THINGS! USE THEM TO OFF. HOW CO YOU BE FOOL LIKE THAT?
RELAX, TIAN! WE'LL JUST RUN THE BUSINESS HERE FOR A WHILE. WE'LL HAVE OUR MONEY BACK IN NO TIME!
THAT'S CORRECT, ABSOLUTELY CORRECT.

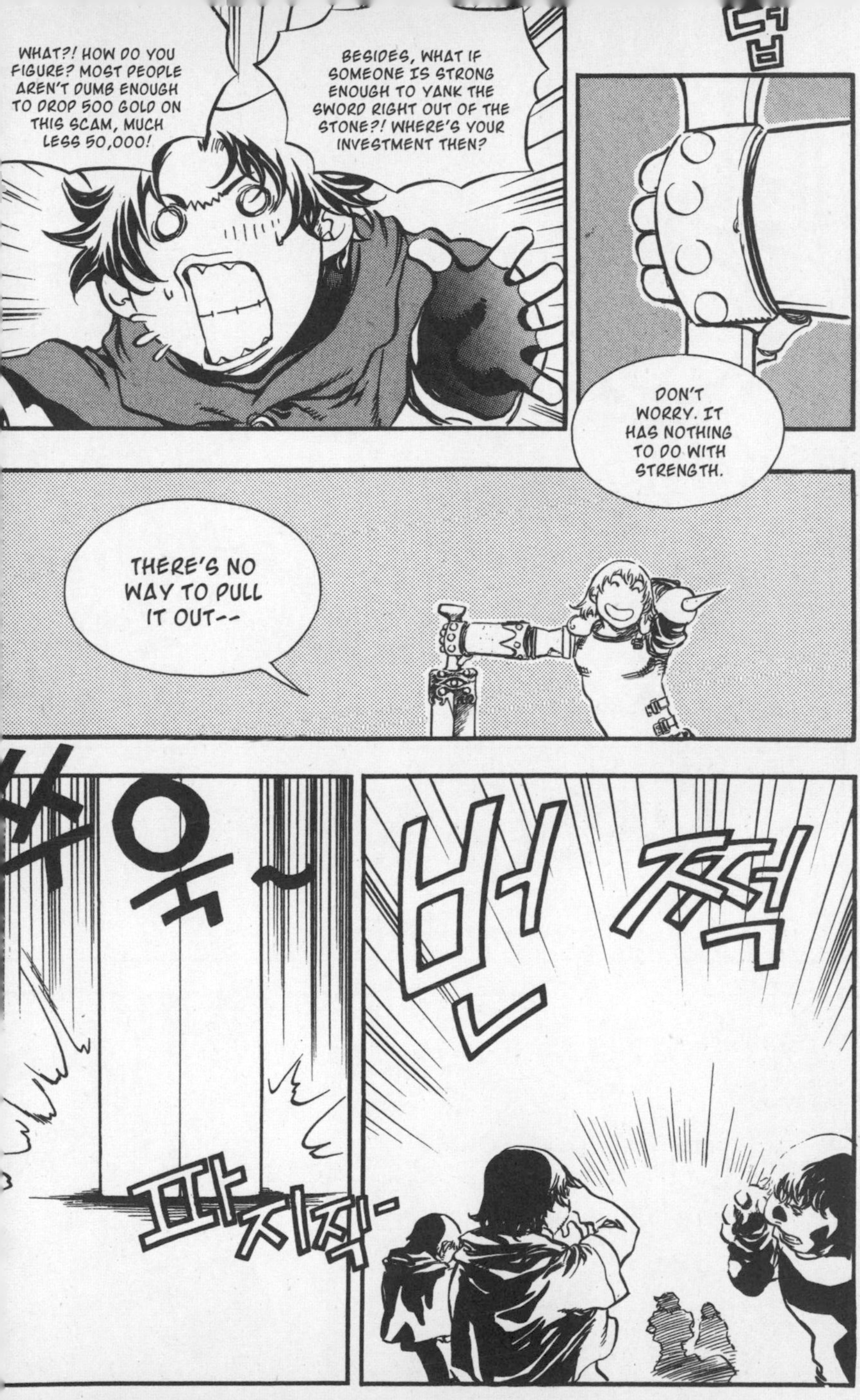
WHAT?! HOW DO YOU FIGURE? MOST PEOPLE AREN'T DUMB ENOUGH TO DROP 500 GOLD ON THIS SCAM, MUCH LESS 50,000!
BESIDES, WHAT IF SOMEONE IS STRONG ENOUGH TO YANK THE SWORD RIGHT OUT OF THE STONE?! WHERE'S YOUR INVESTMENT THEN?
덥
DON'T WORRY. IT HAS NOTHING TO DO WITH STRENGTH.
THERE'S NO WAY TO PULL IT OUT--
쑤욱~
파지직-
번쩍

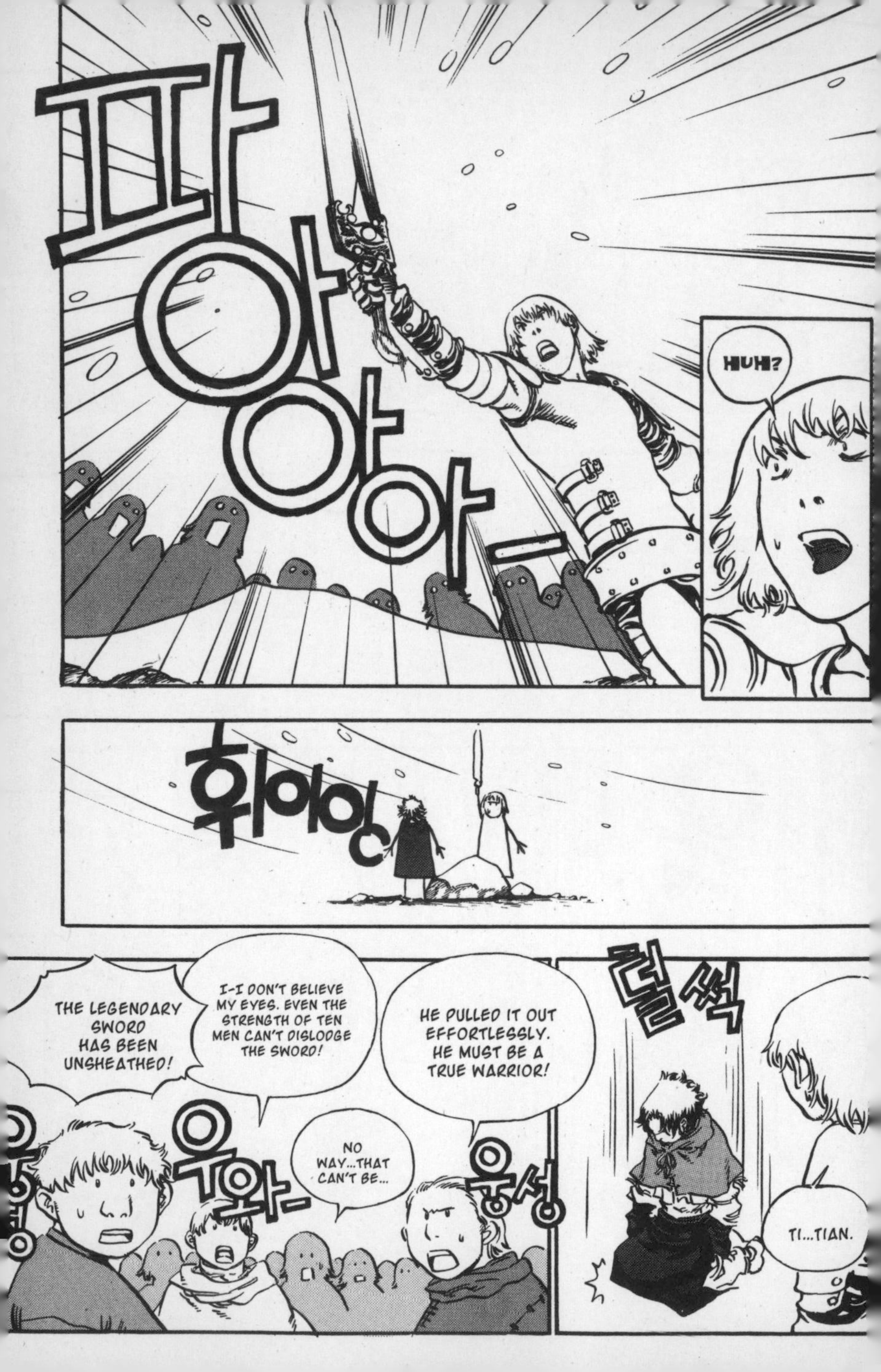
파아아아—
HUH?
휘이이잉
THE LEGENDARY SWORD HAS BEEN UNSHEATHED!
I-I DON'T BELIEVE MY EYES. EVEN THE STRENGTH OF TEN MEN CAN'T DISLODGE THE SWORD!
HE PULLED IT OUT EFFORTLESSLY. HE MUST BE A TRUE WARRIOR!
우와—
NO WAY...THAT CAN'T BE...
웅성
TI...TIAN.

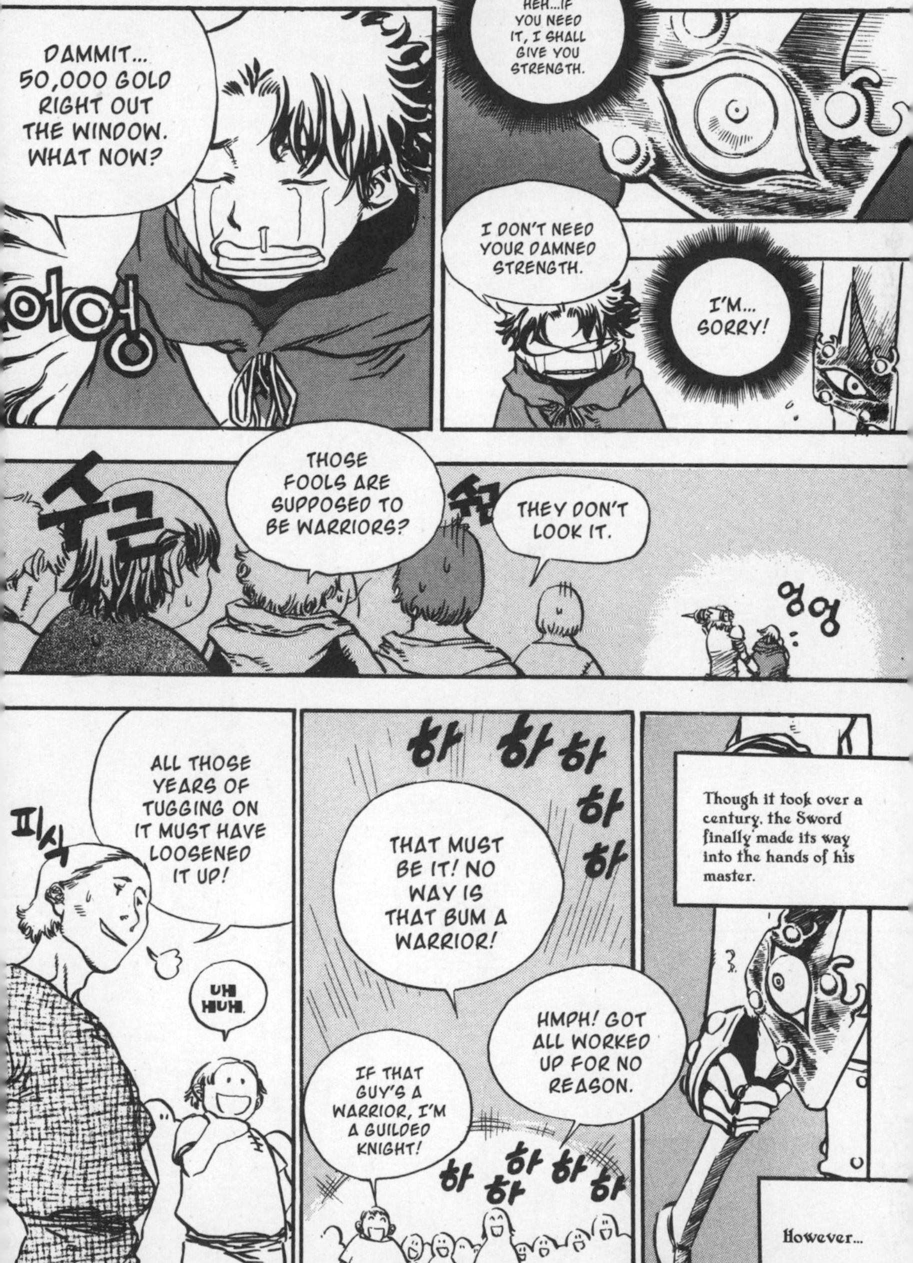
DAMMIT... 50,000 GOLD RIGHT OUT THE WINDOW. WHAT NOW?
HEH HEH HEH...IF YOU NEED IT, I SHALL GIVE YOU STRENGTH.
I DON'T NEED YOUR DAMNED STRENGTH.
I'M... SORRY!
THOSE FOOLS ARE SUPPOSED TO BE WARRIORS?
THEY DON'T LOOK IT.
엉엉
피식
ALL THOSE YEARS OF TUGGING ON IT MUST HAVE LOOSENED IT UP!
UH HUH.
하 하 하 하 하
THAT MUST BE IT! NO WAY IS THAT BUM A WARRIOR!
HMPH! GOT ALL WORKED UP FOR NO REASON.
IF THAT GUY'S A WARRIOR, I'M A GUILDED KNIGHT!
하 하 하 하 하
Though it took over a century, the Sword finally made its way into the hands of his master.
However...

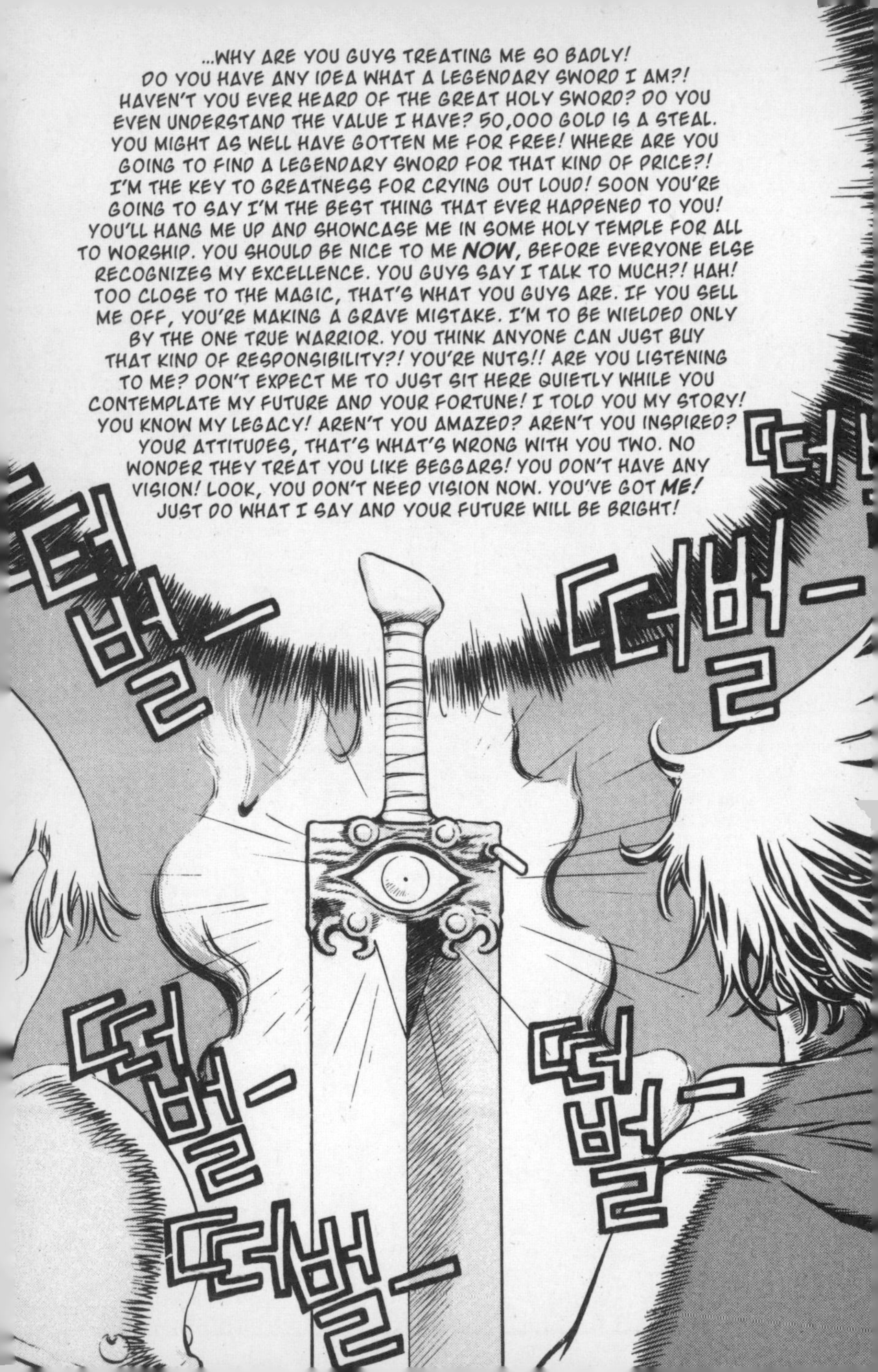
...WHY ARE YOU GUYS TREATING ME SO BADLY! DO YOU HAVE ANY IDEA WHAT A LEGENDARY SWORD I AM?! HAVEN'T YOU EVER HEARD OF THE GREAT HOLY SWORD? DO YOU EVEN UNDERSTAND THE VALUE I HAVE? 50,000 GOLD IS A STEAL. YOU MIGHT AS WELL HAVE GOTTEN ME FOR FREE! WHERE ARE YOU GOING TO FIND A LEGENDARY SWORD FOR THAT KIND OF PRICE?! I'M THE KEY TO GREATNESS FOR CRYING OUT LOUD! SOON YOU'RE GOING TO SAY I'M THE BEST THING THAT EVER HAPPENED TO YOU! YOU'LL HANG ME UP AND SHOWCASE ME IN SOME HOLY TEMPLE FOR ALL TO WORSHIP. YOU SHOULD BE NICE TO ME *NOW*, BEFORE EVERYONE ELSE RECOGNIZES MY EXCELLENCE. YOU GUYS SAY I TALK TO MUCH?! HAH! TOO CLOSE TO THE MAGIC, THAT'S WHAT YOU GUYS ARE. IF YOU SELL ME OFF, YOU'RE MAKING A GRAVE MISTAKE. I'M TO BE WIELDED ONLY BY THE ONE TRUE WARRIOR. YOU THINK ANYONE CAN JUST BUY THAT KIND OF RESPONSIBILITY?! YOU'RE NUTS!! ARE YOU LISTENING TO ME? DON'T EXPECT ME TO JUST SIT HERE QUIETLY WHILE YOU CONTEMPLATE MY FUTURE AND YOUR FORTUNE! I TOLD YOU MY STORY! YOU KNOW MY LEGACY! AREN'T YOU AMAZED? AREN'T YOU INSPIRED? YOUR ATTITUDES, THAT'S WHAT'S WRONG WITH YOU TWO. NO WONDER THEY TREAT YOU LIKE BEGGARS! YOU DON'T HAVE ANY VISION! LOOK, YOU DON'T NEED VISION NOW. YOU'VE GOT *ME!* JUST DO WHAT I SAY AND YOUR FUTURE WILL BE BRIGHT!

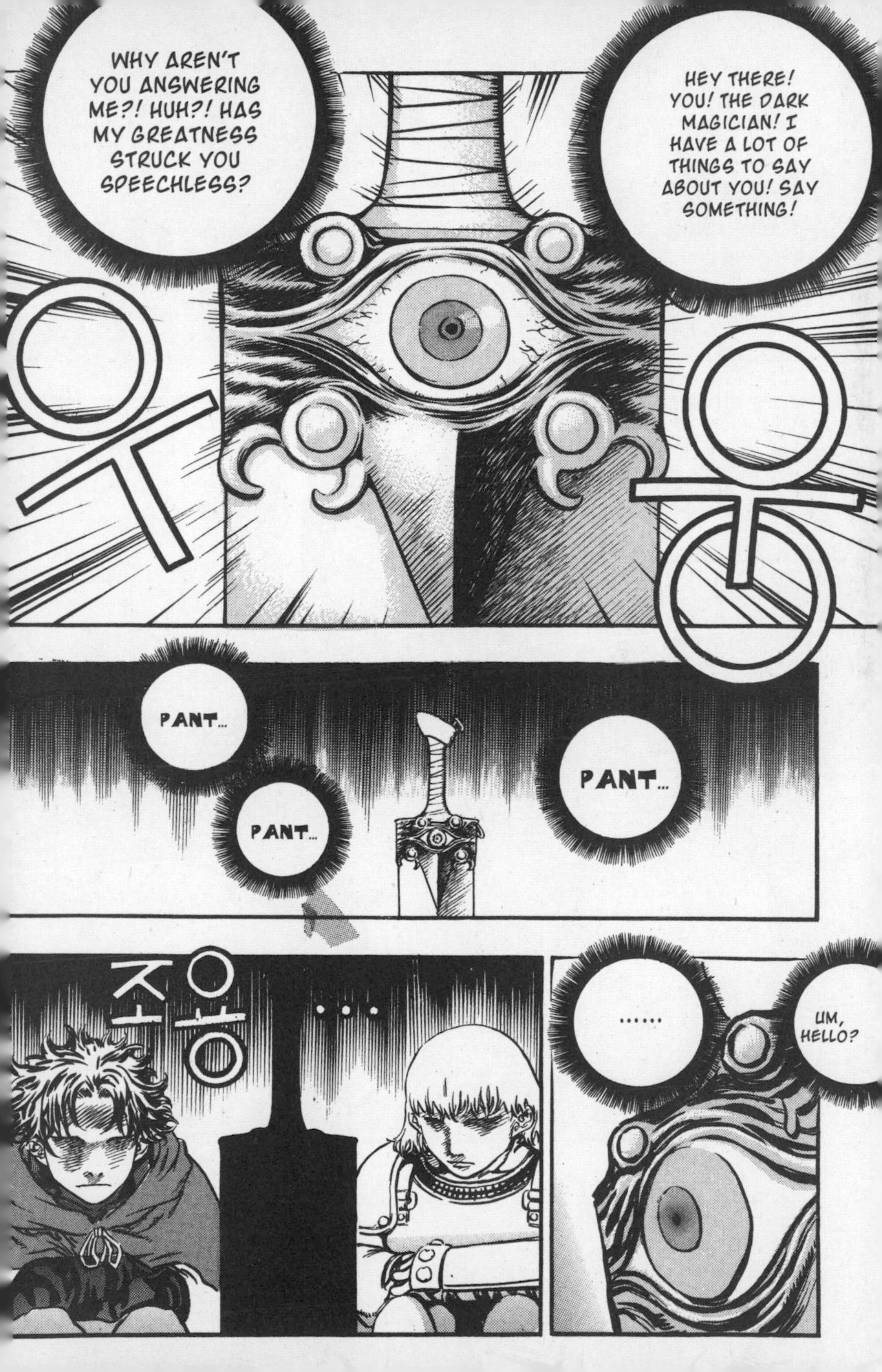
HEY THERE! YOU! THE DARK MAGICIAN! I HAVE A LOT OF THINGS TO SAY ABOUT YOU! SAY SOMETHING!
WHY AREN'T YOU ANSWERING ME?! HUH?! HAS MY GREATNESS STRUCK YOU SPEECHLESS?
PANT...
PANT...
PANT...
...
......
UM, HELLO?

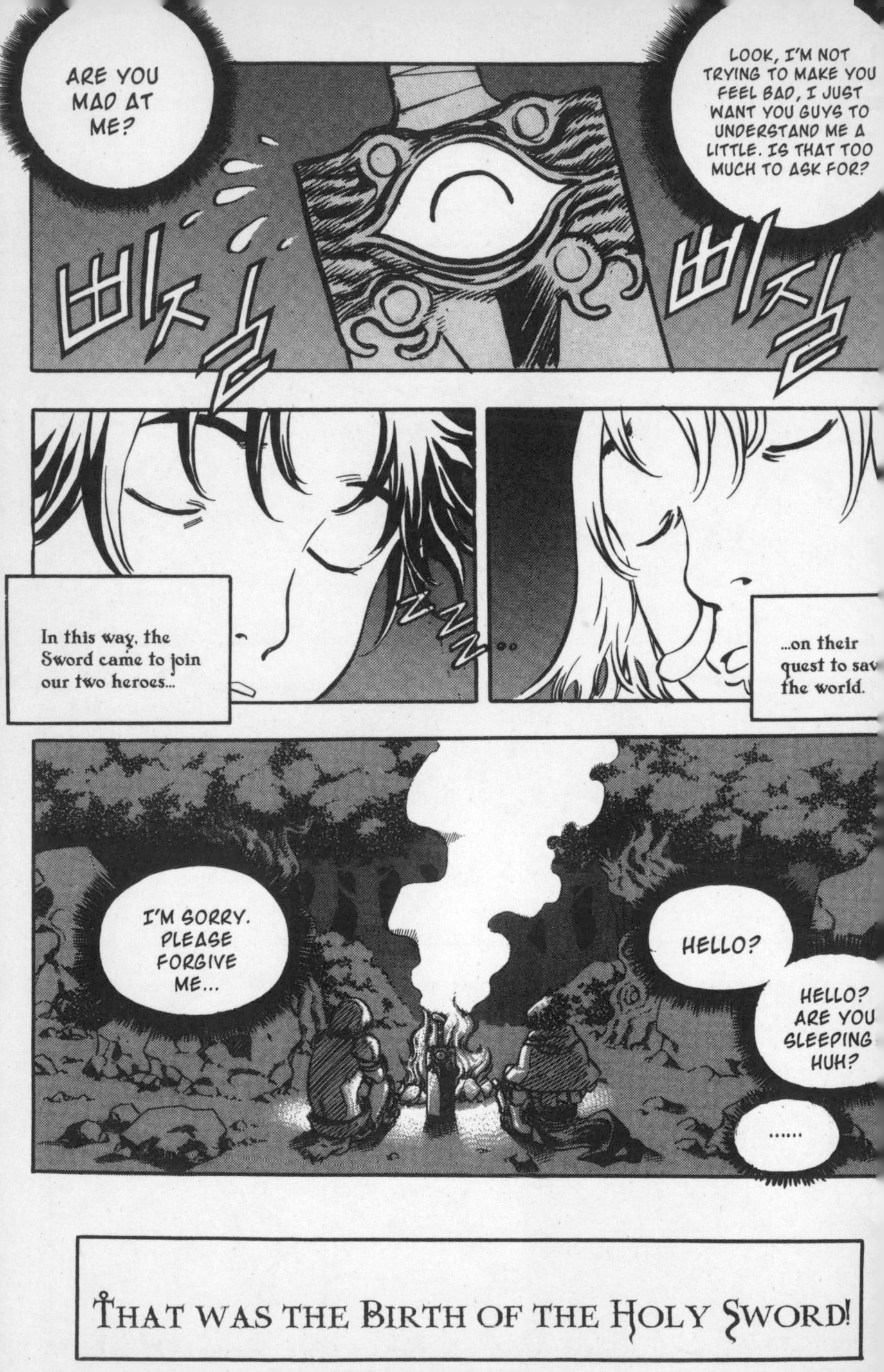
ARE YOU MAD AT ME?
LOOK, I'M NOT TRYING TO MAKE YOU FEEL BAD, I JUST WANT YOU GUYS TO UNDERSTAND ME A LITTLE. IS THAT TOO MUCH TO ASK FOR?
삐질
삐질
In this way, the Sword came to join our two heroes...
ZZZ...
...on their quest to sav the world.
I'M SORRY. PLEASE FORGIVE ME...
HELLO?
HELLO? ARE YOU SLEEPING HUH?
......
THAT WAS THE BIRTH OF THE HOLY SWORD!

Chapter 8

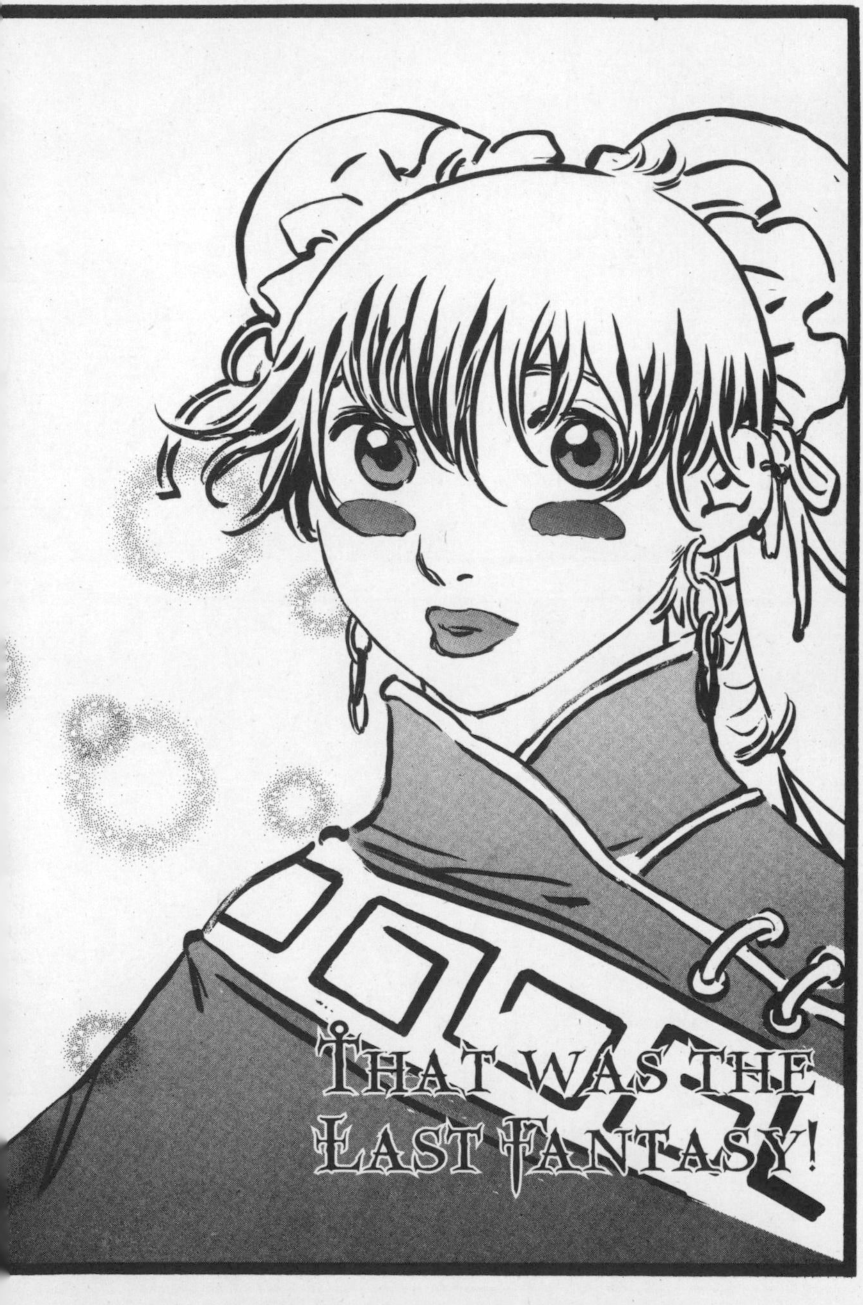
That was the Last Fantasy!

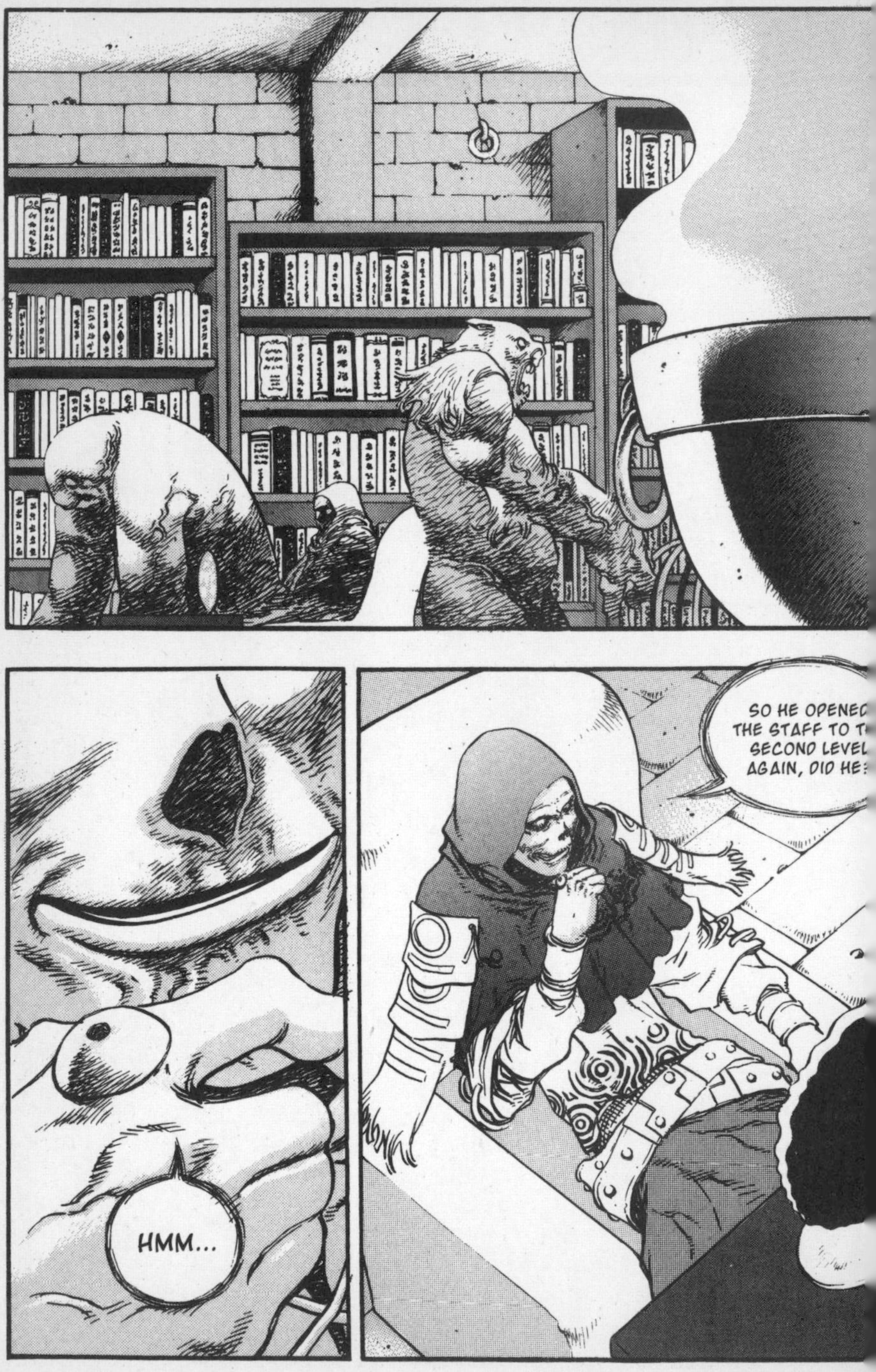
HMM...
SO HE OPENED
THE STAFF TO TH
SECOND LEVEL
AGAIN, DID HE?

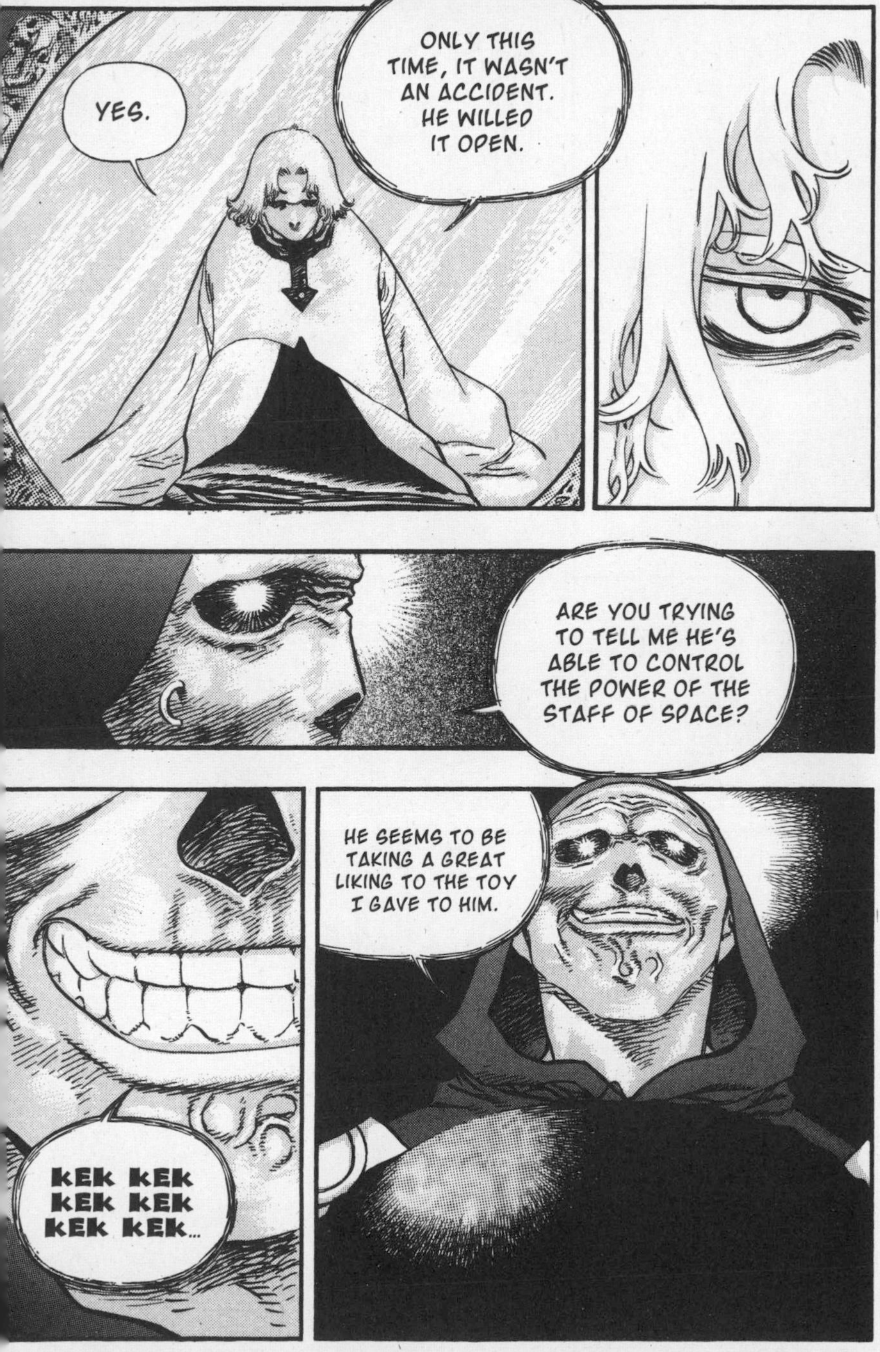
YES.
ONLY THIS TIME, IT WASN'T AN ACCIDENT. HE WILLED IT OPEN.
ARE YOU TRYING TO TELL ME HE'S ABLE TO CONTROL THE POWER OF THE STAFF OF SPACE?
HE SEEMS TO BE TAKING A GREAT LIKING TO THE TOY I GAVE TO HIM.
KEK KEK KEK KEK KEK KEK...

GLACIER... YOU WANT TO KILL TIAN, DON'T YOU?

KEK KEK KEK... I'M SURE YOU DO.

SOON, GLACIER, YOU CAN KILL HIM SOON. I'D LIKE TO STUDY HIM A LITTLE LONGER.

CONTAIN YOURSELF UNTIL I'M FINISHED.

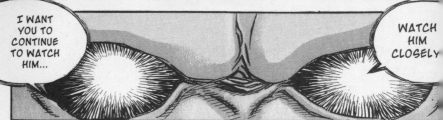

I WANT YOU TO CONTINUE TO WATCH HIM...

WATCH HIM CLOSELY

YES SIR, LORD AGRIPPA!

TIAN...YOU'VE GROWN QUITE A BIT.

HIS STRENGTH IS SUCH NOW THAT HE DEMANDS YOUR ATTENTION, EH, AGRIPPA?

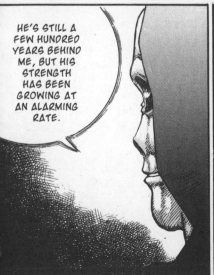

HE'S STILL A FEW HUNDRED YEARS BEHIND ME, BUT HIS STRENGTH HAS BEEN GROWING AT AN ALARMING RATE.

A FEW HUNDRED YEARS? I THINK YOU SAID HE WAS A FEW THOUSAND YEARS BEHIND YOU NOT TOO LONG AGO. HE'LL BE YOUR EQUAL IN NO TIME!

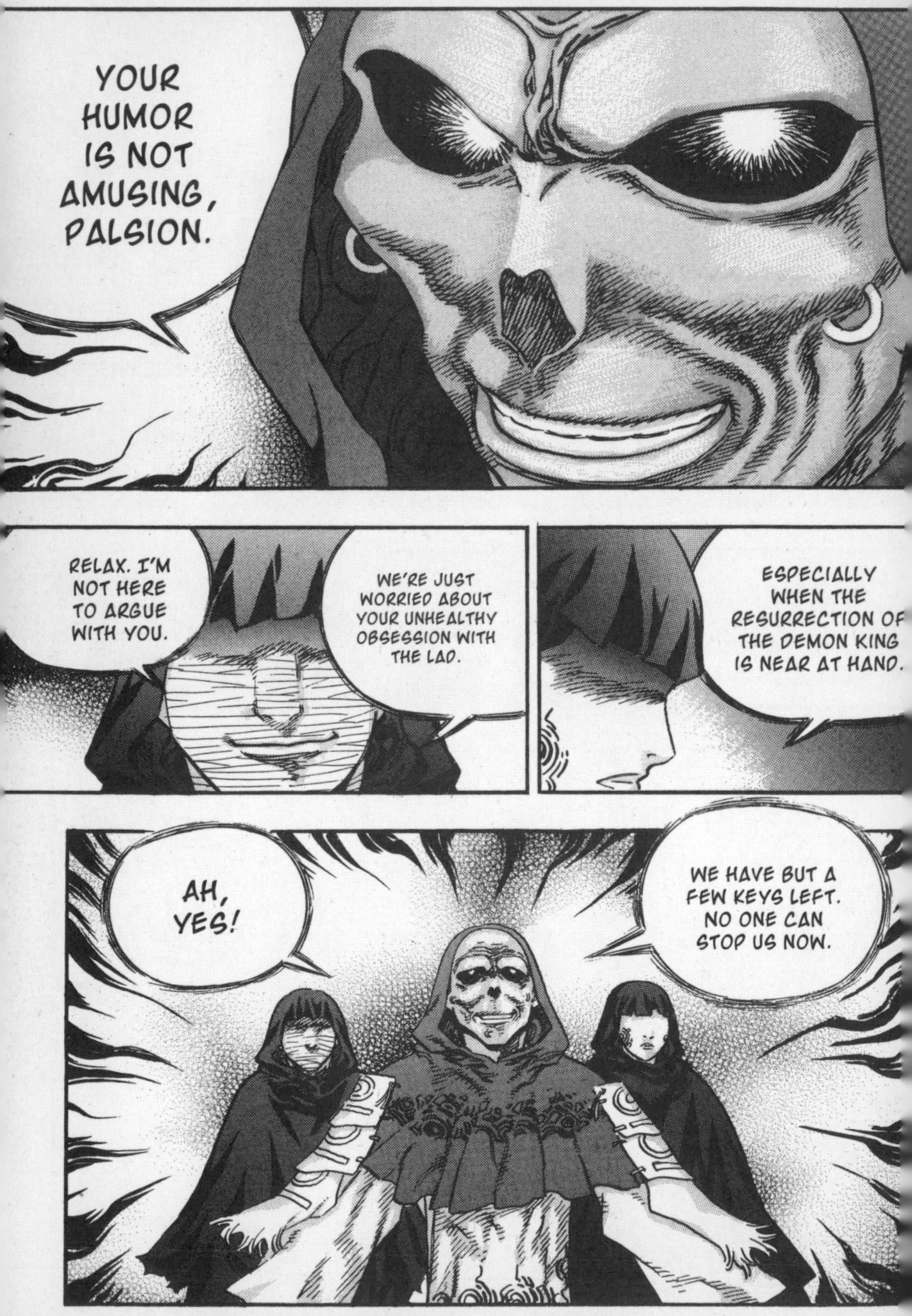
YOUR HUMOR IS NOT AMUSING, PALSION.
RELAX. I'M NOT HERE TO ARGUE WITH YOU.
WE'RE JUST WORRIED ABOUT YOUR UNHEALTHY OBSESSION WITH THE LAD.
ESPECIALLY WHEN THE RESURRECTION OF THE DEMON KING IS NEAR AT HAND.
AH, YES!
WE HAVE BUT A FEW KEYS LEFT. NO ONE CAN STOP US NOW.

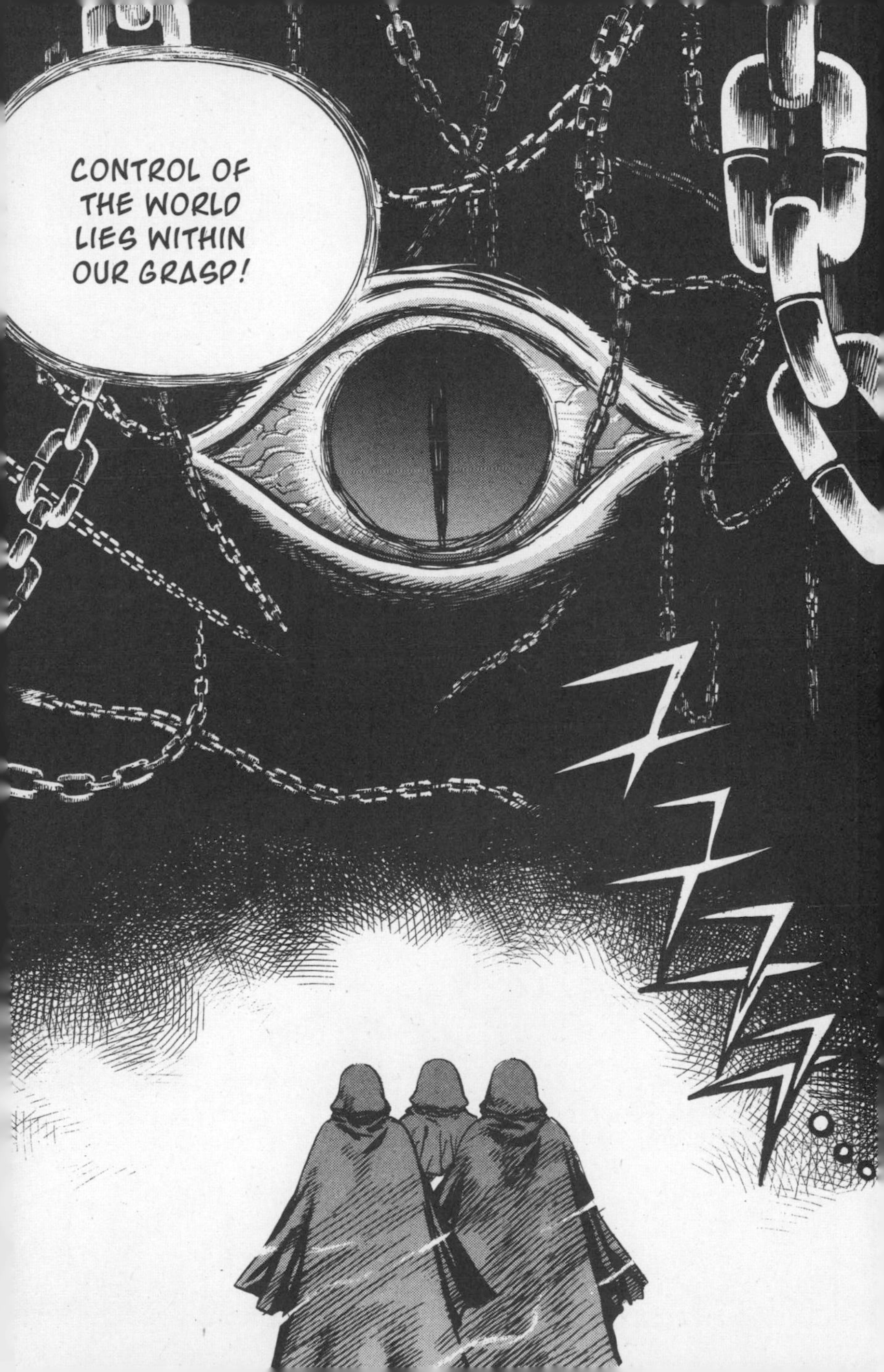
CONTROL OF THE WORLD LIES WITHIN OUR GRASP!

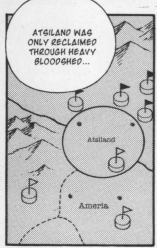

ATSILAND WAS
ONLY RECLAIMED
THROUGH HEAVY
BLOODSHED...

Atsiland

Ameria

HOWEVER, WHAT
USE IS VICTORY
IF WE'VE LOST
THE PRINCE?

SOB...IF ONLY I
HADN'T BEEN SO
OVERZEALOUS!

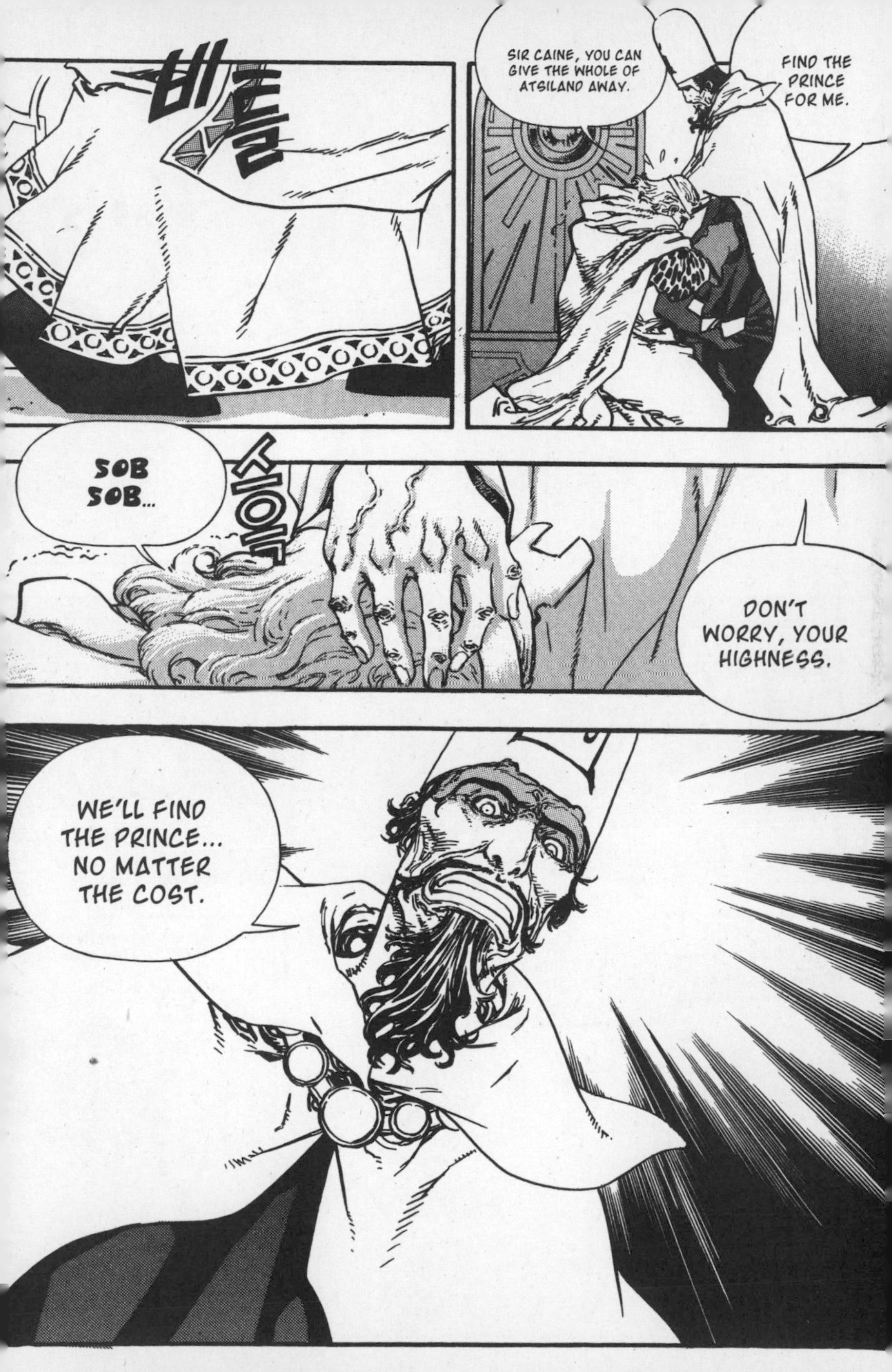
비틀
SIR CAINE, YOU CAN GIVE THE WHOLE OF ATSILAND AWAY.
FIND THE PRINCE FOR ME.
SOB SOB...
스윽
DON'T WORRY, YOUR HIGHNESS.
WE'LL FIND THE PRINCE... NO MATTER THE COST.

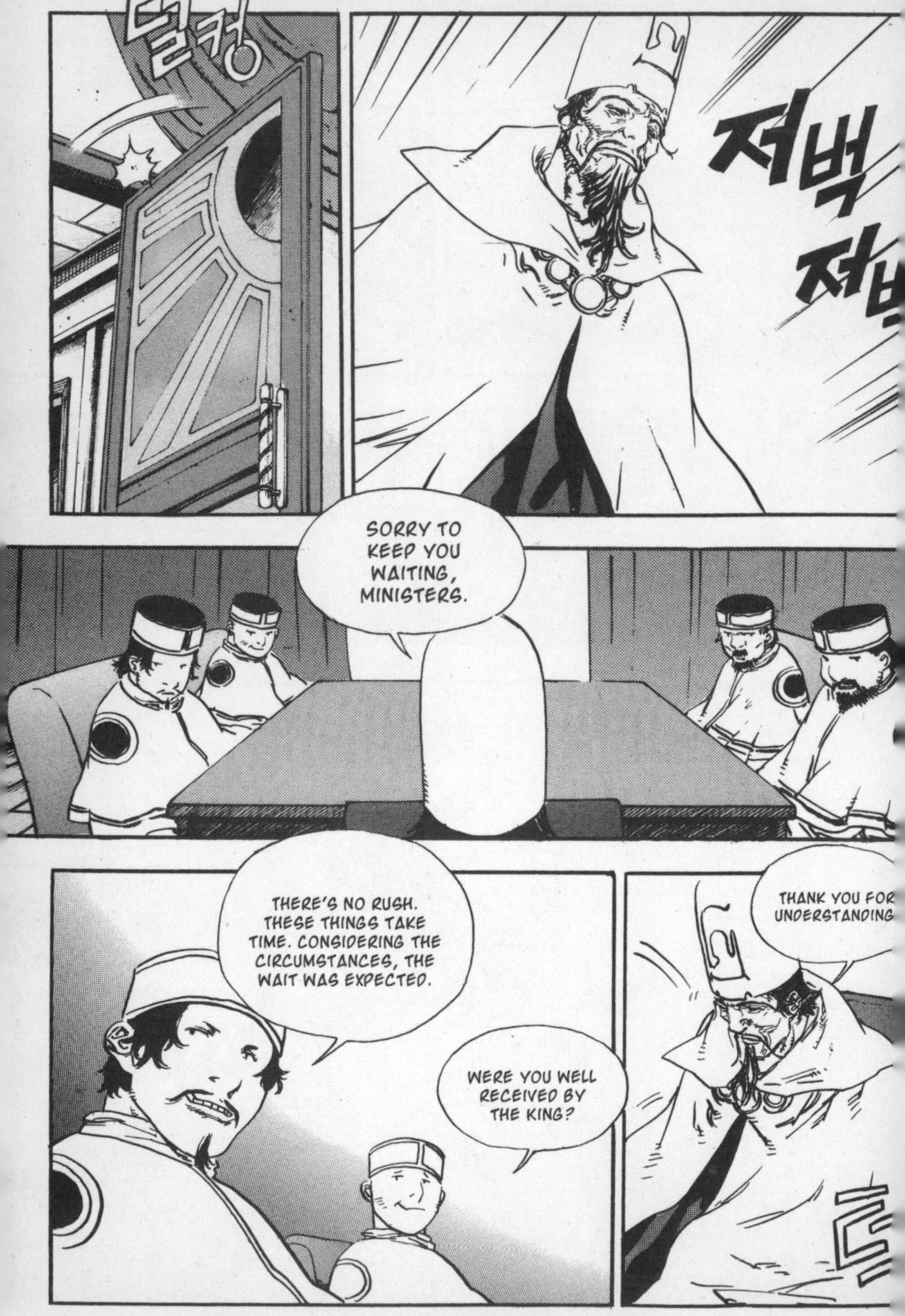

덜컹
저벅 저벅
SORRY TO KEEP YOU WAITING, MINISTERS.
THERE'S NO RUSH. THESE THINGS TAKE TIME. CONSIDERING THE CIRCUMSTANCES, THE WAIT WAS EXPECTED.
WERE YOU WELL RECEIVED BY THE KING?
THANK YOU FOR UNDERSTANDING

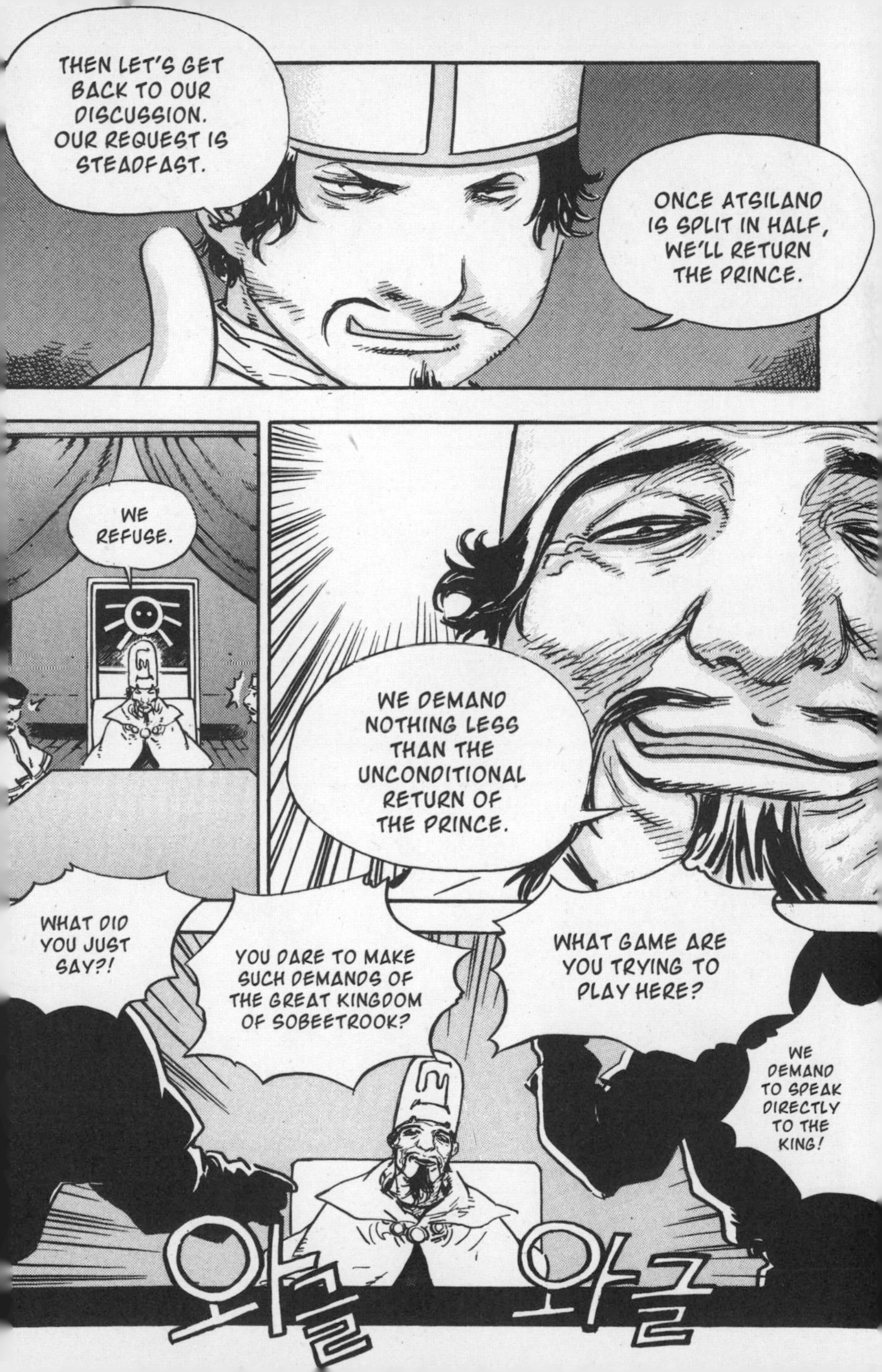
THEN LET'S GET BACK TO OUR DISCUSSION. OUR REQUEST IS STEADFAST.
ONCE ATSILAND IS SPLIT IN HALF, WE'LL RETURN THE PRINCE.
WE REFUSE.
WE DEMAND NOTHING LESS THAN THE UNCONDITIONAL RETURN OF THE PRINCE.
WHAT DID YOU JUST SAY?!
YOU DARE TO MAKE SUCH DEMANDS OF THE GREAT KINGDOM OF SOBEETROOK?
WHAT GAME ARE YOU TRYING TO PLAY HERE?
WE DEMAND TO SPEAK DIRECTLY TO THE KING!
와글 와글

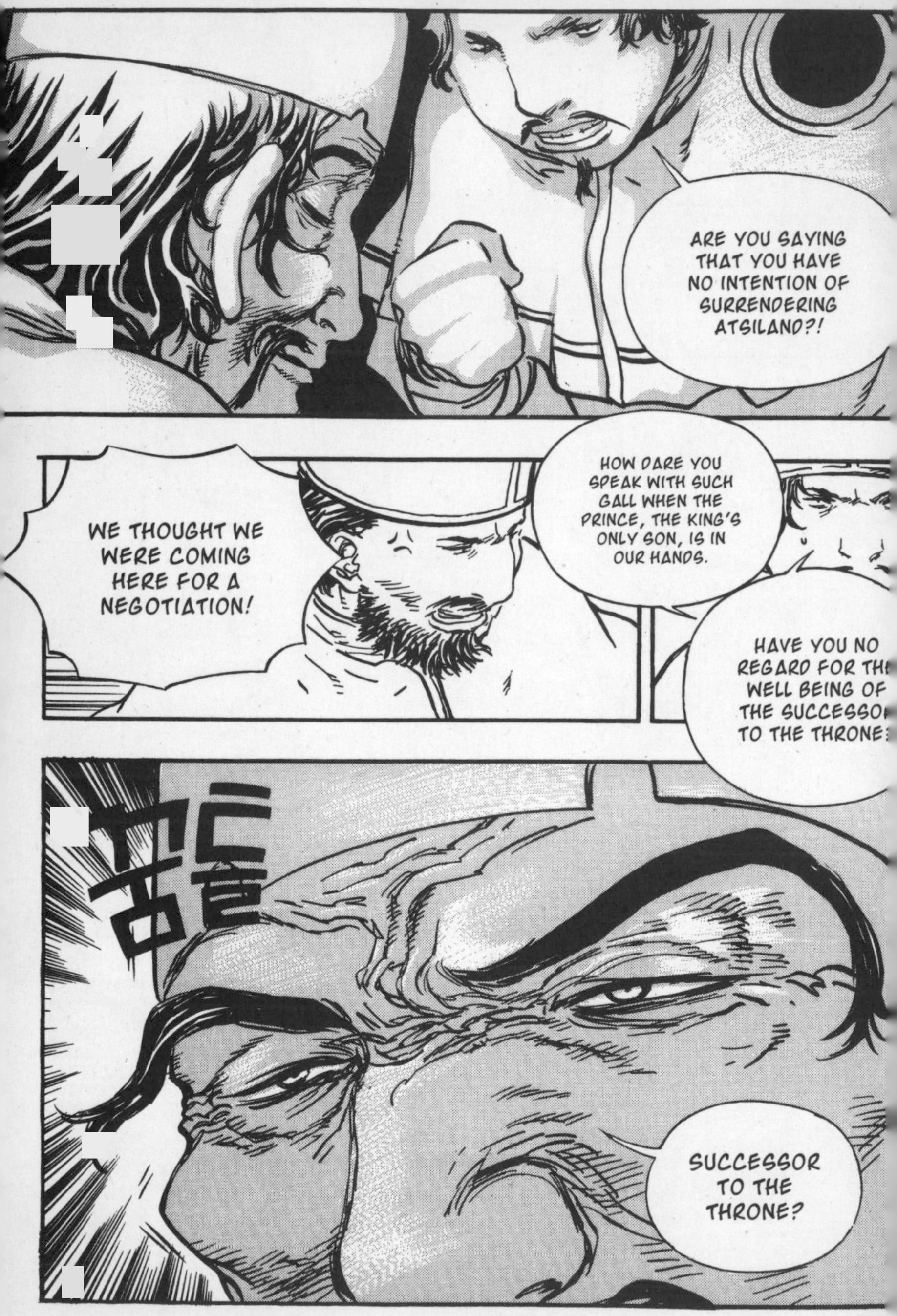
ARE YOU SAYING THAT YOU HAVE NO INTENTION OF SURRENDERING ATSILAND?!
HOW DARE YOU SPEAK WITH SUCH GALL WHEN THE PRINCE, THE KING'S ONLY SON, IS IN OUR HANDS.
WE THOUGHT WE WERE COMING HERE FOR A NEGOTIATION!
HAVE YOU NO REGARD FOR THE WELL BEING OF THE SUCCESSOR TO THE THRONE?!
SUCCESSOR TO THE THRONE?

HEH...

THE SUCCESSOR TO THE THRONE?

DID YOU JUST SAY THE SUCCESSOR TO THE THRONE?

VIOLET...

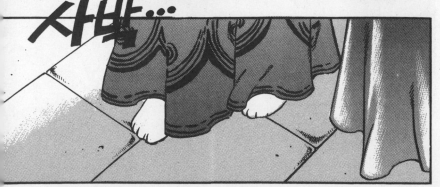

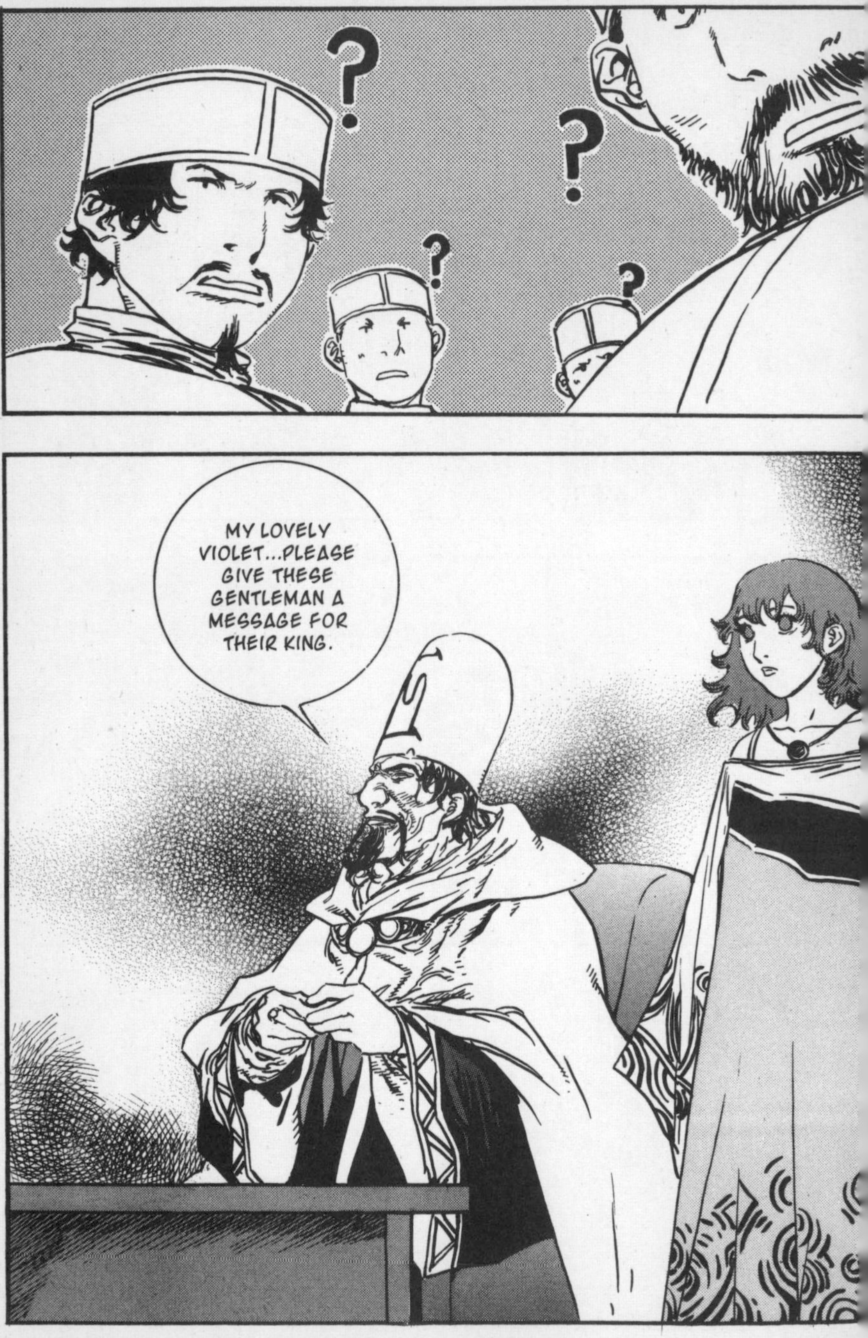
?
?
?
?
MY LOVELY VIOLET...PLEASE GIVE THESE GENTLEMAN A MESSAGE FOR THEIR KING.

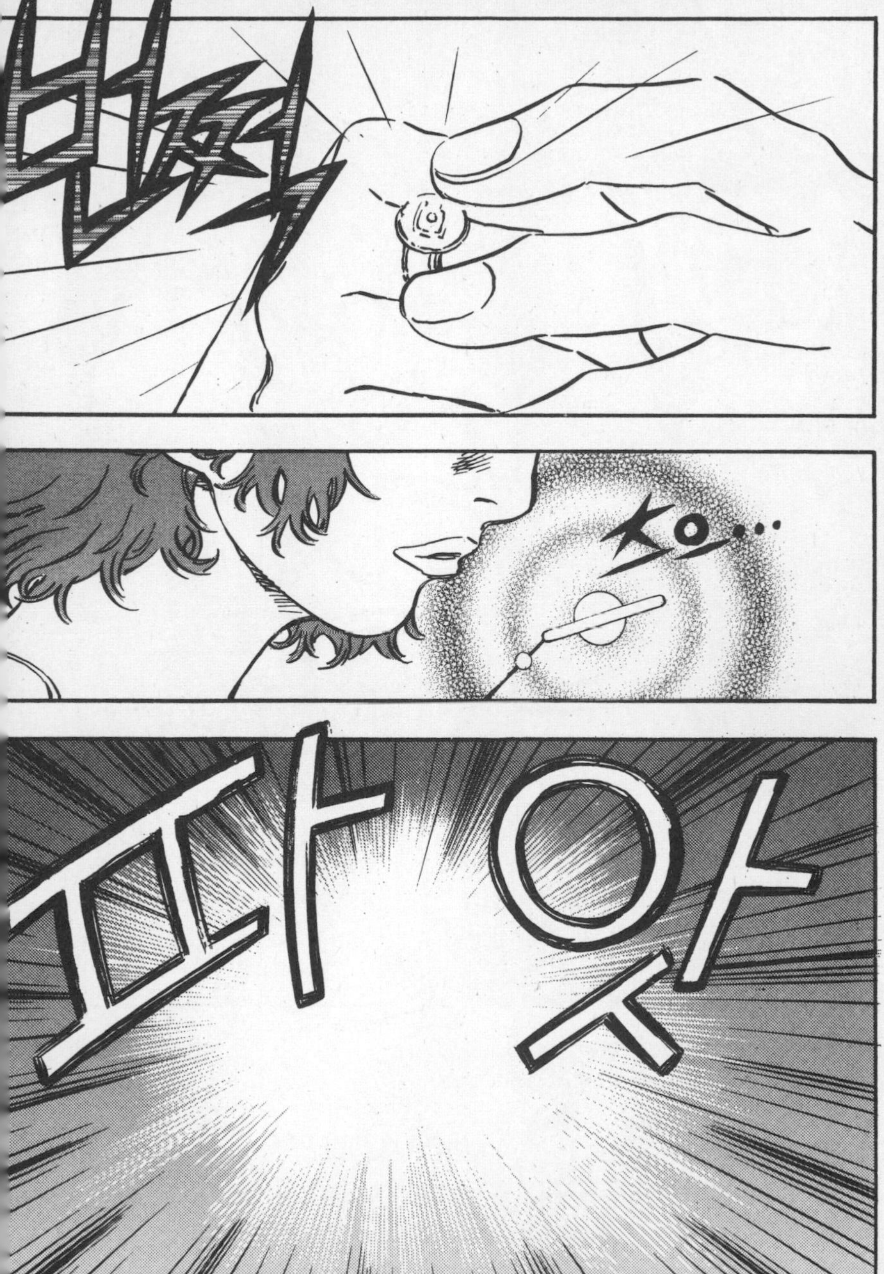
번쩍
파앗

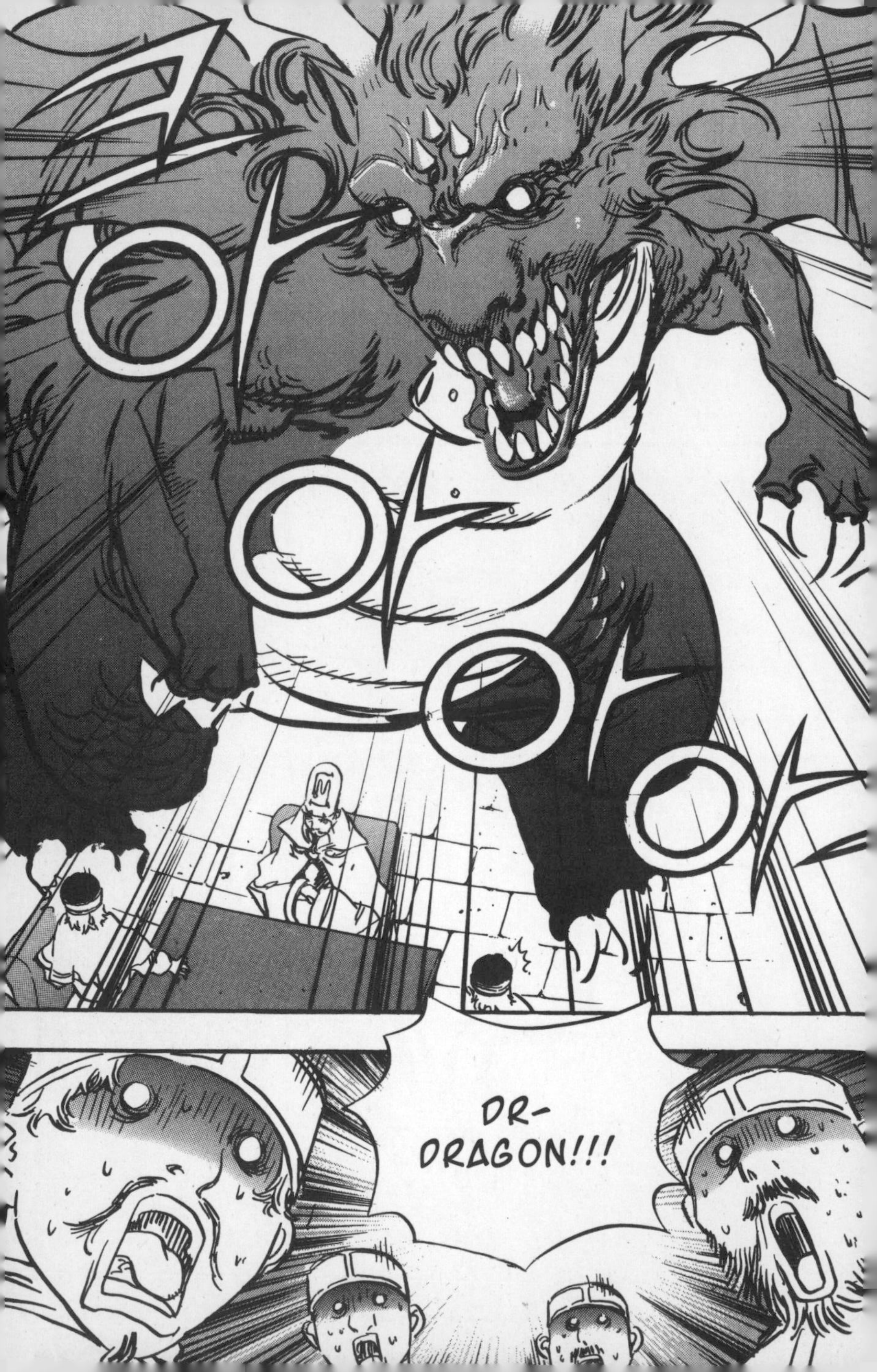
DR-
DRAGON!!!

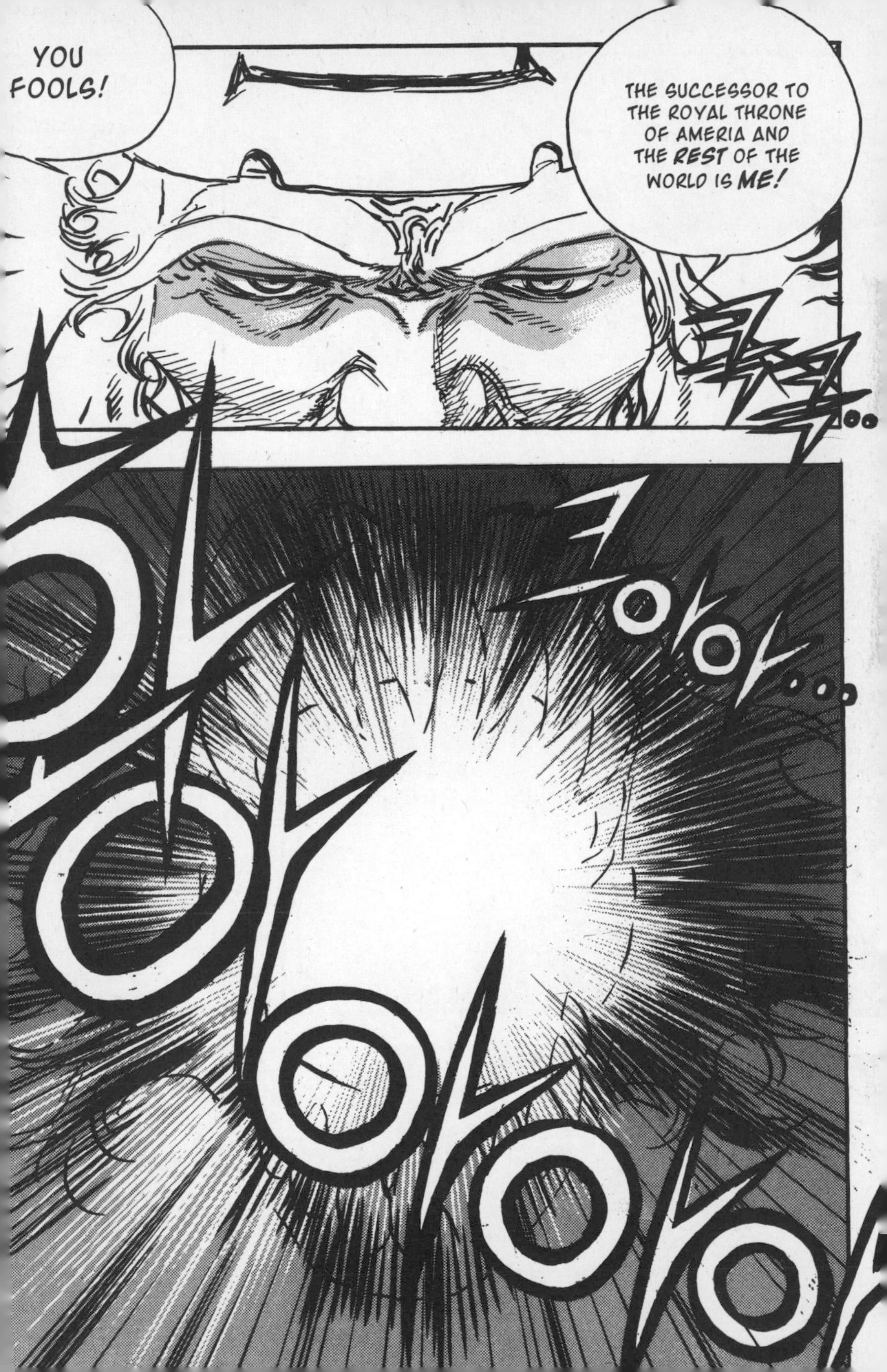
YOU FOOLS!
THE SUCCESSOR TO THE ROYAL THRONE OF AMERIA AND THE REST OF THE WORLD IS ME!

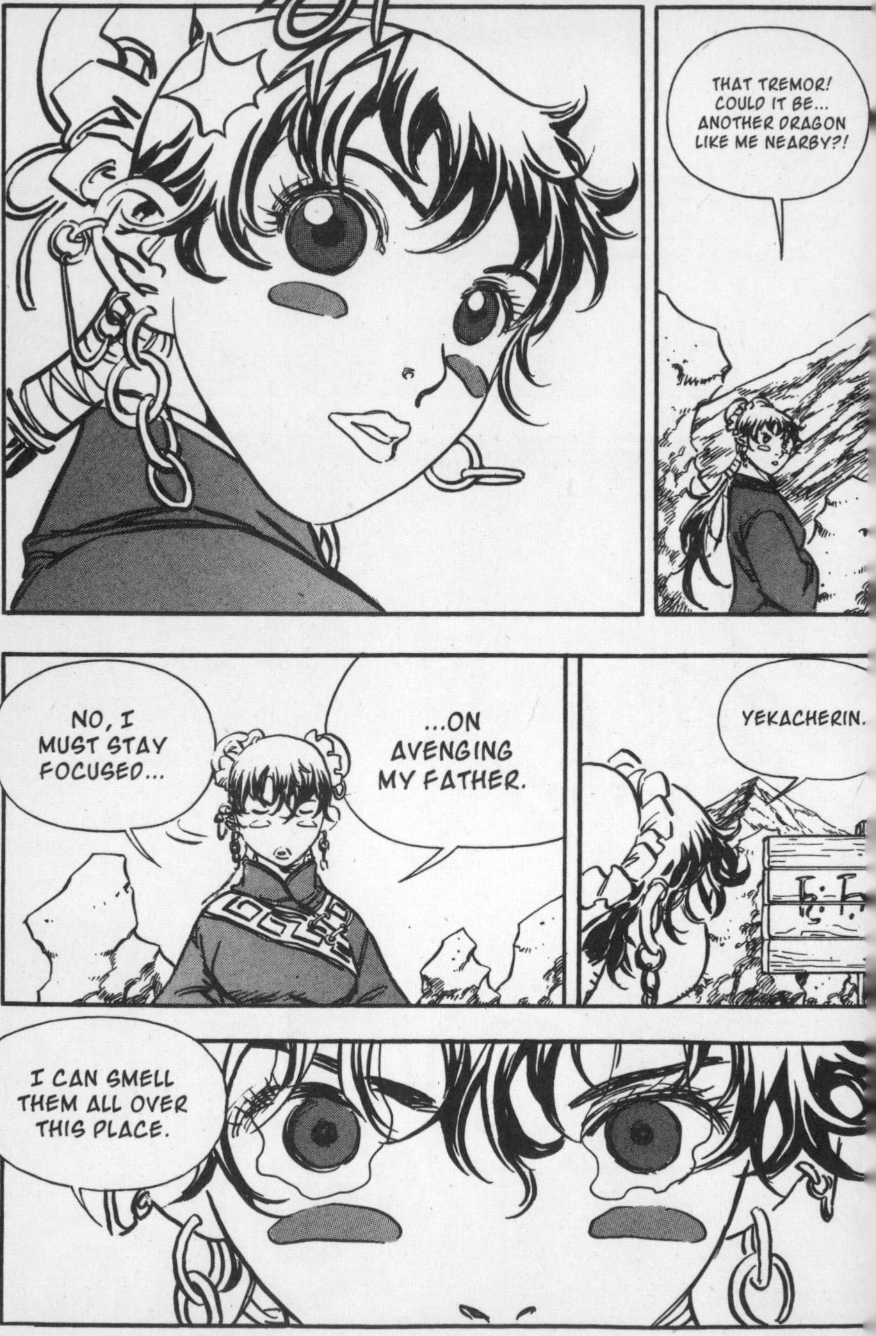
THAT TREMOR! COULD IT BE... ANOTHER DRAGON LIKE ME NEARBY?!
NO, I MUST STAY FOCUSED...
...ON AVENGING MY FATHER.
YEKACHERIN.
I CAN SMELL THEM ALL OVER THIS PLACE.

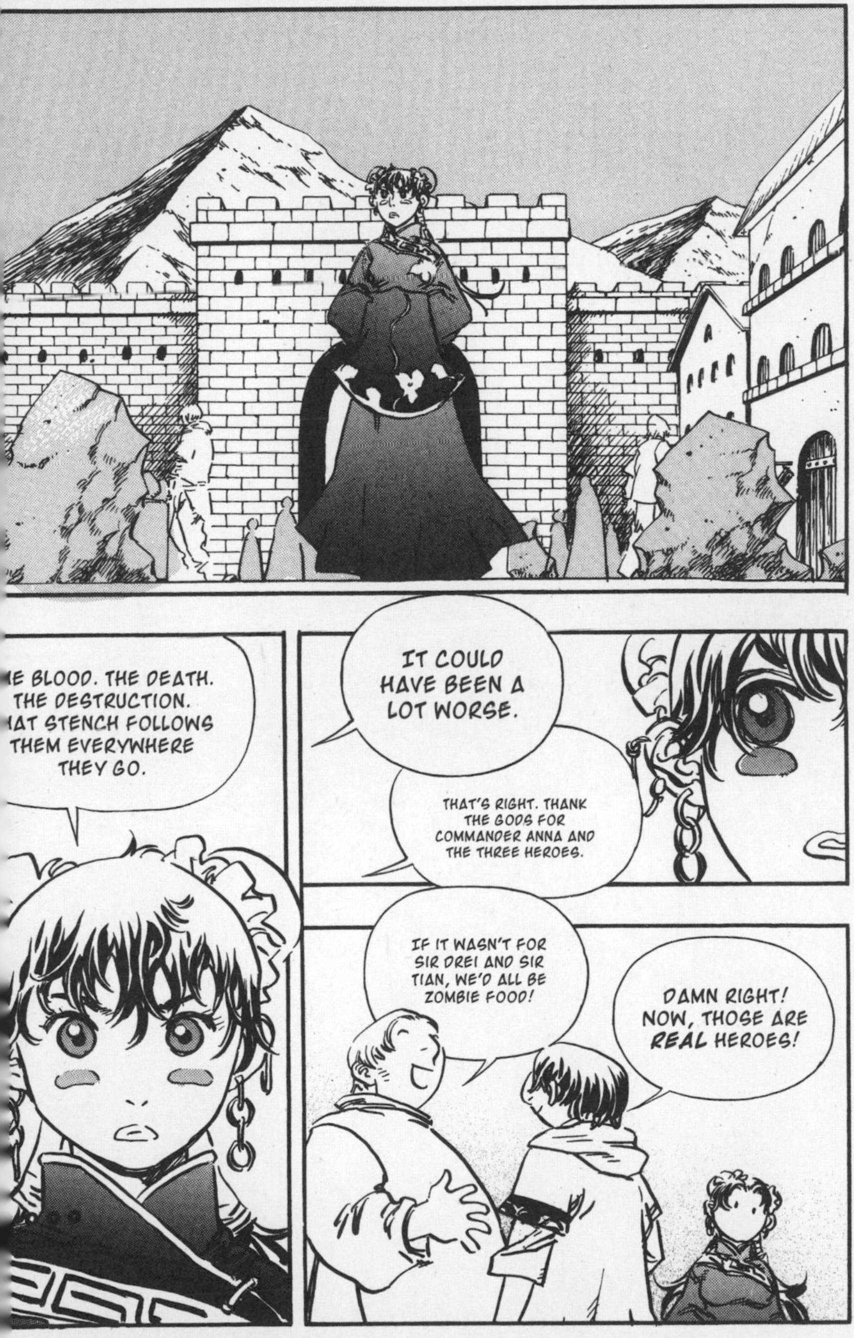

IE BLOOD. THE DEATH. THE DESTRUCTION. IAT STENCH FOLLOWS THEM EVERYWHERE THEY GO.
IT COULD HAVE BEEN A LOT WORSE.
THAT'S RIGHT. THANK THE GODS FOR COMMANDER ANNA AND THE THREE HEROES.
IF IT WASN'T FOR SIR DREI AND SIR TIAN, WE'D ALL BE ZOMBIE FOOD!
DAMN RIGHT! NOW, THOSE ARE *REAL* HEROES!

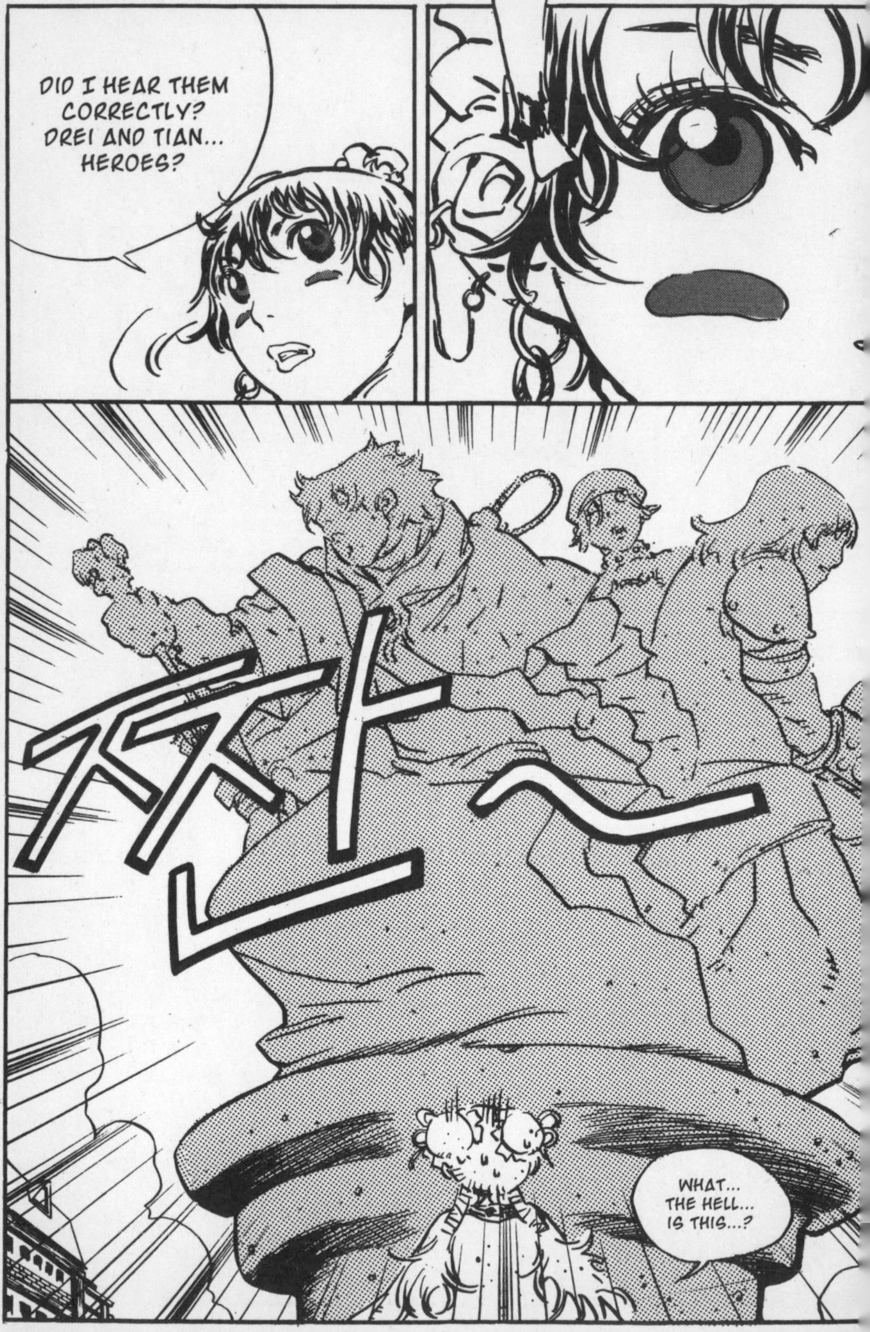
DID I HEAR THEM CORRECTLY? DREI AND TIAN... HEROES?
WHAT... THE HELL... IS THIS...?

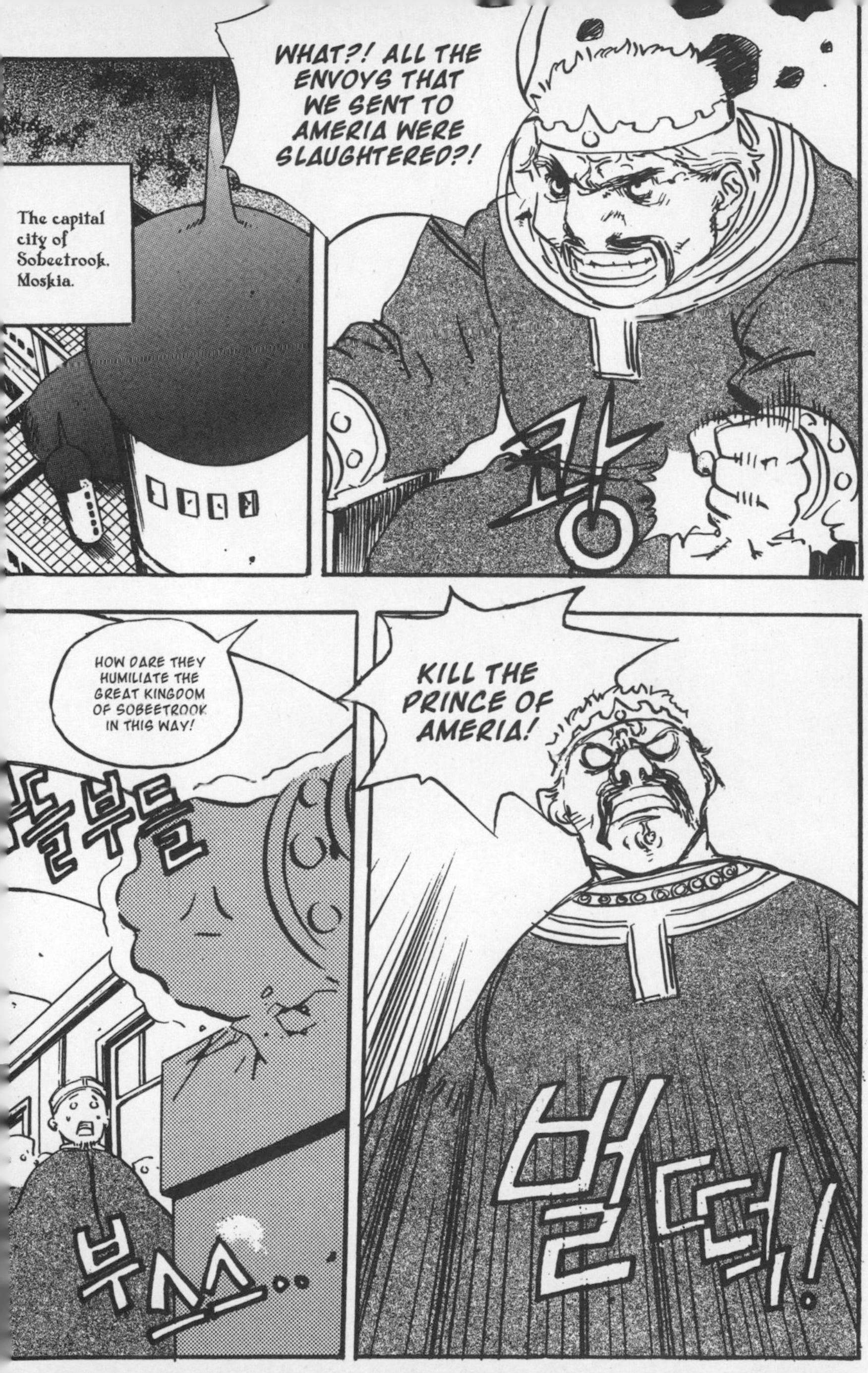

The capital city of Sobeetrook, Moskia.
WHAT?! ALL THE ENVOYS THAT WE SENT TO AMERIA WERE SLAUGHTERED?!
HOW DARE THEY HUMILIATE THE GREAT KINGDOM OF SOBEETROOK IN THIS WAY!
들부들
부스스..
KILL THE PRINCE OF AMERIA!
벌떡!

Last Fantasy

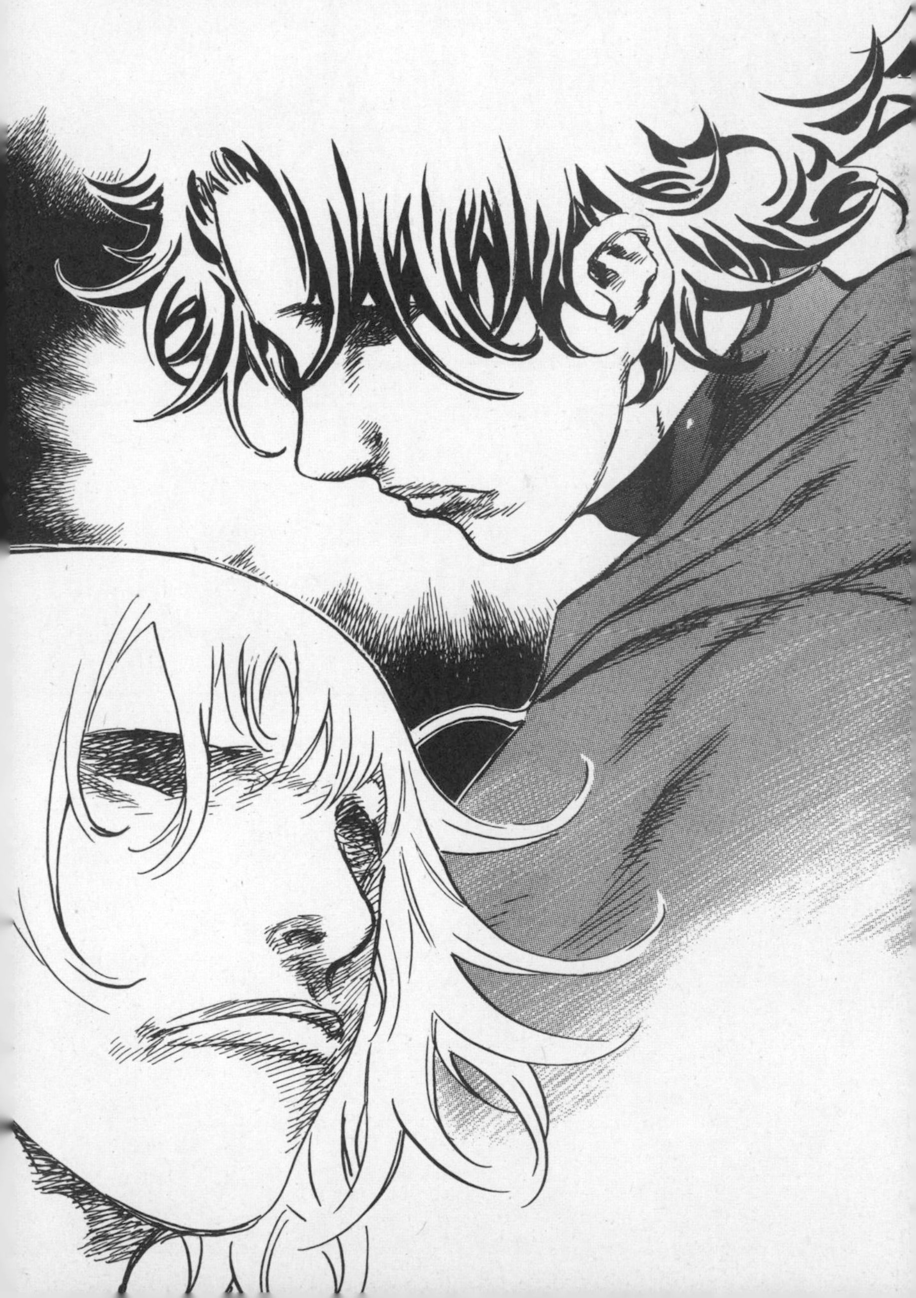

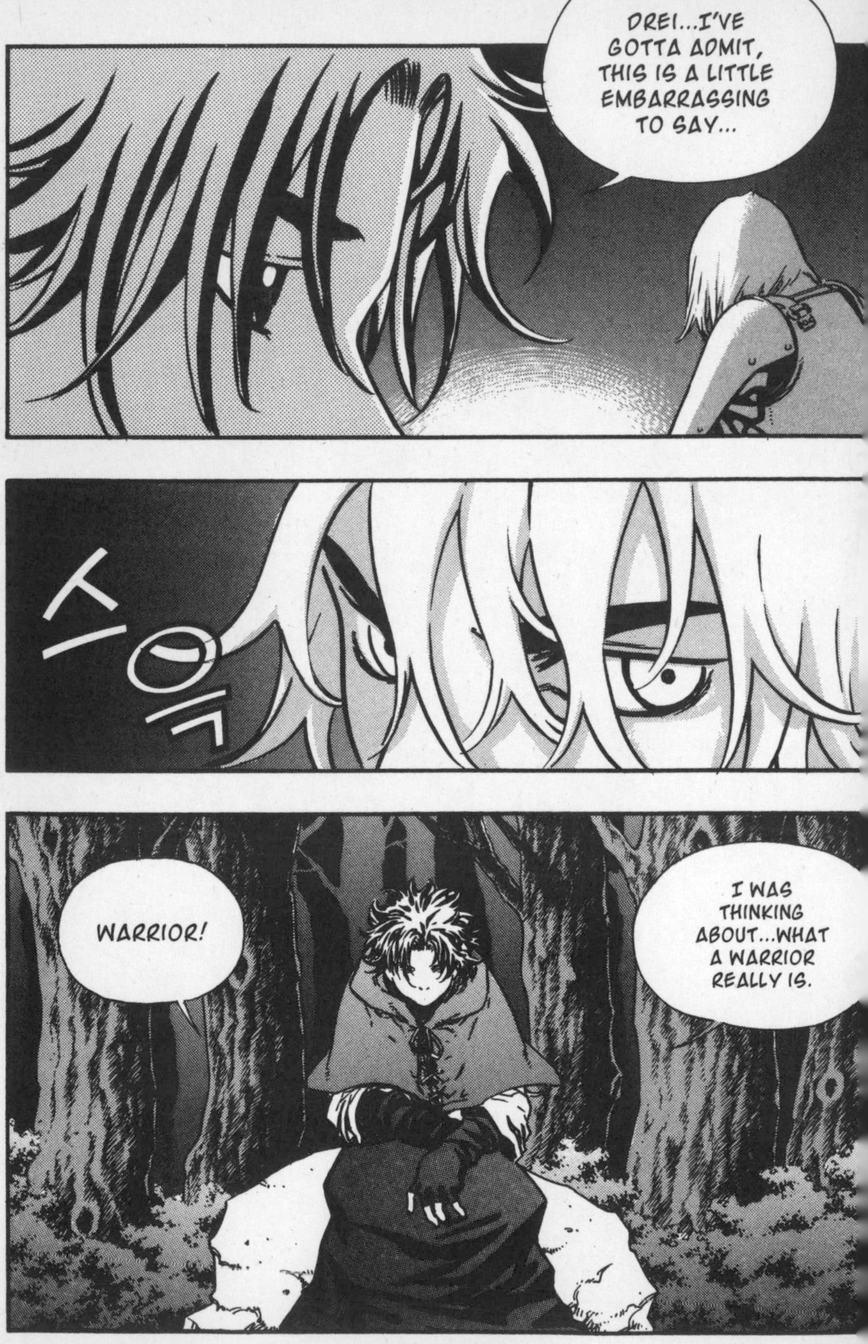
DREI...I'VE GOTTA ADMIT, THIS IS A LITTLE EMBARRASSING TO SAY...
WARRIOR!
I WAS THINKING ABOUT...WHAT A WARRIOR REALLY IS.

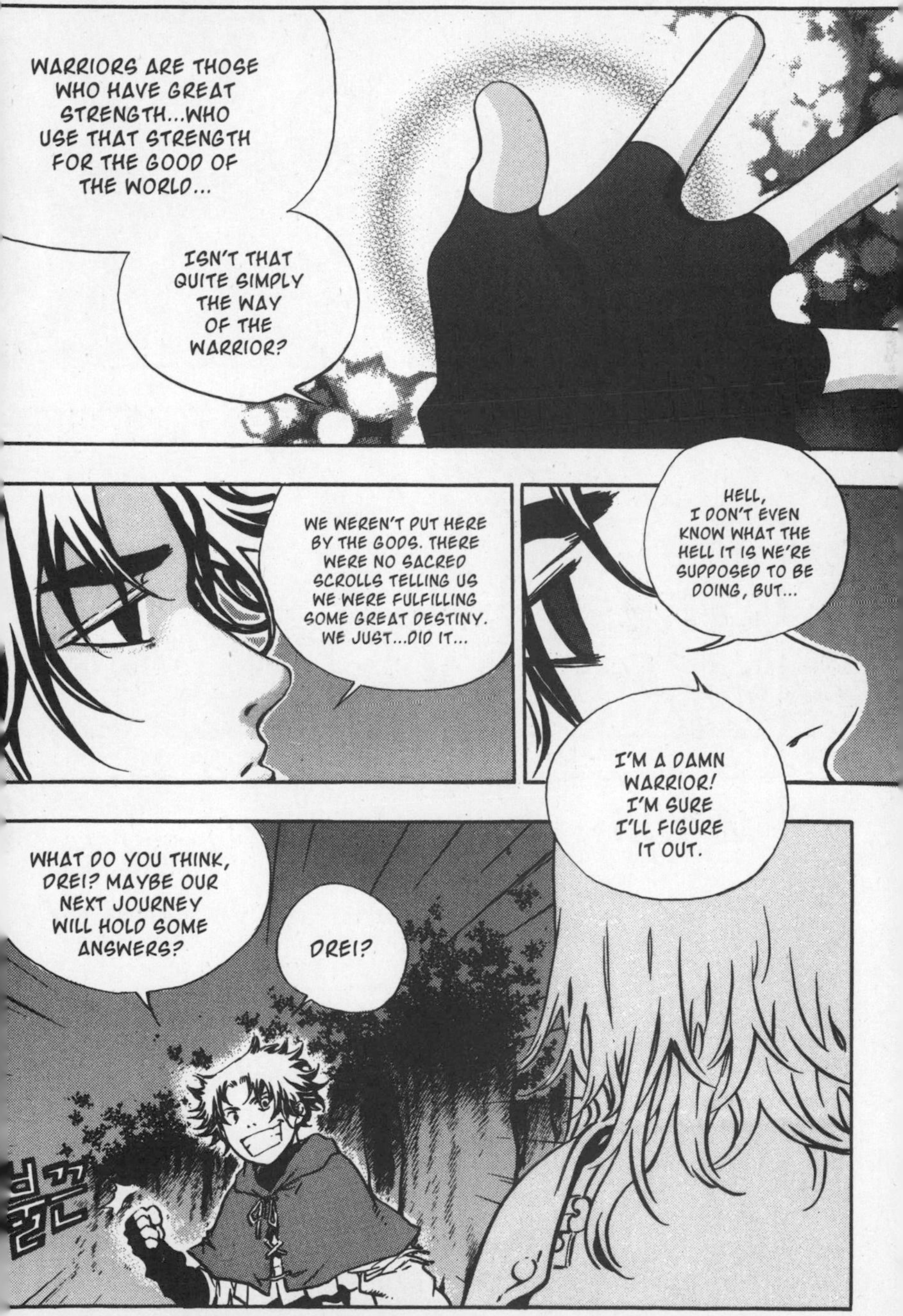
WARRIORS ARE THOSE WHO HAVE GREAT STRENGTH...WHO USE THAT STRENGTH FOR THE GOOD OF THE WORLD...
ISN'T THAT QUITE SIMPLY THE WAY OF THE WARRIOR?
WE WEREN'T PUT HERE BY THE GODS. THERE WERE NO SACRED SCROLLS TELLING US WE WERE FULFILLING SOME GREAT DESTINY. WE JUST...DID IT...
HELL, I DON'T EVEN KNOW WHAT THE HELL IT IS WE'RE SUPPOSED TO BE DOING, BUT...
I'M A DAMN WARRIOR! I'M SURE I'LL FIGURE IT OUT.
WHAT DO YOU THINK, DREI? MAYBE OUR NEXT JOURNEY WILL HOLD SOME ANSWERS?
DREI?

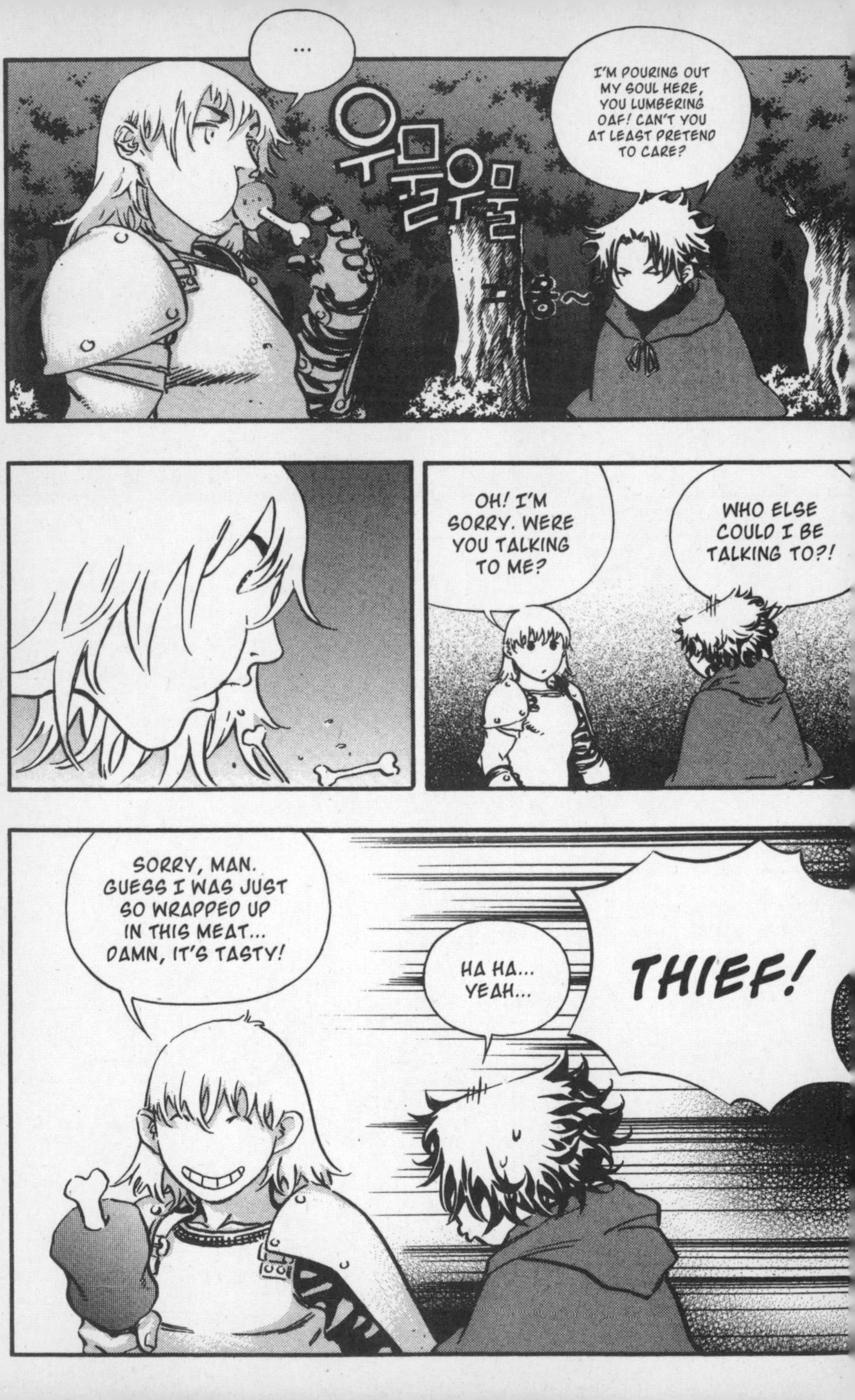
...
우물우물
I'M POURING OUT MY SOUL HERE, YOU LUMBERING OAF! CAN'T YOU AT LEAST PRETEND TO CARE?
OH! I'M SORRY. WERE YOU TALKING TO ME?
WHO ELSE COULD I BE TALKING TO?!
SORRY, MAN. GUESS I WAS JUST SO WRAPPED UP IN THIS MEAT... DAMN, IT'S TASTY!
HA HA... YEAH...
THIEF!

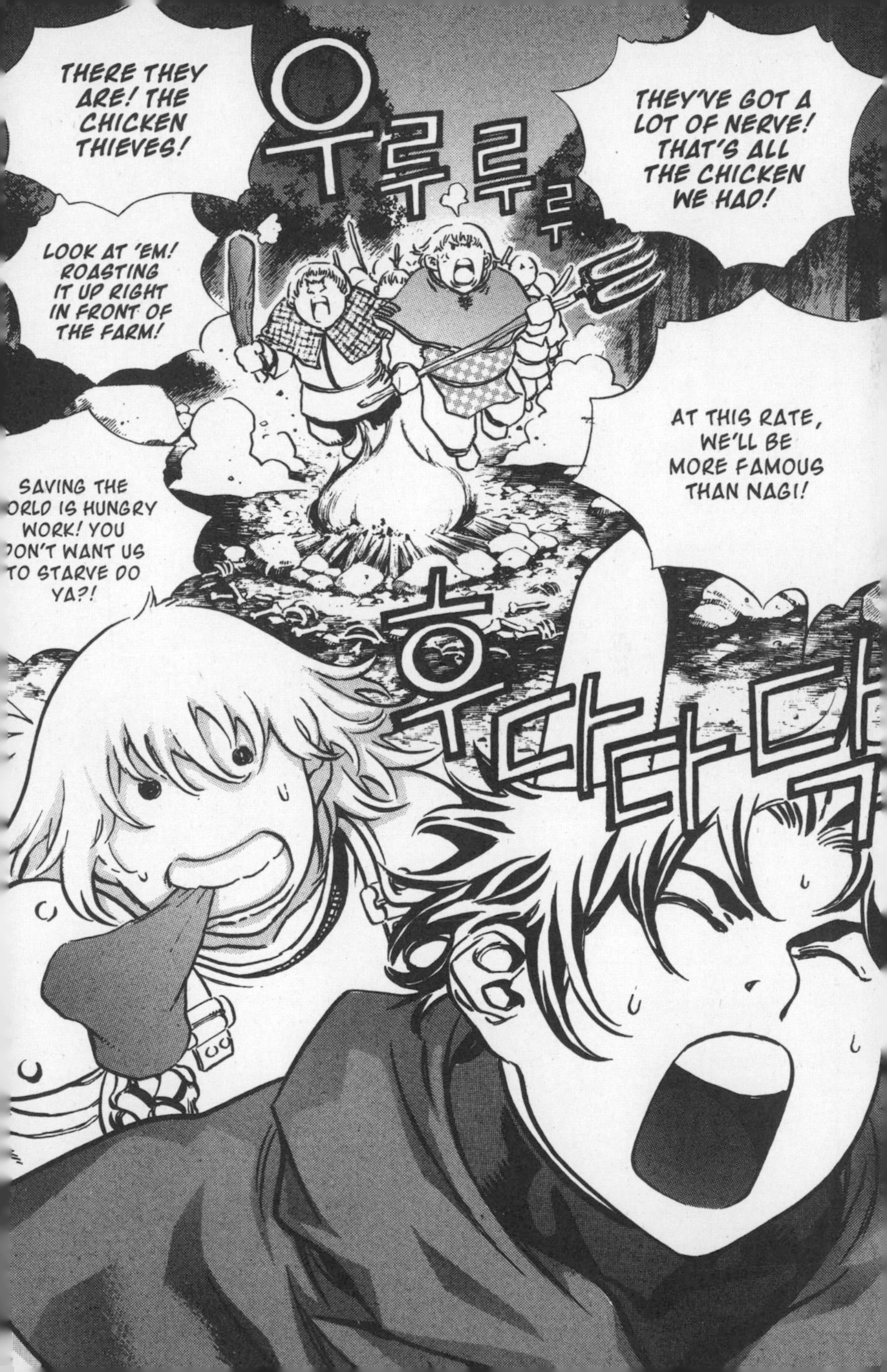
THERE THEY ARE! THE CHICKEN THIEVES!
THEY'VE GOT A LOT OF NERVE! THAT'S ALL THE CHICKEN WE HAD!
LOOK AT 'EM! ROASTING IT UP RIGHT IN FRONT OF THE FARM!
AT THIS RATE, WE'LL BE MORE FAMOUS THAN NAGI!
SAVING THE ORLD IS HUNGRY WORK! YOU ON'T WANT US TO STARVE DO YA?!

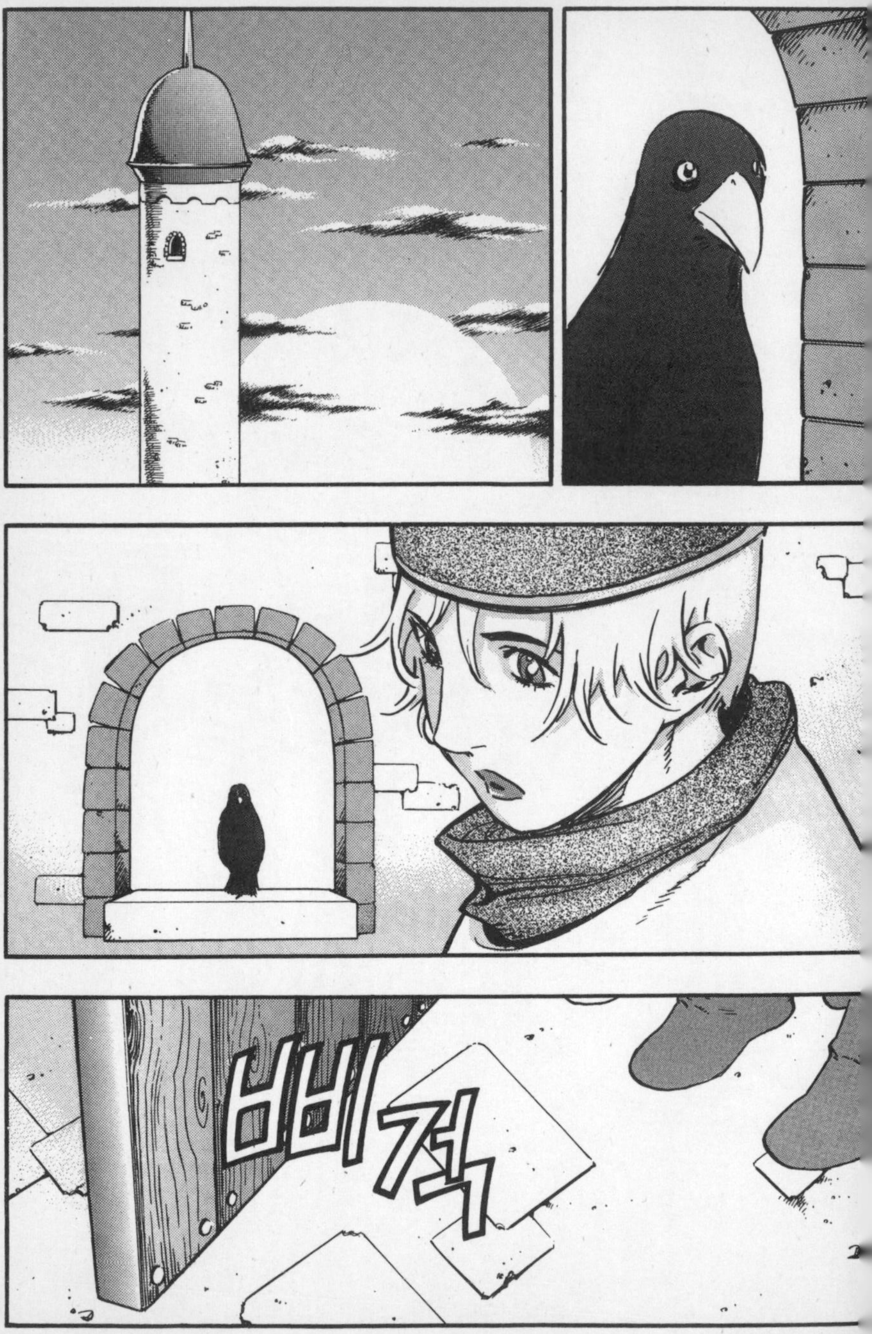
삐걱

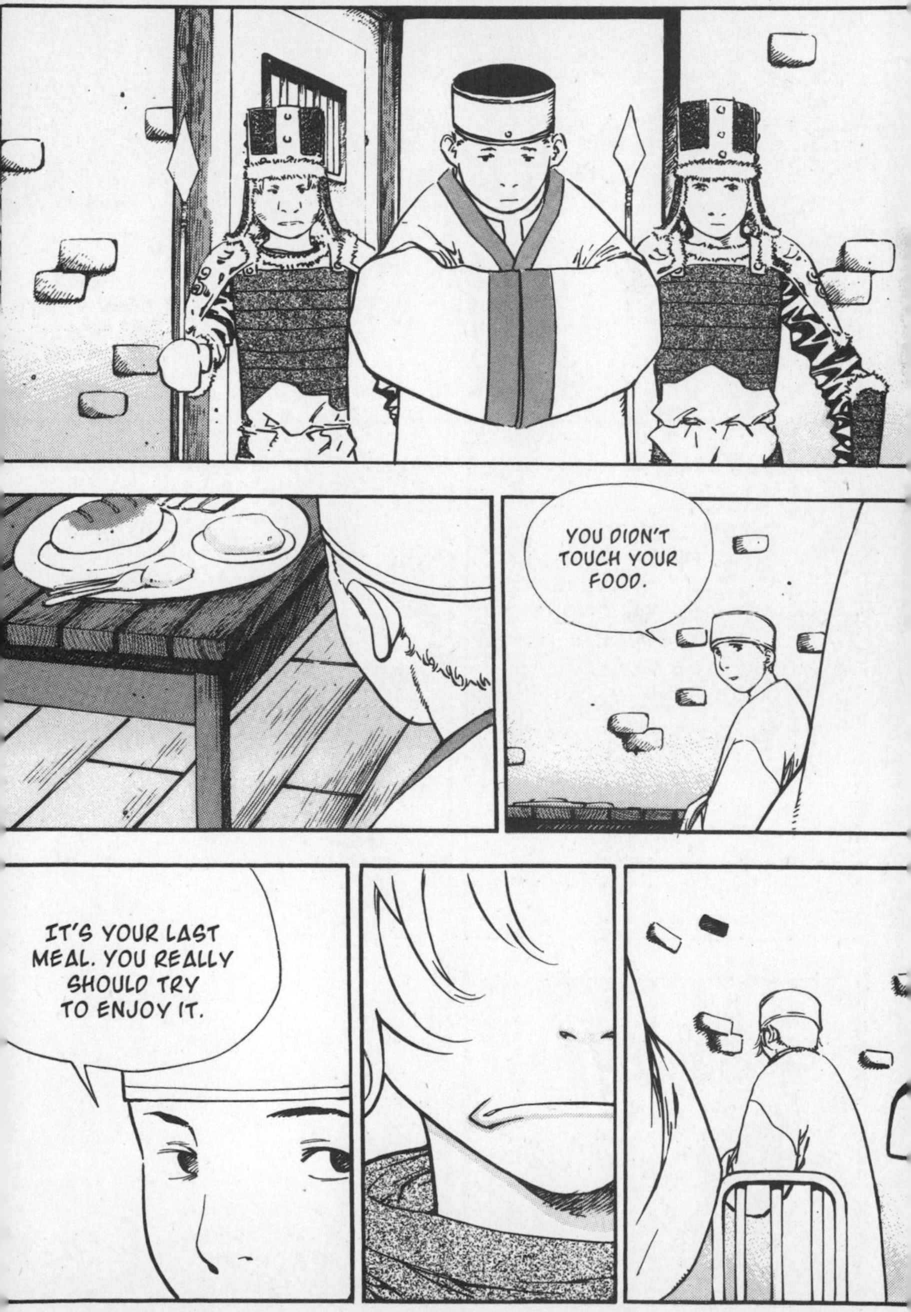

YOU DIDN'T TOUCH YOUR FOOD.
IT'S YOUR LAST MEAL. YOU REALLY SHOULD TRY TO ENJOY IT.

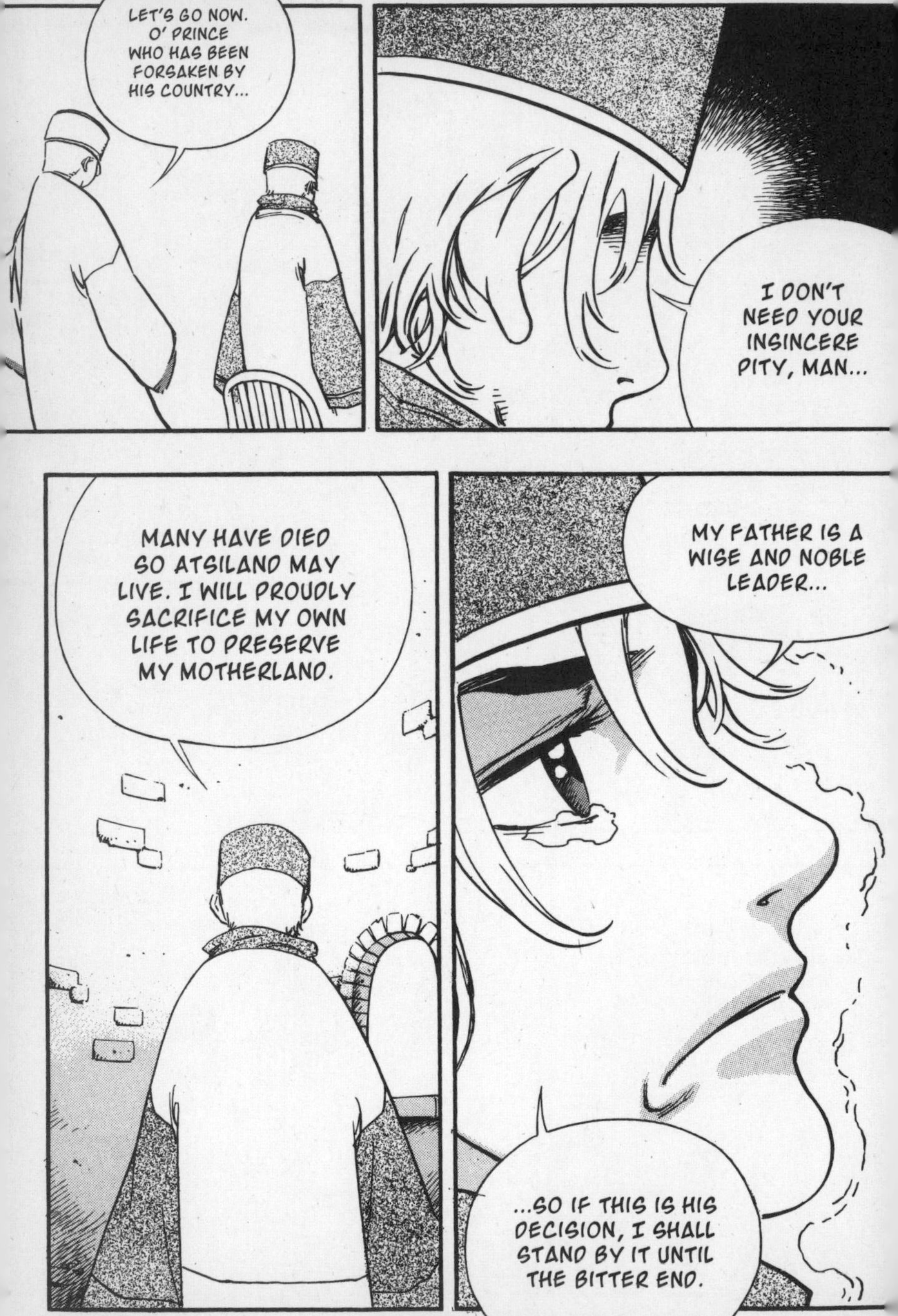
LET'S GO NOW. O' PRINCE WHO HAS BEEN FORSAKEN BY HIS COUNTRY...
I DON'T NEED YOUR INSINCERE PITY, MAN...
MY FATHER IS A WISE AND NOBLE LEADER...
...SO IF THIS IS HIS DECISION, I SHALL STAND BY IT UNTIL THE BITTER END.
MANY HAVE DIED SO ATSILAND MAY LIVE. I WILL PROUDLY SACRIFICE MY OWN LIFE TO PRESERVE MY MOTHERLAND.

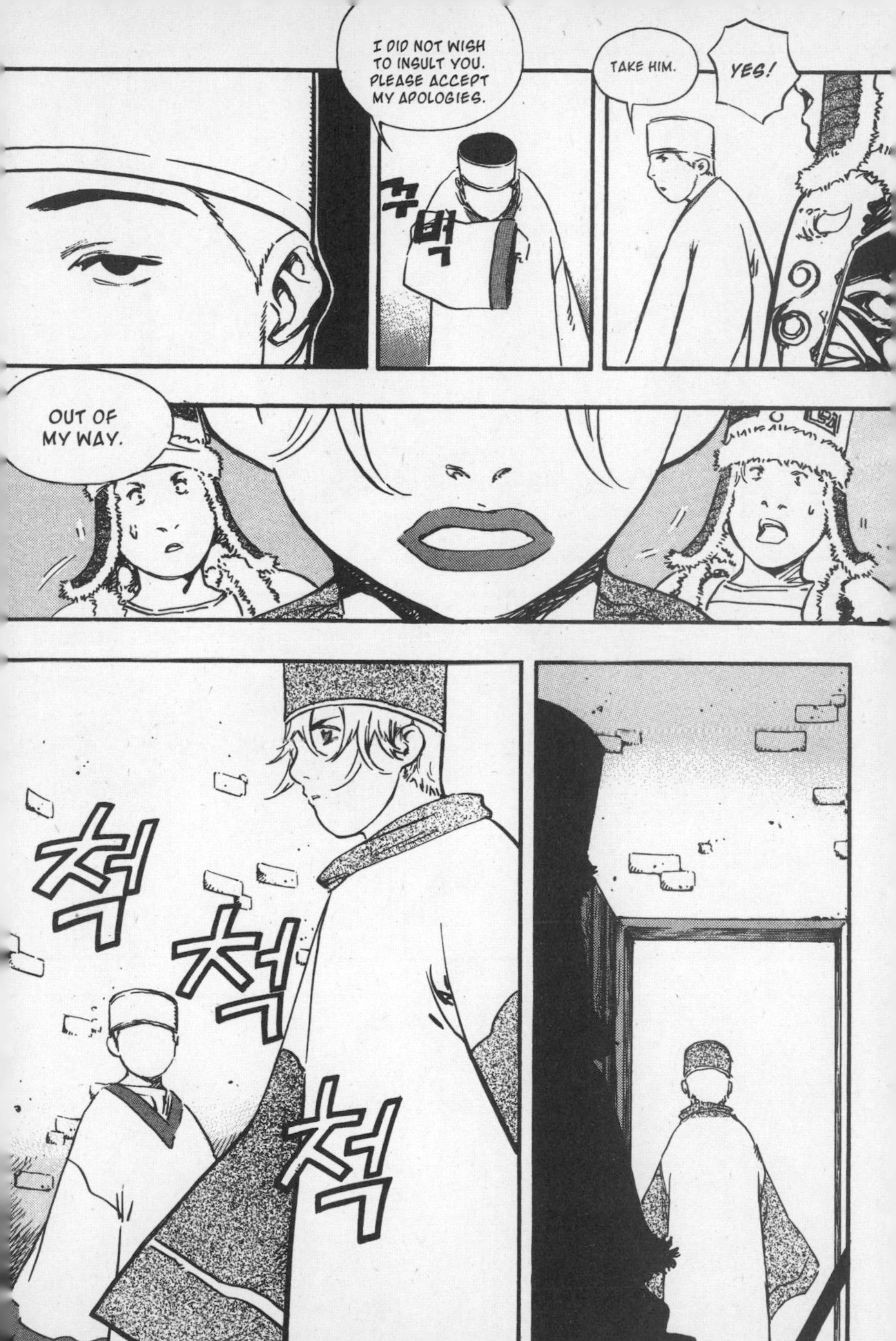
I DID NOT WISH TO INSULT YOU. PLEASE ACCEPT MY APOLOGIES.
꾸벅
TAKE HIM.
YES!
OUT OF MY WAY.
척
척
척

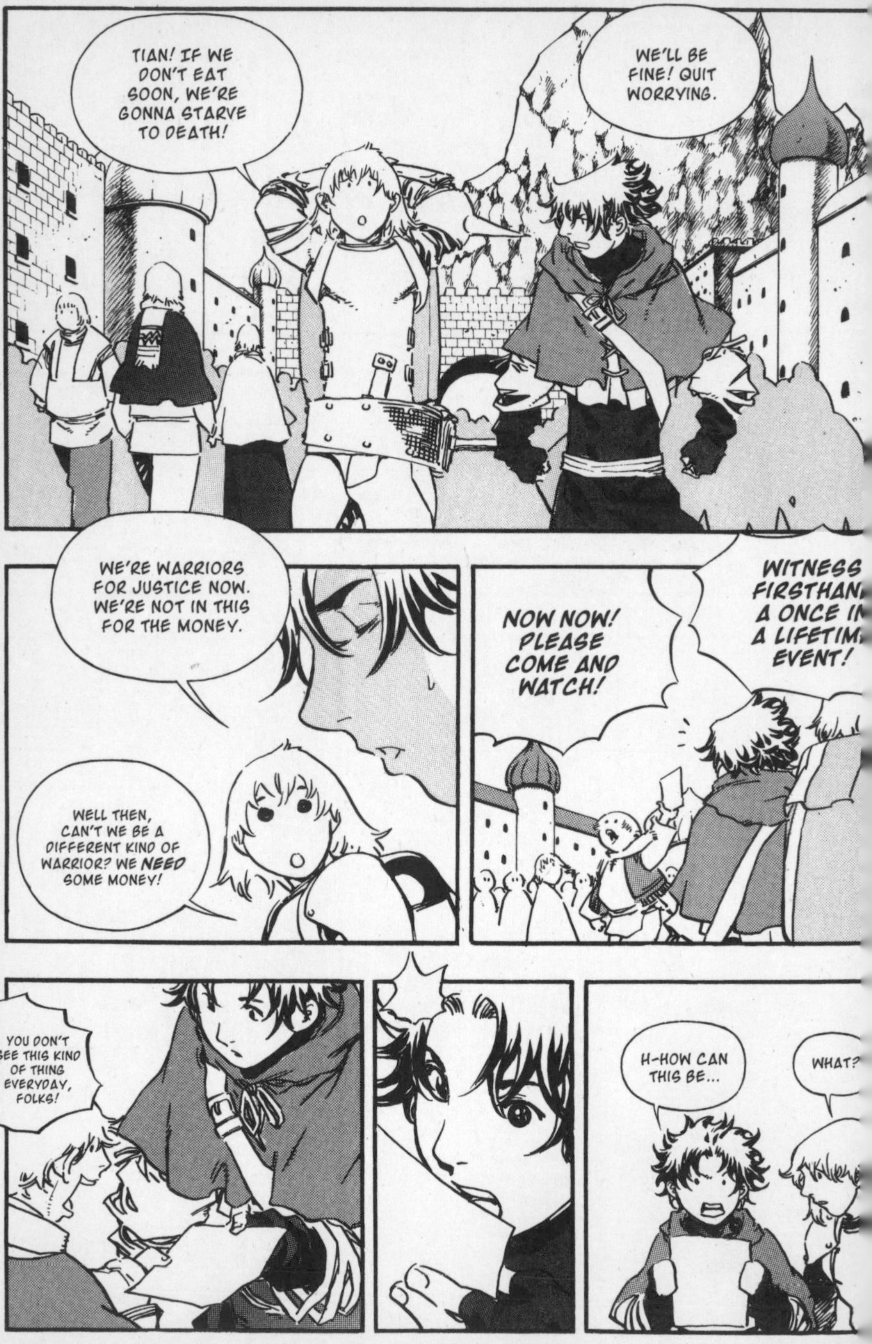
TIAN! IF WE DON'T EAT SOON, WE'RE GONNA STARVE TO DEATH!
WE'LL BE FINE! QUIT WORRYING.
WE'RE WARRIORS FOR JUSTICE NOW. WE'RE NOT IN THIS FOR THE MONEY.
WELL THEN, CAN'T WE BE A DIFFERENT KIND OF WARRIOR? WE NEED SOME MONEY!
NOW NOW! PLEASE COME AND WATCH!
WITNESS FIRSTHAN A ONCE IN A LIFETIM EVENT!
YOU DON'T SEE THIS KIND OF THING EVERYDAY, FOLKS!
H-HOW CAN THIS BE...
WHAT?

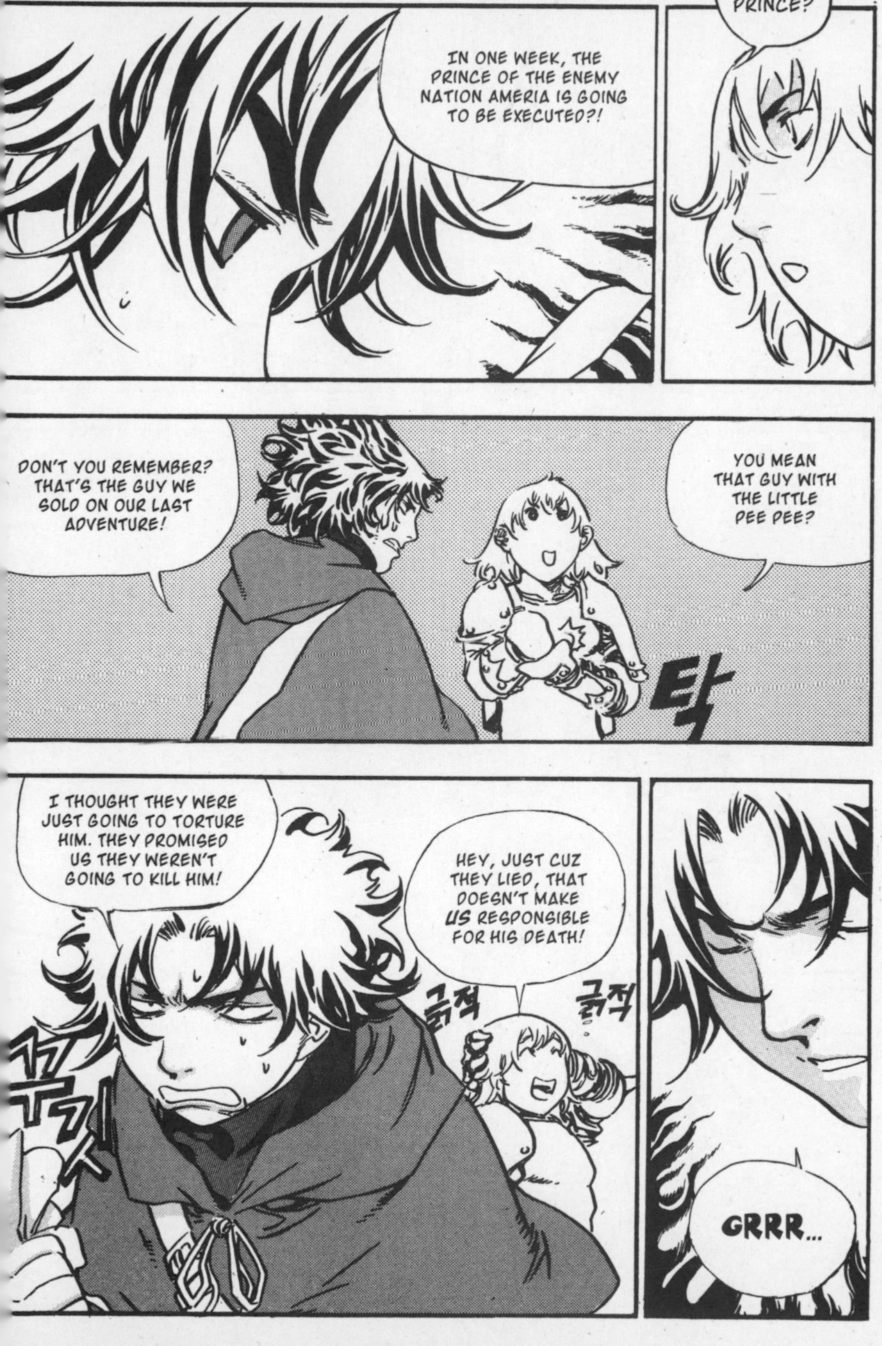
IN ONE WEEK, THE PRINCE OF THE ENEMY NATION AMERIA IS GOING TO BE EXECUTED?!
PRINCE?
DON'T YOU REMEMBER? THAT'S THE GUY WE SOLD ON OUR LAST ADVENTURE!
YOU MEAN THAT GUY WITH THE LITTLE PEE PEE?
탁
I THOUGHT THEY WERE JUST GOING TO TORTURE HIM. THEY PROMISED US THEY WEREN'T GOING TO KILL HIM!
HEY, JUST CUZ THEY LIED, THAT DOESN'T MAKE US RESPONSIBLE FOR HIS DEATH!
긁적
긁적
GRRR...

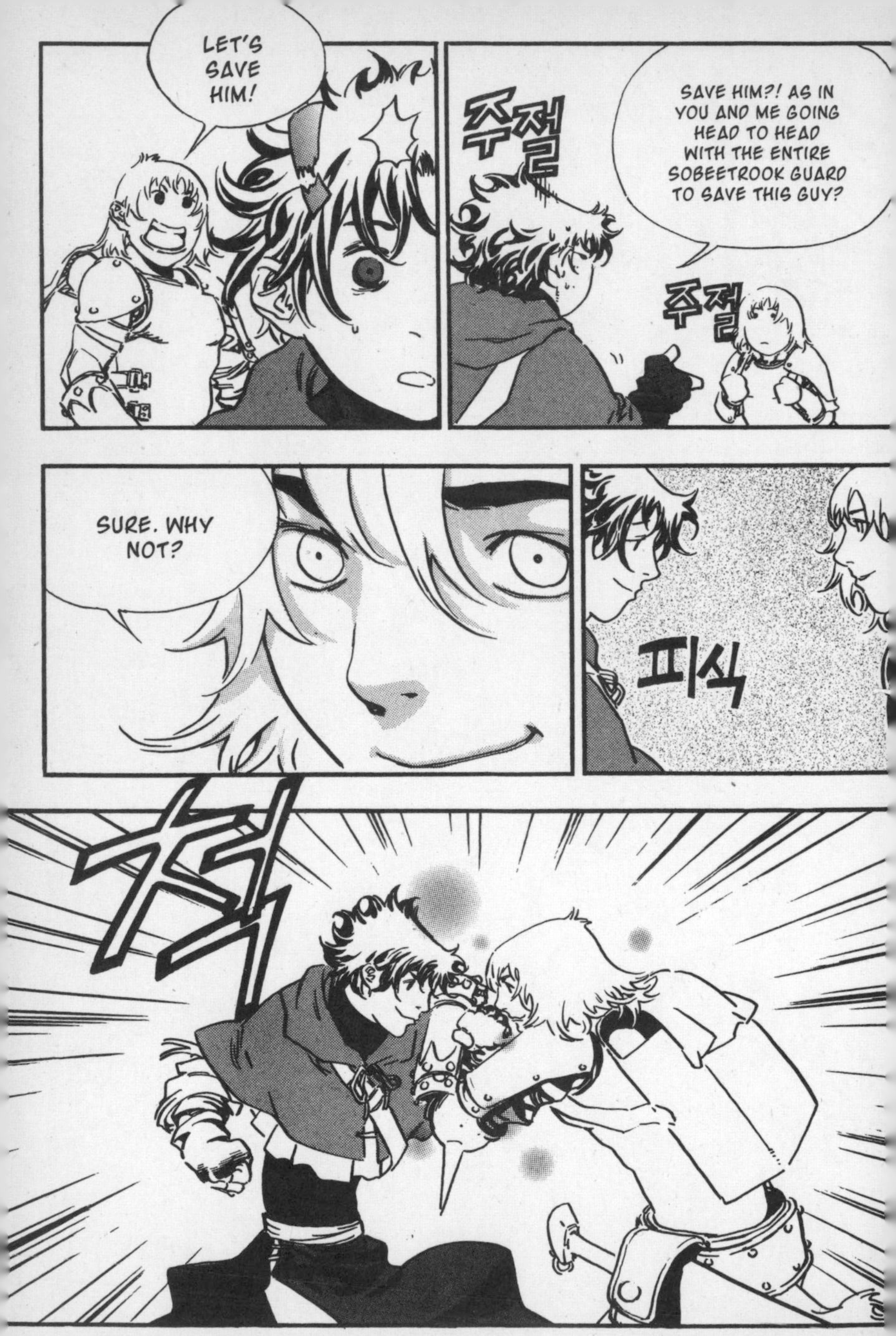
LET'S SAVE HIM!
주절
SAVE HIM?! AS IN YOU AND ME GOING HEAD TO HEAD WITH THE ENTIRE SOBEETROOK GUARD TO SAVE THIS GUY?
주절
SURE. WHY NOT?
피식
척

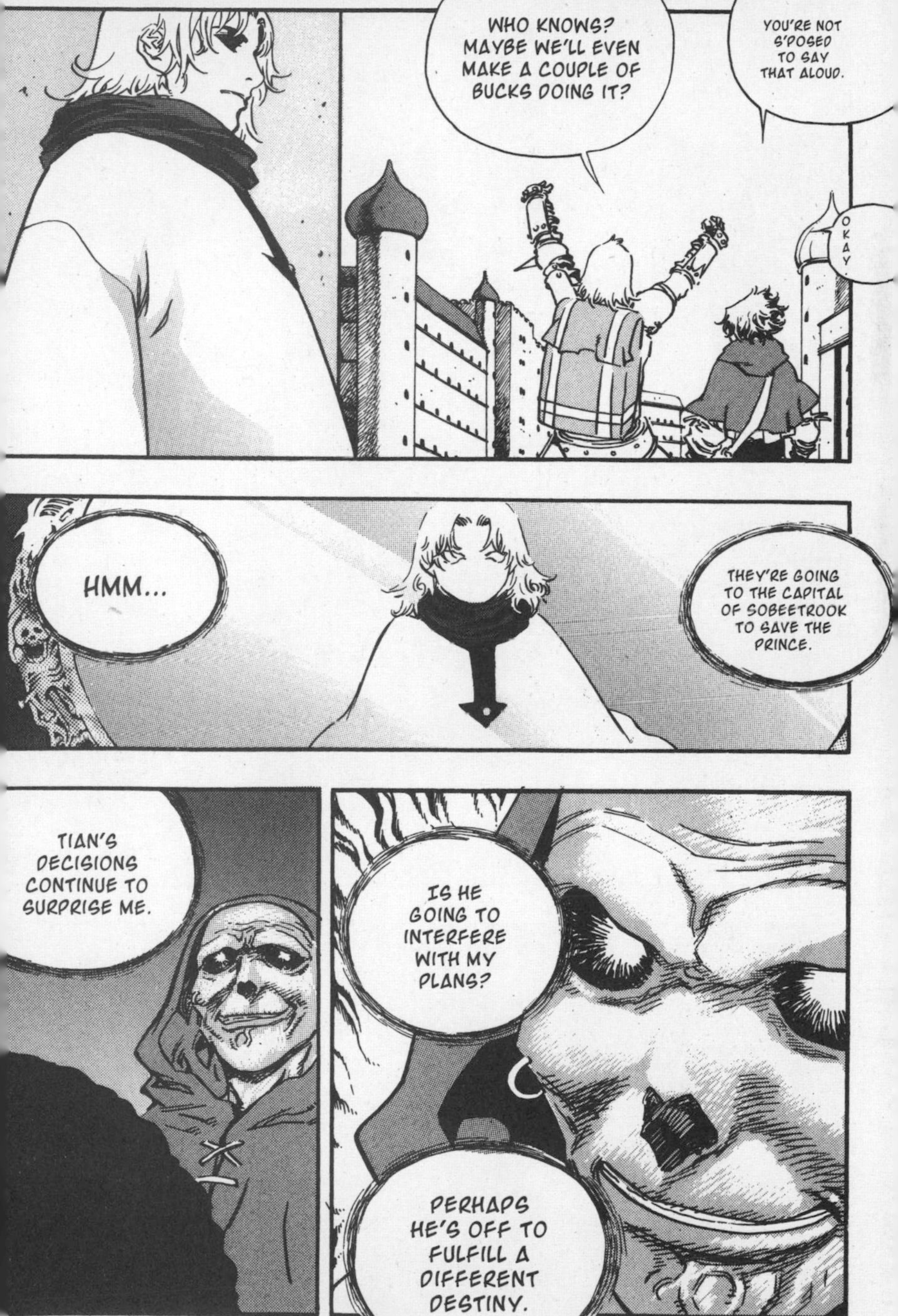
WHO KNOWS? MAYBE WE'LL EVEN MAKE A COUPLE OF BUCKS DOING IT?
YOU'RE NOT S'POSED TO SAY THAT ALOUD.
OKAY.
HMM...
THEY'RE GOING TO THE CAPITAL OF SOBEETROOK TO SAVE THE PRINCE.
TIAN'S DECISIONS CONTINUE TO SURPRISE ME.
IS HE GOING TO INTERFERE WITH MY PLANS?
PERHAPS HE'S OFF TO FULFILL A DIFFERENT DESTINY.

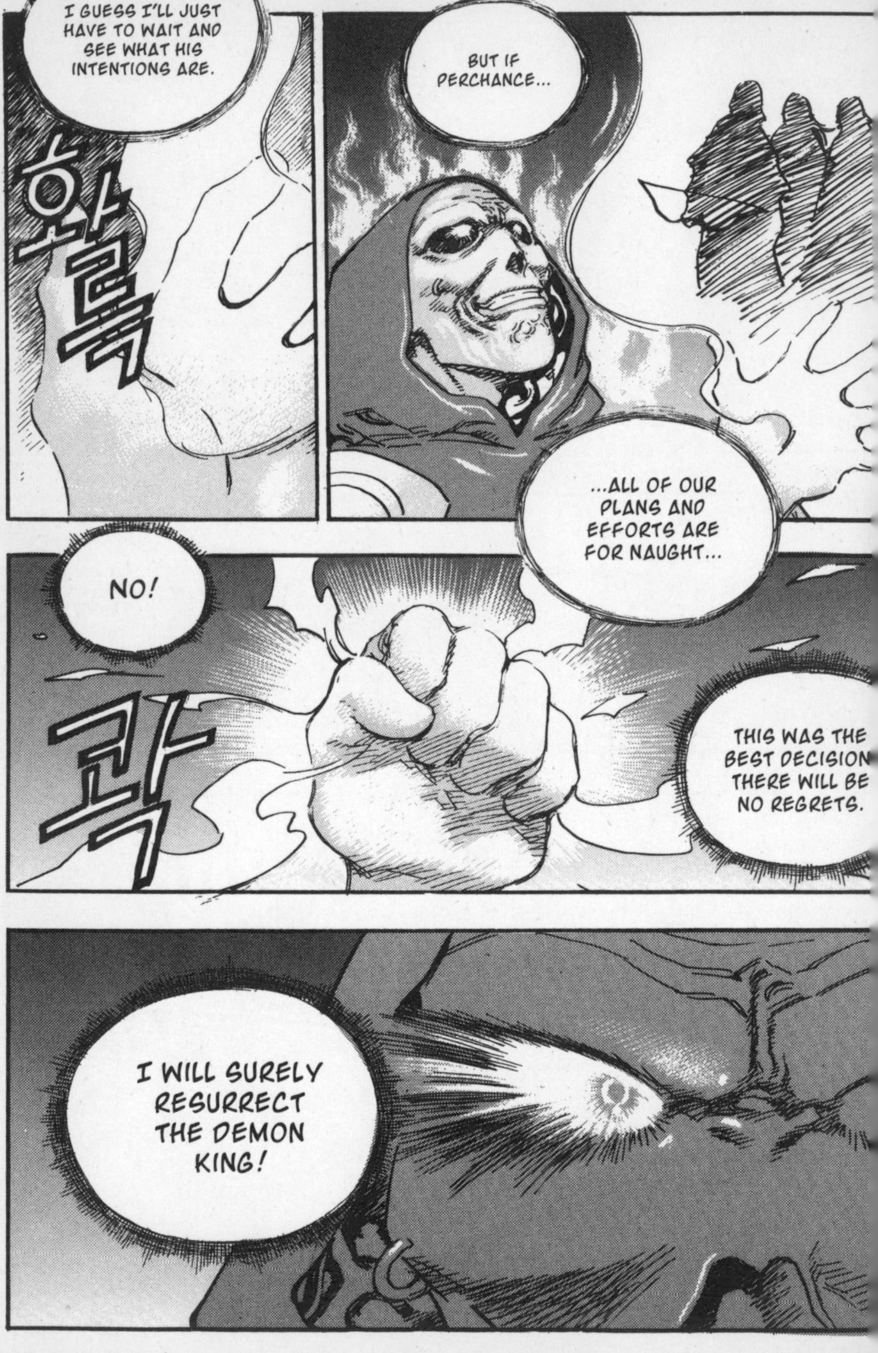
I GUESS I'LL JUST HAVE TO WAIT AND SEE WHAT HIS INTENTIONS ARE.
화륵
BUT IF PERCHANCE...
...ALL OF OUR PLANS AND EFFORTS ARE FOR NAUGHT...
NO!
콱
THIS WAS THE BEST DECISION THERE WILL BE NO REGRETS.
I WILL SURELY RESURRECT THE DEMON KING!

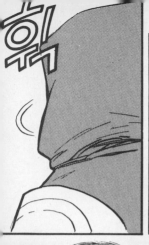

YOU MAY NOT UNDERSTAND ME RIGHT NOW...

HOWEVER, IF YOU EVER ENCOUNTER THE UGLY TRUTH OF THIS WORLD...

...YOU, TOO, WILL WALK THE SAME PATH AS ME.

TIAN...

YOU AND YOUR EXISTENCE...

...HAS GIVEN ME A SMALL FLICKER OF HOPE!

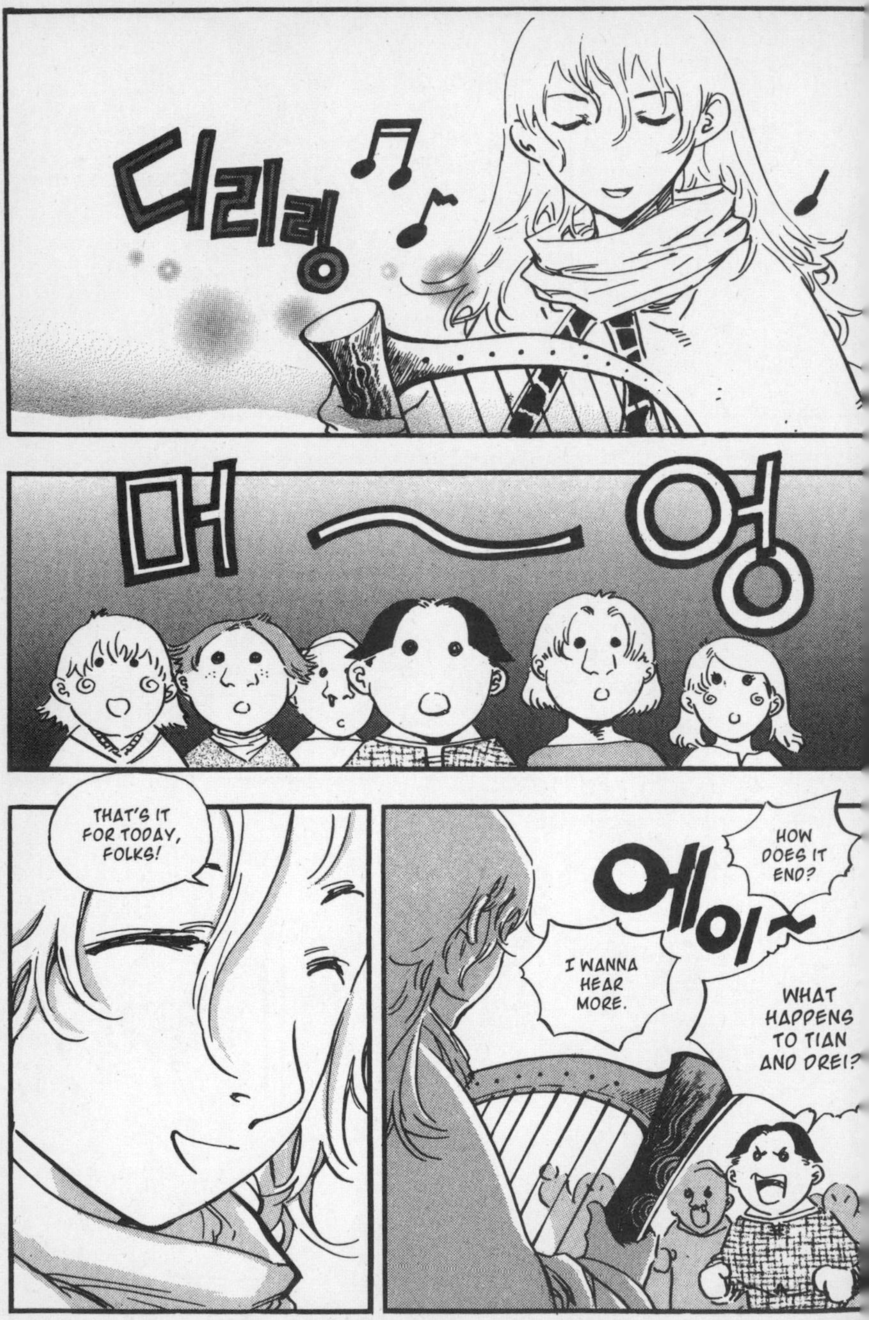
디리링
머~엉
THAT'S IT FOR TODAY, FOLKS!
HOW DOES IT END?
에이~
I WANNA HEAR MORE.
WHAT HAPPENS TO TIAN AND DREI!?

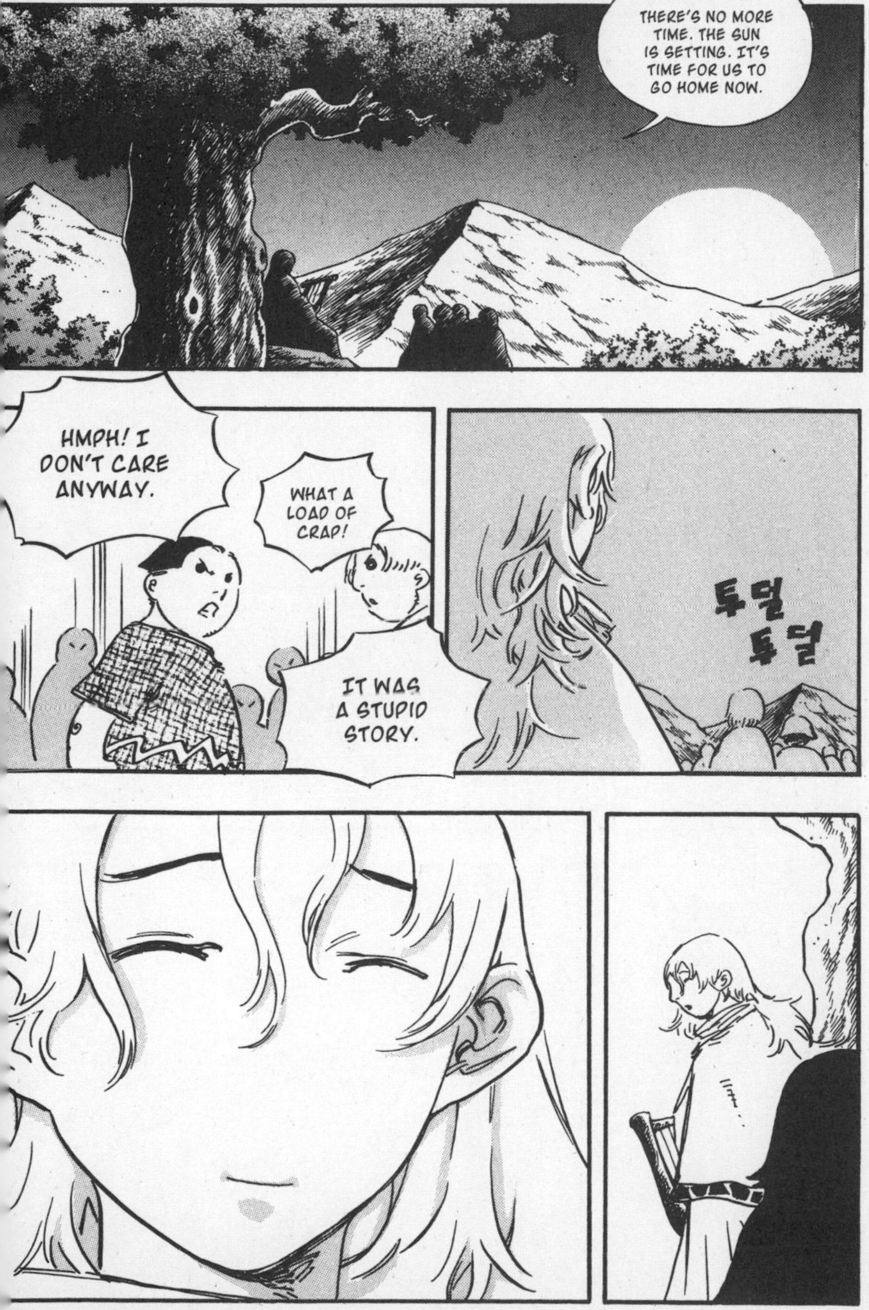
THERE'S NO MORE TIME. THE SUN IS SETTING. IT'S TIME FOR US TO GO HOME NOW.
HMPH! I DON'T CARE ANYWAY.
WHAT A LOAD OF CRAP!
IT WAS A STUPID STORY.
투덜 투덜

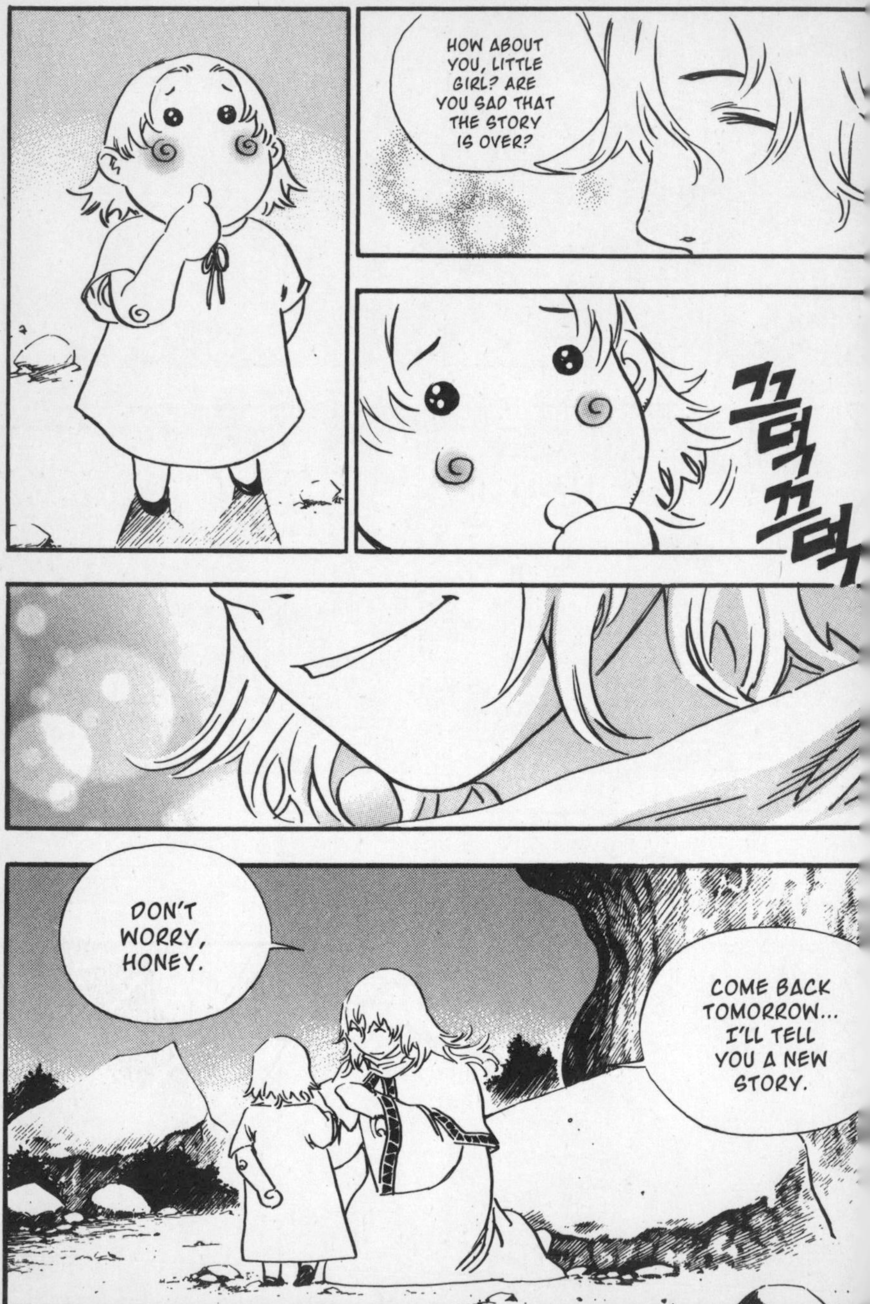
HOW ABOUT YOU, LITTLE GIRL? ARE YOU SAD THAT THE STORY IS OVER?
끄덕 끄덕
DON'T WORRY, HONEY.
COME BACK TOMORROW... I'LL TELL YOU A NEW STORY.

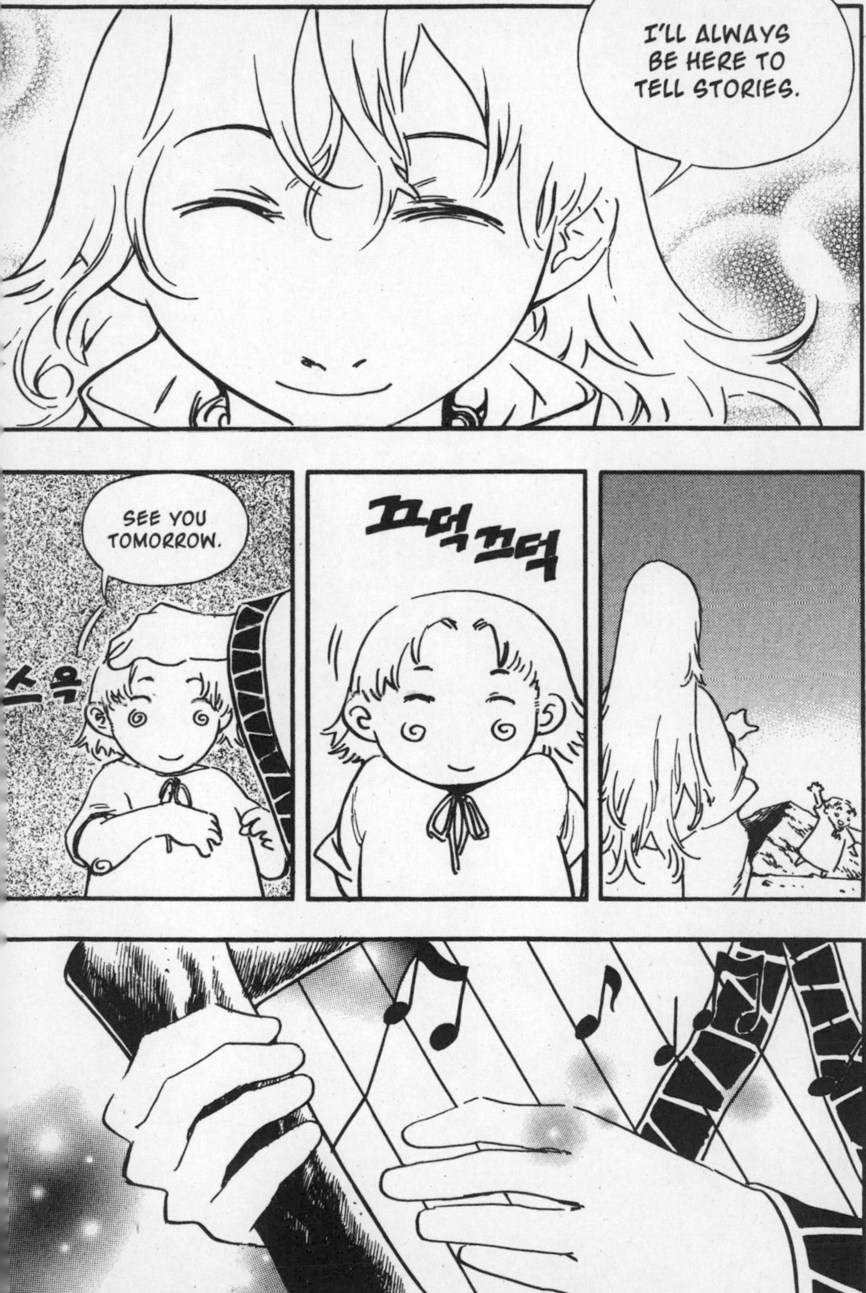
I'LL ALWAYS BE HERE TO TELL STORIES.
SEE YOU TOMORROW.
끄덕끄덕

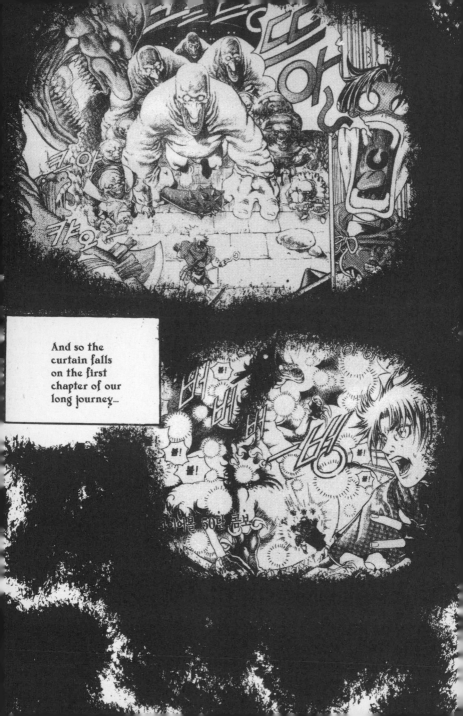

And so the
curtain falls
on the first
chapter of our
long journey...

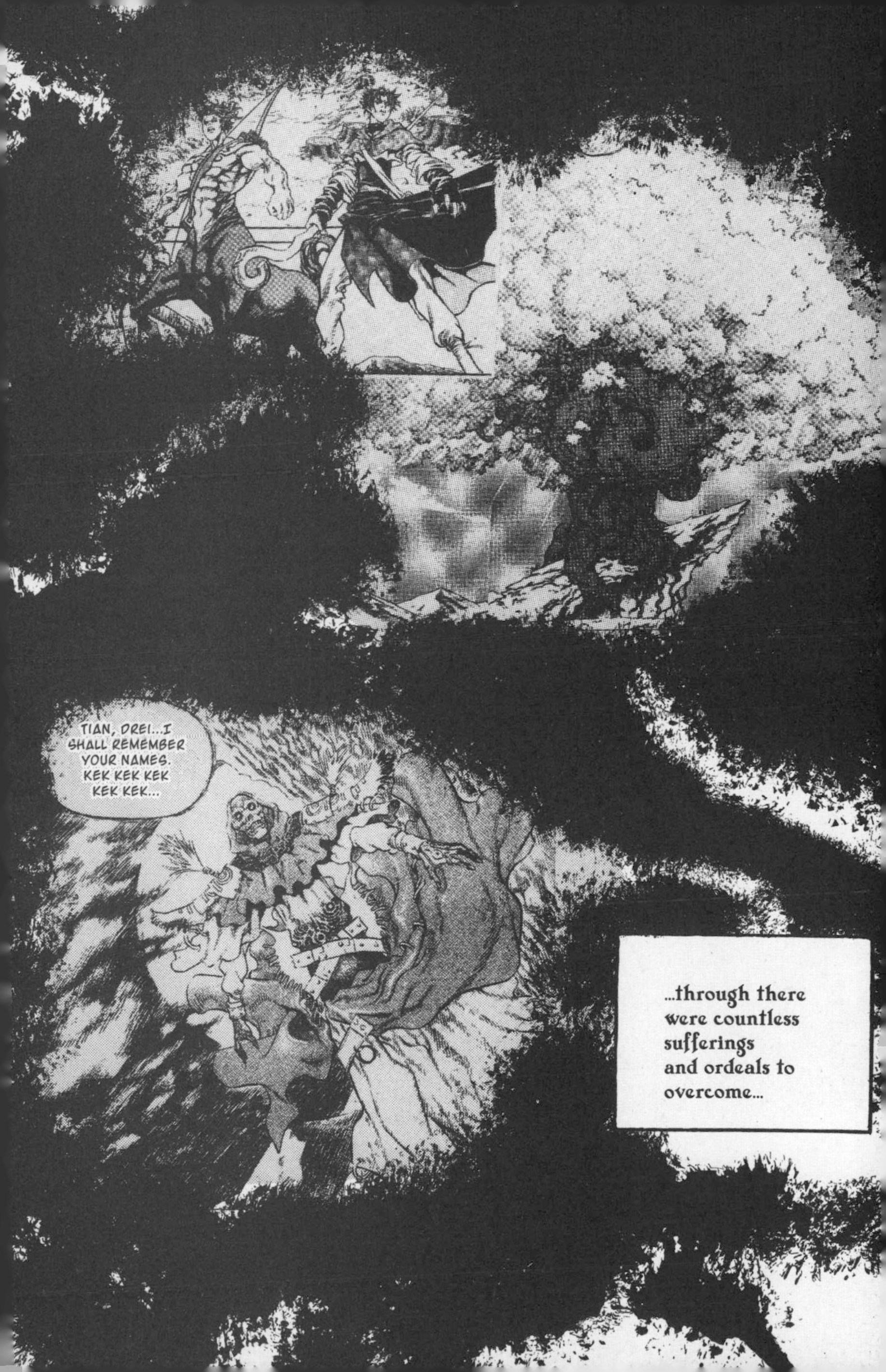
TIAN, DREI...I SHALL REMEMBER YOUR NAMES. KEK KEK KEK KEK KEK...
...through there were countless sufferings and ordeals to overcome...

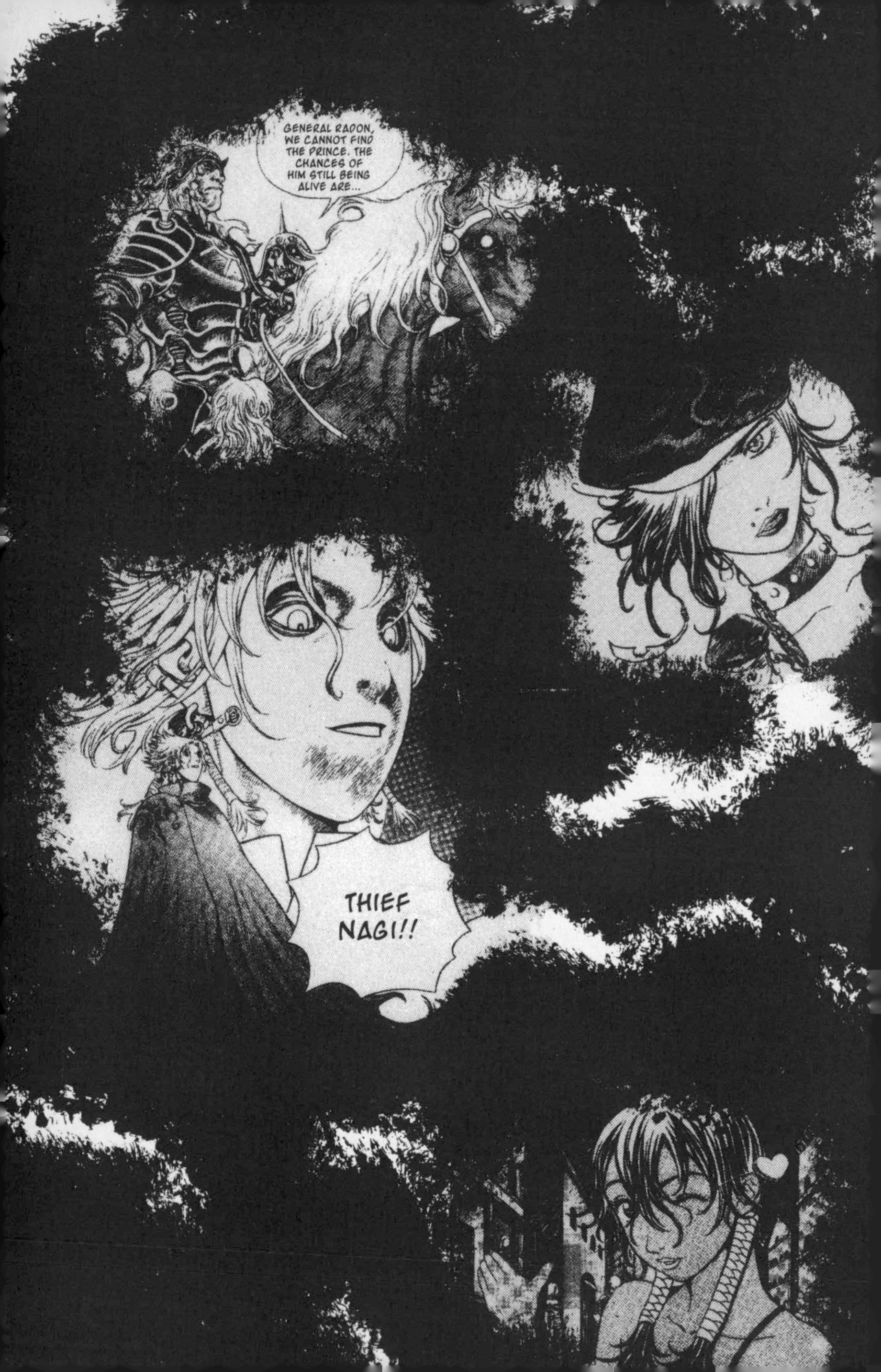
GENERAL RADON, WE CANNOT FIND THE PRINCE. THE CHANCES OF HIM STILL BEING ALIVE ARE...
THIEF NAGI!!

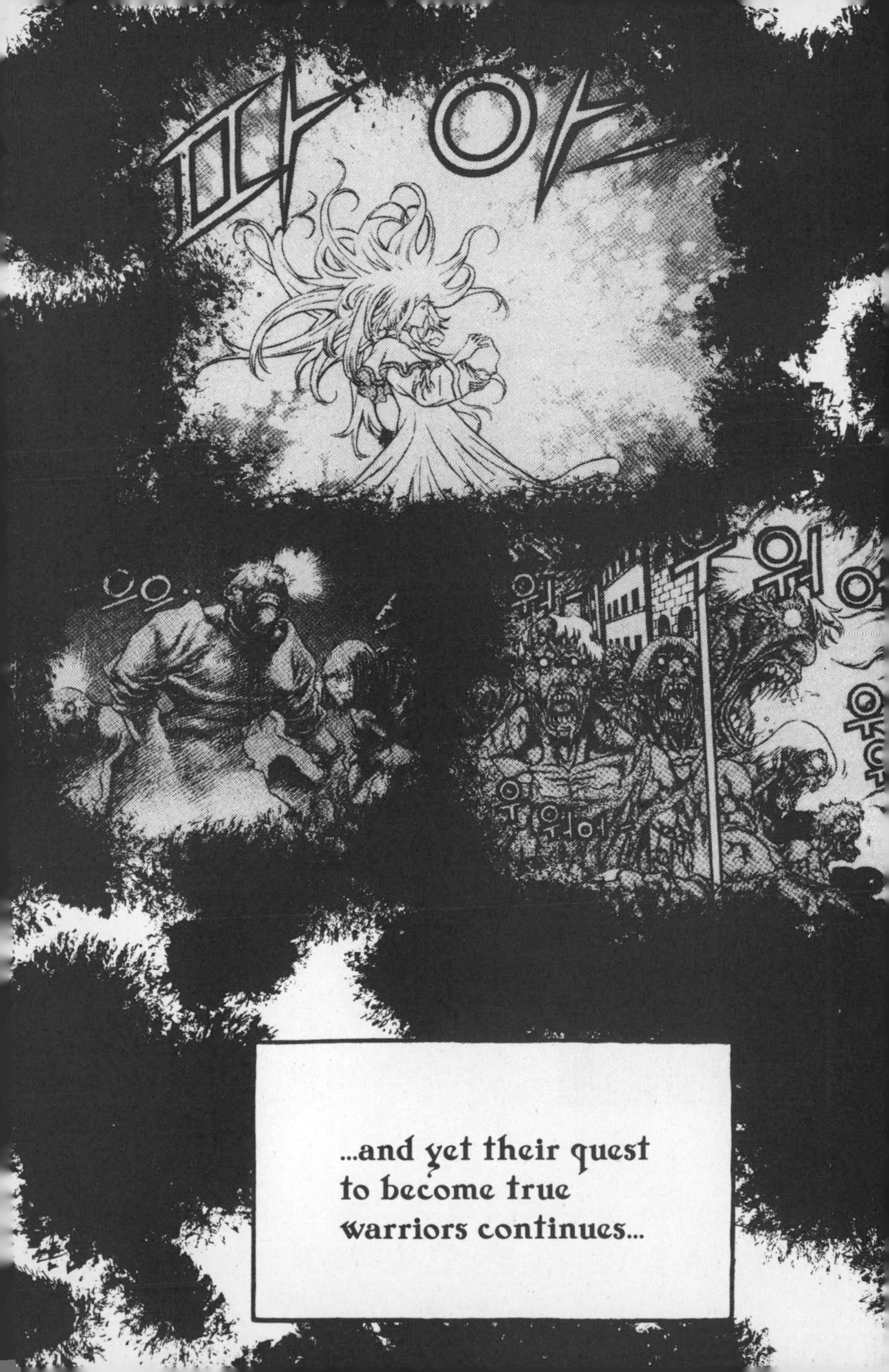

으으..
...and yet their quest to become true warriors continues...

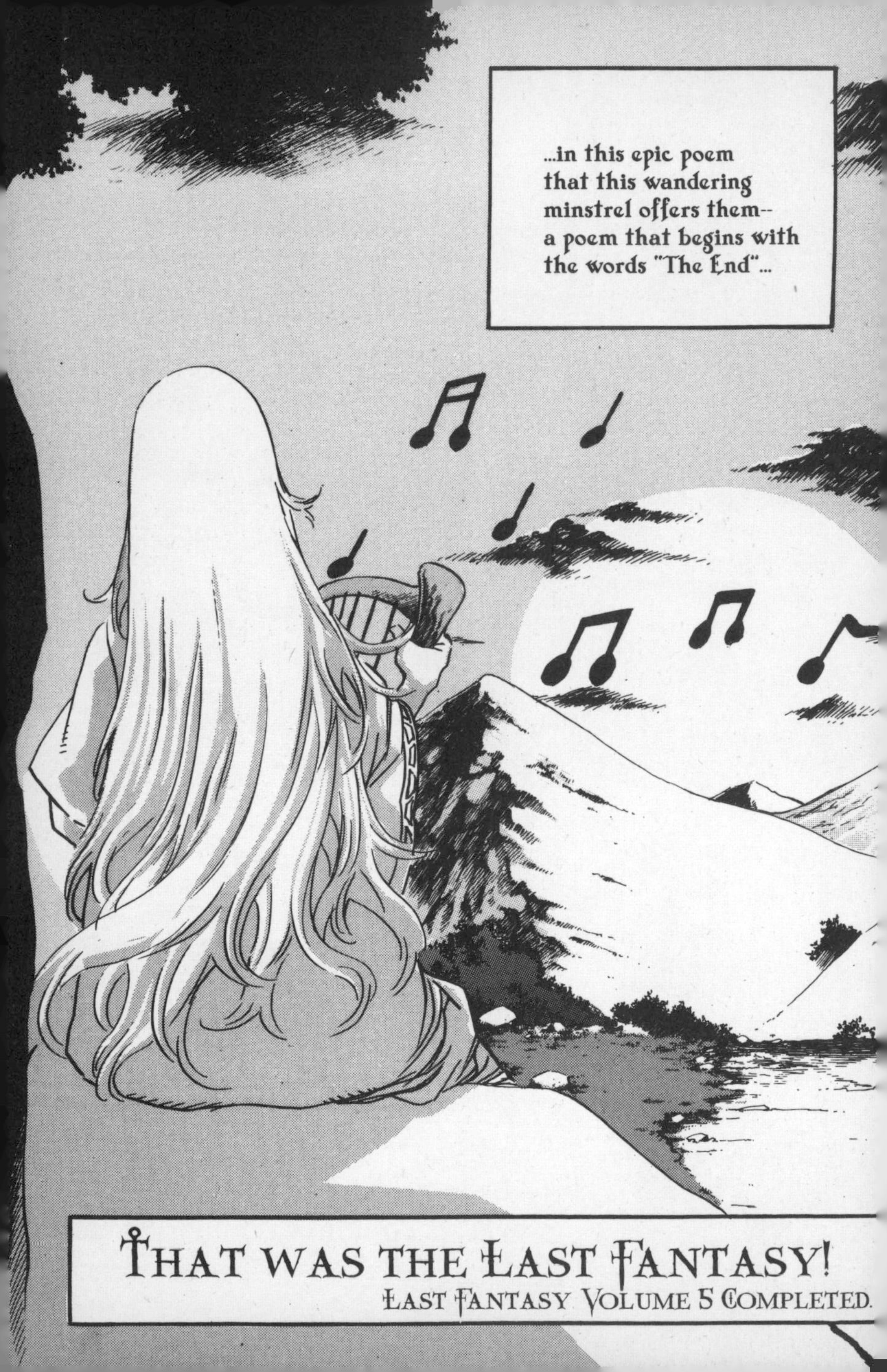
...in this epic poem that this wandering minstrel offers them-- a poem that begins with the words "The End"...
THAT WAS THE LAST FANTASY!
LAST FANTASY VOLUME 5 COMPLETED.

Last Fantasy

vol. 05

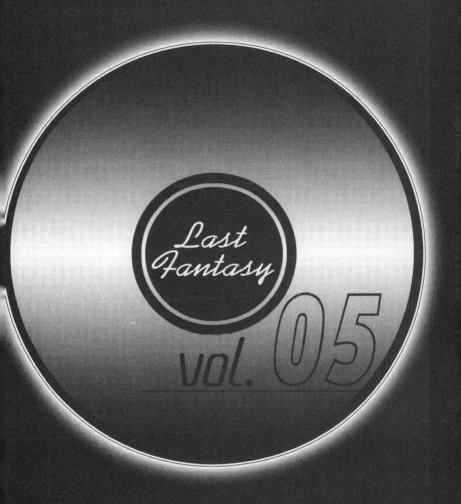

BONUS TRACK

What Though Life Conspire To Cheat You
삶이 그대를 속일지라도

– Aleksandr Sergeyerich Pushkin –
푸슈킨

What though life conspire to cheat you,
삶이 그대를 속일지라도,

Do not sorrow or complain.
슬퍼하거나 노여워말라.

Lie still on the day of pain,
슬픈 날엔 참고 견뎌라,

And the day of joy will greet you.
이제 곧 기쁨의 나날이 오리니.

Hearts live in the coming day.
마음은 미래에 사는 것.

There's an end to passing sorrow.
현재는 한없이 우울한 것.

Suddenly all flies away,
모든 것이 하염없이 날아가버려도,

And delight returns tomorrow.
내일은 기쁨으로 돌아오리라.

JUST LIKE THE WORLD IN WHICH WE ARE LIVING, LIFE ITSELF CAN BE A BIT MUCH TO HANDLE IN THE FANTASY WORLD OF TIAN AND DREI. IT APPEARS THAT THIS LIFE CANNOT BE LIVED WITH THE INNOCENT DREAMS AND VIGOR OF YOUTH. TIAN AND DREI ARE A DEPICTION OF OUR OWN SELVES. THEY WORK HARD AND DILIGENTLY, ONLY TO REPEAT MISTAKE AFTER MISTAKE AND RUIN THEIR INTRICATELY LAID AND IMPORTANT, PLANS. AT TIMES, WE FALL INTO DESPAIR BECAUSE WE ARE UNABLE TO CARRY ON THE BURDENS AND THE RESPONSIBILITIES THAT HAVE BEEN LAID UPON US, AND THERE ARE TIMES AT WHICH WE IGNORE THEM AND RUN AWAY. HOWEVER, IF YOU HAVE THE STRENGTH REMAINING TO STAND UP ONCE AGAIN, CLENCH YOUR FISTS AND RUN TOWARDS TOMORROW, THEN YOU HAVE EVERY RIGHT TO BE CALLED A WARRIOR. ALTHOUGH LIFE MAY CONSPIRE TO CHEAT YOU, THIS WORLD IS ALSO IN DIRE NEED OF A YOUNG WARRIOR LIKE YOURSELF.

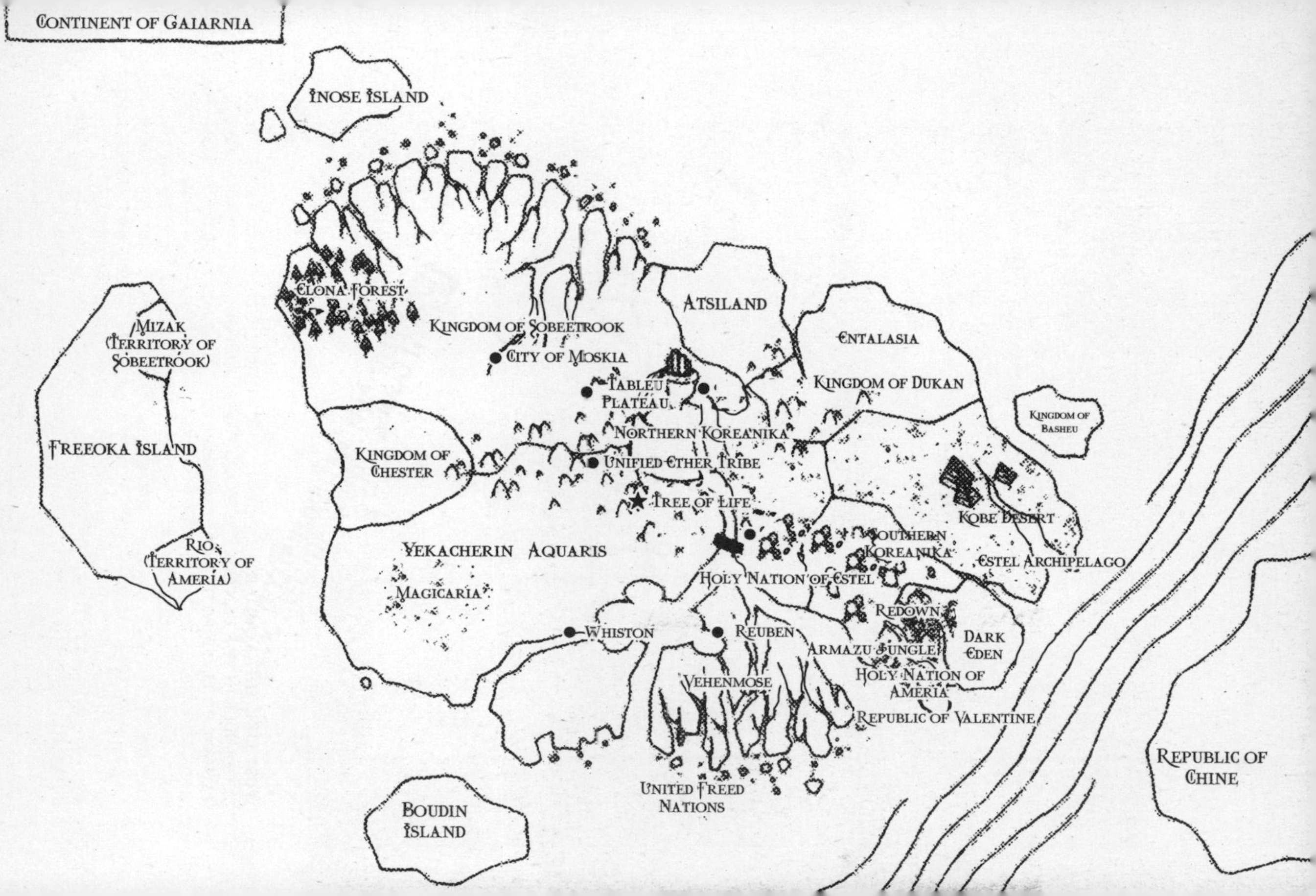
Continent of Gaiarnia
Inose Island
Elona Forest
Kingdom of Sobeetrook
City of Moskia
Mizak (Territory of Sobeetrook)
Freeoka Island
Rio (Territory of Ameria)
Atsiland
Entalasia
Kingdom of Dukan
Tableu Plateau
Northern Koreanika
Kingdom of Basheu
Kingdom of Chester
Unified Ether Tribe
Tree of Life
Kobe Desert
Southern Koreanika
Estel Archipelago
Yekacherin Aquaris
Holy Nation of Estel
Magicaria
Redown
Dark Eden
Whiston
Reuben
Armazu Jungle
Holy Nation of Ameria
Vehenmose
Republic of Valentine
Republic of Chine
United Freed Nations
Boudin Island

THE END